CHRISTIAN MISSION, CONTEXTUAL THEOLOGY, PROPHETIC DIALOGUE

The American Society of Missiology Series, published in collaboration with Orbis Books, seeks to publish scholarly works of high merit and wide interest on numerous aspects of missiology—the study of Christian mission in its historical, social, and theological dimensions. Able presentations on new and creative approaches to the practice and understanding of mission will receive close attention from the ASM Series Committee.

American Society of Missiology Series, No. 57

CHRISTIAN MISSION, CONTEXTUAL THEOLOGY, PROPHETIC DIALOGUE

Essays in Honor of Stephen B. Bevans, SVD

Edited by
Dale T. Irvin and Peter C. Phan

ORBIS BOOKS
Maryknoll, New York 10545

Founded in 1970, Orbis Books endeavors to publish works that enlighten the mind, nourish the spirit, and challenge the conscience. The publishing arm of the Maryknoll Fathers and Brothers, Orbis seeks to explore the global dimensions of the Christian faith and mission, to invite dialogue with diverse cultures and religious traditions, and to serve the cause of reconciliation and peace. The books published reflect the views of their authors and do not represent the official position of the Maryknoll Society. To learn more about Maryknoll and Orbis Books, please visit our website at www.maryknollsociety.org.

Library of Congress Cataloging-in-Publication Data

Names: Irvin, Dale T., 1955– editor. | Phan, Peter C., 1943– editor. |
   Bevans, Stephen B., 1944– honoree.
Title: Christian mission, contextual theology, prophetic dialogue : essays in honor
   of Stephen B. Bevans, SVD / Dale T. Irvin and Peter C. Phan, editors.
Description: Maryknoll, NY : Orbis Books, [2018] | Series: The American Society
   of Missiology ; no. 57 | Includes bibliographical references and index.
Identifiers: LCCN 2018021769 (print) | LCCN 2018046742 (ebook) | ISBN
   9781608337651 (ebook) | ISBN 9781626982994 (pbk.)
Subjects: LCSH: Missions—Theory. | Christianity and culture.
Classification: LCC BV2063 (ebook) | LCC BV2063 .C485 2018 (print) | DDC
   266—dc23
LC record available at https://lccn.loc.gov/2018021769

Photograph by Benjamin Le, SVD

Stephen B. Bevans, SVD

Contents

Part 1

CHRISTIAN MISSION

Part 2
CONTEXTUAL THEOLOGY

Part 3
PROPHETIC DIALOGUE

Part 4
A PERSONAL REFLECTION
FROM STEPHEN B. BEVANS, SVD

Preface to the American Society of Missiology Series

The purpose of the American Society of Missiology Series is to publish—without regard for disciplinary, national, or denominational boundaries—scholarly works of high quality and wide interest on missiological themes from the entire spectrum of scholarly pursuits relevant to Christian mission, which is always the focus of books in the Series.

By mission is meant the effort to effect passage over the boundary between faith in Jesus Christ and its absence. In this understanding of mission, the basic functions of Christian proclamation, dialogue, witness, service, worship, liberation, and nurture are of special concern. And in that context questions arise, including, how does the transition from one cultural context to another influence the shape and interaction between these dynamic functions, especially in regard to the cultural and religious plurality that comprises the global context of Christian life and mission.

The promotion of scholarly dialogue among missiologists, and among missiologists and scholars in other fields of inquiry, may involve the publication of views that some missiologists cannot accept, and with which members of the Editorial Committee themselves do not agree. Manuscripts published in the Series, accordingly, reflect the opinions of their authors and are not understood to represent the position of the American Society of Missiology or of the Editorial Committee. Selection is guided by such criteria as intrinsic worth, readability, coherence, and accessibility to a range of interested persons and not merely to experts or specialists.

The ASM Series, in collaboration with Orbis Books, seeks to publish scholarly works of high merit and wide interest on numerous aspects of missiology—the scholarly study of mission. Able presentations on new and creative approaches to the practice and understanding of mission will receive close attention.

THE ASM SERIES COMMITTEE

Robert Hunt	Paul Hertig
Robert Gallagher	Kristopher W. Seaman
Hendrik Pieterse	Brian Froehle
Peter Vethanyagamony	Francis Adney
Lisa White	

Preface

Barbara E. Reid, OP

The prophet Micah famously wrote that what God requires of us is "to do justice, and to love kindness, and to walk humbly with your God" (Mic 6:8). We would be hard-pressed to find a scholar who embodies these virtues more fully than our beloved colleague Stephen Bevans, SVD. He has spent a lifetime honing his sensitivity to those who cry for justice, and he has extended himself in word and action in their behalf. His kindness and compassion know no bounds, as he has widened the tent of his heart to encompass not only other human beings, but earth itself and all its imperilled inhabitants. One might expect such an acclaimed teacher and world-renowned scholar to be entitled to strut with a bit of an air of superiority. But Steve, as his accomplishments mount, only becomes more humble, available, and open to where God asks him to walk.

Steve's walks with God have taken him to many exotic places, and his wisdom has been widely and generously shared with countless people. We, his colleagues at Catholic Theological Union, count ourselves the most blessed, because he always returns home to Chicago, enriching us with what he has learned—he insists he always learns more than he teaches. His deep sensitivity to other cultures and his skills in interculturality and doing theology contextually have been such a blessing to us. I am particularly fortunate in that I have had the privilege of team teaching a course with Steve every two years for the past thirty on feminist hermeneutics in the Bible and theology. His commitment to justice for women and his openness to hearing the experiences of women from around the globe and to walking with us have led him to create addresses and presentations that are profoundly feminist in nature and delivery.

When Steve decided to retire from full-time teaching in 2015, I was quite distraught, not only as his friend and colleague, but because as the academic dean, I knew he was irreplaceable. In his humble walk with God, Steve was intent on fostering and making way for a younger generation of scholars. As professor emeritus, Steve continues to pour himself out generously in teaching, speaking, writing, preaching, presiding, and serving on boards, committees, and even in interim administrative capacities. This book is not only a fitting tribute to Steve, but hopefully will be another means by which his great spirit can help form the next generation of theologians, showing them how to embrace justice, love kindness, and walk humbly with God in their own unfolding context.

Acknowledgments

This book originated on a beach in Puerto Rico at the annual convention of the Catholic Theological Society of America in June 2016, where Stephen Bevans, a number of contributors, and one of the editors of this volume (Peter Phan) were relaxing "spirit-ually" together. The subject of Steve's upcoming retirement came up, and it suddenly dawned on us that a Festschrift should be organized to honor him and celebrate his legacy. We are grateful to Orbis Books, especially its publisher, Robert Ellsberg, for agreeing to publish it. Indeed, it is highly appropriate that the book finds its home at Orbis, which has published most of Steve's works. We are also deeply grateful to Dr. Jill O'Brien, acquisitions editor at Orbis, for her expert and efficient handling of the editorial process. Another member of the Orbis family to whom we owe a huge debt of gratitude is Dr. William Burrows, a mover and shaker of American Catholic theology through his decades-long editorial activities. He was commissioned to write the final chapter of the book assessing the life and work of Steve, a lifelong friend of his. Unfortunately, his health did not allow him to complete the essay. Happily, Steve's autobiographical essay fills the gap. We also thank Dr. Barbara E. Reid, OP, vice president and academic dean of Catholic Theological Union, for agreeing to write the Preface under very short notice. Lastly, we thank all the contributors of this volume, Tom O'Meara, Steve's doktorvater, fellow SVDs, friends, and colleagues, who have enthusiastically accepted the invitation to honor our beloved Steve. Anyone who knows Steve knows that he is even more active in his "retirement." Carissime Stephane, ad multos annos!

Introduction

Peter C. Phan

Theologians normally can't afford throwing lavish parties, replete with exquisite foods and rare drinks, on cruises to exotic islands to celebrate the achievements of their colleague. And so they resort to doing something they do best—namely, writing essays in their colleague's honor, to be collected into what Germans, with their customary precision, call Festschrift. Sadly, Festschriften are often fated to gather dust on library shelves or, these days, languish as an ebook on some recondite websites.

The achievements of Stephen B. Bevans, SVD, as priest, missionary, professor, theologian, and writer are so numerous and varied; his spiritual impact through his priestly and missionary ministries so deep and vast; his influence through his writings, teaching, and lecturing, on both national and international stages, so profound and long lasting that they cannot be adequately narrated between the covers of a single book, even a thick one. Nor should this narrative be confined to a small circle of esoteric readers and learned scholars. Consequently, to perpetuate Steve's theological legacy and to spread it far and wide, the editors and Orbis Books have decided to celebrate Steve's lifetime achievements not with a garden-variety Festschrift but with a textbook for widespread use by theology students as well as general readers.

In an autobiographical essay, Chapter 14 in this book, Steve describes his intellectual development, with characteristic modesty, as a journey to become a "global theologian." He traces the constant widening of his theological horizon, from the self-assured Catholic theology imbibed in Rome, which he calls "Roman theology," to the disquieting and enriching encounters with other theologies and religious traditions around the globe with their distinctive modes of thought and methodologies, from Rome to Asia, Australia, Africa, Latin America, and of course, the United States, where he has spent most of his professional life. This theological enlargement, over the years and across continents, can easily be documented by taking a look at Steve's bibliography, also appended in this book.

There are, of course, diverse and legitimate ways to give an account of Bevans's theological trajectory, but it is not inaccurate to say that it is fueled by three imaginations: the missiological imagination, the contextual imagination, and the dialogical imagination. These three imaginations serve as the framework with which to organize the materials of this book into three parts: Christian mission, contextual theology, and prophetic dialogue.

One of Bevans's startling claims, one that perhaps many of his colleagues in the more academically oriented universities may find disorienting, is that at the heart of theology lies the church's mission, or more precisely, *missio Dei*. This missiological imagination, as Steve calls it, came to him, he confesses, only after many years of teaching and research. As a major step in his theological development, however, it has shaped his theology, deeply and indelibly, and enables him to integrate theology as a global discipline with theological education. His magnum opus on mission *(Constants in Context: A Theology of Mission for Today),* co-authored with his confrere Roger Schroeder, has been translated into Spanish, Italian, Chinese, Indonesian, Korean, and Vietnamese. It comes as no surprise, then, that the first five chapters of this book (Part I) deal with Christian mission, in the New Testament and in Roman Catholic, Orthodox, Protestant, and evangelical theologies.

The second part touches on what Bevans is known the world over for, namely, contextual theology. His book *Models of Contextual Theology,* which has gone through an expanded edition and has been translated into multiple languages, is a landmark classic in the field and a widely popular textbook. It is fitting, therefore, that the four chapters of the second part discuss what Steve calls the contextual imagination, including the various methods of contextual theology and the many and diverse contexts in which it is practiced, such as European Enlightenment, empire building, racism, and world Christianity.

The third part of the book treats themes conveniently gathered under the rubric "Prophetic Dialogue." In his later writings Bevans, in collaboration with Schroeder, develops a model of mission as prophetic dialogue. By dialogue he means, of course, encounter among different Christian traditions (ecumenical dialogue, in which he has been very active and on which he has published prolifically) and between Christianity and other religions (interreligious dialogue). More important, for Bevans what is required is the dialogical imagination, a fundamental mode of being, for individual Christians as well as for the church, which is deeply marked by respectful listening to the Other, sincere openness of mind and heart, deep intellectual humility, genuine willingness to learn and change, and generous hospitality toward the Other. But this dialogue is prophetic, that is, it must have the courage to speak truth to power to restore justice, to build up peace, and to maintain the integrity of creation. The four chapters of this part deal with various aspects of prophetic dialogue, from liberation to dialogue with cultures, interreligious dialogue, and mission-led ecclesiology.

The final part of the book presents Bevans's reflections on his personal and intellectual journey, as intimated above, to become a global theologian. But Bevans the "global theologian" is also inextricably a "local theologian." To use a neologism, he is a "glocal theologian" par excellence. In his theology he is a missionary, a contextualist, a prophetic dialoguer, all at once and to an unmatched degree. That is Steve's lasting legacy, and his colleagues and students, and may I say, the church as a whole, are forever in his debt. Dear Steve: If this book sells well, the dreamt-of cruise to an exotic island of your choice, in the joyous company of your friends, colleagues, students, and admirers, is not beyond the realm of possibility!

Contributors

Stephen B. Bevans, SVD, is professor emeritus of mission and culture at Catholic Theological Union in Chicago, where he also serves as the faculty advisor for the CTU program "Catholics on Call." He is a commissioner on the World Council of Churches' Commission on World Mission and Evangelism, a member of the Society of the Divine Word's Arnold Janssen Spirituality Team, and a member of his SVD Chicago Province's Provincial Council. He is an editor of the Brill series "Theology of Mission in Global Christianity" and on the editorial board of the *International Review of Mission*. His current work includes research into Pope Francis's thinking on inculturation and on Francis's signature phrase "the culture of encounter."

Carolyn Chau is associate professor of systematic and moral theology at King's University College in London, Ontario, Canada. She is on the executive board of the Centre for Advanced Research in Catholic Thought at King's and has served as a member of the Anglican–Roman Catholic dialogue and the Catholic-evangelical dialogue for the Canadian Conference of Catholic Bishops. Her book *Solidarity with the World: Charles Taylor and Hans Urs von Balthasar on Faith, Modernity, and Catholic Mission* proposes a local ecclesiology of mission for secular cultures in the West.

Gemma Tulud Cruz, a native of the Philippines, taught for several years in the United States before moving to Australian Catholic University where she is senior lecturer in theology at its Melbourne campus. Gemma has written extensively and lectured widely on migration and liberationist theologies. She is author of *Pilgrims in the Wilderness: Toward an Intercultural Theology of Migration* and *Toward a Theology of Migration: Social Justice and Religious Experience*.

José M. de Mesa is a university fellow and past professor of theology at De La Salle University in Manila. He has written several books both in Filipino and in English, including *Bakas: Retrieving the Sense of Sacramentality of the Ordinary, Why Theology Is Never Far Away from Home*, and *José M. de Mesa: A Theological Reader*. He currently teaches systematic theology at the Inter-Congregational Theological Center, the Institute of Formation and Religious Studies, and Maryhill School of Theology, all located in Quezon City, the Philippines.

Dale T. Irvin is president of New York Theological Seminary and professor of world Christianity. He is the co-author with Scott W. Sunquist of *History of the World Christian Movement*. His articles have appeared in a number of journals, among them *Christianity Today, The Ecumenical Review,* and *The Journal of Pentecostal Studies*. He is currently the executive vice president and member of the editorial board of *The Living Pulpit*, a highly acclaimed journal for preaching. He is also a regular teacher and preacher in churches throughout the New York City region.

Veli-Matti Kärkkäinen is professor of systematic theology at Fuller Theological Seminary, Pasadena, California, and docent of ecumenics at the University of Helsinki. A native of Finland, he has also lived and taught theology in Thailand. An ordained Lutheran minister (ELCA) and an expert in Pentecostal-Charismatic theologies, Dr. Kärkkäinen has participated widely in ecumenical, theological, and interreligious work. His projects include the five-volume series *Constructive Christian Theology for the Pluralistic World*, which develops a full-scale Christian systematic theology in critical dialogue with Christian tradition, sciences, and four living faiths.

Leo D. Lefebure is the Matteo Ricci, SJ, Professor of Theology at Georgetown University. He is author of *True and Holy: Christian Scripture and Other Religions; The Buddha and the Christ*; and *Revelation, the Religions, and Violence*. He is co-author with Peter Feldmeier of *The Path of Wisdom: A Christian Commentary on the* Dhammapada. He is vice president of the Society for Buddhist-Christian Studies, research fellow of the Chinese University of Hong Kong, and trustee emeritus of the Council for a Parliament of the World's Religions.

vanThanh Nguyen, SVD, is professor of New Testament studies and the Francis X. Ford, MM, Chair of Catholic Missiology at Catholic Theological Union in Chicago. He is a religious missionary of the Society of the Divine Word and has published several books and numerous articles and book chapters in the areas of Bible, migration, and mission.

Thomas F. O'Meara, a priest of the Dominican Order, grew up in Des Moines, Iowa, and Madison, Wisconsin. After doctoral education in Munich, Germany, he taught at Aquinas Institute and Wartburg Lutheran Seminary in Dubuque, Iowa; Boston College; and the University of Ibadan in Nigeria. He was also a professor at the University of Notre Dame from 1981 to 2002. A past president of the Catholic Theological Society of America, he has authored fifteen books, including *Theology of Ministry* and *Thomas Aquinas Theologian*.

Athanasios N. Papathanasiou is an Orthodox lay theologian living in Athens, Greece. He holds a doctorate in missiology and degrees in theology and law. He teaches missiology, history of religions, canon law, and ecclesiastical law at the Supreme Ecclesiastical Academy of Athens as well as at the Hellenic Open University. He is editor-in-chief of the Greek theological quarterly *Synaxis*. He has done short-term missionary work in Kenya, Nigeria, and Tanzania.

Peter C. Phan, who has earned three doctorates, is the inaugural holder of the Ignacio Ellacuría Chair of Catholic Social Thought at Georgetown University. His research deals with the theology of icons in Orthodox theology; patristic theology; eschatology; the history of Christian missions in Asia; and liberation, inculturation, and interreligious dialogue. He is the author and editor of over thirty books and has published over three hundred essays. His writings have been translated into Arabic, French, German, Italian, Polish, Portuguese, Romanian, Serbian, Spanish, Chinese, Indonesian, Japanese, and Vietnamese, and have received many awards from learned societies. He is the first non-Anglo to be elected president of Catholic Theological Society of America and president of the American Theological Society.

Barbara E. Reid, O.P., has served on the Catholic Theological Union faculty in Chicago since 1988. She served as vice president and academic dean from 2009 to 2018 and has been actively involved in the Association of Theological Schools, including service on their board of directors. A leading scholar in feminist interpretation of the scriptures, she is general editor for the Wisdom Commentary Series, a fifty-eight-volume feminist commentary on the Bible published by Liturgical Press.

Robert Schreiter, CPPS, holds the Vatican Council II Chair of Theology at the Catholic Theological Union in Chicago. He has written in the areas of contextual theology, the mission of the church, and reconciliation and forgiveness. He is past president of the American Society of Missiology and the Catholic Theological Society of America. Among his books are *Constructing Local Theologies, The New Catholicity: Theology between the Global and the Local, Reconciliation: Mission and Ministry in a Changing Social Order*, and *The Ministry of Reconciliation: Spirituality and Strategies*.

Roger Schroeder earned a doctorate degree in missiology from the Pontifical Gregorian University in Rome in 1990. Since then he has taught at Catholic Theological Union in Chicago, where he holds the Louis J. Luzbetak, SVD, Chair of Mission and Culture. His publications include *What Is the Mission of the Church? A Guide for Catholics*, and the following books co-authored with Stephen Bevans: *Constants in Context: A Theology of Mission for Today* and *Prophetic Dialogue: Reflections on Christian Mission Today*. A member of the Society of the Divine Word, he worked as a missionary in Papua New Guinea for six years. His recent writing has been in the areas of world Christianity, interculturality, and indigenous peoples.

Anh Q. Tran, SJ, is associate professor of systematic and historical theology at Santa Clara University's Jesuit School of Theology and Graduate Theological Union at Berkeley. A curious learner, he holds advanced degrees in electrical engineering, health-care ethics, pastoral studies, theology, and theological and religious studies. He is the author of *Gods, Heroes, and Ancestors* and contributor and co-editor, with Jonathan Y. Tan, of *World Christianity: Perspectives and Insights.*

PART 1

CHRISTIAN MISSION

Chapter 1

The Final Testimony of Missio Dei: A Missiological Reading of Revelation

vanThanh Nguyen, SVD

INTRODUCTION

I am an immigrant who became a religious missionary of the Society of the Divine Word, which is an apostolic congregation within the Roman Catholic tradition that serves God's people in over seventy-two countries. Although my parents originally came from North Vietnam, I was actually born and raised in the South of my homeland. After the fall of Saigon in 1975, my family and I immigrated to the United States as refugees, seeking religious freedom and other basic human rights that were no longer available under Vietnam's oppressive political regime. My family certainly knows what it's like to be stripped of all fundamental human rights, especially the freedoms of expression and worship. To live under such conditions as dedicated Christians was not an option! We preferred to die together at sea in a flimsy boat, seeking "a new heaven and a new earth" (Rev 21:1), than to live by accommodating to its atheist ideology and deceptive propaganda.

My mother's resilient faith and unwavering hope have been a great inspiration to my missionary vocation. Even at a very young age I felt a deep call to be a witness. Like John of Patmos, I accepted God's invitation with much enthusiasm—perhaps not to the point of actually eating the scroll (Rev 10:10)—to go wherever God would lead me to proclaim the good news of Jesus Christ in "every nation, race, people, and tongue" (Rev 5:9; 7:9). But working overseas or outside of the United States was not part of God's plan for me. Inspired by Steve Bevans, who is my confrere and former teacher, I followed in his footsteps and pursued an academic career and became a transmitter of God's good word through the ministry of teaching and learning as a religious missionary priest of the Divine Word. Luckily, Steve's footprints were too big to miss and too profound to be washed away by the waves of the sea. In some mysterious ways Steve had a hand in leading me to the Catholic Theological Union, where we have become not only colleagues but friends. His scholarship in the areas of mission theology in general and prophetic dialogue in particular has made him a trailblazer. Steve's encouragement and mentorship have helped me to see the deep connection between Bible and mission.

I am convinced that God's redemptive activity or *missio Dei* is the central and unifying theme of the entire Christian scriptures. From Genesis to Revelation the Bible is a meta-narrative that gives witness to the ultimate mission of God whereby the *missio Dei* is established and restored. Unfortunately, Revelation is usually misinterpreted as a book of judgment and pertaining to specific end-time events. Furthermore, violent descriptions of war and catastrophic scenes of ecological destruction cause many to shy away from this last canonical book of the Bible and therefore "often downplay its importance for mission."[1] A possible source of this misconception is that readers are not patient enough to read all the way to the end of the story—Revelation 21:1–5—to see the breathtaking hope and amazing promises that the book offers. Commenting on the Book of Revelation, Nelson Kraybill states, "No book of the Bible has a more comprehensive and hopeful vision of salvation."[2]

As I shall make clear, the Book of Revelation, or the Apocalypse, is primarily about redemption and salvation by Jesus Christ, who will give the final testimony of *missio Dei*. Biblical scholars and even missiologists too often overlooked the central theme of the mission of God and God's people in Revelation. The aim of this chapter is to read and interpret Revelation missiologically in order to unveil God's missional purpose to redeem the nations and all of creation. Let us begin by examining the literary and historical contexts of this complex and often misinterpreted sacred book.

THE APOCALYPTIC PROPHET OF HOPE

The Book of Revelation belongs to the genre of apocalyptic literature (*apokalypsis* in Greek means "revelation" or "unveiling" by which the book also gets its name, the Apocalypse). Similar to most Jewish apocalypses (1 Enoch, Daniel 7—12, 4 Ezra, Apocalypse of Abraham, 2 Baruch), Revelation too was composed during a time of crisis.[3] When life as a believer was hanging by a thread, Revelation played a crucial role in providing

[1] Dean Flemming, *Why Mission?* (Nashville, TN: Abingdon Press, 2015), 109.

[2] J. Nelson Kraybill, "The New Jerusalem as Paradigm for Mission," *Mission Focus Annual Review* 2 (1994): 123.

[3] Wilfrid J. Harrington, *Revelation*, Sacra Pagina 16 (Collegeville, MN: Liturgical Press, 1993), 1–8.

hope to those in the midst of trial and life's uncertainty.[4] While the main framework of the book is an *apocalypse* revealing "what must happen soon" (1:1), it is also a *prophecy* that gives "witness to the Word of God and to the testimony of Jesus Christ" (1:2). A third interesting feature about this book is that it is written in the form of a *letter*, which identifies the sender ("John") and the addressees ("to the seven churches that are in Asia"), and includes the common greeting "Grace to you and peace" (1:4). The presence of these three literary features has led Dianne Bergant to identify Revelation as "a hybrid document, a visionary apocalyptic writing, expressed in the form of an epistle that functions prophetically."[5] Furthermore, as an "apocalyptic-prophetic-letter," it is meant to be read aloud and heard, for it states, "Blessed is the one who reads aloud and blessed are those who listen to this prophetic message" (1:3).[6]

To the seven scattered Christian communities that were being weighed down by discouragement and fatigue, the author, who identified himself as John (1:1, 4, 9; 22:8), rather than remaining anonymous (or more typically, pseudonymous) wrote to give strength to the faint of heart and security to the despairing. John seemed to have been a wandering Christian prophet (1:3, 10–11; 22:9, 18–19) but is now exiled on the island of Patmos (1:9). The author claimed to be neither an apostle nor an elder (cf. 2 Jn 1:1; 3 Jn 1:1) and therefore most likely had little connection with the rest of the Johannine corpus. Although the world appeared to be collapsing and disappearing (19:11—20:15), this "servant" (1:1; 22:9) and their "brother" (1:9) encouraged his fellow Christians to remain steadfast in faith and boldly to resist the allurement of Rome's imperial cult and the false theological claims of its emperor as god and savior. Consequently, scholars agree that the book was written sometime during the reign of the Roman Emperor Domitian (81–96 CE). Because there is no extra-biblical evidence of systematic persecution at this time, there is no scholarly consensus as to whether the crisis or struggle described in the book refers to a persecution that was initiated by the Emperor Domitian.[7] Nevertheless, it is clear that Revelation was composed during a time of spiritual crisis

---

[4] Gale Z. Heide, "What Is New about the New Heaven and the New Earth? A Theology of Creation from Revelation 21 and 2 Peter 3," *Journal of the Evangelical Theological Society* 40/1 (March 1997): 37.

[5] Dianne Bergant, *A New Heaven, A New Earth: The Bible and Catholicity* (Maryknoll, NY: Orbis Books, 2016), 170.

[6] Ibid., 170; see also Frank J. Matera, *New Testament Theology: Exploring Diversity and Unity* (Louisville, KY: Westminster John Knox Press, 2007), 402.

[7] The sources that are dated to or around the time of the Book of Revelation do not support the popular image of Christian martyrs being thrown to the lions in the Coliseum of Rome or that the Romans tried to stamp Christianity out through relentless persecution. See especially Frederick J. Murphy, *Fallen Is Babylon: The Revelation of John* (Harrisburg, PA: Trinity Press International, 1998), 5–17; Wes

and social calamity, probably in the mid-90s CE, when Christians in Asia Minor (modern Turkey) were facing a challenge even more difficult than persecution.

BEARING FAITHFUL WITNESS

Most scholars today agree that persecution was not the main factor that threatened the existence of the seven Christian communities.[8] While there was minor local opposition, the principal challenge for the early Christians who lived in the midst of the Roman Empire was its attraction.[9] The commodities of Greco-Roman cities and its affluent lifestyles, public baths, theatrical entertainment, and imperial cults seduced many Christian believers.[10] To the seven communities (*ecclesia*), the author wrote *to criticize* those who had lost their prophetic edge and *to energize* those who were experiencing hardships.[11] His threefold message to the seven communities was to resist cultural assimilation, to overcome complacency, and to persevere in times of adversity.[12]

Believers at Ephesus, Pergamum, and Thyatira had compromised their faith through cultural accommodation to the Roman Empire; so much so that the church barely existed anymore. To the Ephesians, John writes, "But I have this against you, that you have abandoned the love you had at first. Remember then from what you have fallen; repent, and do the works you did at first. If not, I will come to you and remove your lampstand from its place, unless you repent" (2:4–5).[13] The message to communities in Pergamum (2:14–16) and Thyatira (2:20–23) is one and the same,

---

Howard-Brook and Anthony Gwyther, *Unveiling Empire: Reading Revelation Then and Now* (Maryknoll, NY: Orbis Books, 1999) 87–118.

[8] Leonard L. Thompson, *The Book of Revelation: Apocalypse and Empire* (Oxford: Oxford University Press, 1990), 116–32.

[9] Howard-Brook and Gwyther, *Unveiling Empire*, 87–119. See also Murphy, *Fallen Is Babylon*, 5–17.

[10] vanThanh Nguyen, "Evangelizing Empire: The Gospel and Mission of St. Paul," *SEDOS Bulletin* 41 (May–June 2009): 99–105.

[11] vanThanh Nguyen, "A Vision of Cosmic Transformation (Rev 21:1–5)," *The Bible Today* 46 (2008): 371–76. These two features of prophecy, *to criticize* and *to energize,* are similar to Bevans's and Schroeder's two natures of prophecy: *speaking against* and *speaking forth*. See Stephen B. Bevans and Roger Schroeder, *Prophetic Dialogue: Reflections on Christian Mission Today* (Maryknoll, NY: Orbis Books, 2011), 42–43.

[12] See Craig R. Koester, "Revelation's Visionary Challenge to Ordinary Empire," *Interpretation* 63 (2009): 5–18; and idem, *Revelation and the End of All Things* (Grand Rapids, MI: Eerdmans, 2001), 1–40.

[13] All biblical quotations are taken from the *New American Bible* (NAB).

namely, to resist cultural assimilation by refusing to eat food sacrificed to idols or practicing fornication. For the prophet John, their assimilation had compromised their Christian faith.

Believers at Sardis and Laodicea faced a different situation. The danger did not seem to come from overt hostility but from the kind of comfortable conditions that led to complacency. Both of these communities were economically affluent and therefore took pride in being self-sufficient. To the community in Laodicea, Christ declares, "I know your works; you are neither cold nor hot. I wish that you were either cold or hot. So, because you are lukewarm, and neither cold nor hot, I am about to spit you out of my mouth. For you say, 'I am rich, I have prospered, and I need nothing.' You do not realize that you are wretched, pitiable, poor, and blind, and naked" (3:15–17). The description gives us a picture of a complacent and apathetic community. While the community is not accused of any major heresy or immoral practices, its self-satisfied complacency and half-hearted commitment were enough to make Christ sick! Similarly, Christ criticized the believers at Sardis, "I know your works; you have a name of being alive, but you are dead" (3:1b). It seems that both the communities, at Sardis and Laodicea, had no zeal or intensity and therefore were ineffective and useless.

Among the seven communities, Smyrna and Philadelphia are the only ones that Christ did not criticize. The messages mainly contain words of commendation and encouragement in times of suffering and persecution. To the community in Smyrna, Christ says, "I know your affliction and your poverty, even though you are rich. I know the slander on the part of those who say that they are Jews and are not, but a synagogue of Satan" (2:9). The community at Philadelphia apparently experienced a similar situation. Its members too were expelled from the synagogue and publicly denounced by the Jewish officials. Without the privileges and protections afforded by the Jews, members of the Philadelphian community were attacked and persecuted by the Romans. Yet, despite suffering and hostility on all fronts, the community remained zealous in its commitment and faith. Its members did not waver in their resistance to the seduction of the empire but rather stood firm in their prophetic witness to Christ as their savior and redeemer. While the door of the local synagogue was closed to the Christian believers, Christ nevertheless promised them a new passage: "I know your works. Look, I have set before you an open door, which no one is able to shut. I know that you have but little power, and yet you have kept my word and have not denied my name" (3:8). The principal message for these two communities is not to be afraid (2:10) and to patiently endure (3:10) during the interim period. Christ assures them: "I am coming soon; hold fast to what you have, so that no one may seize your crown" (3:11). Christ's message to the suffering believers is filled with hope and powerfully reaffirming in the dire straits of their situation.

TESTIMONY TO CHRIST AS CREATOR AND REDEEMER

Descriptions of plagues, violent battle scenes, ecological destruction, the dragon and the beast, 666, Armageddon, just to mention a few, usually cause trepidation in readers. Hence, Revelation is generally considered anything but good news. On the contrary, however, it is heavily Christo-centric, containing seven christological acclamations (see Table 1), seven liturgies honoring the position of Christ (see Table 2), and seven beatitudes (see Table 3).

In addition, there are numerous titles uniquely attributed to Christ, of which seven are worth mentioning (for a complete list, see Table 4):

- Jesus
- Christ
- Son of Man
- Almighty
- Lamb
- Lord of lords and King of kings
- Alpha and Omega

Our brief survey shows that this book is truly a "revelation (*apokalypsis*) of Jesus Christ" (1:1) as triumphal Savior who is the object and focus of the book. The centrality of Christ affirms that he is Lord of the universe; moreover, the Lamb who was once slain and was resurrected is also the redeemer. Since Christ functioned as God, he is the object of worship and adoration. Two texts will suffice to show that Christ is both creator and redeemer. In the vision of the heavenly liturgy, John saw the twenty-four elders throwing down their crowns before the throne, exclaiming: "Worthy are you, Lord our God, to receive glory and honor and power, for you created all things; because of your will they came to be and were created" (4:11; cf. the christological hymn in Colossians 1:15–20). In the vision of the "great multitude," people from every nation, race, and tongue acclaim: "Salvation comes from our God, who is seated on the throne, and from the Lamb" (7:10). Those who are washed white in the blood of the Lamb will "not hunger or thirst any more, nor will the sun or any heat strike them. For the Lamb who is in the center of the throne will shepherd them and lead them to springs of life-giving water, and God will wipe away every tear from their eyes" (7:16–17).

THE TESTIMONY OF *MISSIO DEI*

For John, only Christ is the Almighty One or *pantocrator* (1:8; 4:8; 11:17; 15:3; 16:7; 19:6; 21:22) who will create a new heaven and a new

	Table 1	
	Seven Christological Acclamations	
References	Speakers	Acclamations
1:8	The Lord God	"I am the Alpha and the Omega," says the Lord God, "the one who is and who was and who is to come, the almighty."
5:9–10	Twenty-four elders	"Worthy are you to receive the scroll and to break open the seals, for you were slain and with your blood you purchased for God those from every tribe and tongue, people and nation. You made them a kingdom and priests for our God, and they will reign on earth."
5:12	Countless numbers of angels, living creatures, and elders	"Worthy is the Lamb that was slain to receive power and riches, wisdom and strength, honor and glory and blessing."
5:13	Every creature in heaven and on earth and under the earth and in the sea	"To the one who sits on the throne and to the Lamb be blessing and honor, glory and might, forever and ever."
7:10	A great multitude from every nation, race, people, and tongue	"Salvation comes from our God, who is seated on the throne, and from the Lamb."
11:15	Voices in heaven	"The kingdom of the world now belongs to our Lord and to his Anointed, and he will reign forever and ever."
19:6–8	Sound of a great multitude or rushing water or mighty peals of thunder	"Alleluia! The Lord has established his reign, [our] God, the almighty. Let us rejoice and be glad and give him glory. For the wedding day of the Lamb has come, his bride has made herself ready. She was allowed to wear a bright, clean linen garment."

Table 2
Seven Liturgies Honoring the Position of Christ

Titles	References
"Heavenly Throne Scene"	4:2–11
"The Lamb and the Scroll"	5:8–14
"Song of Victory to the Lamb"	7:9–17
"Song Celebrating the Messianic Empire"	11:15–19
"Enthronement of the Lamb on Zion"	14:1–5
"Song to the King of Nations"	15:2–8
"Song of Victory of God's People"	19:1–8

Table 3
Seven Beatitudes

1:3	"Blessed is the one who reads aloud and blessed are those who listen to this prophetic message and heed what is written in it, for the appointed time is near."
14:13	"Blessed are the dead who die in the Lord from now on."
16:15	"Blessed is the one who watches and keeps his clothes ready, so that he may not go naked and people see him exposed."
19:9	"Blessed are those who have been called to the wedding feast of the Lamb."
20:6	"Blessed and holy is the one who shares in the first resurrection."
22:7	"Blessed is the one who keeps the prophetic message of this book."
11:14	"Blessed are they who wash their robes so as to have the right to the tree of life and enter the city through its gates."

Table 4
The Titles of Christ in Revelation
(adapted from Jean-Pierre Prevost, *How to Read the Apocalypse* [New York: Crossroad, 1993], 6–7)

References	Titles
1:1, 2, 5, 9; 12:17; 14:12; 17:6; 19:10; 20:4; 22:16, 20, 21	Jesus
1:1, 2, 5; 11:15; 12:10; 20:4, 6	Christ
1:5	The faithful witness
1:5	The First-born of the dead
1:5	The Ruler of kings on earth
1:5	Who loves us and has freed us from our sins by his blood
1:6	Who has made us a kingdom of priests to his God and Father
1:13; 14:14	A Son of man
1:17; 2:8; 22:13	The First and the Last
1:18	The Living one; I died, and behold I am alive for evermore, and I have the keys of death and Hades
2:1; 3:1	Who holds the seven stars
2:1	Who walks among the seven golden lampstands
2:8	Who died and came to life
2:12	Who has the sharp two-edged sword
2:18	The words of the Son of God
2:23	I am he who searches mind and heart
3:1	The words of him who has the seven spirits of God and the seven stars
3:7	The words of the Holy One
3:7; 19:11	The True One
3:7	Who has the key of David
3:14	The words of the Amen, the faithful and true witness
3:14	The beginning of God's creation
5:5	The Lion of the tribe of Judah
5:5; 22:16	The Root of David
5:6, 8, 12, 13; 6:1, 16; 7:8, 10, 14; 12:11; 13:8; 14:1, 4, 10; 15:3; 17:14; 19:7, 9; 21:9, 14, 22, 23, 27; 22:1, 3	The Lamb
5:6, 12; 13:8	A Lamb, as though it has been slain
11:8	Their Lord
12:5	A male child, one who is to rule all the nations with a rod of iron
19:13	The Word of God
19:16	King of Kings and Lord of lords
21:6; 22:13	I am the Alpha and the Omega, the First and the Last
22:16	The bright morning Star

earth, fulfilling Old Testament prophecies and promises. "Behold," says the
one who sat on the throne, "I make all things new" (21:5). Furthermore,
the author clearly announces that Christ alone—not Augustus or the Roman imperial economy—has the power to make things new and can bring
order out of the present political and social chaos. Besides, Christ has not
abandoned his creation but fully intends to bring it to fulfillment, for he
says, "Behold, I make all things new" (21:5). Such a christological affirmation must have generated an ecstasy of hope for Christians who were under
trial and distress. It reawakened fervent hope in them as they waited for
the return of Christ by bringing the whole of his creation to its purposed
end, its *telos*, which will be the final victory and triumph of *missio Dei*.

The New Heaven and New Earth

The expression "the new heaven and the new earth" (21:1) is not
unfamiliar in biblical and nonbiblical traditions. It is found in Jewish
apocalyptic literature (1 Enoch 45:4–5; 91:16) and even in targumic and
rabbinic writings (*Tg. Jer.* 23:23).[14] However, in Revelation 21:1–5 John
clearly draws on Isaiah's prophetic promise: "Lo, I am about to create new
heavens and a new earth; the things of the past shall not be remembered
or come to mind" (Isa 65:17; cf. 66:22). The creation motif appears at
various significant junctures in Revelation. The opening and final visions
present God as the "first and last" (1:8; 21:6; 22:13) who is Lord over
all creation and controls human history according to his purposes. God's
work in creation and God's creative work of redemption are manifested
in the actions of the Lamb (4:1–11; 5:1–14). God will restore order out
of chaos by creating things anew (10:5–6; 14:7; 21:1–22:5).

Why is there such a focus on creation language? Second Isaiah provides
important clues for understanding Revelation. As Israel faced near extinction in Babylon, it questioned whether God possessed any more power
to help, for it seemed that God had already deserted his people. To instill
hope and reassert God's faithful promises to his people, Second Isaiah
(40—45) employs creation images to confirm that God is still the creator
and ruler of the whole universe who has not abandoned but favors his
chosen people (see especially Isa 40:28–31; 41:8–10, 14; 42:5–9; 43:1;
44:1–8, 21; 45:1–8).

As in Second Isaiah, Christians in John's day also had to face their own
Babylon, namely, Rome. By employing similar creation language and motifs, John unveiled the false claims that Rome had established world peace
and eternal dominion—*Pax Romana* and *Roma Aeterna*.[15] It is interesting

---

[14] Heide, "What Is New about the New Heaven," 41–43.

[15] Howard-Brook and Gwyther, *Unveiling Empire*, 223–34.

to note that Domitian, like his predecessor Augustus, claimed to embody peace and eternity. On his minted coins the goddess *Aeternitas* is often depicted as holding the sun and moon, which are symbols of eternity. John of Patmos challenged the emperor as guarantor of peace and eternity by asserting that God (7:12), Jesus (1:6; 5:13; 11:15), and followers of the Lamb (22:5) are the ones who truly possess eternity. Like Babylon, Rome too has fallen (18:2), and Christ, the Lamb who was slain, has established a new world peace and order where the Lord and his followers will live "forever and ever" (4:9–10; 10:6; 15:7). John's vision of new cosmic beginning must have brought tremendous comfort and nurtured incredible hope.

The New Jerusalem

Now that Armageddon is over, Satan and the beast are destroyed, and Babylon is judged, John can finally unveil the good news. Consequently, Revelation 21:1–5 is the narrative climax of the book and the pinnacle of hope for John's readers. The question is, What do the new heaven and the new earth look like? The concentric structure of Revelation 21:1–5 points to the heart of the matter:

A – A new heaven and a new earth (v. 1a)
   B – Former heaven and former earth had passed away (v. 1b)
      C – No more sea (v. 1c)
         D – New Jerusalem (vv. 2–3)
      C' – No more death (4a)
   B' – Former things have passed away (4b)
A' – All things made new (5a)

According to John's vision, "the new heaven and a new earth" is none other than the New Jerusalem, the holy and ideal city of God's future home on earth. There are stunning contrasts between Babylon and the New Jerusalem: the whore (17:1) versus the Bride (21:2); the beast (17:3) versus the Lamb (21:9); the great city (17:18) versus the holy city (21:2); darkness (18:23) versus light (21:23); dwelling of demons (18:2) versus dwelling of God (21:3); smoking ruin (18:9) versus splendid garden (22:3); weeping and wailing (18:11, 15) versus no tears or sorrow (21:4); death (18:24) versus life (21:4). The stark contrasts between the two cities reveal them as polar opposites. Since Babylon (Rome) is evil (18:24) and full of vices (21:8) and stands in diametric opposition to the ways of God, Christians must "come out of her" (18:4) in order to enter into the new heavenly city on earth where God and people live side by side under one tent (21:3).

John's vision of the New Jerusalem shares some commonality with Ezekiel's final vision (Ezek 40—48), but there are significant differences.

In the New Jerusalem there is no temple, because God and the Lamb are the temple (21:22);[16] there is no need of sun or moon, for the glory of God and the Lamb are its light and lamp (21:23); there is no need for locked gates, for only those who are righteous and pure may enter it (21:25–27). Its architecture, measurements, and the materials that adorn the city are symbols of perfection, plentitude, and preciousness par excellence. Noticeably, the symbolic number twelve is used repeatedly: twelve gates (21:12, 21), twelve angels (21:12), twelve tribes (21:12), twelve foundations (21:14), twelve names of apostles (21:14), twelve thousand stadia (21:16), 144 cubits (12x12) (21:17), twelve pearls (21:21), and twelve kinds of fruits (22:2). The number twelve commonly represents the tribes of Israel, but here the consecrated number is no longer limited to Israel but represents all nations—a new chosen race that is inclusive and universal. Even foreigners (*ethne*) stream to the holy city with their treasures and are welcomed (21:24, 26). John's vision of God's future home on earth is filled with life (22:1–2) and joy (22:3) so transforming and radical as to be a "new creation" providing comfort to those who dare to dream of a better tomorrow. Perhaps the question of most interest is, When will this take place?

MISSION AS DIALOGUE AND PROPHECY: TRIBUTE AND CONCLUSION

John's apocalyptic vision of a new cosmic beginning is often misunderstood as purely future oriented and therefore has little or nothing to do with the present creation. By means of a literary *inclusio* to remind his readers that Revelation is a prophecy (22:7, 10; cf. 1:3), John of Patmos stands in continuity with the classical prophets of the Bible whose prophetic message is meant to shock people of the present rather than those of the future. Consequently, the vision of the "new heaven and a new earth" is not meant to be an escape from this world, as if we have no participation and responsibility, but rather an invitation to renew our commitment to care for our earth, to work for peace, to fight for justice, and to inaugurate not so much a new creation but rather a renewed and transformed world where war, violence, and human suffering will be no more. This is the *missio Dei*, which is the mission of the church! Barbara Rossing succinctly states:

Today, the vision of the New Jerusalem can empower a renewed commitment to environmental justice, to the health of our cities, rivers, forests, oceans, neighbors, and world. It can shape our vision for addressing our urban and ecological crises—crises such as the

[16] Gregory K. Beale, "Eden, the Temple, and the Church's Mission in the New Creation," *Journal of the Evangelical Theological Society* 48/1 (March 2005): 29.

global market economy that marginalizes millions of people while decimating forests and ecosystems, crises that sap our moral will as environmental problems become both more complex and more urgent. *Revelation* offers nothing less than God's vision of justice and healing for the entire human and natural world—for all of creation.[17]

In our examination of the Book of Revelation, John of Patmos criticized five of the seven communities for having been seduced by the empire. Dean Flemming says, "For John's readers, the call to participate in God's mission is lived out on the dusty streets and in the crowded tenements of the Roman Empire."[18] Perhaps some of our communities have become too assimilated into our culture, and we have accommodated ourselves too fully to be able to criticize our social, political, economic, and religious institutions. Is it possible that our secular lifestyle and globalization have made us complacent, losing some of our original zeal and passion to radically follow Jesus's life and mission? For those of us for whom this may be so, John's admonition is resoundingly clear—"Come out" of the empire and boycott it (18:2–4). Perhaps by resisting the empire, Christians all over the world will re-energize their prophetic vocation and identity. Notice that the Greek word *prophetes* literally means "one who is called or summoned." To be prophetic is indeed an essential character and function of our way of life. Like all biblical characters we are summoned to be a prophetic voice and presence in our contemporary world and church so that God's missional purpose of redemption for the whole cosmos will be realized. If we do this, then we act as "lampstands" (1:12, 13, 20) and thus truly become the light of God to the world around us.

Interestingly, Steve Bevans (along with Roger Schroeder) has written extensively on mission as dialogue and prophecy. According to Bevans and Schroeder, mission is an activity done in dialogue because "God in God's life and activity is dialogical."[19] However, Bevans and Schroeder clarify, saying: "Mission simply *as dialogue* is not enough. Ultimately, we believe, mission is best done in *prophetic dialogue*."[20] As pointed out by the two missionaries, there are two characteristics of prophecy. First, prophecy is "speaking forth" or announcing the good news of the reign of God.[21] Similar to the main thrust of the Book of Revelation, its annunciation is not primarily concerned with future foretelling but rather the vision of

---

[17] Barbara R. Rossing, "For the Healing of the World: Reading Revelation Ecologically," in *From Every People and Nation: The Book of Revelation in Intercultural Perspective*, ed. David Rhoads (Minneapolis: Fortress Press, 2005), 178.

[18] Flemming, *Why Mission?* 117.

[19] Bevans and Schroeder, *Prophetic Dialogue*, 41.

[20] Ibid., 38.

[21] Ibid., 43–46. As has been pointed out above, Bevans's and Schroeder's two natures of prophecy are similar to biblical prophecy, namely, *to energize* (speaking forth) and *to criticize* (speaking against).

the fulfillment of God's awesome plan for humanity and the cosmos. It is precisely the new heaven and a new earth that John of Patmos has envisioned. Second, prophecy is "speaking against" or denouncing that which is contrary to God's reign or the *missio Dei*.[22] These two essential features of prophecy are found in the Book of Revelation, which this essay has unveiled as the final testimony of *missio Dei*. Thus, in every aspect, Bevans's and Schroeder's work on mission as prophetic dialogue is perfectly aligned with the dialogical and prophetic message of the last book of the Bible.

In conclusion, as the early Christians were challenged by the allurement of the Roman Empire, John's vision of the new heaven and the new earth ignited new hope for Christians to continue to bear the gruesome realities of life and to resist the seduction of cultural allurement. Likewise, John's vision of a new cosmic beginning inspires us not to lose hope despite the realities of our own brokenness and violent bloodshed in our cities and throughout our world today. We are invited to faithfully worship Jesus Christ as the one true Creator and Redeemer and to bear witness to his *missio Dei* in the world without compromise. Yet, we know that, despite our best efforts, the new heaven and a new earth will never be fully achieved until Christ returns in glory. Until that day, however, Christians must never cease to act uprightly and responsibly, to give witness to Christ's sovereignty, and to engage in "prophetic dialogue" by boldly *speaking forth* the good news of the reign of God and *speaking against* that which is contrary to the *missio Dei*.

---

[22] Ibid., 46–48.

Chapter 2

Mission in Roman Catholic Theology

Roger Schroeder

The understanding of mission has developed in great depth in Roman Catholic theology since the mid-twentieth century. However, it is important to situate this within the broader panorama of the church's history. The first section of this chapter provides a brief overview of how mission was perceived in various contexts from the beginning until the nineteenth century. The second and major portion treats the extensive developments of mission during the twentieth century primarily by focusing on official church documents and major Catholic missiological schools. The third section sketches the major theologies of mission today, particularly as articulated by Catholic theologians and Pope Francis, and then briefly introduces the most recent trends in mission theology of the twenty-first century.

BEGINNINGS THROUGH THE NINETEENTH CENTURY

Tracing mission in Roman Catholic theology over two thousand years would require a book-length treatment and reveal a rich and complex (and sometimes contradictory) development. Stephen Bevans has made a very significant contribution to such an endeavor as part of his co-authored ecumenical and global treatment of mission theology and history in *Constants in Context: A Theology of Mission for Today*. Here, I simply provide a snapshot of five periods of mission before the twentieth century. It is important to note that the word *mission* itself began to be used in our current sense only in the sixteenth century. Before that it was understood in a theological sense of the Father sending the Son, and the Father and Son sending the Spirit. The Jesuits, founded in 1540, "began using *mission* in a generic sense of carrying out whatever the pope requested. . . . [But soon] the meaning of *mission* specified the idea of being sent, but not necessarily beyond one's local area."[1] However, we shall now look at the theology and practice of mission through the church's history from today's broader understanding of mission.

Mission in the early church (100–301)[2] was grounded in a theology that tightly linked church, mission, and baptism. This was evident in the catechumenate process. "By baptism they became soldiers in an army which waged war not through physical force but through . . . [the] witness of a holy life and of love, not by the sword."[3] While the faith spread through the influence of traveling evangelists, bishops, apologists, teachers, and martyrs, the primary agents of mission were ordinary Christians who, according to Michael Green, were "gossiping the gospel"[4] in their daily interactions—at home, in the marketplace, and along trade routes. Likewise, women played a central role in the growth of Christianity through "official ministries," martyrdom, and in daily life.

During the six centuries of the post-Constantinian period (313–907), diverse theologies of mission were expressed primarily through a variety of vibrant monastic movements from the Mediterranean area across Asia to China.[5] The Roman Catholic understanding of mission drew heavily from the theologies of Augustine of Hippo and Anselm of Canterbury, with the beginnings of the "ecclesiasticization" of salvation and the theology of atonement through the satisfactory death of Jesus, respectively. The Catholic mission practice was represented by the forced conversion of the Saxons by Charlemagne, as one extreme, and by the gentle approach of Irish, Benedictine, and Anglo-Saxon monks and nuns, on the other end of the spectrum.

In the Middle Ages (1000–1453) the Catholic Church continued to understand salvation "fundamentally as otherworldly, individualistic and ecclesial."[6] Aquinas wrote that mission with those who had never been Christian was to be done without force.[7] This theology was generally followed by the women and men of the multiple forms of the Franciscan, Dominican, and beguine movements.[8] Francis of Assisi's gentle encounter with the sultan is an outstanding example of this. Ramon Llull, considered

[1] Stephen B. Bevans and Roger P. Schroeder, *Constants in Context: A Theology of Mission for Today* (Maryknoll, NY: Orbis Books, 2004), 173–74.

[2] See ibid., 74–98.

[3] E. Glenn Hinson, *The Evangelization of the Roman Empire* (Macon, GA: Mercer University Press, 1981), 87.

[4] Michael Green, *Evangelism in the Early Church* (Grand Rapids, MI: Eerdmans, 1970), 173.

[5] See Bevans and Schroeder, *Constants in Context*, 99–136.

[6] Ibid., 164.

[7] Thomas Aquinas, *Summa Theologiae* II-2. q. 10, a. 8.

[8] See Bevans and Schroeder, *Constants in Context*, 141–60.

"the first to develop a theory of missions,"[9] encouraged the use of reason in engaging Muslims. One should remember that the Crusades "were not intended to be instruments for spreading the Christian faith."[10]

Many outside Europe felt the Western impact as colonialism and mission joined hands over the next three centuries (1492–1773).[11] The pope gave the Catholic countries of Spain and Portugal the rights and responsibilities for mission. There were also two contrasting theologies of mission. In the Americas the prominent conquest model of the "cross and the sword" was opposed by a prophetic model that respected the human dignity and religious freedom of the indigenous. The theology of Ginés de Sepúlveda endorsed the former, De Vittorio the latter. In Asia the conflict between the imperial *tabula rasa* and the Jesuits' accommodational approaches reached its height in the Rites Controversy. Bañez and Suárez represented these two theologies, respectively.

Mission in the nineteenth century—between the French Revolution and World War I (1792–1914)—was situated within the three C's of colonialization, commerce, and Christianity.[12] The earlier Catholic prophetic and accommodational theologies of mission disappeared almost completely. "Regarding ecclesiology and soteriology, the Catholic Church continued with the operative though not official theology of 'outside the church, no salvation,'"[13] and "church" referred exclusively to the Roman Catholic Church. However, Catholic missionaries "like Libermann, Lavigerie and Comboni promoted a more positive appreciation of and adaptation to indigenous culture."[14] Pope Leo XIII's 1891 encyclical *Rerum novarum* addressed social concerns of the day and initiated the tradition of Catholic social teachings and a more holistic understanding of mission.

TWENTIETH CENTURY

The description by Robert Schreiter of the twentieth-century Roman Catholic missionary movement in terms of the following four periods

---

[9] Stephen Neill, *History of Christian Missions*, rev. ed. (New York: Penguin Books, 1986), 114–15.

[10] Bevans and Schroeder, *Constants in Context*, 138.

[11] See ibid., 171–205.

[12] See ibid., 206–38.

[13] Ibid., 235. Official Catholic theology accepted baptism by water, blood, and desire. The third form acknowledged the possibility for people to be saved without explicit faith in Christ. However, the operative theology was evident in missionary motivation and popular Catholic understanding.

[14] Ibid.

provides a fine framework for this section—certainty, ferment, crisis, and rebirth.[15]

Certainty: From Maximum Illud to the Second Vatican Council

We will trace the understanding of mission from World War I until Vatican II mainly by examining the major missiological schools[16] and the major mission encyclicals[17] during this period. After the war the Catholic Church revived its missionary efforts with the theological understanding of mission from the nineteenth century. The primary motivations for mission were the salvation of souls *(conversio animarum)* and the establishment of the visible church *(plantatio ecclesiae)*—normally under a Western form. This was based on the belief that the Catholic Church had an exclusive claim to the truth.

Josef Schmidlin, inspired by the Protestant missiologist Gustav Warneck, was the leading figure in the development of Catholic missiology[18] and the founder of what became known as the Münster School of missiology. Those at the University of Münster considered the conversion of non-Christians the central goal of mission. In his 1917 *Einführung in die Missionswissenschaft* (introduction to missiology) Schmidlin laid the foundations in scripture and church tradition for this understanding of mission.[19] A second Catholic theological stream, the Louvain School of missiology, placed the planting of the church as the primary goal of mission. Pierre Charles was the first chief proponent of this theology, which also promoted a certain degree of cultural adaptation or acculturation.[20] He initially outlined his theology of mission in his manual of missiology, *Les*

---

[15] Robert J. Schreiter, "Changes in Roman Catholic Attitudes toward Proselytism and Mission," in *New Directions in Mission and Evangelization 2: Theological Foundations*, ed. James A. Scherer and Stephen B. Bevans (Maryknoll, NY: Orbis Books, 1994), 113–25. For parallel developments of conciliar and evangelical understandings of mission within this same four-stage framework, see Bevans and Schroeder, *Constants in Context*, 255–64.

[16] Francis Anekwe Oborji, "Catholic Missiology 1910–2010," in *A Century of Catholic Mission*, ed. Stephen Bevans, 133–54, Regnum Edinburgh Centenary Series 15 (Oxford: Regnum Books International, 2013).

[17] James Kroeger, "Papal Mission Wisdom: Five Mission Encyclicals 1919–1959," in Bevans, *A Century of Catholic Mission*, 93–100.

[18] See Karl Müller, "Joseph Schmidlin, 1876–1944: Pioneer of Catholic Missiology," in *Mission Legacies: Biographical Studies of Leaders of the Modern Missionary Movement*, ed. Gerald Anderson, et al., 402–9 (Maryknoll, NY: Orbis Books, 1994).

[19] Josef Schmidlin, *Einführung in die Missionswissenschaft* (Münster: Aschendoff, 1917).

[20] See Joseph Masson, "Pierre Charles, SJ, 1883–1954: Advocate of Acculturation," in Anderson et al., *Mission Legacies*, 410–15.

Dossiers de l'Action Missionnaire (1927–29).[21] Rather than viewing these two schools in opposition, one can consider each of them as providing the theological grounding for the two main missionary goals or motivations, respectively, leading up to the Second Vatican Council.[22]

Maximum Illud—subtitled *On Spreading the Catholic Faith around the World*—by Pope Benedict XV in 1919, which emphasized the formation of well-prepared indigenous clergy, was the first mission encyclical after World War I. However, it was Pope Pius XI[23] who did much to situate mission at the center of the church. His mission document *Rerum ecclesiae* in 1926 fostered missionary zeal, encouraged the ongoing efforts to prepare local clergy, and called for the ordination of indigenous bishops. This latter initiative was carried out by Cardinal Willem van Rossum, the prefect of the Sacred Congregation of the Propagation of the Faith, and further sparked by the prophetic voice of the missionary Vincent Lebbe. He insisted that "Chinese Christians should not have to become like foreigners in their own society, and that missionaries should distance themselves from European nationalistic interests to the point of missionaries becoming naturalized Chinese citizens in order to identify as closely as possible with the Chinese."[24] Lebbe, who has been compared with the outstanding Protestant missionary Hudson Taylor,[25] signaled a critique of the link between mission and colonialism. Pius XI also recognized two faculties of missiology in Rome—the Gregorian University in 1932 and the Urban University in 1933.

Pope Pius XII issued *Evangelii praecones* in 1951. It proposed further principles and norms for missionary activity. "Perhaps, the greatest novelty in *Evangelii praecones* is the emphasis on preserving the positive elements found in 'the special customs and time-honored observations of pagan peoples.'"[26] In 1957 Pius XII promulgated the encyclical *Fidei donum (Gift of Faith)*, which focused on the particular mission needs in Africa, encouraged diocesan priests to join the missionary efforts, and acknowledged the important contribution of the laity in mission. Newly elected Pope John XXIII just two years later issued the mission document *Princeps pastorum (Prince of Shepherds)*, in which he highlighted new developments in mission, including the point that "the time of any attitudes or approaches reminiscent of 'colonial mission' is definitely past."[27] He had also announced the convocation of the Second Vatican Council. Alongside

---

[21] Pierre Charles, *Les Dossiers de l'Action Missionnaire* (Louvain: Editions de L'Aucam, 1938).

[22] See Oborji, "Catholic Missiology 1910–2010," 134.

[23] Josef Metzler, "Pius XI, 1857–1939: The Missionary Pope," in Anderson et al., *Mission Legacies*, 56–61.

[24] Bevans and Schroeder, *Constants in Context*, 244.

[25] Neill, *History of Christian Missions*, 412.

[26] Kroeger, "Papal Mission Wisdom," 97.

[27] Ibid., 99.

these last three mission encyclicals, the theological understanding of mission continued to develop in the two Catholic schools of missiology. From the Münster School, most notably Thomas Ohm filled in "some lacunae in Schmidlin's theory of mission."[28] Two key names in the Louvain School were Joseph Masson (Louvain) and André Seumois (Rome).

Many events and mission practices were also shaping a broader Catholic theology of mission. In addition to Lebbe's call for denationalizing mission and de-Westernizing Christianity in China and the further involvement of diocesan priests and laity in mission, the mission models of presence in Algeria by Charles de Foucauld, of medical mission by Anna Dengel in India, of the Catholic Students' Mission Crusade founded in 1918, of missionary anthropology by Wilhelm Schmidt,[29] and of social outreach in the United States by Dorothy Day and the Catholic Worker movement represent other such developments. During World War II, Henri Godin and Yvan Daniel wrote a small paperback titled *France, pays de mission?* (France, a mission country?), describing a "pagan" France. This challenged the geographical understanding of mission as one-way traffic from the Christian West to the rest of the world. In the following year the Priest Worker movement—calling for priests to leave the rectories and work in the factories—was initiated in France by Cardinal Emmanuel Suhard.

This pre–Vatican II period of Catholic mission can be characterized as a period of certainty. The primary goals and theologies of mission—salvation of souls and planting the church—were quite clear and could be measured fairly concretely, for example, in terms of the number of baptisms. However, at the same time there were also signs of the winds of change in the encyclicals, Catholic theology of mission, and mission practice.

Ferment: Second Vatican Council

The Second Vatican Council (1962–65) has "often been called the most significant theological and religious event of the twentieth century."[30] In terms of mission, our focus is on the *Decree on the Church's Missionary Activity (Ad gentes)* (AG), but it is important to note that mission was central to what the entire council was about.[31] Schreiter highlights three major theological

---

[28] Oborji, "Catholic Missiology 1910–2010," 137–38.
[29] Louis J. Luzbetak, "Wilhelm Schmidt, SVD, 1868–1954: Priest, Linguist, Ethnologist," in Anderson et al., *Mission Legacies*, 475–85.
[30] Stephen Bevans, "Mission at the Second Vatican Council: 1962–1965," in Bevans, *A Century of Catholic Mission*, 101–11.
[31] See Stephen Bevans and Jeffrey Gros, *Evangelization and Religious Freedom: Ad Gentes, Dignitatis Humanae* (New York: Paulist Press, 2009).

developments in *Ad gentes* and other council documents that shape the shift in the understanding of mission in Catholic theology.[32]

First of all, *the Trinity is the center and origin of mission.* "The pilgrim Church is missionary by its very nature. For it is from the mission of the Son and the mission of the Holy Spirit that she takes her origin, in accordance with the decree of God the Father. This decree flows from 'that fountain of love,' or charity within God the Father" (AG 2). The church is important only because it is part of God's mission *(missio Dei).* In other words, "the church doesn't have a mission, but the mission of God has a church."[33] Proclamation is the prominent form of a mission, but Christian presence and witness may be the only appropriate means in some situations (AG 6). Furthermore, every aspect and activity of the church now needs to be seen from the perspective of the church's missionary nature, which reaffirms the theological interconnectedness of church, mission, and baptism in the early church.

Second, Vatican II offered *an expanded understanding of the church.* While some former hierarchical portraits of the church are found in the conciliar material, the main ecclesiological image in the decree on the church, *Lumen gentium* (LG), is that of the pilgrim people of God. "With this image, the church's nature is seen as more provisional, imaging a group of people in a common search for the fulfillment of the kingdom or reign of God."[34] The church "in Christ" is also the sacrament of salvation (LG 1) and is to witness to God's reign (LG 5). The *Pastoral Constitution on the Church in the Modern World (Gaudium et Spes)* adds that the church should discern the "signs of the times" (GS 4), the flow of the fountain of God's love (AG 2) outside the Catholic Church. This major theological shift led to a much greater appreciation for the movement of God's Spirit in other Christian denominations/churches (ecumenism), all cultures (especially non-Western ones), society in general, and other religions.

Third, building upon the previous shift, the Second Vatican Council brought a *new understanding of the nature of other religions.* They can serve not only as "preparations for the Gospel" (AG 3), but the conciliar document on the relationship of the church to other religions, *Nostra aetate* (NA), calls the church to respect the rays of Truth found in them and "to enter with prudence and charity into discussion and collaboration with members of other religions" (NA 2). "While the document certainly affirmed that salvation for all is through Christ and that Christians have the duty to witness to their own faith, it opened the door for the theological

---

[32] Schreiter, "Changes in Roman Catholic Attitudes toward Proselytism and Mission," 116.

[33] Roger P. Schroeder, *What Is the Mission of the Church? A Guide for Catholics,* rev. and exp. edition (Maryknoll, NY: Orbis Books, 2018), 28.

[34] Bevans and Schroeder, *Constants in Context,* 250.

debate regarding the role of salvation in other religions and the role of the church in this context."[35]

These three theological shifts in Catholic theology form the foundations for the new understanding and practice of mission. While this will develop into a rich and complex sense of mission, the initial impact also caused some chaos.

Crisis: The Decade after the Council

The ten years following Vatican II was a period of change and transition not only within the church but also throughout the world. The steady movement of former colonies to political independence prompted many to ask whether mission, which had been so closely aligned with colonialism, was also finished. There were calls for a missionary moratorium from some former colonies. "In a historically significant address, Ronan Hoffman shocked the US Catholic audience at the 1967 annual meeting of the mission-sending societies with his declaration of the end of the foreign missionary era, as it has been known."[36] Three years earlier Stephen Neill had stated that "the age of missions is at an end; the age of mission has begun."[37]

Furthermore, the threefold theological shift of the Second Vatican Council, described above, shook the foundations of the pre–Vatican II motivations for mission of saving souls and planting the church. Now the church recognized that the movement of God's grace includes but also extends beyond explicit faith in Christ and membership in the Catholic Church. SEDOS,[38] founded by missionary congregations soon after Vatican II as a resource center for themselves and the church, treated the question of "Why mission at all?" at its first international conference in 1969.[39] According to Schreiter, the paper by Johannes Schütte "remains the best articulation of a theological response to the missionary dilemma of that period."[40] Schütte stated, "The goal of mission is to help in bringing everything ultimately together in Christ (Eph 1:10) by proclaiming Christ at the center of human history, by continuing the process of Christ's incarnation into every culture, and by working for peace and reconciliation, which are to

---

[35] Ibid.

[36] Ibid., 251.

[37] Neill, *History of Christian Missions*, 572.

[38] Acronym for *Service of Documentation and Study of Global Mission*.

[39] See Mary Motte, "Historical Perspectives on Catholic Mission Theology," in *Contemporary Mission Theology: Engaging the Nations*, ed. Robert Gallagher and Paul Hertig (Maryknoll, NY: Orbis Books, 2017), 161–62.

[40] Schreiter, "Changes in Roman Catholic Attitudes toward Proselytism and Mission," 121.

be signs of Christ's imminent return and the establishment of his reign."[41] A new theology of mission was developing.[42]

In another situation the Conference of Latin American Bishops (CELAM), formed in 1955, held its first General Assembly after the Second Vatican Council in Medellín, Colombia, in 1968. Looking beyond development and revolution, CELAM committed itself to the transformation of unjust structures in society. After an analysis of its reality *(realidad)*, it moved toward communal action. This laid the grounds for the birth of liberation theology. Gustavo Gutiérrez published his landmark *A Theology of Liberation* in 1971.[43] This overall movement had an impact on the entire Catholic Church as the 1971 Synod of Bishops in Rome discussed the integral relationship between mission and justice.

Catholics in other parts of the world were also seriously discerning the "signs of the times" in their own contexts—interreligious dialogue in Asia, the interaction between faith and culture in Africa, the conversation between Christianity and secularization in Europe and Australia, the potential of ecumenism in North America, and the role of Christian life and rapid social change in the Pacific Islands. Other signs of renewal included the Cursillo lay spirituality movement and the emergence of basic Christian (ecclesial) movements. The dissolution in 1969 of the *jus commissionis* meant that missionary congregations were not assigned "mission territories." Instead, bishops now had the responsibility for mission within their own local church. "Mission was not to be defined geographically, and every local church, to be 'fully church,' was missionary by its very nature."[44]

Rebirth: Evangelii nuntiandi *to* Dialogue and Proclamation

Following the post–Vatican II decade of transition toward something new, several church documents laid solid theological foundations for the rebirth of the Catholic understanding of mission.

Evangelii nuntiandi (1975)

A Synod of Bishops was held in Rome on the theme of evangelization in the modern world in 1974. Based on these deliberations Pope Paul VI

---

[41] Bevans and Schroeder, *Constants in Context*, 252. See also Schreiter, "Changes in Roman Catholic Attitudes toward Proselytism and Mission," 121.

[42] For the proceedings of the 1969 SEDOS seminar, see *Foundations of Mission Theology*, ed. SEDOS, trans. John Drury, (Maryknoll, NY: Orbis Books, 1972).

[43] Gustavo Gutiérrez, *A Theology of Liberation: History, Politics, and Salvation* (Maryknoll, NY: Orbis Books, 1973); originally published as *Teologia de la liberación, Perspectival* (Lima: CEP, 1971).

[44] Bevans and Schroeder, *Constants in Context*, 253.

issued the apostolic exhortation *Evangelii nuntiandi* (EN) the following year. "Probably in an effort to avoid identifying mission with colonization, the term 'evangelization' was used rather than 'mission.'"[45] While *evangelization* is sometimes identified in a limited sense with proclamation, Paul VI used the term in a broader way to encompass all forms of mission. Therefore, *evangelization* and *mission* are treated here as interchangeable terms. We shall now highlight three significant contributions of *Evangelii nuntiandi* to the rebirthing of the Catholic theology of mission.

First of all, rather than beginning with the *missio Dei* theology of *Ad gentes*, Paul VI centers the theology of the church and mission around the *reign of God*. "As an evangelizer, Christ first of all proclaims a kingdom, the Kingdom of God; and this is so important that, by comparison, everything else becomes 'the rest,' which is 'given in addition.' Only the Kingdom therefore is absolute, and it makes everything else relative" (EN 8). The kingdom of God was central to Jesus's mission in his words (parables), actions (healings and exorcisms), and behavior (table fellowship). Therefore, "evangelizing is in fact the grace and vocation proper to the Church, her deepest identity" (EN 14). The pope insists that the church must also be evangelized itself by constant renewal (EN 15), that there is an inseparable link between Christ's mission and the church (EN 16), and that every member of the church is to participate in this mission (EN 15).

Second, *Evangelii nuntiandi* presented an *expanded understanding of mission* that not only included direct proclamation and planting the church, but also "bringing the Good News into all strata of humanity, and through its influence transforming humanity from within and making it new" (EN 18). Paul VI describes the latter as an evangelization of cultures, "not in a purely decorative way as it were by applying a thin veneer, but in a vital way, in depth and right to their very roots" (EN 20).

Third, drawing upon the earlier Synod of Bishops in 1971 on justice and mission, *Evangelii nuntiandi* stated that "evangelization involves an explicit message . . . about life in society, about international life, peace, justice and development—a message especially energetic today about liberation" (EN 29). "This is the first appearance of the word *liberation* in an official Catholic document, and it clearly reflects the influence of the theology of liberation that was so important in the 1970s."[46] The pope also points to the need for a balance between mission and justice, whereby the former is not reduced to only material projects. Also, the church is against all forms of violence. The reign-of-God theology provides the foundation for a more integrated understanding of mission and for the necessity of engaging the world and society.

---

[45] Roger Schroeder, "Catholic Teaching on Mission after Vatican II: 1975–2007," in Bevans, *A Century of Catholic Mission*, 112–20.

[46] Bevans and Schroeder, *Constants in Context*, 306.

Over the next fifteen years Catholic gatherings developed aspects of mission in their particular situations. The Third General Assembly of CELAM, held in Puebla, Mexico, in 1979, reaffirmed the importance of liberation and the preferential option for the poor. In 1986, the Fourth Plenary Assembly of the Federation of Asian Bishops' Conferences (FABC) affirmed the mission of the laity in Asian societies, the Association of Member Episcopal Conferences of Eastern Africa (AMECEA) addressed issues of inculturation, and the United States bishops published *Economic Justice for All: Catholic Social Teaching and the US Economy*. An important international 1981 SEDOS seminar described the four "principal activities" of the church's mission as proclamation, dialogue, inculturation, and liberation of the poor.[47]

Redemptoris missio (1990)

Pope John Paul II issued the encyclical *Redemptoris missio* (RM) in 1990, which some consider "the best articulation of a systematic reflection on mission in official Catholic documents."[48] While the pope affirmed the *missio Dei* and reign of God theologies, he was also concerned that some theologians and missionaries were losing focus on Jesus Christ as the unique savior and judge of cultures and on the importance of the role of the church in mission. "A third issue is that an over-emphasis on the all-encompassing nature of mission for the church, universal and local, in every part of the world, and on the multiplicity of the forms of mission could lead to losing focus on mission *ad gentes* and proclamation."[49] Three aspects of the theological understanding of mission can be highlighted from this comprehensive and lengthy document.

First, John Paul II presents a *christocentric theology* (in chapter I) in addressing the first two concerns mentioned in the preceding paragraph. Although it is possible to be saved outside the church and explicit faith in Christ (RM 10), the church's mission is still to witness to and proclaim Jesus Christ as the universal savior (RM 5). Humanity has a right to the truth of the gospel, but this must be presented in a way that respects human freedom (RM 7–8). *Redemptoris missio* then affirms and nuances the reign of God theology and trinitarian theology in chapters II and III, respectively. "These three foundational chapters, while building upon *AG* and *EN*, highlight the specificity of Christ and the necessity of proclaiming Jesus' lordship."[50]

---

[47] "Agenda for Future Planning, Study, and Research in Mission," in *Trends in Mission: Toward the Third Millennium,* ed. William Jenkinson and Helene O'Sullivan (Maryknoll, NY: Orbis Books, 1991), 399–414.

[48] Schroeder, "Catholic Teaching on Mission after Vatican II: 1975–2007," 115.

[49] Ibid., 116.

[50] Ibid.

Second, John Paul II offers a detailed *expanded idea of mission* in terms of the "horizons" (chapter IV) and the "paths" of mission (chapter V). The "horizons" of mission are (1) where Christ is unknown or the church is immature (*ad gentes*; mission in its proper sense); (2) pastoral care of the Christian faithful; and (3) where people are no longer Christian (called new evangelization or reevangelization). Regarding the latter, the pope refers to Paul's encounter in the Areopagus to describe the modern Areopagi or cultural sectors that include a "commitment to peace, development and the liberation of peoples; the rights of individuals and peoples, especially those of minorities; the advancement of women and children; safeguarding the created world" (RM 37c). As for the "paths" of mission, John Paul II begins by stating that "mission is a single but complex reality, and it develops in a variety of ways" (RM 41), and then proceeds to name some of the forms of mission—beginning with witness and proclamation (RM 42–45)—that can lead to conversion and baptism (RM 46–49). He continues by mentioning other paths, such as inculturation, interreligious dialogue and works of charity (RM 52–60). In this treatment of the "horizons" and "paths," John Paul II "clarified and expanded the idea of mission for a post–Vatican II church that is 'missionary by nature.'"[51]

The third important contribution of *Redemptoris missio* is its treatment of *interreligious dialogue*. While Vatican II and later *Evangelii nuntiandi* had affirmed the positive elements of other religions and the Secretariat for Non-Christians had described interreligious dialogue as an integral part of evangelization in "The Attitude of the Church toward the Followers of Other Religions,"[52] *Redemptoris missio* was the first papal encyclical to include such dialogue as "part of the Church's evangelizing mission" (RM 55). The church is to engage in respectful dialogue, while always keeping in mind that "*salvation comes from Christ and that dialogue does not dispense from evangelization*" and that "*the Church is the ordinary means of salvation* and that *she alone* possesses the fullness of the means of salvation" (RM 55). At the same time, interreligious dialogue should not be done out of "tactical concerns or self-interest," but rather with a spirit of "truth, humility and frankness, knowing that dialogue can enrich each side" (RM 56).

Dialogue and Proclamation (1991)

The third above-mentioned significant issue in *Redemptoris missio*—the relationship of Christianity and other religions—was the most pressing theological and practical challenge for mission at the end of the twentieth century. Using the framework of exclusivist, inclusivist, and pluralist

---

[51] Ibid., 117.

[52] Secretariat for Non-Christians, "The Attitude of the Church toward the Followers of Other Religions: Reflections and Orientations on Dialogue and Mission," *Bulletin Secretariatus Pro Non-Christianis* 56/13 (1984): 126–41.

perspectives on the question of salvation and interreligious dialogue, the work of Catholic theologians such as Michael Amaladoss, Gavin D'Costa, Jacques Dupuis, Paul Knitter, and Aloysius Pieris "represents a serious effort to overcome simple exclusivism and simple pluralism."[53]

Within a few months of the distribution of *Redemptoris missio*, the Pontifical Council for Interreligious Dialogue (formerly known as the Secretariat for Non-Christians) and the Congregation for the Evangelization of Peoples (formerly known as the Sacred Congregation for the Propagation of the Faith) jointly published the 1991 document *Dialogue and Proclamation* (DP). While it does not carry the same ecclesial authority as *Ad gentes, Evangelii nuntiandi,* and *Redemptoris missio,* this official church publication elaborates on the important connection between two key components of mission.[54]

First, *Dialogue and Proclamation* presents a well-developed theology of religions and the four forms of interreligious dialogue—of life, action, theological exchange, and religious experience.[55] It spells out both the requirements (DP 47–50) and obstacles (DP 54) related to such dialogue. Second, *Dialogue and Proclamation* offers a fine treatment of the mandate and urgency of proclamation. From the perspective of dialogue the church is reminded that the followers of other religions "may have already been touched by the Spirit and in some ways associated unknowingly with the paschal mystery of Jesus Christ (cf. *Gaudium et Spes* 22)" (DP 68). The document again describes both the requirements (DP 70) and obstacles (DP 73–74) of proclamation. Finally, the document shows the connection between these two elements of mission.

> Interreligious dialogue and proclamation, though not on the same level, are both authentic elements of the Church's evangelizing mission. . . . They are intimately related, but not interchangeable; true interreligious dialogue on the part of the Christian supposes the desire to make Jesus Christ better known, recognized and loved; proclaiming Jesus Christ is to be carried out in the Gospel spirit of dialogue. (DP 77)

The theological questions of interreligious dialogue and the uniqueness of Christ continued to draw much attention. The Vatican Congregation for the Doctrine of the Faith issued the declaration *Dominus Iesus* (DI) in 2000 and a document entitled "Doctrinal Note on Some Aspects of Evangelization" in 2007. Both emphasized the centrality of Christ as Savior and underrepresented the Catholic belief in God's grace outside of Christianity.

---

[53] Bevans and Schroeder, *Constants in Context,* 254; see also 378–85.

[54] See William Burrows, *Redemption and Dialogue: Reading* Redemptoris Missio *and* Dialogue and Proclamation (Maryknoll, NY: Orbis Books, 1993).

[55] DP 42. Originally in "The Attitude of the Church toward the Followers of Other Religions."

"However, these two documents were not intended to offer a systematic theology of mission, but rather were responding to the particular issues of relativism, the uniqueness of Christ, and to some degree the role of the church."[56] Discussions of Christology in Catholic theology are fundamental not only for interreligious dialogue but also for inculturation.

TWENTY-FIRST CENTURY

Having traced the dynamic and complex understanding of mission in Catholic theology through the twentieth century, we now turn to the twenty-first century. We start by reviewing how Catholic theologians and missiologists have developed and/or integrated the three current major theologies of mission presented above. Second, we look briefly at further developments in this century through *Evangelii gaudium* and several emerging trends.

Three Theologies of Mission

While the following major theologies of mission are also rich resources beyond the Roman Catholic Church, we focus our treatment primarily on how they have been developed by Catholic theologians and on the strengths and potential weaknesses of each mission theology.

Mission as Participation in the Mission of the Triune God *(missio Dei)*

Ad gentes maintains, according to Bevans and Schroeder, that "the church is in mission because it has been graciously caught up in the *missio Dei*, the very mission of God in creation, redemption and continual sanctification."[57] Yves Congar has noted that this trinitarian perspective can be traced historically to (1) "divine missions" developed by Augustine and thirteenth-century theologians like Bonaventure, Albert the Great, and Thomas Aquinas; (2) the missionary ecclesiology of Cardinal Pierre de Bérulle and missiologist André Rétif; and (3) twentieth-century Protestant thinking.[58] Orthodox documents and theologians have also developed the trinitarian theology of mission in great depth.[59] The renewed Catholic interest in trinitarian theology is often linked to an essay by Karl Rahner, which included the famous statement: "*The 'economic' Trinity is the 'immanent'*

---

[56] Schroeder, "Catholic Teaching on Mission after Vatican II: 1975–2007," 119.
[57] Bevans and Schroeder, *Constants in Context*, 288.
[58] Ibid., 289–90.
[59] Ibid., 288–89.

Trinity and the 'immanent" Trinity is the 'economic' Trinity."[60] Important writings on the Trinity, with its connection to ecclesiology and mission, have been developed by Catholic theologians such as Leonardo Boff, Catherine Mowry LaCugna, Elizabeth Johnson, and David Cunningham, and by Catholic missiologists such as Anthony Gittins, Robert Schreiter, and Stephen Bevans.[61]

The strengths of this theology for mission are the invitation to the unfathomable mystery of God, the acknowledgment of God's surprising presence outside of Christianity, and the grounding of the church itself in God's mission. A potential danger of such a theology is a weak appreciation of the uniqueness of salvation through Christ and of the role of the church.

Mission as Liberating Service of the Reign of God

The apostolic exhortation *Evangelii nuntiandi* was grounded in the theology of the reign of God, which was witnessed to, served, and preached by Jesus. The church and every Christian are to continue that mission. "Here lies the touchstone of evangelization: it is unthinkable that a person should accept the Word and give himself to the kingdom without becoming a person who bears witness to it and proclaims it in his turn" (EN 24). The World Council of Churches has also developed the reign-of-God theology for mission.[62] As for Catholics, New Testament scholar Rudolf Schnackenburg in his 1959 book *Gottes Herrschaft und Reich* (God's rule and kingdom), and Hans Küng, in his 1967 classic *The Church*, provided solid biblical, theological, and ecclesiological foundations for the reign-of-God theology.[63] Gustavo Gutiérrez and other liberation theologians like Alvaro Quiroz Magaña, Leonardo Boff, Juan Luis Segundo, and Michael Amaladoss have grounded this theology within their Latin American and Asian contexts.[64] Amaladoss writes, "Mission as service to the reign of God means that it is 'a call to conversion, *a challenge to change* . . . an urge to enter the creative dynamism of God's action in the world, making all things new."[65]

The strengths of this theology for mission are its holistic approach, clear link with the concrete ministry of Jesus, prophetic aspect in the dialogue with the world, and strong commitment to the marginalized. The potential dangers are the reduction of mission to mere humanization and lack of appreciation for the role of the church in mission.

---

[60] Karl Rahner, *The Trinity* (New York: Herder and Herder, 1970), 22.

[61] See Bevans and Schroeder, *Constants in Context*, 291–93.

[62] See ibid., 307–10.

[63] Rudolf Schnackenburg, *Gottes Herrschaft und Reich* (Freiburg: Herder, 1959); Hans Küng, *The Church* (London: Continuum, 1967).

[64] See Bevans and Schroeder, *Constants in Context*, 312–16.

[65] Michael Amaladoss, "Mission as Prophecy," in Scherer and Bevans, *New Directions in Mission and Evangelization 2*, 68.

Mission as Proclamation of Jesus Christ as Universal Savior

The encyclical *Redemptoris missio* addressed the main question—why mission?—by stating clearly that "the Church's universal mission is born of faith in Jesus Christ" (RM 4). While Jesus has always been central to Christian theology and mission, this christocentric emphasis among Catholics, and many evangelical and Pentecostals, "has emerged with particular urgency in light of the challenges . . . to the validity of mission in general, and to the uniqueness and absoluteness of Jesus Christ as universal Savior in particular."[66] Catholic theologians who have developed this theology include Cardinal Josef Tomko, Sebastian Karotemprel, Karl Müller, Adam Wolanin, Cardinal Walter Kasper, and Claude Geffré.[67] While the publication of Karotemprel's *Following Christ in Mission*,[68] which developed this theology, "neither denies nor is opposed to trinitarian or reign of God perspectives of mission—indeed, it clearly endorses them—it presents them in a way that does not jeopardize the centrality of Jesus for evangelization, for interpretation of God's reign and for understanding the church."[69]

The strengths of this theology are its clear statement of the particularity of Christ and of Christian faith and its ability to motivate people for explicit evangelizing mission activity. The potential dangers are compromised commitments to inculturation, interreligious dialogue, and the pursuit of justice.

Prophetic Dialogue

The three major streams of theology of the last thirty-five years of the twentieth century—outlined above and described earlier within their historical development—provide solid foundations for the Catholic understanding and practice of mission in the twenty-first century. Each has strengths and potential weaknesses. Bevans and Schroeder proposed bringing them together into a synthesis or creative tension called *prophetic dialogue*.[70]

On the one hand, the dialogical life and mission of the Trinity provide the basis for mission as *dialogue*.[71] "In other words, God's very *nature* is to be in dialogue: Holy Mystery ('Father'), Son (Word) and Spirit in an eternal movement or flow of openness and receiving, a total giving and

---

[66] Bevans and Schroeder, *Constants in Context*, 330–31.

[67] See ibid., 323–24, 332–34.

[68] Sebastian Karotemprel et al., eds., *Following Christ in Mission: A Foundational Course in Missiology* (Boston: Pauline Books, 1996).

[69] Bevans and Schroeder, *Constants in Context*, 333.

[70] See ibid., 348–52; and Stephen B. Bevans and Roger P. Schroeder, *Prophetic Dialogue: Reflections on Christian Mission Today* (Maryknoll, NY: Orbis Books, 2011).

[71] See Bevans and Schroeder, *Prophetic Dialogue*, 19–39.

accepting, spilling over into creation and calling creation back into communion with Godself."[72] Therefore, as the church participates in God's mission, it should respectfully acknowledge and engage the riches of the reign of God already present in all individuals, churches, cultures, and religions, and in society, the world, and all of creation.

At the same time, mission must be *prophetic*.[73] To begin with, prophets must be rooted in dialogue as people "who have listened carefully to God, who are able to discern the signs of the times."[74] Second, the church should with and without words "speak forth" the reign of God and the gospel of Jesus Christ. This is the *annunciation* aspect of prophecy. Third, the church is, both with and without words, to "speak against" those things that are contrary to (1) God's reign, and (2) what John Paul II calls the "gospel of life."[75] This is the *denunciation* element.

Bevans and Schroeder consider prophetic dialogue a way of drawing upon the strengths of the three Catholic mission theologies and of minimizing their potential weaknesses. After Vatican II the bishops of Asia (FABC) spoke of mission as dialogue with the poor, cultures, and religions. However, after about fifteen years of experience and reflection, they concluded that the church should (1) both share in the life of the poor and speak out against what keeps the poor in that situation; (2) both appreciate culture and critique aspects of each culture that are contrary to God's reign; and (3) both engage the truth in other religions and maintain the conviction that Jesus is the Way, the Truth, and the Life (Jn 14:6). Furthermore, prophetic dialogue is spirituality. In a similar way David Bosch spoke of doing mission in "bold humility."[76] Part 3 of the present volume nuances the theology of prophetic dialogue in more depth.

Evangelii gaudium *and Pope Francis*

In 2013, following the synod on the new evangelization, the newly elected Pope Francis issued the lengthy and rich apostolic exhortation *Evangelii gaudium (The Joy of the Gospel)* (EG). The pope presented a powerful vision of the church, "missionary by its very nature" (AG 2), as a "community of missionary disciples" (EG 24, 120). In comparison with the recent major Catholic documents on mission—*Ad gentes, Evangelii nuntiandi,* and *Redemptoris missio*—*Evangelii gaudium* "is less theological,

---

[72] Ibid., 26.

[73] See ibid., 40–55.

[74] Ibid., 42.

[75] *Evangelium Vitae,* 1.

[76] David J. Bosch, *Transforming Mission: Paradigm Shifts in Theology of Mission* (Maryknoll, NY: Orbis Books, 1991), 489.

and more pastoral or homiletic in tone and style."[77] However, Francis draws heavily from these three magisterial statements and mission theologies, as well as regional and national church proceedings, especially the 2007 *Aparecida Document* of the Fifth General Conference of CELAM. The church as a "*mystery* rooted in the Trinity*" (EG 111) is to carry out its mission with "the primacy of the proclamation of Jesus Christ in all evangelizing work" (EG 110), and the "Gospel is about the *kingdom of God*" (EG 180).

The pope "emphasizes that the church grows not from proselytizing but 'by attraction' (EG 14), and the words 'mercy' and 'tenderness' are featured prominently throughout the apostolic exhortation."[78] His description of "informal preaching" that "can happen unexpectedly and in any place" (EG 128) is reminiscent of the inspiring "gossiping the gospel" example of the early church. This calls for authentic Christian witness and credibility. The apostolic exhortation also maintains the necessary theological balance or creative tension. Missionary discipleship "seeks to communicate more effectively the truth of the Gospel in a specific context, without renouncing the truth" (EG 45). This is done through a process of dialogue that "is always respectful and gentle" (EG 128). "Evangelization and interreligious dialogue, far from being opposed, mutually support and nourish one another" (EG 251).

The exhortation *Evangelii gaudium* and the entire papacy of Francis offer an inspiring and challenging call to the entire church to be "a community of missionary disciples" today. It represents a development of the Catholic theology, practice, and spirituality of mission from the last thirty-five years of the twentieth century and into the twenty-first century.

Emerging Trends

From the many ongoing approaches to mission in Catholic theology today, we briefly highlight three. The first is reconciliation as a major model of mission. The consequences of the fall of the Berlin Wall in 1989 and the upsurge of armed conflicts around the world since the 1990s were accompanied by the advance of globalization. In response to the growth in violence and division, "the theme of reconciliation began to surface as a compelling response to all that was happening in terms of mission."[79] Robert Schreiter, the leading author on this topic, states that "Christian

---

[77] Roger Schroeder, "Interculturality as a Paradigm of Mission," in *Intercultural Mission*, vol. 2, ed. Lazar T. Stanislaus and Martin Ueffing (Sankt Augustin, Germany: Steyler Missionswissenschaftliches Institut; New Delhi, India: ISPCK, 2015), 161.

[78] Ibid.

[79] Robert J. Schreiter, "Reconciliation as a Model of Mission," in Bevans, *A Century of Catholic Mission*, 234.

mission as reconciliation may be able to contribute something significant to the realization of the *missio Dei* and a better, more peaceful, and sustainable world."[80]

Second, the movement to promote more mutuality in mission among peoples has surfaced in several ways. Jonathan Tan proposed the use of the term *inter-gentes* to reflect the shift in mission strategy "that is geared not to *(ad)* the Asian peoples, but rather, among *(inter)* the Asian peoples . . . for the sake of the Kingdom of God . . . [that is] a qualitative approach that seeks to transform and heal the brokenness in Asian cultures and Asian realities."[81] A number of missiologists have followed up on this idea. Other Catholic writers, who very recently have been developing the more general topic of interculturality and mission, include Anthony Gittins, Lazar Stanislaus, Martin Ueffing, and Roger Schroeder.[82]

The third issue receiving more attention is the integrity of creation. While concern for environmental issues had been voiced by Paul VI, John Paul II, and Benedict XVI,[83] and by Roman Catholic bishops around the world for some time,[84] the 2015 encyclical *Laudato si': On Care for Our Common Home* of Pope Francis has lifted up the care of creation more clearly into Catholic consciousness and within Catholic social teachings. "The urgent challenge to protect our common home includes a concern to bring the whole human family together to seek a sustainable and integral development" (LS 13). Furthermore, this is an "integral ecology." "Concern for the environment thus needs to be joined to a sincere love for our fellow human beings and an unwavering commitment to resolving the problems of society" (LS 91).

CONCLUSION

The practice of mission has taken many forms in the church since the Acts of the Apostles. There has always been an underlying operative the-

---

[80] Ibid., 238.

[81] Jonathan Tan, "*Missio inter Gentes*: Towards a New Paradigm in the Mission Theology of the FABC," *Mission Studies* 21/1 (2004): 90.

[82] See Anthony J. Gittins, *Living Mission Interculturally: Faith, Culture, and the Renewal of Praxis* (Collegeville, MN: Liturgical Press, 2015); Lazar T. Stanislaus and Martin Ueffing, eds. *Vol. 1: Intercultural Living, Vol. 2: Intercultural Mission* (Sankt Augustin, Germany: Steyler Missionswissenschaftliches Institut; and New Delhi, India: ISPCK, 2015); Roger Schroeder, "Prophetic Dialogue and Interculturality," in *Mission on the Road to Emmaus: Constants, Context and Prophetic Dialogue*, ed. Cathy Ross and Stephen B. Bevans (London: SCM Press, 2015), 215–26.

[83] Denis Edwards, "Ecology at the Heart of Mission: Reflections on Recent Catholic Teachings," in Bevans, *A Century of Catholic Mission*, 206–15.

[84] See Bevans and Schroeder, *Constants in Context*, 376.

ology, and sometimes this has been explicit and/or official. However, the latter has never been so strong as in the past seven decades. Tracing mission in Roman Catholic theology demonstrates a major shift from a pre–Vatican II to a post-conciliar understanding, and a major development of a rich and complex theology of mission into the twenty-first century—with such images as missionary disciples, prophetic dialogue, *inter-gentes*, and integral ecology. Finally, this theology of mission continues to both shape and be shaped by the practice and spirituality of mission.

Chapter 3

Mission in Orthodox Theology

Athanasios N. Papathanasiou

It is my pleasure and privilege to have been given the opportunity to pen an essay in honor of Professor Stephen Bevans, a prominent worker in modern missiology. I am happy to express my gratitude to a person with whom my own thoughts have been in dialogue for a long time. Professor Bevans is quite aware of both the contribution of Orthodoxy (the Orthodox Church and Orthodox theology) and the quest for orthodoxy (the correct belief), which is a major missiological theme.[1] His work is marked by his willingness to search out the criteria for a meaningful Christian witness in every context, and I believe that this good labor will bear bountiful fruits for the ecumenical discourse. Having this in mind and in heart, I will try to sketch out Orthodox theology's basic missiological criteria in the limited space of this essay.

It is often said that Orthodox theology was shaped in Byzantine times, as the theology of Eastern Christianity, in gradual juxtaposition to Western Christianity, especially after the Great Schism (1054), which signaled the formation of separate Christian bodies. This description, however, is unsatisfying, insofar as Orthodox theology is unwilling to understand itself in confessional terms. On the contrary, it claims to have creatively continued the theology of the ancient undivided church. At the same time, it sees the Christian division as a painful event and acknowledges that Orthodoxy has to take into account Western thought and experience, avoiding any sort of isolationism.[2] So, in order to approach the Orthodox understanding and practice of mission, given this complex framework, one has to trace

---

[1] See Stephen B. Bevans, *Models of Contextual Theology* (Maryknoll, NY: Orbis Books, 2002), 22–25 (for orthodoxy), and Stephen B. Bevans and Roger P. Schroeder, *Constants in Context: A Theology of Mission for Today* (Maryknoll, NY: Orbis Books, 2004), 227–28, 288–89 (for Orthodox theology).

[2] Georges Florovsky, *Aspects of Church History* (Belmont, MA: Nordland, 1975), 47.

the distinct characteristics of Orthodox theology and discern how these characteristics shape the Orthodox perception of mission.

I will try to respond to this task, inevitably through a personal approach. I mean that my contribution will not be merely a mirror of the ideological environment. More than that, it is a theological essay, that is, an essay opting and arguing for the elements from Orthodox tradition that I see as vital and inclusive, in contrast to trends toward cultural propaganda or traditionalist fossilization, which have sadly accompanied the historical path of the Orthodox churches. This option and argumentation are somehow a manifestation of "theology not so much as a particular *content*, but as an *activity*, a process," in the meaningful words of Bevans.[3] Here, I think, Bevans meets Georges Florovsky, a prominent Orthodox theologian of the twentieth century, who is traditional yet not a traditionalist:

> Loyalty to tradition means not only *concord* with the past, but, in a certain sense, *freedom from the past*, as from some outward formal criterion. Tradition is not only a protective, conservative principle; it is, primarily, the principle of growth and regeneration.[4]

SOME HISTORY

Orthodoxy's missionary perspective is emblematically expressed by the work of Saints Cyril and Methodius, Byzantine missionaries to Great Moravia (approximately within the area of the modern-day Czech Republic and Slovakia) in the ninth century.[5] Though they were eventually accepted by the pope, the strong opposition they faced from German clerics—including persecution of both them and their disciples—marked an essential difference between Eastern and Western understanding, a difference that lasted until the modern era.

The issue at stake was the adoption of the vernacular. The Byzantine missionaries took for granted the right of each people to use its own language in church life, while the said Western clerics maintained the sanctity (and therefore the legitimacy) of only three languages—Latin, Greek, and Hebrew—on the basis that the inscription on the cross of Jesus was written in these languages. Cyril and Methodius simply expressed the ages-long

[3] Stephen B. Bevans, *An Introduction to Theology in Global Perspective* (Maryknoll, NY: Orbis Books, 2009), 1.

[4] Georges Florovsky, *Bible, Church, Tradition: An Eastern Orthodox View* (Belmont, MA: Nordland, 1972), 47.

[5] For the history of Orthodox missions, see Luke Alexander Veronis, *Missionaries, Monks, and Martyrs: Making Disciples of All Nations* (Minneapolis: Light and Life, 1994). See also Ihor Ševčenko, "Religious Missions Seen from Byzantium," *Harvard Ukrainian Studies* 12–13 (1988–89): 7–27.

conviction of Eastern Christianity, which favored the acceptance of the vernacular tongue and local art, the appointment of native clergy, and so on, that is, forms of inculturation. This does not mean that Byzantine society lacked arrogance about the superiority of Greek culture over others. In fact, imperial policy used the Christianization of neighboring peoples as a significant tool for the stabilization of the empire. However, in spite of these attitudes, which might well have led to several distortions of evangelical witness, the pro-inculturation principles prevailed throughout the eleven centuries of Byzantium and colored the missions to Goths, Huns, Heruli, Iberians, Armenians, Russians, Chinese, and so forth.

It is notable that many missions were due to the initiatives of monks, traders, and captives who found themselves in foreign lands and co-existed with people of other nations. By way of example one could mention the dialogical missionary stance of the captives: Saint Nino to Iberia (now Georgia) in the fourth century, and Saint Gregory Palamas to the Muslim Chionae in the fourteenth century. Byzantine missions disseminated the values of their own culture, but at the same time the predominant respect for otherness contributed to the development of the self-awareness of the evangelized peoples. Especially in cases where the missionaries created a written form of the (until then only oral) language for the first time, the evangelized peoples obtained the capacity to develop their own literature, reinforce their identity, and enter a cultural exchange with other nations. In an attempt to summarize the diversity of Byzantine missions in modern missiological vocabulary, we could say that they belong mainly to the paradigm of the extension of the church, yet with several forms of nonaggressive proclamation of the faith: interreligious dialogue, personal invitation, witness through personal sainthood, and so on.

The expansion of Islam, which came to a climax with the fall of Constantinople to the Ottoman Turks in 1453, signaled the subjugation to Muslim political rule for almost four centuries of extensive parts of the Orthodox world (the Balkans, Asia Minor, the Middle East). Mission in its traditional form was impossible to practice. Instead, martyrdom sometimes functioned as a kind of public witness (as in the ancient church), which attracted respect for and interest in the martyr's faith. Evangelism was nevertheless performed by the Russian Church, mostly applying Cyril's and Methodius's method. As always, evangelism was never practiced in uniformity. Russian imperial policy encouraged the "Russification" of the other peoples, while many missionaries implemented various types of inculturation. For centuries missionary work was aimed at several nations within the vast empire or to peoples invading it (such as the Mongols, the Tartars, Siberian tribes). The nineteenth and early twentieth centuries in particular were marked by the endeavors of Innocent Veniaminov (1797–1879) in Alaska, Innocent Figurovsky (1863–1931) in China and Nikolai Kasatkin (1836–1912) in Japan. The Bolshevik Revolution of 1917 impeded missionary efforts.

Due to these events and conjunctures the Orthodox churches did not really participate in the colonial expedition that marked modernity after the so-called discovery of the New World. Only the Russian mission to Alaska was connected to the annexation of new territories, but even in this case the mission was initiated and founded by monastics who defended the native population from the voracity of the Russian (and nominally Orthodox) merchants who pervaded the region. Furthermore, Nikolai Kasatkin represents the type of missionary who acted through personal encounters after his own integration into the culture of the people to whom he addressed himself.

The twentieth century found the Orthodox world at a crossroads. The capacity in Orthodox theology for witness and historical action was heavily opposed by an introversion stemming from its mystical disposition, always inherent in Eastern Christianity, and to the nationalism that has captured considerable parts of Orthodox peoples since approximately the nineteenth century. The thirst for a decisive openness, however, was expressed as early as 1902 and 1920 by the Ecumenical Patriarchate in Constantinople, which issued two encyclical letters proclaiming the need for Christian unity and Christian witness in a changing world. These documents have been considered forerunners of the ecumenical movement. At that time the common understanding among other Christians was that Orthodoxy was nested in a self-sufficient collectivism, being by nature indifferent to mission. It is true that indifference did occur to a great degree, but it is unfair to consider it to be a perennial characteristic of Orthodox theology. We would rather say that many Orthodox had forgotten their missionary tradition.

It is not by chance that the only Orthodox invited to the momentous World Missionary Conference in Edinburgh in 1910 was Nikolas Kasatkin of Japan, though he ultimately did not participate. Almost twenty years later, however, a political upheaval facilitated the encounter between Western and Orthodox Christians. After the establishment of the Bolshevik regime in Russia (1917), many Russian intellectuals migrated to Western Europe and Orthodox theology began to figure prominently in ecumenical circles. The missionary vision of Orthodox theology was now expressed more clearly, yet rather sporadically and indirectly. Things changed even more drastically with the approach of the 1960s, when a massive trend for renewal reverberated throughout the Orthodox world and questioned the dominant centripetal feelings.

In 1961, "Syndesmos, The World Fellowship of Orthodox Youth," established a pan-Orthodox missionary center called Porefthentes (a Greek word meaning "Go ye," after Matthew 28:19). This center functioned as the catalyst for awaking the missionary consciousness of the Orthodox churches and encouraged ecumenical cooperation. Anastasios Yannoulatos, now archbishop of the Orthodox Church in Albania, has played a critical role in this renewal, together with the late Elias Voulgarakis (1927–99), later professor of missiology, and others. Since then Orthodox missions have been active in Africa, the Far East, and Latin America (belonging to the jurisdiction of the Patriarchate of Alexandria and the Patriarchate of Constantinople) and, of special importance, Orthodox missiology is developing significantly alongside axes I now describe.

GOD, A FELLOWSHIP LONGING FOR FELLOWSHIP

The Orthodox Divine liturgy (which comes down to us from the fourth century) begins not with the remembrance of the past, as most narratives do, but with an explicit turning toward the future. Namely, it starts with an invocation of the expected eschatological kingdom of the triune God: "Blessed is the kingdom of the Father, and of the Son, and of the Holy Spirit." This formula manifests and summarizes the pivotal framework of Orthodox theology, that is, the belief in the trinitarian God and in a pending cosmic renewal, the kingdom of God. Trinitarian theology invests missiology with an understanding of real life as communion, thereby evading the danger of Christomonism, which has tantalized church life and its missionary practice.

Mission is witness to the outpouring of the life of the Holy Trinity to the entire world. God is love insofar as God is Trinity, that is, a communion of three unique Persons. The root of the creative activity of God, which brought the world into existence, is a loving turning toward the other. The Persons spur one another on toward love, and thus the Trinity created the world in order to share its own life—its love—with more partners. This loving "opening up" is the rationale behind all God's initiatives in history. That means that mission is comprehended not simply as the propagation of an ideology or the diffusion of a doctrine, but mostly as the ministry of the love of the triune God and as an invitation to this love. Thus mission aims not only at individual souls, but also at the entirety of creation, seen as a gift that also has to be liberated from the bonds of death. It is not by chance that in Orthodox tradition the scriptural text Matthew 28:16–20—which in the nineteenth century became the motto of imperialistic missions—is interpreted primarily as a testimony to Trinitarianism, which cherishes mission as an invitation to a fellowship.[6] The scriptural texts that the Orthodox approach to mission prefers to use are rather those that emphasize God's unconditional love (such as Jn 3:16, 17:23) and God's promise that the entire creation will ultimately be headed to the kingdom of love (such as 1 Corinthians 15:26–28).

---

[6] Petros Vassiliadis, *Eucharist and Witness: Orthodox Perspectives on the Unity and Mission of the Church* (Geneva; Brookline, MA: WCC Publications/Holy Cross Orthodox Press, 1998), 33–38.

CHRISTOLOGY AND PNEUMATOLOGY

Trinitarian theology does not downgrade Christ's centrality and finality. On the contrary, Triadology serves as the sound basis for the exaltation of Christology, always in organic connection with Pneumatology.

The incarnation of the Son of God was the sublime manifestation of God's love. His *kenosis* (self-emptying; Phil 2:5–7) and the assumption of humanity fully (meaning, among other things, the assumption of human will and creativity, which leads to a positive approach to human cultures) have been major missiological criteria. In the seventh century Saint Maximus the Confessor declared that "God's Word, being God himself, that is, the Son of God, desires the mystery of his incarnation to be activated continuously and everywhere."[7] This results in stances friendly toward inculturation and contextualization. The backbone of Christian life, wrote Saint Basil the Great (4th century), is the imitation of Christ "according to the extent of his incarnation."[8] As a matter of fact, doctrine, praxis, and witness are inseparably intertwined.

At the same time Orthodox ecclesiastical life has a strong pneumatological basis and a profound *epicletic* character (*epiclesis* = invocation). Every divine liturgy and every sacrament is not performed *ipso jure;* rather, the worshiping community asks the Holy Spirit to act anew, here and now. So, the question about the relationship between Christ and the Holy Spirit comes to the fore, because one-sided emphasis on Christ alone has been charged with institutionalizing the church and its mission and has restricted the role of the Spirit. Against this monism, Orthodox theology has made a significant contribution to the ecumenical discourse, especially since the 1960s. Contrary to the Spirit's "subordination" to the Son within the framework of the *Filioque*, the insistence by some Orthodox theologians that there are two distinctive economies, that of the Son and that of the Spirit, opened up new horizons.[9] These thinkers brought to the fore the role of the Holy Spirit, not only as the Person who is being sent by Christ or as the Person whose work is merely included in Christ's work, but as the Person who has been creatively present throughout the world from the very first moment of creation and who even made the Son's incarnation possible. This was emphatically stressed in 1944 by the Orthodox theologian (and Russian emigre to Paris) Vladimir Lossky.[10] This aware-

---

[7] Maximus, "Ambigua," *Patrologia Graeca* 91, 1084C-D (my translation).

[8] Basil the Great, "Longer Rules," 43, *Patrologia Graeca* 31, 1028B.

[9] See Athanasios N. Papathanasiou, "If I Cross the Boundaries, You Are There! An Affirmation of God's Action outside the Canonical Boundaries of the Church," *Communio Viatorum* 53/3 (2011): 40–55.

[10] Vladimir Lossky, *The Mystical Theology of the Eastern Church* (New York: St Vladimir's Seminary Press, 1976), 159.

ness of the distinct economies has triggered, ever since, the recognition of the Spirit's universal action. In 1971 and again in 1990 the Orthodox Bishop Georges Khodr from Lebanon appealed to Lossky and stressed the "hypostatic independence" of the Persons, while at the same time emphasizing that "between the two economies there is reciprocity and a mutual service." He underlined that the Spirit's salvific work with the prophets of the Old Testament preceded the historical Jesus and has been taking place everywhere, and concluded that, as Saint Irenaeus (2nd century) affirmed, there is but one and the same God who continuously comes in assistance to humankind through various economies.[11]

Several Orthodox theologians have worked on this distinction, either from a positive or a critical point of view,[12] while certain theologians of various denominational origins were inspired, so that in the following decades missiology experienced an explosion of interest in Pneumatology. However, many pushed "hypostatic independence" to its extremes, developing Pneumatologies almost in opposition to Christology—something that apparently was not part of Lossky and Khodr's intention.[13] For some of these theologians Christology has to do with the institutional church only (consequently, it can hardly be related to the universal activity of God), while Pneumatology comprises the process of opening up to the world. But this dichotomy is highly questioned by Orthodox theology.

"Hypostatic independence" needs to be approached in ways that neither fragment the Trinity nor negate Christ's finality. In Old Testament times it was not only the Spirit that acted worldwide, but it was also the Logos, the yet pre-incarnate Son (Jn 1:1–5, 9–10), whose role has cosmic dimensions, since the *logoi*, the reason of existence of all the beings, are rooted in the God Logos.[14] We might also speak about the universal action of Christ. Christ is incarnate as well as risen. That means that Christ is not only the "historical Jesus." Through the action of the Spirit, the incarnate Son has been a historical reality but also an eschatological intervention free from

---

[11] Georges Khodr, "An Orthodox Perspective of Inter-Religious Dialogue," *Current Dialogue* 19 (1991): 26. Irenaeus's quotation is from "Contra Haereses" 3, 12, 13, *Patrologia Graeca* 7, 907A.

[12] See Papathanasiou, "If I Cross the Boundaries," 43.

[13] Kirsteen Eim, *The Holy Spirit in the World: A Global Conversation* (Maryknoll, NY: Orbis Books, 2008), 54. Paul Knitter, "Can Our 'One and Only' Also Be a 'One among Many'? A Response to Responses," in *The Uniqueness of Jesus: A Dialogue with Paul F. Knitter*, ed. Leonard Swidler and Paul Mojzes (Maryknoll, NY: Orbis Books, 1997), 181. Khodr maintains that Christ himself is mystically present in every well-intended human deed, even in the realm of other religions.

[14] Torstein Theodor Tollefsen, *The Christocentric Cosmology of St. Maximus the Confessor* (Oxford: Oxford University Press, 2008).

the bondage of history.[15] The recognition that both the Holy Spirit and
Christ (in their individual ways) have cosmic dimensions is of immense
importance, since it takes into account the biblical assurance that the entire creation is going to encounter Christ at the eschaton (1 Cor 15:28).
The conclusion of the Book of Revelation notes that both the church and
the Spirit are longing for the eschatological Christ (Rev 22:17, 20). My
conviction is that we should rather talk about the apparent paradox of
"relational independence," in which the Spirit is free to act wherever it
pleases, in an unlimited universality, but which always leads mystically to
the Trinity and its kingdom.[16] Christians bear witness to this and invite
all to the all-embracing love of the Trinity.

ESSENCE AND ENERGIES: A PERSONAL GOD AT WORK

A special characteristic of Orthodox theology, perhaps its most striking difference from the Western theology, is the distinction that Orthodox
theology makes about God: the distinction between the divine essence and
the divine energies.[17] For the Orthodox this distinction elaborates the fundamental biblical antinomy that God is both transcendent and immanent.
God is wholly unknowable in the essence, yet God is self-revealed in the
energies. Yet both the essence and the energies are uncreated, which means
that God is immediately present and active in the world. If one accepts the
divine energies as created, then a gap emerges between God and the world.
This distinction permeates patristic thought in general, but was systematically developed by Saint Gregory Palamas in the fourteenth century. As
Kallistos Ware aptly puts it: "The God of Palamas is not a remote God,
not a detached and distant architect, but a living and personal God, an
involved God, unceasingly present and at work in all that he has made."[18]

---

[15] John D. Zizioulas, *Being as Communion: Studies in Personhood and the
Church* (New York: St. Vladimir's Seminary Press, 1985), 130. This approach
might well enter a dialogue with crucial issues such as those raised by Peter Phan,
The Joy of Religious Pluralism: A Personal Journey (Maryknoll, NY: Orbis Books,
2017), 75–98.

[16] See Papathanasiou, "If I Cross the Boundaries," 46–47.

[17] See Constantinos Athanasopoulos and Christoph Schneider, eds., *Divine
Essence and Divine Energies: Ecumenical Reflections on the Presence of God in
Eastern Orthodoxy* (Cambridge: James Clarke, 2012), esp. Nikolaos Loudovikos,
"Striving for Participation: Palamite Analogy as Dialogical Syn-energy and Thomist
Analogy as Emanational Similitude," 122–48.

[18] Kallistos Ware, "God Immanent Yet Transcendent: The Divine Energies ac-
cording to Saint Gregory Palamas," in *In Whom We Live and Move and Have
Our Being: Panentheistic Reflections on God's Presence in a Scientific World*, ed.
Philip Clayton and Arthur Peacocke (Grand Rapids, MI: Eerdmans, 2004), 165.

In the field of missiology Yannoulatos elaborated on this distinction, very often using the term "glory (Greek: *doxa*) of God" instead of or in parallel with the term *energies*. The glory of God is God's real and unmediated presence in history.

> It is a fervency of divine presence, inconceivable, inaccessible, but directly perceptible. It is a matter of the dynamic, creative, transfiguring energy of the super-essential Holy Trinity. The glory of the Triune God embraces the universe, and brings "everything" into the range of His love and the redemptive grace. . . . In this doxological perspective, mission is not understood as a method for the proselytizing and attracting of new members to a closed community living for itself, but as a polyphonic, multi-dimensional manifestation of the glory of God through the Church that is glorifying God by each God-glorifying believer, whose basic purpose is the mobilization: a) of the whole of human existence to appropriate and to declare the glory of God, and then b) mobilize all of humanity to a common journey within the space that is illumined by the glory of God and to contribute to the return of all creation to the doxological rhythm.[19]

This perspective leads us to a crucial question: What is the nature and the mission of the church, given that its Lord is a God constantly at work in history?

THE CHURCH AND THE KINGDOM

For Orthodox theology, the church is much more than an anthropocentric, sociological entity. It participates in the divine Mystery, as the Nicene Creed shows. In reciting the creed the faithful manifest their faith in the Father, the Son, and the Spirit, as well as the one, holy, catholic and apostolic church.

Of special importance here is the reference to the apostolicity of the church. Ecclesiastical bureaucracy that overemphasizes the role of the clergy—especially that of bishops—at the expense of conciliarity often interprets apostolicity solely as apostolic succession, that is, the unbroken chain of episcopal ordinations from the twelve apostles all the way down to the present day. But, beyond this, the church is apostolic insofar as it participates in God's work in history. The adjective *apostolic* derives from the Greek verb *apostellein*, which means "to send out" (in Latin, *mittere*, hence the noun *missio*). In short, *mission* means "sending out." According

---

[19] Archbishop Anastasios of Albania, "The Doxological Understanding of Life and Mission" (1984).

to the scriptures, the Father sent the Son into the world (Mt 10:40; Jn 3:17; Gal 4:6) and then Christ, the apostle ("he who is sent") par excellence, sends his disciples into the world (Heb 3:1; Jn 20:21). The sending—that is, the mission—of Christ into the world coincides not only with what he did, but also with what he has become; the fleshless Second Person of the Holy Trinity assumed human nature and became Christ, the God-human. All of this means that the church is *apostolic* insofar as (and provided that) it is both sent and sending. But once more we have to make a clarification here. This sending out is actually synonymous with the "opening up" of love, not an imperialistic invasion into foreign lands or an intrusion into the life of others. The "sending" and the "being sent" always have to be performed in Christ's way: in self-emptying *(kenosis)*.

The church is called to function in history as a token of the kingdom, a token that is a community. In other words, the future kingdom of love is to be actualized in history through the life of a community. This fits Orthodox anthropology, which does not share a post-Augustinian dichotomy between nature and grace and does not understand the human being as a closed, autonomous, and static entity.[20] The human subject is invited to be a partner in relationships—relationships with God and with fellow humans. But these relationships are not something additional (and therefore secondary) to human existence. Quite the contrary, they make up the vital condition for human existence to reach its fullness and—according to the established Orthodox vocabulary—become a *person*, an event of communion, not an autonomous individual.[21]

So the church community is commissioned to be a sign and a foretaste of the kingdom, living as the minister of the invitation that God addresses to the entire creation. The church does not *have* a mission; it *is* mission. The very self and the raison d'être of the church are to be the first fruits and the servant of the kingdom. So, mission is not only a matter of word (preaching) or a matter of extraordinary activities, but it also coincides with the very being of the church.

> The Church is the divinely appointed and permanent witness to the very truth and the full meaning of this message, simply because the Church belongs itself to the revelation, as the Body of the Incarnate Lord. The proclamation of the Gospel, the preaching of the Word of God, obviously belongs to the *esse* of the Church. . . . The primary task of the historical Church is the proclamation of another world "to come."[22]

---

[20] Petros Vassiliadis, "Theological Foundations of Mission: An Orthodox Perspective," in *Orthodox Perspectives on Mission*, ed. Petros Vassiliadis (Oxford: Regnum Books, 2013), 192.

[21] John D. Zizioulas, *Communion and Otherness: Further Studies on Personhood and the Church* (London: T & T Clark, 2006).

[22] Florovsky, *Bible, Church, Tradition*, 26, 68–69.

Mission . . . is the organic need and task of the Church in the world, the real meaning of the Church's presence in history between the first and the second advents of her Lord.[23]

So the faithful have to act in this perspective, living out the profound missionary character of their ecclesial identity. This approach, combined with the traditional Orthodox doctrine of *synergia* (cooperation)—which means that humans have the responsibility to respond to God's work, and that God's grace does not violate human free will—has actually anticipated the notion of *missio Dei*, which liberated Christian mission from the bonds of institutionalized or authoritative ecclesiologies.

THE BOUNDARIES OF THE CHURCH
AND A BOUNDLESS MISSION

The kingdom has been inaugurated with Christ's resurrection, but it hasn't reached its fullness yet. The eschaton coincides with salvation, which is not conceived as a matter of individualistic atonement, but rather as the transformation of the entire creation to the status of resurrection, meaning the abolition of sin and the annulment of every kind of death, both biological and ethical (exploitation, racism, slavery, and so on). The church witnesses to this expectation and works so that the kingdom is manifested in history—not only inside the church community but also beyond it.

As Nikos Nissiotis (1924–86) puts it, the church, as the body of Christ, is

neither confining the Spirit of God to her institutional organization seen as a sociological unit, nor imprisoning the individual by human authority. . . . There are no limitations to the grace of God, but, within this limitless grace, the Church represents the new action of God in Christ, through the Spirit, as an act of redeeming and of gathering all people into One fellowship.[24]

Orthodox ecclesiology is inclusive. The motto of Saint Cyprian of Carthage (3rd century), *Extra ecclesiam nulla salus* was never fully accepted by Orthodox ecclesiology, which recognizes that the canonical and the charismatic boundaries of the church do not coincide. We have already spoken about the continuous and limitless loving mission of God, especially that of the incarnate Son and the Spirit. This also affects the role of the church. Christ, the head of the church, is not imprisoned in it but

---

[23] Alexander Schmemann, "Orthodoxy and Mission," *St. Vladimir's Seminary Quarterly* 3/4 (1959): 41.

[24] N. A. Nissiotis, "An Orthodox View of Modern Trends in Evangelism," in *The Ecumenical World of Orthodox Civilization: Essays in Honor of Georges Florovsky*, ed. Andrew Blane (Paris: Mouton, 1973), 189–90.

acts wherever it pleases him, not annihilating the church but surprisingly widening its boundaries in mystical ways. The Byzantine Saint Nicholas Cabasilas (14th century) emphasized that Christ himself baptizes in secrecy where the church is absent.[25] In that case those who mystically encounter Christ and are mystically baptized become members of the church, though not members of any historical Christian community. It is obvious that all these factors in the mystery of salvation—the economies of the Son and the Spirit, the outward activities of the church, and the unseen activities of God—have to be correlated without being mutually exclusive.

Christ's mystical extension of the church's boundaries complements the work of the Spirit. The mission of the church, therefore, is both an invitation to itself and a witness to God's universal action. The church's mission "is to read through the mystery of which it is the sign, all other signs sent by God through all times and in various religions in view of the full revelation at the end of history."[26]

This approach offers the dynamics for the formation of a theology from below. The church is not a mechanism to impose ideological formulas or customs, but it is the prophet sent by God to teach people to be open to the Lord of surprises, to untamable sacrificial love. This prophetic role is programmatically experienced in the divine liturgy and the Eucharist, which is the heart of the ecclesial life for Orthodox.

THE EUCHARIST AND . . . : *AND,* NOT *VERSUS*

It has been noted that the liturgy is conceived not simply as one of a body's activities but as the event that makes the church truly exist qua church. In the celebration of the Eucharist the life of the world (represented by the bread and the wine) is offered to God, then imbued with the divine life, and eventually the community becomes an outpost of the kingdom. This scheme necessitates the historical action of the faithful—their opening up to the world, in order to invite it into the church. Orthodox devotion, however, always runs the danger of degenerating into a mysticism that paralyzes its sensitivity to history and its impulse for witness to the world. It is true that some Orthodox see the Eucharist in juxtaposition with mission and social engagement, claiming that the essence of the church is the Eucharist alone, while mission and social involvement are something secondary, if not diversions that jeopardize the genuineness of the spiritual life. Views like this, however, limit the fullness of Christian life and undermine its evangelical ecumenicity. It is thus important to discern the parameters which reveal that the liturgy and Eucharist are missionary events by nature.

---

[25] Nicholas Cabasilas, *The Life in Christ,* trans. Carmino J. De Catanzaro (New York: St. Vladimir's Seminary Press, 1974), 88–89, 92–93.

[26] Khodr, "An Orthodox Perspective of Inter-Religious Dialogue," 26.

Important Orthodox theologians have observed that the Eucharist is not an isolated ritual or an esoteric event, but the font of Christians' attitude in everyday life. The very word *liturgy* (Greek: *leitourgia*) consists of the Greek words *litos* ("pertaining to the people") and *ergon* ("work"). All members of the community are commissioned to become bearers of the divine gifts. So, when the liturgy ends, all members of the community have to return to everyday life radiant with what they experienced in the liturgy. This had already been brought to the fore in the 1960s,[27] but it was Anastasios Yannoulatos who gave it a strong missiological orientation. In 1975 he coined the term "liturgy after the liturgy," meaning the diffusion of what has been achieved in the worship to everyday life and the entire society, in the form of witness to the hope and struggle for liberation from all demonic structures: injustice, exploitation, poverty, nihilism, and so on. In this perspective what happens after the liturgy is acknowledged not as an annex to the liturgy but as a substantial dimension of the liturgy itself.[28] As Ion Bria pointed out, this formula connected the theology of the church (ecclesiology) and the theology of mission (missiology) in an organic way.[29]

The missionary perspective of the liturgy transcends the conviction that the Eucharist is the sole sign of the kingdom and that the whole life of the church is just the fruition of the Eucharist.[30] It is certainly no accident that, in the liturgy, certain deeds—the bringing in of the bread and wine, the confession of faith, and reconciliation with our fellow human beings—precede the Anaphora, that is, that specific part of the liturgy when the celebration of the Eucharist is culminated. The sacrament of the brother conditions the liturgy. According to Christ's words, "If you bring your gift to the altar, and there remember that your brother has something against you, leave your gift before that altar and go your way. First be reconciled to your brother, and then come and offer your gift" (Mt 5:23–24). So, the sacrament of the brother it is not simply the outcome of the liturgy.[31] Moreover, the clear missiological character of the liturgy is also manifested in the Great Entrance, which also precedes the Anaphora. In the Great Entrance the priest comes out from the sanctuary from a side door into the main church and then solemnly enters the sanctuary through its central, main door. With this movement the bread and wine are carried from the Prothesis (a

---

[27] Paul Evdokimov, *La Prière de l'Eglise d'Orient: La Liturgie Byzantine de Saint Jean Chrysostome* (Mulhouse, France: Salvator, 1966).

[28] Athanasios N. Papathanasiou, "The Social Engagement as Part of the Call to Deification in Orthodox Theologies," *Logos: A Journal of Eastern Christian Studies* 57/1–4 (2016): 82.

[29] Ion Bria, "The Liturgy after the Liturgy," in Vassiliadis, *Orthodox Perspectives on Mission*, 46.

[30] For example, see John D. Zizioulas, *The Eucharistic Communion and the World* (London: T & T Clark, 2011), 68.

[31] Athanasios N. Papathanasiou, "The Church as Mission: Fr. Alexander Schmemann's Liturgical Theology Revisited," *Proche-Orient Chrétien* 60 (2010): 21–25.

special place on the north side of the sanctuary), to be placed on the altar and therefore offered to God. This movement symbolizes a real entrance: the movement of all human life, toil, and creativity into an encounter with God and their transformation into materials for the kingdom. From this perspective the Eucharist is not merely the result of a vertical action of the Spirit alone, but also a historical *movement*. The Great Entrance signifies the prior opening up of the faithful to the "fields" of the world. For these reasons it has recently been proposed that the formula "liturgy after the liturgy" be accompanied by the "liturgy before the liturgy."[32]

All of this brings to the fore the significance of praxis and the practical way of life. Mission is both the witness to and the serving of the Holy Trinity's outpouring of life to the entire world. This means that solidarity with the victims of history witnesses to the gospel, even without any verbal proclamation. The Eucharist is a model of sharing in a suffering world,[33] and solidarity becomes a sign of the kingdom.[34] Not only does the church have to practice occasional charity, but it must also imitate Christ's self-emptying, suffer with the marginalized, and imbue life with a vision for a new world. Christians experience the crucifixion as the victory of sacrificial love against the demonic powers that rage in history and dehumanize life. From this perspective the church witnesses to the liberating good news in word as well as in deeds of solidarity, away from pseudo-theologies such as the health-and-wealth gospel, which justify inequality, praise individual success, and bypass the sacrament of the cross. The liberating mission of the church also implies an especially critical stance toward culture. I mean that every culture should not be thought of as a compact entity. On the contrary, it should be acknowledged that every culture is composed of subcultures and class inequalities, elites and non-privileged strata. The faithful have to meet this reality without pursuing neutrality. God's preferential option for the suffering and the marginalized is the ecclesiastical Great Commission.

Emphasis on *orthodoxy,* the right doctrine, should not overshadow the emphasis on *orthopraxy,* the right way of life. Actually, following the narrative of the Gospel about the last judgment, where Christ welcomes those who practice love, beyond any prerequisite of orthodoxy, Saint Gregory

---

[32] Athanasios N. Papathanasiou, "Journey to the Center of Gravity: Christian Mission One Century after Edinburgh 1910," in *2010 Boston: The Changing Contours of World Mission and Christianity*, ed. T. M. Johnson, R. L. Petersen, G. A. Bellofatto, and T. L. Myers (Eugene, OR: Pickwick, 2012), 70–71. Geevarghese Mor Coorilos, "Mission as Liturgy before Liturgy and as Contestation," in Vassiliadis, *Orthodox Perspectives on Mission*, 175–76.

[33] Emmanuel Clapsis, "The Eucharist as Missionary Event in a Suffering World," in Vassiliadis, *Orthodox Perspectives on Mission*, 60–66. Vassiliadis, *Eucharist and Witness*, 49–66.

[34] Papathanasiou, "Social Engagement," 79–80. Cf. Evi Voulgaraki-Pissina, "Reading the Document on Mission of the Holy and Great Council from a Missiological Point of View," *International Review of Mission* 106/1 (2017): 136–50.

the Theologian, patriarch of Constantinople (4th century), writes: "Just as many of us do not belong really to us, because their own way of life cuts them off from the common body, in the same manner many of those who do not belong to the church are really near us, because they reach the Christian identity through their way of life, and the only thing that they are missing is their designation as Christians."[35] Saint Cosmas of Aitolia (18th century), who performed extensive missionary work among the populations under the Ottoman yoke in Greece and in the Balkans, courageously crushed any lapse into sacramentalism that undermines the liberating core of Christian life. Cosmas said that even if all the priests, bishops, and patriarchs absolve an exploiter of other people, the perpetrator remains unforgivable if he is not forgiven by the person wronged, whether Orthodox Christian, Western Christian, or Jew.[36]

DIALOGUE AND CONVERSION: PARTNERS IN MISSION

In 1943, Lev Gillet (1893–1980), a French convert to Orthodoxy, published an article in the historic *International Review of Missions* (later *International Review of Mission*). He proposed something that sounded new at that time: mission as dialogue. Gillet argued that this concept was rooted in the ancient Christian tradition and had been expressed characteristically in the second century in Saint Justin Martyr's *Dialogue with a Jew Named Trypho*.[37] Three decades had to pass after Gillet's article before mission as dialogue came to the forefront of the ecumenical movement.[38] Dialogue has been acknowledged as a precious, complex, and multifaceted procedure that can be carried out in various ways: through argumentation as well as through an open and caring way of life.

There are missionaries who are saints and saints in the Orthodox tradition who were missionaries. The world, however, is healed and transfigured more by the praying saint than by the thundering preachers. It is the saint who, manifesting God's tender love and receiving his creatures in divine hospitality, is genuinely sensitive to the riches of other religions, to different cultures, to "all sentient beings." The

[35] Gregory of Nazianzus, "Sermon 18, Obituary to the Father," *Patrologia Graeca* 35, 992 BC.
[36] John Menounos, *Kosma tou Aitolou Didaxes* [The teaching of Kosmas of Aitolia] (Athens: Tenos, 1979), 45 [in Greek]; Papathanasiou, "Social Engagement," 79.
[37] Lev Gillet, "Dialogue with Trypho," *International Review of Missions* 31 (1942): 172–79.
[38] Athanasios N. Papathanasiou, "Tradition as Impulse for Renewal and Witness: Introducing Orthodox Missiology in the IRM," in Vassiliadis, *Orthodox Perspectives on Mission*, 161.

crusading missionary is afire with the message he proclaims, but can be totally lacking in receptivity and sensitivity. Perhaps this is a stereotyped image of the past. Today we need to combine in our experience of our Church the true saint and the genuine missionary whose sole concern is manifesting the Kingdom and not annexing new territories.[39]

Dialogue means two things at the same time: testifying to the truth that inspires one's life, and keeping open to God's revelation. Dialogue is neither superficial public relations nor pretext and deceit. It is a path to deepening the experience of the good news through encounter with the Other (probably after an interior dialogue first),[40] through learning from the Other's experience, through honest debate and through discernment of the spirits (1 Jn 4:1), since all human realities (religions, cultures, and so on) have not only bright sides but also dark ones. Contradictory as it may sound, dialogue does not impede conversion. The call for conversion lies at the heart of the gospel and is something totally different from proselytism, which means aggressive recruitment, forced change, colonization of consciousness, and so forth. Proselytism is "the corruption of witness."[41] But free and wholehearted conversion is rooted in the precious capacity of humans to choose their own spiritual orientation. Without it, humans degenerate into a mere product of biological, cultural, and ethnic randomness.

People are invited to convert to God's love, and this applies to all circumstances, either when someone enters the church or when someone does not share the Christian faith but opts for love (and experiences the mystical action of God) instead of perpetuating the violence inherent in natural and social Darwinism.[42] Even for the evangelists themselves conversion has to be a constant and always renewed process. The Orthodox voices that clarify the meaning of conversion are of particular importance because they confront the collectivism that lurks in traditionally Orthodox societies and maintains that one is "born" Orthodox or that Orthodoxy lies in the DNA

---

[39] K. M. George, "Mission for Unity or Unity for Mission? An Ecclesiological/Ecumenical Perspective," in Vassiliadis, *Orthodox Perspectives on Mission*, 112.

[40] See Francis X. Clooney, "Comparative Theology—as Theology," in *Interreligious Hermeneutics in Pluralistic Europe: Between Texts and People*, ed. David Cheetham, Ulrich Winkler, and Oddbjørn Leirvik (Amsterdam: Rodopi, 2011), 138.

[41] World Council of Churches, "Towards Common Witness: A Call to Adopt Responsible Relationships in Mission and to Renounce Proselytism" (Geneva: WCC, 1997).

[42] Athanasios N. Papathanasiou, "Reconciliation: The Major Conflict in Postmodernity: An Orthodox Contribution to a Missiological Dialogue," in *Come Holy Spirit, Heal and Reconcile! Report of the WCC Conference on World Mission and Evangelism, Athens, Greece, May 2005*, ed. Jacques Matthey (Geneva: WCC Publications, 2008), 178–86; also Vassiliadis, "Theological Foundations of Mission," 191.

of the people. Consequently, whenever nationalism and phyletism influence a missionary activity, they try to impose their own fossilized traditionalism on people of other cultures, violating the fact that both nationalism and phyletism were condemned by the Synod of Constantinople in 1872[43] and again renounced by the Great Synod of the Orthodox Churches in Crete in 2016.[44] Contrary to these perversions Orthodox theology has to face broader questions of contextualization—for example, how its traditional dogmatic assets can be assimilated into the vocabularies of people unfamiliar with Greco-Roman ontological categories. A few attempts have been made in this area from the time of the so-called Nestorian mission to China (7th–14th centuries) to our days.[45] But the issue extends beyond the traditional cultures. The postmodern narrative method of doing theology is also a challenge, yet not foreign to church tradition, since narration is the biblical method to a great degree.

Witness articulated in dialogue has to claim a significant role in public space today. In opposition to the illusion that religion belongs to the private sphere, Christians have to testify to the good news in the midst of the agora, without using unrelatable and non-inclusive terminology. They have to become partners in public deliberation, facing issues important for common life and using the current language of the society, the verbal language as well as the language of action and hospitality.[46] This means that Christians have to discuss their point of view not only with people of other faiths but also with atheists and agnostics, thus undertaking a kind of incarnation of the Logos in current reality.

The correlation between the assertion of the truth and dialogue means that the church is commissioned to a "prophetic dialogue," to use the powerful expression of Stephen Bevans and Roger Schroeder.[47] Something similar happens with the seeming antithesis between the missionary

---

[43] Cf. Pantelis Kalaitzidis, "New Wine into Old Wineskins?: Orthodox Theology of Mission Facing the Challenges of a Global World," in *Theological Education and Theology of Life: Transformative Christian Leadership in the Twenty-First Century*, ed. Atola Longkumer, Po Ho Huang, and Uta Andree (Oxford: Regnum Books, 2016), 119–47.

[44] "Encyclical of the Holy and Great Council of the Orthodox Church, Crete 2016."

[45] Cf. the attempt of Hieromonk Damascene, *Christ the Eternal Tao* (Platina, CA: St. Herman of Alaska Brotherhood, 1999). See also Athanasios N. Papathanasiou, "Christos, o Progonos kai Adelfos: Mia Afrikaniki Christologia" ("Christ, the Ancestor and Brother: An African Christology"), *Bulletin of Biblical Studies* 25/1 (2007): 59–82.

[46] Cf. Luke Bretherton, "Translation, Conversation, or Hospitality? Approaches to Theological Reasons in Public Deliberation," in *Religious Voices in Public Places*, ed. Nigel Biggar and Linda Hogan (Oxford: Oxford University Press, 2009), 85–109.

[47] Stephen B. Bevans and Roger P. Schroeder, *Prophetic Dialogue: Reflections on Christian Mission Today* (Maryknoll, NY: Orbis Books, 2011).

paradigms of liberation, on one hand, and reconciliation, on the other. What is needed is a prophetic synthesis of both. Reconciliation includes liberation, because reconciliation is impossible without "breaking down the dividing wall" (Eph 2:14). If reconciliation is meant as toleration of the dividing walls of hatred, injustice, and death, then it ends up surrendering to the old world that fights against the gospel of the resurrection.

CONCLUSION

The mission of Orthodox missiology is to participate in serving the free Spirit in an exhausted world that is becoming more and more narrow; more and more claustrophobic; more and more allured by narcissism, bigotry, and fundamentalism. Orthodoxy has to bring its own wealth to the vision of the New Jerusalem, yet with a humble disposition, self-critical readiness, and always in the spirit of discipleship.

Chapter 4

Mission in Protestant Theology

Dale T. Irvin

Stephen B. Bevans is one of the most important voices in world Christian theology in our generation. His work has ranged widely across the fields of historical and dogmatic theology. His global perspective has been one that embraces the multiplicity of local contextual methods and experiences, and connects them not only with one another but with the history of Christian traditions through the past. Drawing upon the insight of Vatican II that "the pilgrim Church is missionary by her very nature" (*Ad gentes* I.1), Bevans has sought to articulate a "full-blown Catholic missionary ecclesiology" for today.[1] In line with a number of his insights, this chapter looks at the Protestant tradition as fundamentally a missionary ecclesiology. Protestantism is at its heart a movement committed to the renewal of the church brought about through a continuing encounter with the good news (*euangélion* in Greek) heard in the person and work of Jesus Christ.

Protestantism in all of its branches throughout the world traces its genealogy in one way or another back to the sixteenth century and a cluster of reform movements launched in Western Europe within the Catholic Church. What began as a series of intended reforms quickly gave rise to a new group of ecclesial formations that were separated not only from the Roman Catholic tradition but in many cases from one another as well. Protestantism today is a diverse global reality embracing a wide range of beliefs and practices.[2] Holding it together as a distinct tradition are its

---

[1] See Stephen B. Bevans, SVD, and Roger P. Schroeder, SVD, "Missionary Ecclesiology: Evangelical, Ecumenical, and Catholic Developments in 'Engaging the Nation,'" in *Contemporary Mission Theology: Engaging the Nations: Essays in Honor of Charles E. Van Engen*, ed. Robert L. Gallagher and Paul Hertig (Maryknoll, NY: Orbis Books, 2017), 58.

[2] See Todd M. Johnson, Gina A. Zurlo, Albert W. Hickman, and Peter F. Crossing, "Christianity 2017: Five Hundred Years of Protestant Christianity," *International Bulletin of Mission Research* 41/1 (January 2017): 41–52.

twin historic commitments to the Bible being the primary or sole source of authority in matters of faith and identity *(sola scriptura)*, and to human beings having direct access to God through faith *(sola fide)*.[3] Not surprisingly, these twin commitments have characterized Protestant theologies of mission over the past five centuries.

Most histories cite October 31, 1517, as a convenient starting point for the Protestant Reformation when a German monk and university professor named Martin Luther is reported to have posted his *Ninety-Five Theses* on the door of the castle church in Wittenberg.[4] The theses concerned a number of reforms that the young German monk wished to defend in an academic disputation. Luther sent a copy to Archbishop Albert of Mainz, ensuring that they were seen by church authorities. Albert forwarded them to Pope Leo X in Rome, who the following year charged Luther with heresy. The *Ninety-Five Theses* were soon translated from the Latin in which Luther wrote them into German and made widely available through the new commercial instrument known as the printing press. Luther's fame spread through the region of Saxony. He was summoned to Rome to face the charges but chose instead to engage in a series of debates nearer to home. Several more documents critical of Rome were penned by Luther, put into print, and circulated commercially, to a wider readership. Finally in January 1521, Leo X issued the papal bull *Decet Romanum Pontificem,* formally excommunicating Luther as a heretic as well as those others "whatever their authority and rank, who have recked naught of their own salvation but publicly and in all men's eyes become followers of Martin's pernicious and heretical sect, and given him openly and publicly their help, counsel, and favor."[5]

Luther initially had no intention of leaving the Roman Catholic Church. His goal was to address issues that he deemed theologically incorrect, doing so—in his words from the opening line of the *Ninety-Five Theses*—"out of love for the truth and from desire to elucidate it."[6] His excommunication led Luther and his supporters to organize a separate communion around a common confessional identity. The name Protestant became associated with these efforts in 1529 when a group of princes and representatives

---

[3] Douglas Jacobson, *The World's Christians: Who They Are, Where They Are, and How They Got There* (New York: Wiley Blackwell, 2011), 38.

[4] The full title of the document was *A Disputation of Doctor Martin Luther on the Power and Efficacy of Indulgences*, but it is most widely known simply as *The Ninety-Five Theses*. On the historical basis for Luther posting or not posting his theses on the door of the church, see Joachim Ott and Martin Treu, eds., *Faszination Thesenanschlag: Faktum oder Fiktion Gebundene* (Berlin: Evangelische Verlagsanstalt, 2017).

[5] The text can be found in Denis R. Janz, ed., *A Reformation Reader: Primary Texts with Introductions*, 2nd ed. (Minneapolis: Fortress Press, 2008), 384.

[6] Martin Luther, *Works of Martin Luther: With Introductions and Notes*, vol. 1 (Philadelphia: A. J. Holman Company, 1915), 29.

of free cities in Germany issued a "Letter of Protestation" against an imperial edict that rescinded an earlier decision to allow them to reform the churches in their regions along lines that Luther was proposing. The movement spread to other parts of Europe and eventually took on institutional shape in the form of a number of separate communions. What united them was mostly their common rejection of the universal teaching authority of Rome and the papacy.

Not all of the reform movements of the sixteenth century ended up outside the Roman Catholic Church.[7] Those that did formed themselves into three major confessional families or communions: Lutheran, Reformed, and Anabaptist. In England the established church under the Archbishop of Canterbury was separated from Rome in the sixteenth century by royal decree without opting for the confessional commitments of Luther and the other Protestant reformers. By the middle of the sixteenth century the Anglican Church, as it came to be known, had a strong Protestant wing, but it also retained its Catholic identity to a greater degree than many of the other Protestant communions. Further divisions arose within the churches of England in the seventeenth century that gave rise to Baptists and others who were called Non-Conformists or Dissenters. In England the diverse communions came to be called denominations in the eighteenth century, replacing the earlier, more dismissive, terminology of sects. The number of Protestant communions or denominations continued to multiply through the nineteenth century as divisions arose around social, political, and religious issues.[8] The irruption of the global Pentecostal movement at the beginning of the twentieth century added to the expanding ranks of Protestant communions or denominations. By the end of the twentieth century many observers had come to regard Pentecostals and churches in the closely related Charismatic movement as forming a separate stream of Christianity that was distinct from Protestantism.[9]

Luther's ideas spread rapidly throughout Europe in the first decades of the sixteenth century. A key factor promoting the dissemination of his ideas was the development of the printing press. Printers throughout Germany were soon turning out thousands of copies of Luther's various writings in a highly readable form that were sold and circulated throughout Europe.[10] Other reformers soon picked up the practice and published their works.

---

[7] See Carter Lindberg, *The European Reformations*, 2nd ed. (New York: Wiley-Blackwell, 2009).

[8] The classical statement of this thesis is H. Richard Niebuhr, *The Social Sources of Denominationalism* (New York: Henry Holt and Co., 1929).

[9] Jacobson, *The World's Christians*, 9–10.

[10] Andrew Pettegree, *Brand Luther: How an Unheralded Monk Turned His Small Town into a Center of Publishing, Made Himself the Most Famous Man in Europe—and Started the Protestant Reformation* (New York: Penguin Books, 2016).

The rapid spread of the Protestant Reformation in its early days was in no small part due to publishing and books.

One book in particular came to define the Protestant movement: the Bible. Luther's translation of the Bible into German is among his most important contributions to world Christianity. Before becoming a reformer, Luther was already part of a wider movement of scholars in Europe who came to be known as Humanists. The Humanists were committed to investigating the cultural, literary, and philosophical works of the Greco-Roman world of antiquity, which generally meant before the year 500 CE. One of their rallying cries for scholarship was *ad fontes* ("to the fountains," that is, "sources"). For Luther and the other Protestant reformers who identified with his cause, the source to which they sought to return was the Bible. Luther, the Swiss Reformers Huldrych Zwingli and John Calvin, and many others in the Protestant movement preferred the term *evangelical* to describe their efforts. The word is derived from the Greek *euangélion* and means "good news." The use of the term by the Protestant reformers was meant to emphasize the priority they gave not only to the Bible as a whole as their primary source of authority for doctrine and practice in the church, but especially to the first four books of the New Testament, which are the primary source for our knowledge of the good news of Jesus Christ. Energizing their efforts was not simply a hoped-for increase in biblical literacy, but a deepening of understanding and relationship with Jesus Christ.

Here then is the heart of the Protestant understanding of mission from the inception of the movement. Protestants in all streams of the movement (Lutheran, Reformed, Anabaptist, Baptist, and others) argued that one's salvation was attained through direct faith in Jesus Christ and not through the mediations of the church. Justification by faith was the doctrine on which the movement was founded. As Luther wrote in 1532 in a commentary on Psalm 130, "quia isto articulo stante stat Ecclesia, ruente ruit Ecclesia," which can be translated, "if this article [justification] stands, the church stands; if it collapses, the church collapses."[11] The mission that Luther, Calvin, and others undertook was to proclaim this message of justification or salvation through faith in Jesus Christ alone to the members of their congregations. They did not dispute that Jesus Christ was mentioned in other churches. Lutheran and Reformed branches of the movement did not dispute the validity of baptism that was practiced by Roman Catholics (Anabaptists did). Protestants of all branches agreed, however, that greater attention to preaching was needed in worship in order to direct or call members of the church continually to faith in Jesus Christ.

---

[11] Martin Luther, *D. Martin Luthers Werke: Kritische Gesammtausgabe*, vol. 40/3 (Weimar: Hermann Böhlau Nachfolger, 1930), 352. See Alister E. McGrath, *Iustitia Dei: A History of the Christian Doctrine of Justification*, 3rd ed. (Cambridge: Cambridge University Press, 2005), 188–240.

In this sense the Protestant reformers were driven primarily by pastoral concerns. Members of their churches needed to hear in a variety of ways the good news that they were justified not by any works that they performed, whether moral or sacramental. Rather, they were justified by what Christ through the power of the Spirit has already accomplished through his life, death, and resurrection. Justification was received through faith, which the Holy Spirit brought about through preaching and the sacraments. In the words of the Heidelberg Catechism of 1563 in Question 62, good works neither in whole nor in part could make one righteous before the judgment seat of God. God rewarded us in the life to come not because of our good works but as an act of grace. This did not obliterate the need for action on the part of believers, however; as Question 64 explained, "it is impossible that those who are implanted into Christ by true faith should not bring forth fruits of righteousness."[12] The mission of the church was to proclaim this message and apply it to the daily lives of believers; this would then lead them into action, living holy or righteous lives.

Luther spelled out some of the implications of this doctrine of justification in his 1523 pamphlet *Concerning the Ordering of Divine Worship in the Congregation.*[13] Several major problems have crept into the life of the church in worship, he argued. "The first—God's Word has been silenced, and only reading and singing remain in the churches." This has led to the introduction of "fables and lies" by which he meant stories of the saints that take the place of the Bible. Furthermore, it appeared to Luther, worship had become a work that Christians performed in order to earn God's favor. "The result of this was that faith disappeared and instead every one gave to churches, established foundations, and wanted to become priests, monks and nuns." In order to correct these problems, said Luther, "the Christian congregation never should assemble unless God's Word is preached and prayer is made, no matter for how brief a time this may be. . . . Where God's Word is not preached, it is better that one neither sing nor read, nor even come together."[14] Luther argued that the daily mass or eucharistic service should be abolished "for the importance is in the Word and not in the masses."[15] The Eucharist would continue to be part of the weekly Sunday worship service under Luther's directives and would be available at other times as pastoral needs arose, but one accessed God through reading and hearing the word, which for Luther was found primarily in the Bible. Luther did not equate the Bible with the word. The Bible, he said, was the manger in which the Christ child was laid and the swaddling

---

[12] Philip Schaff, ed., *The Creeds of Christendom,* vol. 3, *The Evangelical Protestant Creeds,* 4th ed. (New York: Harper and Brothers, 1877; reprinted Grand Rapids, MI: Baker Books, 1977), 328.

[13] Martin Luther, *Works of Martin Luther,* vol. 6 (Philadelphia: A. J. Holman Company, 1915), 47–50.

[14] Ibid., 47.

[15] Ibid., 49.

cloth that bound him. It was the task of the preacher to become the living voice of Christ once again in worship, not merely reading the Bible but finding what Christ was saying from it for the faithful and interpreting it afresh for the present day.[16]

Like Luther, Calvin taught that a sermon was to be a part of every regular worship service, that it was to be based upon a biblical text, and that it was to be in the language that the people understood (the vernacular). Like Luther, he taught that all Christians needed to be able to read the Bible for themselves. This led Calvin along with the other Protestant Reformers to support universal literacy, including education for women so they too could read and understand the Bible for themselves.[17] Unlike Luther, Calvin did not publish his own translation of the Bible into French, the dominant language spoken in Geneva, but relied on a translation that his cousin Pierre Robert Olivétan produced and published in Neuchâtel, Switzerland, in 1535. Calvin followed Luther's lead in replacing the daily eucharistic celebration in the churches of Geneva with a daily sermon offered by a preacher. Calvin himself preached several times a week from the pulpit of his home church, St. Pierre's Cathedral, in Geneva. Looking at Calvin's reform of worship, Wesley A. Kort writes:

> His crucial acts were to move the practice of reading Scripture from the monastery and from clerical circles to all Christians, to exchange the centrality of receiving the sacraments for the centrality of reading Scripture, and to make the reading of Scripture the determining and defining practice of Christian life.[18]

To support this shift, Kort says, Calvin developed a new hermeneutic regarding reading and the text. Calvin often called the act of reading the actual text of scripture hearing the word. Reading scripture for Calvin, in other words, was an act of reception. Furthermore, reading was not confined to the eyes. Reading and hearing blur to become one act in worship. Calvin also spoke of ingesting the word, shifting the sacramental weight to the sermon in worship. Calvin, like Luther, argued for the real presence in the Eucharist, but he agreed with Luther that the Eucharist sealed what one received through the word in the sermon. The sermon expounds on the word, thereby exposing all who hear it to the presence of God. As the

---

[16] Roland H. Bainton, "The Bible in the Reformation," *The Cambridge History of the Bible*, vol. 3, *The West from the Reformation to the Present Day*, ed. Stanley L. Greenslade (Cambridge: Cambridge University Press, 1963), 21.

[17] See Rebecca A. Giselbrecht, "Women from Then to Now: A Commitment to Mutuality and Literacy," in *The Protestant Reformation and World Christianity: Global Perspectives*, ed. Dale T. Irvin (Grand Rapids, MI: Eerdmans, 2017), 65–95.

[18] Wesley A. Kort, *"Take, Read": Scripture, Textuality, and Cultural Practice* (University Park: Pennsylvania State University Press, 1996), 25.

Second Helvetic Confession of 1566 puts it, "The preaching of the word of God is the word of God."[19]

Preaching was the primary means by which the Holy Spirit united believers with Christ in worship for both Luther and Calvin.[20] In a sermon on John 15, Luther explained:

> When I am converted by the Gospel, the Holy Spirit is present. He takes me as clay and makes of me a new creature, which is endowed with a different mind, heart, and thoughts, that is, with a true knowledge of God and a sincere trust in His grace. To summarize, the very essence of my heart is renewed and changed. . . . Now I am like Him and of His kind. Both He and I are of one nature and essence, and I bear fruit in Him and through Him.[21]

It is important to note that conversion here for Luther did not mean an initial act of becoming a Christian. Luther considered it an ongoing process of change and renewal in which one is continuously being brought into union with Christ. Luther, Calvin, and the other Protestant reformers believed that individual believers and the church as a whole could fall away from this union with Christ and that they had to be continuously renewed, just as the material body had to be continuously fed. Salvation meant being grafted onto or joined in nature to Christ. As Calvin wrote in the *Institutes*, "We do not, therefore, contemplate him [Christ] outside ourselves from afar in order that his righteousness may be imputed to us, but because we put on Christ and are engrafted into his body—in short, because he deigns to make us one with him."[22] This relationship required constant attention, however.

Mission in Protestant theology starts with the worshiping community encountering Christ and being continuously revived or renewed through the power of his Spirit. Mission is not external to the life of the church; it

---

[19] *Second Helvetic Confession* I.4. See also J. Mark Beach, "The Real Presence of Christ in the Preaching of the Gospel: Luther and Calvin on the Nature of Preaching," *Mid-America Journal of Theology* 10 (1999): 77–134.

[20] See Carl E. Braaten and Robert W. Jenson, *Union with Christ: The New Finnish Interpretation of Luther* (Grand Rapids, MI: Eerdmans, 1998); and Richard A. Muller, "Union with Christ and the *Ordo Salutis*: Reflections on Developments in Early Modern Reformed Thought," in *Calvin and the Reformed Tradition: On the Work of Christ and the Order of Salvation*, 204–43 (Grand Rapids, MI: Baker Books, 2012).

[21] Martin Luther, *Luther's Works*, vol. 24, *Sermons on the Gospel of St. John: Chapters 14–16*, ed. Jaroslav Pelikan, Hilton C. Oswald, and Helmut T. Lehmann (Saint Louis: Concordia Publishing House, 1961).

[22] John Calvin, *Institutes of the Christian Religion*, 3.11.10, trans. Ford Lewis Battles, ed. John T. McNeill (Philadelphia: Westminster Press, 1960), 737.

is found at the very heart of Christian life, in worship, in the reception of the word of Jesus Christ, who through the Spirit has been sent by God into the world. It extends out from worship into the world, where the witness of Christ is carried by believers. All Christians are called to participate in these activities, those who are recognized as ministers as well as those who are not. In his 1520 pamphlet *To the Christian Nobility of the German Nation* Luther asserted that all Christians are consecrated as priests in their baptism. They serve God both in worship and by carrying out their everyday work in the world. Luther and Calvin both sought to unleash the spirituality that they believed had previously been wrongly confined to monastic life. They taught that one served God through one's work or trade in the world, becoming evangelists and missionaries through their work and witness to the glory of God.[23] Luther and Calvin both called their efforts evangelical in this sense of witnessing in the world. Evangelism and mission, in other words, were one and the same. In the twentieth century this insight would be regained in Protestant theology through the notion of *missio Dei*[24] and in the "missional church" movement.[25] As the twentieth-century Protestant theologian Johannes C. Hoekendijk provocatively states, "That which cannot serve as 'order of missions' has no right to exist as order of the church."[26]

The sixteenth-century Protestant reformers and their successors could not find sufficient consensus among themselves theologically to allow them to gather in a common church. The fragmentation of European Christendom was no small matter. Armies went to war at times over religious divisions.[27] Families divided, as did whole kingdoms.[28] In the midst of these unresolved divisions Protestant leaders found their movements facing political, social, and cultural pressures to institutionalize. Most did so along the traditional lines of Christendom in the West, forging new ties

---

[23] Michal Valèo, "Martin Luther's Views on Mission and Christianization," in *Oxford Research Encyclopedia of Religion* (2016).

[24] See Georg F. Vicedom, *The Mission of God: An Introduction to a Theology of Mission* (Saint Louis: Concordia Press, 1965); and John G. Flett, *The Witness of God: The Trinity, Missio Dei, Karl Barth, and the Nature of Christian Community* (Grand Rapids, MI: Eerdmans, 2010). A concise analysis of the concept can be found in David J. Bosch, *Transforming Mission: Paradigm Shifts in Theology of Mission* (Maryknoll, NY: Orbis Books, 1991), 389–93.

[25] See Darrell Gruder, ed., *Missional Church: A Vision for the Sending of the Church in North America* (Grand Rapids, MI: Eerdmans, 1998).

[26] Johannes C. Hoekendijk, *The Church Inside Out* (Philadelphia: Westminster Press, 1964), 159.

[27] It should be noted that the major reasons for military conflicts among European rulers in the period were financial in nature. See, for instance, James D. Tracy, *Emperor Charles V, Impresario of War: Campaign Strategy, International Finance, and Domestic Politics* (Cambridge: Cambridge University Press, 2010).

[28] See Eamon Duffy, *Reformation Divided: Catholics, Protestants, and the Conversion of England* (London: Bloomsbury Continuum, 2017).

between their churches and the ruling political authorities of their era, whether princes, kings, and queens or the councils of the emerging free cities. Only the Anabaptists refused to align their faith communities with temporal rulers, doing so out of their commitment to nonviolence and their rejection of the power of the sword.[29]

The institutionalization process for what came to be called the magisterial Reformation among Lutheran, Reformed, and Anglican churches took place mostly around formal confessions of faith that set out in considerable detail nuances of theological understanding fixed in verbal forms. The stress on doctrine seemed, to some at least, to diminish the direct personal dimensions of faith that the original Protestant reformers had emphasized. Within a century of the publication of Luther's *Ninety-Five Theses,* Protestant churches were finding movements for spiritual renewal arising from within their own ranks and challenging their established leadership. In Germany the publication of Johann Arndt's four-volume *True Christianity* from 1605 to 1610 was a watershed in the history of spirituality. The starting point for Arndt's work was a sober assessment of the need of baptized Christians to confront their sinful nature, which he said was not washed away in their baptism and, if left unaddressed, prevented them from experiencing full fellowship with God. Christians needed to grow in grace and holiness, which is the work of the Holy Spirit in one's inward life. Arndt placed far more emphasis upon the work of the Spirit in the inward dimensions of one's life than Luther or Calvin before him. "Faith," he wrote, "is a sincere confidence, and a firm persuasion of the grace of God promised to us in Christ Jesus, for the remission of sin and eternal life; and it is enkindled in the heart, by the word of God and the Holy Spirit."[30]

Arndt's work helped to inspire a movement within Lutheranism known as Pietism. Pietists emphasized the inward dimensions of religious experience and the need for personal spiritual renewal. It increased attention to biblical study and the work of the Holy Spirit not just in the church as a whole, but in one's own life. Inspired by Arndt's work, the Lutheran pastor and theologian Philipp Jakob Spener in 1670 in Frankfurt am Main began organizing small groups for prayer and spiritual renewal that he called *collegia pietatis.* He referred to these small groups as *ecclesiola in ecclesia* ("little churches within the church"). Spener's influence, along with that of other Pietists who followed him, spread to other Protestant communions, most notably to England where it helped shape a movement within the

---

[29] Not all Anabaptists refused political establishment, but the majority of these movements did so out of a commitment to nonviolence. See Meic Pearse, *Great Restoration: The Religious Radicals of the Sixteenth and Seventeenth Centuries* (Milton Keynes: Paternoster, 1998).

[30] Johann Arndt, *True Christianity: A Treatise on Sincere Repentance, True Faith, the Holy Walk of the True Christian, Etc.* (Philadelphia: The Lutheran Book Store, 1868), 71.

Anglican Church known as Puritanism. In the eighteenth century the Anglican priest John Wesley, the major figure in the founding of Methodism
in England, was greatly influenced by both Puritanism and Pietism, the
latter especially through its Moravian expressions led by Count Nikolaus
Ludwig von Zinzendorf from Germany. Wesley and Zinzendorf were
among the key figures in launching the evangelical revivals or awakenings
of the eighteenth century that have had a lasting impact on Protestant
theology generally.[31]

It has been common in mission studies over the past century to read
that the sixteenth-century Reformers were not concerned about carrying Christian faith beyond the confines of their own European nations.
Gustav Warneck, who is considered by many the founder of the discipline
of missiology or mission studies today, in 1882 wrote, "We miss in the
Reformers not only missionary action, but even the idea of missions, in
the sense in which we understand them today."[32] David J. Bosch, in his
landmark introductory textbook *Transforming Mission,* corrects Warneck's
perception, but only partially so.[33] Warneck argued that Protestant efforts
to engage in global missions began with Pietism. Pietists and Methodists
were important movements in expanding Protestantism on a global scale
beginning in the eighteenth century.[34] But the assertion that Luther, Calvin,
and the other first-generation Reformers of the sixteenth century were not
concerned with extending Christian faith beyond their immediate European
churches and locations has been decisively proven to be untrue. Both Luther and Calvin regularly asserted that the church was called to proclaim
the message of Jesus Christ to all peoples and nations on earth.[35] Luther,
David D. Daniels III has recently demonstrated, had an active ecumenical
interest in the life of the church in Ethiopia both because of the esteemed
place Ethiopia commanded in the Bible and because the church of Ethio-

---

[31] See Michael J. McClymond, "Theology of Revival," in *The Encyclopedia of
Christianity,* vol. 5, ed. Erwin Fahlbusch, Jan Miliè Lochman, John Mbiti, Jaroslav
Pelikan, and Lukas Vischer (Grand Rapids, MI: Eerdmans, 2008), 431–49.

[32] Gustav Warneck, *Outline of a History of Protestant Missions from the Reformation to the Present Time: A Contribution to Modern Church History* (New
York: Fleming H. Revell Co., 1901), 9.

[33] Bosch, *Transforming Mission,* 248–51.

[34] See Daniel Jeyaraj, *Der Beitrag der Dänisch-Halleschen Mission zum Werden
einer indisch-ein-heimischen Kirche, 1706–1730* (Erlangen: Verlag der Ev.-Luth.
Mission, 1996); Jon Sensbach, *Rebecca's Revival: Creating Black Christianity in
the Atlantic World* (Cambridge, MA: Harvard University Press, 2005); and Charles
Yrigoyen Jr., ed., *The Global Impact of the Wesleyan Traditions and Their Related
Movements* (Lanham, MD: Scarecrow Press, 2002).

[35] See Ingemar Oberg, *Luther and World Mission: A Historical and Systematic
Study with Special Reference to Luther's Bible Exposition* (St. Louis: Concordia
Publishing House, 2007); and Michael A. G. Haykin and C. Jeffrey Robinson Sr.,
To the Ends of the Earth: Calvin's Missional Vision and Legacy (Wheaton, IL:
Crossway, 2014).

pia in his view was older than the church of Rome (Luther assumed the Ethiopian church began with the conversion of the Ethiopian official in Acts).[36] John Calvin sent several pastors as part of a Huguenot effort to establish a colony in Rio de Janeiro, Brazil, as early as 1557.[37] Daniels has shown that the issues concerning the global South were on the agenda of Reformed theology at the Synod of Dort in 1619.[38]

The global expansion of Protestantism was very much tied to the colonial expansion of predominantly Protestant European nations in the modern era.[39] British and Dutch merchants around 1600 began to form trade companies that, with the support of their national governments, launched colonial expeditions in Asia and the Americas. The Scandinavian nations soon followed. Clergy from various Protestant communions were part of these early colonial ventures. At first they went along to provide for the religious needs of the colonial merchants. By the end of the century they were turning their attention to spreading Christian teachings and planting churches among peoples they encountered outside their European settler communities. New organizations supporting these efforts, such as the Society for the Propagation of the Gospel in Foreign Parts in England, which was founded in 1700, emerged. William Carey's *An Enquiry into the Obligations of Christians to Use Means for the Conversion of the Heathens*, published in 1792, turned attention to the instructions that Jesus had given to his disciples to go into all the world.[40] *An Enquiry* opens by stating that Christ laid upon his original disciples the obligation "to disperse themselves into every country of the habitable globe, and preach to all the inhabitants, without exception, or limitation."[41] The command was never repealed, said Carey. It remains as binding upon Christians of the present as it was upon the first apostles. Carey in effect moved world missions and the call to convert the nations into an order of the church. Carey's pamphlet helped launch what turned out to be a century of enormous expansion in Protestant world missions.

Protestant mission works were as diverse as the communities and communions that sponsored them. Two commonalities emerge from the

[36] David D. Daniels III, "Honor the Reformation's African Roots," op. ed. in *Commercial Appeal* (October 31, 2017).

[37] Eduardo Galasso Faria, "Calvin and Reformed Social Thought in Latin America," in *John Calvin Rediscovered: The Impact of His Social and Economic Thought*, ed. Edward Dommen and James D. Bratt (Louisville, KY: Westminster John Knox Press, 2007), 93.

[38] David D. Daniels III, "The Global South: The Synod of Dort on Baptizing the 'Ethnics,'" in Irvin, *The Protestant Reformation and World Christianity*, chap. 4.

[39] See Peter C. Phan, "The Protestant Reformations in Asia: A Blessing or a Curse?" in Irvin, *The Protestant Reformation and World Christianity: Global Perspectives*, 120–53.

[40] William Carey, *An Enquiry into the Obligations of Christians to Use Means for the Conversion of the Heathens* (1792).

[41] Ibid., Sect. 1.

history of these efforts, however. Both are reflective of the commitments
of the initial Reformers in the sixteenth century. The first has been Bible
translation. In almost every instance Protestant missionaries undertook
translation of scriptures as their first and most important task. The impact,
argues Lamin Sanneh, was multifaceted. First, by translating the Bible
into indigenous languages Protestant missionaries, in many cases without intending to do so, helped to preserve local languages and dialects.
Translating the Bible into local languages also helped to facilitate a more
rapid contextualization process. Quite often Protestant translations used
an indigenous name for God. The effect was to facilitate the transfer of
attributes from the existing religious worlds out of which converts were
coming to the Christian understanding of God.[42]

Over the course of the nineteenth century Protestant world missionary
activity was increasingly dominated by those coming from the evangelical
or revival wing of the tradition. They tended to emphasize the personal
and relational dimensions of the faith, resonating with the strong emphasis placed on knowing Christ for one's self that was part of the original
message of the sixteenth-century Reformers. Anglo-American evangelical
missionaries in particular tended to place more emphasis upon an initial
conversion experience and to emphasize the personal over the ecclesial
dimensions of Christian faith. Where Catholic missionaries often produced
catechisms in the local language, Protestants were content to translate the
Bible. The liturgical services of evangelicals and revivalists tended to be
simpler and began to contextualize more quickly. The overall impact was
less attention paid to ecclesial formations and greater attention to encouraging personal acts of faith. Evangelicalism fostered a democratization of
faith that was passed along in its missionary efforts. Jay Riley Case notes,
"By inadvertently encouraging religious dissent and empowering marginalized Christians, American evangelicalism had a way of turning around
and challenging its own established leaders. A similar process unfolded in
places like Burma and South Africa."[43] One is reminded of Luther's commitment to evangelical freedom.[44]

By the end of the nineteenth century the Protestant world missionary
effort had become extensive. Some fifteen thousand persons from the
United States alone were working in almost every nation on earth, trying
to convince people to abandon whatever previous religious commitments
they had and become Christian. The missionary zeal was making its way
onto university campuses as a younger generation began to emerge. In

---

[42] See Lamin Sanneh, *Translating the Message: The Missionary Impact on Culture* (Maryknoll, NY: Orbis Books, 1989).

[43] Jay Riley Case, *An Unpredictable Gospel: American Evangelicals and World Christianity, 1812–1920* (Oxford: Oxford University Press, 2012), 8.

[44] Brett Muhlhan, *Being Shaped by Freedom: An Examination of Luther's De-velopment of Christian Liberty, 1520–1525* (Eugene, OR: Pickwick Publications, 2012), 11.

1877 the YMCA in North America began organizing students on college campuses to meet for Bible study and fellowship. In 1886 the evangelist Dwight Moody teamed up with the leadership of these intercollegiate YMCA groups to hold a summer student conference at the Mount Hermon School he had helped to found in Northfield, Massachusetts. Some 250 students showed up for the week-long event, one of them a young student from Cornell University named John R. Mott. Following the 1886 conference Mott and others organized the Student Volunteer Movement for Foreign Missions (SVM), which was designed to bring college students into the foreign missionary movement. Mott went to work for the YMCA nationally and used his position to begin traveling to other campuses, first in North America but soon around the world, organizing chapters in what were now being called Student Christian Movements (SCMs) supporting SVMs. In 1895 Mott and a small handful of other student leaders from several nations met in Vadstena, Sweden, to organize the World's Student Christian Federation (WSCF). The leadership of the twentieth-century ecumenical movement emerged from that network.

The ecumenical movement was deeply grounded in evangelical Protestantism, but Mott was not limited by that vision. Beginning around 1900 he began reaching out to leaders working among Orthodox Christian students in Russia. Mott was a key figure in the organization of the 1910 World Missionary Conference held in Edinburgh, Scotland. One of the decisions made by the organizers of that conference was to remove Latin America from being listed on the agenda of Protestant mission work. The move was done out of deference to the Anglo-Catholic wing of the Church of England, which vigorously opposed the efforts of other Protestants to convert Roman Catholics. Mott agreed. The following year he visited the Middle East and met with a number of Orthodox leaders. Then, in Istanbul, he helped to organize an Orthodox SCM, and finally led a move to change the constitution of the WSCF to admit students of all Christian traditions, not just Protestants. These efforts set in motion a revolt among some of the more conservative evangelical student movements such as the Cambridge Inter-Collegiate Christian Union, which saw Mott's actions in embracing Catholic or "high church" forms of Christianity a direct rejection of the central principles of Protestant faith, namely, the doctrine of justification by faith alone. By 1920 these evangelical student groups were organizing their own network, which in 1928 became the Inter-Varsity Fellowship of Evangelical Unions.[45] This split in the ecumenical movement would have lasting effects on Protestant mission theology for the rest of the twentieth century.

Toward the end of the Edinburgh conference a Continuation Committee was appointed to carry the work in missionary cooperation forward.

---

[45] See Douglas Johnson, ed., *A Brief History of the International Fellowship of Evangelical Students* (Lausanne: The International Fellowship of Evangelical Students, 1964), 37–41.

Delegates agreed that a more permanent agency that could engage in study, advise mission boards and agencies, and provide an interconfessional forum for discussion was desirable. Eventually these efforts led to the formation of the International Missionary Council (IMC) in 1921. Seven years later the IMC held its first international conference in Jerusalem. Among the challenges that delegates to Jerusalem 1928 addressed were the relationships between churches that had sent mission workers and churches that had been formed out of these mission efforts; racism and its effects on world missions; the challenges of growing secularization in the West; and the problems associated with global industrialization. The question of whether other religions have salvific value was a hot issue. Various options ranging from exclusivist to fulfillment theory were voiced. Zhao Zichen (Chao Tzu-chen) and Wei Zhuomin (Wei Cho Min, also known in the West as Francis Wei) from China, and Pandipeddi Chenchiah from India led the way in arguing that Christianity was the fulfillment of what was good and true in all religions and therefore had a role to play in helping adherents of other religions to understand their own faith more fully.[46]

The next IMC international conference took place in 1938 on the campus of the Madras Christian College in Tambaram, India. A majority of the delegates at Tambaram were of Asian and African rather than European descent. During the conference they received a report that two other major international conference movements—Faith and Order, and Life and Work—had decided to merge to form the World Council of Churches (WCC). The Tambaram delegates voiced their belief that indigenous leadership from the churches of Asia and Africa should vote not to become part of the WCC (out of a concern that members from Asia and Africa would not be sufficiently represented in the new WCC).

The relationship between Christianity and other religions, and especially the question of whether salvation was only possible through Christian religion, was again a main concern on the agenda. Hendrik Kraemer, a former lay missionary from the Dutch Reformed Church to Indonesia and now a professor of history of religion at the University of Leiden, had written one of the preparatory texts for Tambaram, which he published as *The Christian Message in a Non-Christian World*.[47] In its pages he defended what is best called the exclusivist paradigm of Christianity as a revealed religion of absolute truth. Christianity is founded on the event of Jesus Christ. The narrative of Christ stands on its own as the word without any human corroboration. Thus the Christian message cannot be regarded as being on the same level with the message of any other human religious

---

[46] See Dennis Tak Wing Ng, "Chinese Christianity: The Study of Indigenous Theology in Twentieth-Century China," *Journal of World Christianity* 7/2 (2017): 101–22; and Jan van Lin, *Shaking the Foundations: Religious Plurality and the Ecumenical Movement* (Amsterdam: Rodopi, 2002), 57–59.

[47] Hendrik Kraemer, *The Christian Message in a Non-Christian World* (New York: Harper and Brothers, 1938).

teacher. Christ's message had given rise to the church, which for the greater part of its history, argued Kraemer, was found in Europe. Christians who lived in the West had the benefit of this revelation throughout their history. Christians in Asia and Africa lacked such historical resources and thus only had a connection to Christ through the history of Christianity coming from the West. Christians in Asia were left with no option but to take a stance against their cultural and religious heritage.

Kraemer's arguments did not go unopposed at Tambaram. A group of Indian theologians in particular took up the case against him. Their book, *Rethinking Christianity in India*,[48] was also published in advance of the conference. Its pages provided an alternative argument. G. V. Job, for instance, argued that the builder of Indian Christianity and the Indian church was God, not missionaries, and that God was using resources from the religious heritage of India as well as that of the West. India's religious and cultural heritage was a critical and constructive resource for Christianity in India, and that as Christians empowered by the Spirit of God they were free to draw from this heritage as they saw fit. Luther's evangelical freedom was not cited in their arguments, but one can hear the echoes of it in the Protestant arena in Asia. The dichotomy of mission and church was no longer operative for them.

The third IMC international conference was held in Whitby, Canada, in 1947. Whitby forcefully challenged not only the divide between church and mission that had found a home in a number of places in Protestant theology during the colonial era, but also the equally problematic divide between what were often called older churches and younger churches. Churches throughout the world were instead called to a new level of relationship defined by partnership and solidarity in common obedience to God. The realization that all stand equally before God was picked up five years later in 1952 at the IMC conference held in Willingen, Germany. At Willingen the concept *missio Dei* emerged in a compelling manner. It held that mission is not the work of the church, but of God. Also, God does not depend upon missions; rather, mission derives from what God is doing. The church engages in mission work in response to what God is doing, so that both mission and church derive from what God is doing in and for the world.

Engagement with the wider world was becoming radicalized in the 1950s. M. Richard Shaull's 1955 publication *Encounter with Revolution* engaged with a new kind of missionary discourse and activity emerging from Latin America.[49] From India, J. Russell Chandran, in a paper titled "The Christian Mission and the Judgment of History," argued in favor of the emerging theological diversity that was the result of churches

---

[48] D. M. Devasahayam and A. N. Sudarisanam, eds., *Rethinking Christianity in India* (Madras: Hogarth Press, 1938).

[49] M. Richard Shaull, *Encounter with Revolution* (New York: Association Press, 1955).

responding to diverse historical situations around the globe. The theology
of mission must undergo changes as well, he said, in light of their failures,
such as their complacency with colonialism, but also the new challenges
the churches face in diverse locations, such as the revolutionary message
of Communism being heard around the world. Communism, he argued,
resulted from the church's failure to preach liberation to the socially and
economically dispossessed.[50]

Delegates for the IMC gathered one last time in 1958 in Achimota on
the outskirts of Accra, Ghana. The postcolonial era was fully upon them.
Mission boards in the West were being forced to relinquish their govern-
ing power to local churches in Asia, Africa, and Latin America. Regional
conferences of Protestant churches in Asia, Africa, and Latin America had
formed and were carrying on the work of decolonization and liberation.
Some declared that the age of global missions was over. The title of James
Scherer's 1964 study summed it up: *Missionary, Go Home! A Reappraisal
of the Christian World Mission.*[51] The other route was to seek a greater
integration of mission into the life of the church. This was essentially the
path that emerged from Achimota with the decision for the IMC to join
the WCC. In 1961, at the New Delhi assembly of the WCC, the IMC
became the Commission on World Mission and Evangelism (CWME)
within the WCC.

Two years later the CWME held its first gathering in Mexico City; the
theme was "mission on six continents." The Mexico City gathering was the
first to be committed explicitly to overcoming the division of the Protestant
global community into church and mission that had characterized the
movement since the eighteenth century. At Mexico City the dichotomies
of older and younger churches, or Christian lands and mission lands, were
rigorously challenged. Delegates were invited to replace the traditional
framework of Europe and North America being the home base, or of
some churches sending missions and others only receiving missions. In
its place they were invited to think of the church on six continents with
mission being from all and to all places. Thinking along these lines, the
divide that had emerged in the eighteenth century between mission, which
was directed toward those located outside Christendom, and evangelism,
which was directed toward those who lived within Christendom, likewise
was challenged.[52]

---

[50] J. Russell Chandran, "The Christian Mission and the Judgment of History,"
in *Missions under the Cross: Addresses delivered at the Enlarged Meeting of the
Committee of the Inter Missionary Council at Willingen (Germany), 1952* (London:
Edinburgh House Press, 1953), 93–106.

[51] James Scherer, *Missionary, Go Home! A Reappraisal of the Christian World
Mission* (Englewood Cliffs, NJ: Prentice-Hall, 1964).

[52] See Ronald K. Orchard, ed., *Witness in Six Continents: Records of the Meeting of the CWME of the WCC Held in Mexico City, 1963* (Geneva: WCC, 1967).

Engagement with the world continued to expand geographically and deepen methodologically through the 1960s. A study project launched by the Department on Studies in Evangelism within the WCC, "Missionary Structure of the Congregation," sought to extend the missional theology that had emerged from Willingen and was associated with such names as Lesslie Newbigin and Johannes C. Hoekendijk. The study culminated in 1967 with the publication of its findings in book form, titled *The Church for Others and The Church for the World: A Quest for Structures for Missionary Congregations.*[53] The document provocatively proposed that we should think of the direction of mission not as being from God to the church to the world, but rather from God to the world to the church.[54] The result was a shift from an ecclesiocentric theology to "an *oikocentric* perspective."[55] Two years later, in the United States, James H. Cone published *Black Theology and Black Power,*[56] followed the next year by *A Black Theology of Liberation.*[57] At nearly the same time in Lima, Peru, Gustavo Gutiérrez published *Teología de la liberación.*[58]

At a meeting of the All Africa Conference of Churches in Lusaka, Zambia, in 1974, John Gatu called for a moratorium on all Western missions to Africa. Two years later a group of theologians from Africa, Asia, and Latin America organized the Ecumenical Association of Third World Theologians (EATWOT).[59] African Americans and other minority people joined the following year in what became a two-decade process of seeking convergences and divergences in liberation theologies from across the world. The emergence of theologies of liberation was not disconnected from the wider realm of Protestant mission theology. Letty M. Russell was one of the first generation of leaders in feminist liberation theology among European American women. She was one of the members of the study project "The Missionary Structure of the Congregation" and one of the authors of *The Church for Others.* By the early 1970s, she noted, she had undergone a shift from "mission" to "liberation." "I think of God's

---

[53] *The Church for Others and the Church for the World: A Quest for Structures for Missionary Congregations* (Geneva: WCC, 1967).

[54] Ibid., 69–71.

[55] Letty M. Russell, *Church in the Round: Feminist Interpretation of the Church* (Louisville, KY: Westminster/John Knox Press, 1993), 88–89. *Oikos* means "family" or "household" in Greek.

[56] James H. Cone, *Black Theology and Black Power* (New York: Harper and Row, 1969).

[57] James H. Cone, *A Black Theology of Liberation* (New York: J. B. Lippincott, 1970).

[58] Gustavo Gutiérrez, *Teología de la liberación* (Lima: CEP, 1971); published in English as *A Theology of Liberation: History, Politics, and Salvation,* trans. Caridad Inda and John Eagleson (Maryknoll, NY: Orbis Books, 1973).

[59] See M. P. Joseph, *Theologies of the Non-Person: The Formative Years of EATWOT* (New York: Palgrave Macmillan, 2015).

Mission or action in the world as equivalent to God's liberating action or liberation."[60]

Alongside the emergence of liberation theologies in Protestant mission theologies in the late twentieth century, another development took place that would challenge traditional conceptions of mission at their core. It had long been assumed that central to the practice of missions was belief that those who adhered to other faith commitments needed to abandon these other religions in order to receive salvation. Mission work entailed proclaiming that salvation was obtained through the redeeming work of Jesus Christ alone. As noted above, challenges to the exclusivist position began to appear in Asian Protestant theologies in the 1920s. Challenges also began to appear from Western mission scholars such as Daniel Johnson Fleming, the first person to hold a chair in missions at Union Theological Seminary in New York.[61] The 1932 publication of *Re-Thinking Missions: A Laymen's Inquiry after One Hundred Years*, which was produced by a special commission drawn from among seven US church mission boards chaired by William Ernest Hocking, found a change in attitude toward other religions taking place among many Western Protestants serving in Asia. Members of the commission reported that they found members of various religious communities joining together to oppose secularism and materialism. A shift was taking place, they reported, from a confrontational attitude of conquest of other religions to an attitude of tolerance, association, and even appreciation.[62]

Two decades later, in 1955, the World Council of Churches undertook an initial study entitled "The Word of God and the Living Faiths of Men."[63] The East Asia Christian Conference in 1964 issued a brief statement titled "Christian Encounter with Men of Other Beliefs," which asserted that "witness" was better understood in Asia as "encounter."[64] Christians in Asia, in particular, were challenged to learn ways of relating to their religious neighbors and other faith communities in ways that did not seek to convert them or extinguish their beliefs. By the end of the 1960s the terminology that had emerged to dominate these discussions was *dialogue* with other religions. From 1968 until 1971, Stanley J. Samartha worked with the Living Faiths project until the WCC set up a full subunit, Dialogue with People of Living Faiths and Ideologies, which he headed. *Dialogue* was now firmly a part of the ecumenical vocabulary regarding mission

[60] Russell, *Church in the Round*, 90.

[61] See Daniel Johnson Fleming, *Whither Bound in Missions* (New York: Association Press, 1925).

[62] The Commission of Appraisal, William Ernest Hocking, chair, *Re-Thinking Missions: A Laymen's Inquiry after One Hundred Years* (New York: Harper and Brothers, 1932), 29–36.

[63] See Douglas Pratt, *The Church and Other Faiths: The World Council of Churches, the Vatican, and Interreligious Dialogue* (Bern: Peter Lang, 2010), 46–48.

[64] Published in *The Ecumenical Review* 16/4 (July 1964): 451–55.

and evangelism, at least within the WCC and in deliberations related to it, such as those of EATWOT.

The divide between ecumenical and evangelical Protestant efforts that first appeared at the beginning of the twentieth century did not diminish over the decades. In the 1960s, following the integration of the IMC into the WCC, it reemerged with renewed force. Evangelical mission leaders sponsored two major conferences in 1966, in Wheaton, Illinois, and in Berlin. Buoyed by the success of these initial gathering, evangelicals in 1974 convened an International Congress on World Evangelization in Lausanne. The gathering was a watershed in the evangelical Protestant movement globally. The Lausanne Covenant that emerged from the gathering, which evangelical leaders were invited to endorse, stated that the primary task of Christians throughout the world is to communicate the message of salvation that is offered to the world in Jesus Christ and which brings about both the forgiveness of sins and incorporation into the body of Christ, or the church. Divine judgment of injustice and oppression in the world flows from this forgiveness, according to the covenant, establishing a clear theological priority that places personal salvation in front of social transformation. Following the 1974 gathering the Lausanne Committee for World Evangelization (LCWE) was organized as a permanent body supporting global efforts in mission and evangelism. Over the decades that followed successive conferences convened under the auspices of LCWE have moved progressively toward a more integrated understanding of the personal and social dimensions of salvation and justice, bringing it into the trajectory of the IMC and its deliberations of more than half a century earlier.

A year before evangelicals gathered for the Lausanne Congress, Taiwanese theologian Shoki Coe published "In Search of Renewal in Theological Education" in the US journal *Theological Education*; the article would have a lasting impact on world Christianity in all of its branches.[65] Coe had grown up under Japanese colonial rule and gone to school in Japan and England before returning to serve in ministry under the Nationalist Chinese (Kuomintang or KMT) government that had retreated to Taiwan in 1947. Forced by the KMT into exile, he became a British citizen in 1967 and director of the Theological Education Fund of the WCC. Coe was attentive to the processes of secularization, urbanization, and rapid social change taking place across Asia. As a Taiwanese living first under Japanese occupation and then under the KMT, he was familiar with political oppression. He was also fully immersed in the ecumenical movement and the discussions that had been taking place within the IMC regarding

---

[65] Shoki Coe, "In Search of Renewal in Theological Education," *Theological Education* 9/4 (summer 1973): 233–43. The name Shoki Coe is Anglicized from the Japanese version of his original name. See Huang Po Ho, "Ng Chiong Hui (Shoki Coe, Hwang Chang Hui)," in *A Dictionary of Asian Christianity*, ed. Scott W. Sunquist (Grand Rapids, MI: Eerdmans, 2001), 601; and Jonah Chang, *Shoki Coe: An Ecumenical Life in Context* (Geneva: WCC, 2012).

the churches in Asia, Africa, and later Latin America. Since the nineteenth century, key Protestant mission leaders had been calling for the indigenization of the churches that had formed as a result of initial Western Protestant missionary activities in these regions. These efforts accelerated during the 1950s and 1960s.

Coe's 1973 essay moved the discussion forward in a significant way. "Indigenous, indigeneity, and indigenization all derive from a nature metaphor, that is, of the soil, or taking root in the soil," he argued.[66] The model was that of taking a plant from one location to another. Although it was now potted in different soil, the plant remained the same. Over time it might eventually adapt to or be changed by the elements encountered in its new location, but concerning the nature of the church itself, the process was essentially static. Coe noted, "Indigenization tends to be used in the sense of responding to the Gospel in terms of traditional culture. Therefore, it is in danger of being past-oriented."[67] A more dynamic model was needed, he argued, one that entailed a more critical assessment of the radical social, political, and cultural situation of diverse contexts around the world, and one that was more open to change and the future.[68] Coe called this new process "contextualization." He argued that it entailed first an act of contextuality, which he described as "missiological discernment of the signs of the times, seeing where God is at work and calling us to participate in it."[69] This in turn engendered the capacity to respond in a new way to "contextualize" the faith. "Contextualization" was the result at a doctrinal level, manifested in what was to be taught in theological education.

Renewal was the operative word in this process for Coe. The concept of contextualization reached deeply into the Protestant memory to articulate in a fresh way a call to reform and revival. In one sense Coe was opening the door to an entire new era of theological production in world Christianity. *Contextual theology* and *contextualization* quickly caught on and became part of the vocabulary of contemporary theology. But in another sense Coe was reformulating the originating theology of the sixteenth-century Protestant Reformation. The critical process of contextuality, which entailed participation in the full social, political, cultural, and religious life of the people, echoed Luther's originating call for translation of the scriptures into the vernacular of the people. Translation is always a process of contextualization to some degree. The result was a deeper and more authentic understanding of "the catholicity of the gospel." Coe was arguing that catholicity did not entail repetition of what has been in the past. Theologians in Africa, Asia, and Latin America were given permission

---

[66] Coe, "In Search of Renewal in Theological Education," 240.

[67] Ibid.

[68] Ibid., 240–41.

[69] Ibid., 241.

to bypass theologies (those potted plants) received from churches in the North Atlantic world or the West in favor of a fresh encounter with "the Word which became flesh and dwelt among us at a particular time and place." He continued, "I believe, in fact, that the incarnation is the divine form of contextualization, and if this is so, the way we receive this gift [of catholicity] is also through our following His way. That is what I mean by contextualization."[70] As with the doctrine of justification by faith, Coe was calling for a direct encounter with the living Word that was incarnate in the person of Jesus Christ, to whom we are to respond faithfully in our own time and place. Regarding such responses, he writes:

> Ours can only be in following in His steps as an ongoing process of the pilgrim people. But in doing so we can accept our relativity with hope and even with joy, as we see in our faithful responses the sign of the divine contextualization unfolding its purpose for the liberation and salvation of mankind.[71]

The call to contextualization, on the one hand, was a fresh hearing of the originating message of the Protestant movement to recover the theological mission of the church. On the other hand, Coe's turn to catholicity at the end of his essay marked a significant ecumenical advance. The Roman Catholic communion had only fully entered the twentieth-century ecumenical movement a decade earlier through Vatican II. Through such agencies as the Secretariat for Promoting Christian Unity (known since 1988 as the Pontifical Council for Promoting Christian Unity), the Roman Catholic Church at its highest levels of authority has engaged in ecumenical dialogue with various other Christian communions. Roman Catholics became active dialogue partners globally in the field of mission studies as well. One of the places where this new dialogue has been most fruitful is in contextual theology. One of the most important voices in the field is that of the Roman Catholic theologian Stephen B. Bevans, SVD. Bevans's 1992 *Models of Contextual Theology* marked a major milestone in the development of contextual theology at a methodological level.[72] In that work Bevans sketched six distinct models of contextual theology that he discerned having emerged over the previous quarter-century or so globally. Just as important, he invited readers to work to develop their own models as well.

According to Bevans, "Theology that is contextual realizes that culture, history, contemporary thought forms, and so forth are to be considered,

[70] Ibid., 242.
[71] Ibid., 243.
[72] Stephen B. Bevans, SVD, *Models of Contextual Theology* (Maryknoll, NY: Orbis Books, 1992; revised and expanded edition, 2002).

along with scripture and tradition, as valid sources for theological expression."[73] He presses this insight further when he writes:

> If the ordinary things of life are so transparent of God's presence, one can speak of culture, human experience, and events in history—of contexts—as truly sacramental and so revelatory. Culture, human experience, and history, if we are true to a real dynamic in Christianity's self-understanding, must be "unpacked" of its sacredness.[74]

But this, in turn, leads him to affirm diversity in theological thought:

> Rather than a bland uniformity, Christianity is endowed with a dynamic that moves toward unity through a rich diversity, through conversation and even argument among people of particular personal, cultural, and historical experience.[75]

Bevans fittingly adds that theology cannot be only contextual but must be ready to engage in dialogue if it is to realize the call for enrichment and renewal that is at the heart of the Protestant theology of mission.[76]

In one sense it may seem somewhat ironic that a contemporary Roman Catholic theologian such as Stephen B. Bevans has become a major theological force in articulating the dynamic processes of translation, contextualization, and revitalization or renewal that this chapter argues are the heart of Martin Luther's theology and the broader Protestant understanding of mission. The irony is mitigated considerably by the realization that we are living now in an ecumenical era, and especially by the advances over the past two decades in Lutheran–Roman Catholic dialogue. One thinks immediately of *The Joint Declaration on the Doctrine of Justification* that was formally approved by the Roman Catholic Church and the Lutheran World Federation in 1999, and signed by the heads of both communions on October 31. The document declares "that on the basis of their dialogue the subscribing Lutheran churches and the Roman Catholic Church are now able to articulate a common understanding of our justification by God's grace through faith in Christ."[77] One thinks also of Cardinal Walter

---

[73] Bevans, *Models of Contextual Theology* (2002), 4. See also idem, *An Introduction to Theology in Global Perspective* (Maryknoll, NY: Orbis Books, 2009), 18–26.

[74] Bevans, *Models of Contextual Theology* (2002), 13.

[75] Ibid., 14–15.

[76] Bevans, *An Introduction to Theology in Global Perspective*, 5.

[77] "Preamble," *Joint Declaration on the Doctrine of Justification by the Lutheran World Federation and the Catholic Church*," para. 5; see also William G. Rusch, ed., *Justification and the Future of the Ecumenical Movement: The Joint Declaration on the Doctrine of Justification* (Collegeville, MN: Liturgical Press, 2003).

Kasper's appreciative volume, *Martin Luther: An Ecumenical Perspective.*[78] As the Orthodox theologian Vladimir Latinovic writes:

> Luther's legacy does not consist wholly of the Protestant churches, but belongs more generally to all Christian churches and to all humanity. . . . In the past five hundred years, all churches, almost without exception, have moved in the direction of the Reformation and have adopted many of the changes that Luther called for regarding the Roman Catholic Church. The Reformation influenced all Christian churches in one way or another.[79]

This chapter has argued that at its heart the Protestant understanding of mission is one of renewal and revitalization through the conversion of life that comes through an encounter with God. That means first and foremost that mission begins in and with the life of the church. Because mission constitutes and characterizes the trinitarian life of God, who sends and receives love, it must constitute and characterize the life of the church. It cannot be confined to the church, however, for God is the God who loves all peoples and indeed all creation. Mission thus overflows into witness and proclamation to all peoples, dialogue with other religions, engagements in social movements for justice and transformation, concern for ecology and the broader environment, and what Peter C. Phan, among others, calls a dialogue of life.[80] The Protestant movement has highlighted the manner in which mission is grounded in the renewal that comes through an encounter with the good news (the *euangélion*) that is found in Jesus Christ. We are reminded by contemporary theologians of all Christian traditions that this good news is always first and foremost to be good news to the poor.[81]

---

[78] Cardinal Walter Kasper, *Martin Luther: An Ecumenical Perspective*, trans. William Madges (New York: Paulist Press, 2016).

[79] Vladimir Latinovic, "Contemporary Challenges: The Reformation and the World Today," in Irvin, *The Protestant Reformation and World Christianity: Global Perspectives*, 154n1.

[80] See, for instance, Peter C. Phan, *Being Religious Interreligiously: Asian Perspectives on Interfaith Dialogue* (Maryknoll, NY: Orbis Books, 2005), 237–39. For a fuller discussion of mission as dialogue, see Stephen B. Bevans and Roger P. Schroeder, *Prophetic Dialogue: Reflections on Christian Mission Today* (Maryknoll, NY: Orbis Books, 2011).

[81] See the entire issue of *Missio Dei: A Journal of Missional Theology and Praxis* 2/1 (February 2011), which is on the theme "Good News to the Poor."

Chapter 5

Mission in Pentecostal Theology

Veli-Matti Kärkkäinen

A MOVEMENT WITH A MISSION

While very few, if any, outside observers would be willing to ignore or undermine the staggering numerical growth of the global Pentecostal missionary movement,[1] many are wondering, what is the theological input behind such expansion and enthusiasm? Although numbers, of course, do not directly affect theology, neither are they meaningless—particularly for a movement whose first century of existence has brought it from zero to

---

This essay was first presented as "Mission and Salvation: A Pentecostal Perspective," at the Annual Reformed-Pentecostal International Dialogue in Antalya, Turkey, December 2–6, 2015. It draws directly (and without constant referencing) from my two recent essays, "Pentecostal Mission and Encounter with Religions," in *The Cambridge Companion to Pentecostalism*, ed. Cecil M. Robeck and Amos Yong (Cambridge: Cambridge University Press, 2014), 294–312; and "Pentecostal Mission: A Theological Appraisal," in *Festschrift for Dr. Opoku Onyinah*, ed. Lord Elorm Donkor, African Christian Series (Eugene, OR: Wipf & Stock, forthcoming). It also repeats materials from other recent essays of mine, particularly "The Pentecostal Understanding of Mission," in *Pentecostal Mission and Global Christianity*, ed. Wonsuk Ma, Veli-Matti Kärkkäinen, and J. Kwabena Asamoah-Gyadu, Regnum Edinburgh Centenary Series 20 (Oxford: Regnum Books International, 2014), 26–44.

[1] Annual statistics provided in the January issue of *International Bulletin of Missionary Research* give the most up-to-date survey of the spread of Christian churches and movements, including Pentecostals, for each year. For a healthy cautionary note to Pentecostals not to glory in numbers, see Gary B. McGee, "Pentecostal Missiology: Moving beyond Triumphalism to Face the Issues," *Pneuma* 16/2 (1994): 275–81.

hundreds of millions of people.[2] Questions such as the following inspire and guide this inquiry into the theological basis of the global Pentecostal family: Why do Pentecostals focus so much on mission? What is the missionary agenda? What are the underlying motifs—or resources?

Engaging this kind of *theological* (as opposed to, say, merely sociological or phenomenological or anthropological) appraisal is all the more important in light of the dearth of such literature until recent years. As is widely known, first-generation Pentecostals have been more "doers" than "thinkers." Rather than writing theological treatises, the first Pentecostals produced evangelistic tracts.[3]

A theological assessment of the movement's missionary ethos and principles is an ecumenical task and call. On one hand, other churches may glean valuable lessons from the Pentecostal experience. On the other hand, Pentecostals themselves would do well to listen to critical-yet-sympathetic observers and analysts of their work.

The purpose of this chapter is to seek to discern as accurately as possible—for brevity's sake, in the form of a sketch rather than an overly schematized system—some key theological resources that stand behind Pentecostal mission work. That these theological resources most likely were not discerned as such by the early Pentecostal missionaries (and perhaps even by many contemporary Pentecostals whose main interest may lie in praxis) does not make this kind of after-the-fact exercise either futile or useless. Analysts just have to remind themselves constantly of the tentative and constructive nature of such work.

Before attempting a five-tiered theological sketch of leading theological factors birthing and facilitating Pentecostal mission theology, two descriptive reports are in order: first, concerning some of the most common ways of profiling Pentecostal mission, and second, regarding the slow evolvement and recent maturing of Pentecostal theology in written (more or less) academic style.

---

[2] The definitive current history of Pentecostal missions is Allan Anderson, *Spreading Fires: The Missionary Nature of Early Pentecostalism* (Maryknoll, NY: Orbis Books, 2007). Also important is idem, *An Introduction to Pentecostalism: Global Charismatic Christianity* (Cambridge: Cambridge University Press, 2004). See also L. Grant McClung, *Azusa Street and Beyond: Pentecostal Missions and Church Growth in the Twentieth Century* (South Plainfield, NJ: Bridge Publishing, 1986); Gary B. McGee, *This Gospel Shall Be Preached: A History and Theology of Assemblies of God Foreign Missions to 1959*, 2 vols. (Springfield, MO: Gospel Publishing House, 1986, 1989).

[3] See further, Russell J. Spittler, "Suggested Areas for Further Research in Pentecostal Studies," *Pneuma* 5/2 (1983): 39–56. Nicaraguan Carlos Sediles Real ("Pentecostalisms in Nicaragua: General Aspects of Their Foundations, Growth, and Social Participation," *Exchange* 36 [2007]: 386–96) attempts to discern key themes of Pentecostal theology of mission as they appear in songs, hymns, and choruses of worship and liturgy. While not academic or discursive in nature, they allow access to central theological intuitions.

A TYPICAL PROFILE OF PENTECOSTAL MISSION ETHOS

A historically important, very early Pentecostal statement of the self-identity of the fledgling movement from 1906—widely regarded as the "birthdate" of the American Pentecostal movement whose influence rapidly spread like a fire to other continents[4]—wonderfully highlights the centrality of mission, evangelization, and social concern. Here is the "mission statement" of the first local church of the modern Pentecostal church, namely, the Apostolic Faith Mission[5] in Los Angeles, California:

> THE APOSTOLIC FAITH MOVEMENT stands for the restoration of faith once delivered unto the saints—the old time religion, camp meetings, revivals, missions, street and prison work and Christian Unity everywhere.[6]

Importantly, this new movement called itself an apostolic movement, thereby establishing the connection with New Testament roots; not incidentally, Pentecostals unabashedly considered themselves the direct followers of the church of the first apostles, as narrated particularly in the Book of Acts, the dearly beloved book among them. These Pentecostals viewed themselves as restoring the apostolic faith by the power of the Holy Spirit, and its immediate effect was an amazing missionary fervor. It led Pentecostals to spread the gospel through revivals, tent meetings, faith missions, and other creative forms of proclamation.[7] But not only that, this same apostolic restoration also inspired Spirit-filled men and women to launch massive social programs in prisons, for orphans, on the streets, and elsewhere. Amazingly, this mission statement also called for an ecumenical impulse: seeking "Christian Unity everywhere," whatever precise forms this search might have taken.

Seeking to capture these and related mission impulses, the American missiologist Gary McClung's oft-cited listing of typical features of Pen-

---

[4] Mentioning here the year 1906 as the birthdate of the *American* Pentecostal movement implies that this was not the only and not necessarily the first instance of what we nowadays call the Pentecostal movement. Indeed, we know of Pentecostal outpourings and emerging movements from the same time period (and even earlier), for example, from India. (And even on the American scene the year 1901 is routinely stated as the date for the influential outpouring of the Spirit in Topeka, Kansas, from where the impulse soon traveled to Los Angeles.) The current essay, understandably, is not in a place to engage such complex questions of origins and historiography.

[5] Its original name; it is now the Apostolic Faith Church.

[6] *Apostolic Faith* 2/1 (September 1906).

[7] See Allan H. Anderson, "The Vision of the Apostolic Faith: Early Pentecostalism and World Mission," *Svensk Missionstidskrift/Swedish Missiological Themes* 97/3 (2009): 295–314.

tecostal mission ethos is as representative as any.[8] According to him, Pentecostal mission is

- experiential and relational,
- deeply biblical,[9]
- extremely urgent,
- prioritizing evangelization, but not to the exclusion of social concern,
- aggressive and bold in its approach,
- interdependent (both among various Pentecostal/charismatic groups and in relation to older churches and their mission endeavors),
- unpredictable as to the future.

With regard to mission methods and practices Pentecostals have been pragmatists. Consequently, flexibility in choosing methods, strategies, and structures—or lack of structures!—has been a trademark of Pentecostal missiology. In their mission and church structures, Pentecostals embrace all the possible variations from episcopal (for example, former Eastern Europe, Africa) to presbyterian (mainly in the English-speaking world) to polities emphasizing total autonomy of local churches (Scandinavian Pentecostals and their mission fields, for example, in some Latin American countries).

THE EVOLVEMENT AND MATURING OF PENTECOSTAL MISSIOLOGY: A REPORT

The first missiological treatises came from the pen of Pentecostal missionary and missiologist Melvin L. Hodges. His 1953 *The Indigenous Church* and its sequel, *Theology of the Church and Its Mission* (1977), echoed and followed evangelical mission theology and social action.[10] It

---

[8] L. Grant McClung Jr., "Pentecostal/Charismatic Perspectives on a Missiology for the Twenty-First Century," *Pneuma* 16/1 (Spring 1994): 11–21. For a somewhat similar profiling, see Veli-Matti Kärkkäinen, "Missiology, Pentecostal and Charismatic," in *The New International Dictionary of Pentecostal and Charismatic Movements*, ed. Stanley M. Burgess and Eduard M. van der Maas, rev. and expanded ed. (Grand Rapids, MI: Zondervan, 2002), 877–85.

[9] For a useful discussion, see Richard Burgess, "Nigerian Pentecostal Theology in Global Perspective," *PentecoStudies* 7/2 (2008): 29–63.

[10] Melvin L. Hodges, *The Indigenous Church: A Complete Handbook on How to Grow Young Churches* (1953) and *Theology of the Church and Its Mission* (Springfield, MO: Gospel Publishing House, 1977). For an evaluation, see McGee, *This Gospel Shall Be Preached*, 2:157–58.

was quite natural for Pentecostals to align themselves with evangelicals, since the mainline ecumenical movement seemed too liberal both theologically and in its mission agenda.[11] Both Pentecostals and evangelicals share conservative doctrinal views regarding the inspiration and authority of the Bible, the lostness of humankind without Christ, and justification by faith, as well as the priority of evangelism over social action.

It was not until 1991—when the major compendium of Pentecostal missiology titled *Called and Empowered: Global Mission in Pentecostal Perspective*[12] came out—that some theologically serious perspectives were offered by a younger generation of Pentecostal academics. The book contains biblical, theological, strategic, cultural, and religious viewpoints on global Pentecostal mission and provides a fascinating analysis of its latest developments at the time.

An important impulse for evolving Pentecostal thinking on mission has come from a wide interest in the biblical theology of the Holy Spirit. Of great interest, understandably, to Pentecostal biblical scholars and missiologists has been the work of the Spirit in Luke-Acts.[13] The well-known American missionary-missiologist Robert P. Menzies's *Empowered for Witness*[14] has highlighted the nature of the church as a charismatically endowed prophetic community prepared for missionary service. Australian J. M. Penney's *The Missionary Emphasis of Lukan Pneumatology* contends that the reason Acts has been so dear to Pentecostals is that it "is more than history for the Pentecostal: it is a missionary manual, an open-ended account of the missionary work of the Holy Spirit in the church, concluding, not with ch. 28, but with the ongoing Spirit-empowered and Spirit-directed gospel preaching of today."[15]

A significant recent contribution to Pentecostal missiology comes from the leading Korean missionary-missiologist couple Julie and Wonsuk Ma.

---

[11] Gary B. McGee, "Pentecostal and Charismatic Missions," in *Toward the Twenty-first Century in Christian Mission: Essays in Honor of Gerald H. Anderson*, ed. James M. Phillips and Robert T. Coote (Grand Rapids, MI: Eerdmans, 1993), 43.

[12] M. W. Dempster, B. D. Klaus, and D. Petersen, eds., *Called and Empowered: Global Mission in Pentecostal Perspective* (Peabody, MA: Hendrickson, 1991).

[13] Some missiological insights can be gleaned from Roger Strondtandt, *A Charismatic Theology of St. Luke* (Peabody, MA: Hendrickson, 1984), with its idea of the transference of the Spirit from Jesus to his followers.

[14] Robert P. Menzies, *Empowered for Witness: The Spirit in Luke-Acts* (Sheffield: Sheffield Academic Press, 1994). See also the earlier work, Robert P. Menzies, *The Development of Early Christian Pneumatology with Special Reference to Luke-Acts* (Sheffield: Sheffield Academic Press, 1991).

[15] J. M. Penney, *The Missionary Emphasis of Lukan Pneumatology* (Sheffield: Sheffield Academic Press, 1997), 12.

Their jointly produced *Mission in the Spirit: Towards a Pentecostal/Charismatic Missiology* (2010)[16] makes a number of significant contributions to Pentecostal mission theology. The book develops a robust and holistic account of the work of the Spirit of God, beginning from the Old Testament with the work of the Spirit of Yahweh in creation. The turn to the Old Testament is a needed corrective to the one-sided focus on the New Testament. Hence, a pneumatological creation theology is developed first (chap. 2) and only then does the work of the charismatic Spirit of God come into play (chap. 3), including signs and wonders (chap. 5).[17] Importantly, this missionary pneumatology also supports care for the environment as an essential part of mission work and affirms and in no way ignores the Spirit's role in the world's complex sociopolitical and religious contexts (chaps. 6 and 7).

Having made these introductory descriptions and reports of the centrality of mission enthusiasm in Pentecostalism and its typical features, as well as mission theology's evolvement among Pentecostal writers, we turn to the central task of the essay, that is, to discern key elements of Pentecostal theology of mission and tasks for the future. Five dimensions or factors are lifted up and discussed.

PENTECOSTAL THEOLOGY OF MISSION
IN FIVE DIMENSIONS

A proper Pentecostal theology of mission has to be based on key intuitions of Pentecostal spirituality and theology at large, lest it suggest something external to the core of the movement. A tentative presentation of leading theological motifs includes the following interrelated aspects:

---

[16] Julie Ma and Wonsuk Ma, *Mission in the Spirit: Towards a Pentecostal/ Charismatic Missiology* (Oxford: Regnum International, 2010). For a discussion of the role of pneumatology in Pentecostal spirituality and theology, see Veli-Matti Kärkkäinen, "Pentecostal Pneumatologies in the Matrix of Systematic Theology," in *Studying Global Pentecostalism: Theories and Methods*, ed. Allan Anderson, Michael Bergunder, André Droogers, and Cornelis van der Laan (Berkeley and Los Angeles: University of California Press, 2010), 289–313; and "'The Spirit Poured Out on All Flesh': Pentecostal Testimonies and Experiences of the Holy Spirit," in *Lord and Life-Giver: Spirit Today*, Concilium 4 (London: SCM Press, 2011): 78–86.

[17] The Canadian Pentecostal theologian Steve Studebaker has issued a similar call to appreciate the Spirit's role as the principle of life and creation in "Christian Mission and the Religions as Participation in the Spirit of Pentecost," in *The Wide Reach of the Spirit: Renewal and Theology of Mission in a Religiously Plural World*, ed. Amos Yong and Clifton Clarke (Lexington, KY: Emeth Press, 2011).

- eschatological enthusiasm and urgency of mission
- Jesus Christ and the Full Gospel
- the Holy Spirit and charismatic empowerment
- salvation and the holistic vision
- church and the Spirit of *Koinonia*

Eschatological Enthusiasm and Urgency of Mission

It is a scholarly consensus that two interrelated factors lie at the center of Pentecostal spirituality and the evangelistic-missional impulse: eschatological fervor and the crucial role of the Holy Spirit. Pentecostals believe that they have been called by God in the "last days" (Acts 2:17)[18] to be Christlike witnesses in the power of the Spirit. The hope in the imminent coming of the Lord has energized Pentecostal churches and movements in their worldwide missionary enthusiasm and activity.[19]

The most well-known charismatic gift among Pentecostals, *glossolalia*, the capacity to speak in tongues,[20] coupled with eschatological urgency, led many early followers of the movement to launch into mission fields to finish the job just on the eve of the coming End. Indeed, there was an unwarranted optimism that the ability to speak in tongues would be given by the Holy Spirit to help finish the evangelization of the world before the imminent return of Christ.[21] That this expectation was unwarranted—a fact soon noticed by Pentecostal missionaries who then, in their typical pragmatism, adopted the conventional forms of missionary preparation with language learning—should not lead us to dismiss, let alone ridicule, the expectation. This somewhat naive urgency is a powerful indication of the centrality of eschatology and pneumatology as catalysts for missionary expansion, hallmarks for which even the Pentecostal movements of the third millennium are still well known.

---

[18] Based on the messianic-apocalyptic prophecy of Joel, the verse, highly regarded and often cited by Pentecostals, proclaims: "And in the last days it shall be, God declares, that I will pour out my Spirit upon all flesh, and your sons and your daughters shall prophesy, and your young men shall see visions, and your old men shall dream dreams."

[19] See Veli-Matti Kärkkäinen, "Mission, Spirit, and Eschatology: An Outline of a Pentecostal-Charismatic Theology of Mission," *Mission Studies* 16/1 (1999): 73–94.

[20] When tongues are known languages, the scholarly technical term *xenolalia* is used; when that is not the case, *glossolalia* is the chosen term.

[21] Douglas Petersen, *Not by Might, Nor by Power: A Pentecostal Theology of Social Concern in Latin America* (Oxford: Regnum, 1996), 9–13.

Jesus Christ and the Full Gospel

Differently from the most persistent mistaken assumptions of uninformed outside observers, it is not necessarily pneumatology, the doctrine of the Holy Spirit, but rather Christology that stands at the center of Pentecostal spirituality. Indeed, at the heart of Pentecostal spirituality lies the idea of the Full Gospel, the template of Jesus Christ in his fivefold role as Savior, Sanctifier, Baptizer with the Spirit, Healer, and Soon-Coming King.[22] On this robust "Spirit-Christology" stands the Pentecostal missiological vision:

> Thus, the outpouring of the Spirit at Pentecost constituted the church as an eschatological community of universal mission in the power and demonstration of the Spirit. The tongues at Pentecost and Peter's subsequent sermon meant that the church in general and each Spirit-filled individual are to be and to give a witness to the mighty acts of God in saving humanity. This witness centers in Jesus Christ and must therefore be given in the power of the Spirit if it is to have continuity with his ministry and fulfill the promise of the Father through Christ. The "full gospel" of the Jesus who is Savior, Sanctifier, Healer, Baptizer in the Holy Spirit and coming King can and should be proclaimed in the fullness of the Spirit so that the kingdom will be manifested in the midst of the world in words and deeds.[23]

The term *Full Gospel* was coined by Pentecostals to signify this desire to embrace all the gifts that Christ in the power of the Spirit might donate. In their enthusiastic search for this Full Gospel, Pentecostals wondered if older traditions were missing some crucial aspects.[24] Pentecostals were glad to hear Lutherans, Reformed, and other Protestants preach the gospel

---

[22] The classic study is Donald W. Dayton, *Theological Roots of Pentecostalism* (Grand Rapids, MI: Zondervan, 1987). It seems to me the "Full Gospel" template, with a robust "Spirit-Christology," is a valid interpretation even in light of the important and useful criticism coming from the Singaporean Pentecostalist Tan-Chow May Ling (*Pentecostal Theology for the Twenty-First Century: Engaging with Multi-Faith Singapore* [Aldershot, UK: Ashgate, 2007], 102–3), according to which a robust christological and trinitarian focus may be missing in Pentecostal theology.

[23] Steven J. Land, *Pentecostal Spirituality: A Passion for the Kingdom*, Journal of Pentecostal Theology Supplement Series 1 (Sheffield: Sheffield Academic Press, 1993), 60–61.

[24] Of course, the early Pentecostals at times were guilty of an ideological use of the term *Full Gospel*. They were not only sincerely concerned about the well-being of other churches, but sometimes used the Full Gospel template as a way of criticizing, making pejorative comments, and even condemning others' "dead" spiritual life. That human fallibility, unfortunately, is not limited to Pentecostals; however, misuse of the term is hardly a reason to ignore its positive contribution.

of justification by faith and Methodists/Holiness movements highlight the importance of sanctification. What they did not hear in the preaching of other churches and their missionaries were the dynamic New Testament testimonies to the healing power of Jesus, the One who is the same yesterday, today, and tomorrow (Heb 13:8).[25] Similarly missing were the themes of the Spirit's charismatic empowerment and such an enthusiastic expectation of the end that would catalyze a missionary urgency. And so forth.

The Holy Spirit and Charismatic Empowerment

Highlighting the centrality of Christology at the core of Pentecostal spirituality is, of course, not an attempt to undermine in any way the Spirit's robust role. It is just a correction of the prevalent misconception of Pentecostalism as a Spirit-movement without a proper focus on the Son (and the Father). Indeed, similarly to Gospel writers, Pentecostals have discerned a charismatically endowed Man of Spirit in Jesus of Nazareth and, as his followers, they seek to emulate the same. This desire comes to the fore in their emphasis on the Spirit's power—not merely an elusive presence of the Spirit in the community, as important as that may be in itself.

While this empowerment often manifests itself in spiritual gifts such as speaking in tongues, prophecy, and healings, even when those manifestations are absent, it is still felt and sought by Pentecostals. The main function of the Pentecostal worship service is to provide a setting for an encounter with Jesus, the embodiment of the Full Gospel, to receive the (em)power(ment) of the Spirit.[26] As important as sermon, hymns, and liturgy are, they all take second place to the "meeting with the Lord," as they put it.

Part of the texture of enthusiastic missions ethos is a spirituality that incorporates the importance of visions, healing, dreams, dance, and other archetypal religious expressions. The noted observer of global Pentecostalism, Harvard scholar of religion Harvey Cox, remarks that "the reemergence of this primal spirituality came—perhaps not surprisingly—at just the point in history when both the rationalistic assumptions of modernity and the strategies religions had used to oppose them (or to accommodate

---

[25] Korean Samuel Yull Lee (*Grace and Power in Pentecostal and Charismatic Theology* [Apeldoorn: Theologische Universiteit Apeldoorn, 2002], 109–10) forges an integral connection between Christ, Full Gospel, and healing of the body, a central theme of Pentecostal spirituality. See further, Vernon Purdy, "Divine Healing," in *Systematic Theology: A Pentecostal Perspective*, ed. Stanley M. Horton (Springfield, MO: Logion Press, 1999), 508–9.

[26] See Daniel E. Albrecht, *Rites in the Spirit: A Ritual Approach to Pentecostal/ Charismatic Spirituality* (Sheffield: Sheffield Academic Press, 1999).

them) were all coming unraveled."[27] No wonder gifts of the Spirit such as prophesying, prayer for healing, and works of miracles are enthusiastically embraced and sought by Pentecostals. A related belief commends the Spirit-given capacity to engage in "spiritual warfare"[28] and exorcise demonic spirits.[29]

Salvation and the Holistic Vision

In their search for the Full Gospel, Pentecostals have not been content with merely a "spiritual" or otherworldly vision of salvation. Theirs has been a holistic soteriological vision, and it has funded their missionary work in a remarkable manner. In this template (again, most probably unknowingly), Pentecostals seem to echo not only the mindset of much of Christianity in the global South but also the postmodern insistence on a holistic understanding of the body-mind relationship, as has been noted by some scholars of Pentecostalism[30] and Pentecostal theologians.[31] The common features between the two movements—Pentecostalism and postmodernism—include embodiment, holism, as well as attention to "experientialism," values too often marginalized particularly in the post-Enlightenment Protestant spirituality. As Harvey Cox has stated, Pentecostalism "has succeeded because it has spoken to the spiritual emptiness of our time by reaching beyond the levels of creed and ceremony into the core of human religiousness. . . . Pentecostals have touched so many people because they have indeed restored something."[32] In their yearning and search for a holistic account of the Full Gospel, Pentecostals came

[27] Harvey Cox, *Fire from Heaven: The Rise of Pentecostal Spirituality and the Reshaping of Religion in the Twenty-first Century* (Reading, MA: Addison-Wesley, 1995), 81–82.
[28] Ogbu U. Kalu, "Preserving a Worldview: Pentecostalism in the African Maps of the Universe," *Pneuma* 24/2 (2003): 122.
[29] See Opoku Onyinah, "Deliverance as a Way of Confronting Witchcraft in Contemporary Africa: Ghana as a Case Study," in *The Spirit in the World: Emerging Pentecostal Theologies in Global Contexts*, ed. Veli-Matti Kärkkäinen (Grand Rapids, MI: Eerdmans, 2009).
[30] See especially Cox, *Fire from Heaven*, 299–301.
[31] An important contribution here is Jackie David Johns, "Pentecostalism and the Postmodern Worldview," *Journal of Pentecostal Theology* 7 (1995): 73–96. Lately, however, more modest and self-critical remarks have emerged, such as those found in John C. Poirier and B. Scott Lewis, "Pentecostal and Postmodernist Hermeneutics: A Critique of Three Conceits," *Journal of Pentecostal Theology* 15/1 (2006): 3–21.
[32] Cox, *Fire from Heaven*, 81.

to embrace the notion of "holistic salvation" long before the term gained fame in some mainline theologies.[33]

In an important essay titled "Materiality of Salvation: An Investigation in the Soteriologies of Liberation and Pentecostal Theologies," Yale theologian Miroslav Volf, who comes originally from the Pentecostal Church of Croatia, former Yugoslavia, has argued that with all their differences, these two Christian movements share a vision of salvation in this-worldly, physical, material, embodied terms.[34] While neither of the movements, of course, leaves behind the eschatological, future-oriented hope, relegating salvation merely to the future will not do. True, liberationists focus their efforts on sociopolitical (including gender) liberation, while for Pentecostals it is more about the individual's release from sicknesses and ailments, physical or emotional—however, not to the exclusion of sociopolitical dimensions.

The importance of social concern as an integral part of a holistic vision of salvation comes to the fore in Pentecostals' investment in building schools, hospitals, and orphanages, as well as care for the poor, disadvantaged, and marginalized. While giving priority to evangelism and individual conversion, Pentecostals have not been oblivious to social concern, even though that myth exists among outside observers of Pentecostalism.[35] Indeed, unbeknown to many outside observers, with all their problems with "otherworldliness," Pentecostals have not been lazy in their efforts to better the conditions of this world. Pentecostal mission for a long time has been characterized by a commitment to social justice, empowerment of the powerless, and a "preferential option for the marginalized" tracing back to its roots at Azusa Street as a kind of paradigm of marginalization.[36] Where the difference from the older traditions, particularly Roman Catholic social ethics, may surface has to do with the Pentecostal priority on personal rather than structural change as the origin of social improvement.

At the same time, as many Pentecostal missiologists are the first to point out in a constructive self-critical way, the idea of the materiality of salvation in the hands of too many Pentecostals and charismatics has also turned

---

[33] Amos Yong, *The Spirit Poured Out on All Flesh: Pentecostalism and the Possibility of Global Theology* (Grand Rapids, MI: Baker Academic, 2005), 82.

[34] Miroslav Volf, "Materiality of Salvation: An Investigation in the Soteriologies of Liberation and Pentecostal Theologies," *Journal of Ecumenical Studies* 26 (1989): 447–67.

[35] See Veli-Matti Kärkkäinen, "Are Pentecostals Oblivious to Social Justice: Theological and Ecumenical Perspectives?" in *Missiology* 29, no. 4 (2001): 417–31.

[36] See the important discussion by the Hispanic Pentecostal ethicist Eldín Villafañe, *The Liberating Spirit: Toward an Hispanic American Pentecostal Social Ethic* (Grand Rapids, MI: Eerdmans, 1993), 218.

into a gross materialistic search for financial and other benefits. Health and wealth are sometimes made prime indicators of God's blessings, and spiritual techniques for reaching them are fine-tuned by ever-new itinerant charismatic preachers. That said, it is true that this is a problem far less with established Pentecostal communities and much more among more recent independent charismatic constituencies and groups.

Related, Pentecostalism also at times suffers from the same kind of "spiritualist" reductionism that is not far from many evangelical and other traditional theologies, that is, prioritizing the salvation of the "soul" to the point where the wholeness of the human being as an embodied *imago Dei* is being missed. In Pentecostal preaching and witnessing one can hear both voices simultaneously: seeking for wholeness of salvation, and emphasis on the salvation of the soul.

Church and the Spirit of Koinonia

While only a few Pentecostals have joined the vibrant ecumenical conversation about communion theology,[37] in their aggressive and creative church-planting work they have intuited the importance of communal dimensions and communities in a way that may be closer to the testimony of the New Testament than the practice of many older traditions. Indeed, despite the lack of a fully developed ecclesiology, a good case can be made for the claim that "Pentecostal soteriology and pneumatology point . . . unmistakably in the direction of an ecclesiology of the fellowship of persons."[38]

On the other hand, in a regrettable opposition to this communion orientation, much of Pentecostalism, especially in the global North and

---

[37] See Veli-Matti Kärkkäinen, "The Church as the Fellowship of Persons: An Emerging Pentecostal Ecclesiology of Koinonia," *PentecoStudies* 6/1 (2007): 1–15. An exciting collection of essays on Pentecostal ecclesiology focused on the Full Gospel template is *Pentecostal Ecclesiology: The Church and the Five Fold Gospel*, ed. Chris Thomas and William Kay (Lexington, KY: Emeth Press, 2010). Similarly, the theme issue of the *International Journal for the Study of the Christian Church* 11/4 (2011) is "The Ecclesiology of the Pentecostal Churches," guest editor Veli-Matti Kärkkäinen.

[38] Peter Kuzmic and Miroslav Volf, "*Communio Sanctorum*: Toward a Theology of the Church as a Fellowship of Persons," Pentecostal Position Paper Read at the International Roman Catholic–Pentecostal Dialogue, Riano, Italy, May 21–26, 1985 (unpublished), 2 (manuscript with the author of this essay). See also Veli-Matti Kärkkäinen, *Spiritus ubi vult spirat: Pneumatology in Roman Catholic-Pentecostal Dialogue (1972–1989)*, Schriften der Luther-Agricola-Gesellschaft 42 (Helsinki: Luther-Agricola Society, 1998), 100–121.

as a result of missions work from the North, has tended to foster the hyper-individualism of the post-Enlightenment mentality.[39] That said, there is no denying the fact that a charismatically conceived communion theology, with an inclusive vision, has supported Pentecostal mission efforts and led to a mushrooming of communities that have experienced the multifaceted *koinonia* described in Acts 2:42–44, a passage dear to Pentecostals.[40]

Before some concluding thoughts, a topic at the center of contemporary missiology and theology of mission should be briefly considered: the challenge of religious pluralism and interfaith encounters. No current mission theology can—or should—ignore this vital question. How would Pentecostals fare in this regard?

WHAT ABOUT THE ENGAGEMENT OF OTHER FAITH TRADITIONS?

In keeping with the general evangelical caution and prejudice, not surprisingly, for a long time Pentecostals took it for granted that the topic of religious plurality has little need for reflection. A typical conservative-fundamentalistic exclusivism was taken for granted. Not for nothing did the late sympathetic observer of Pentecostalism, Clark Pinnock of Canada, note this: "One might expect the Pentecostals to develop a Spirit-oriented theology of mission and world religions, because of their openness to religious experience, their sensitivity to the oppressed of the Third World where they have experienced much of their growth, and their awareness of the ways of the Spirit as well as dogma."[41] Yet to date that expectation has gone unfulfilled.

In keeping with exclusivism, it has been common for Pentecostals to raise grave doubts about any kind of saving role of the Spirit apart from the proclamation of the gospel. They have either tended to limit the Spirit's saving work to the church (except for the work of the Spirit preparing for

---

[39] See Frank Macchia, *Baptized in the Spirit: A Global Pentecostal Theology* (Grand Rapids, MI: Zondervan, 2006), 203, 205.

[40] In the third phase of the Roman Catholic–Pentecostal International Dialogue the theme of communion was studied in some detail, leading to an important ecumenical document: *Perspectives on Koinonia: The Report from the Third Quinquennium of the Dialogue between the Pontifical Council for Promoting Christian Unity of the Roman Catholic Church and Some Classical Pentecostal Churches and Leaders (1985–1989)*, available on the vatican website, among others.

[41] Clark Pinnock, *Flame of Love: A Theology of the Holy Spirit* (Downers Grove, IL: InterVarsity Press, 1996), 274.

receiving the gospel),[42] or have ignored outright any reflection on what their otherwise strong insistence on the principle *spiritus ubi vult spirat* ("the Spirit blows where it wills," Jn 3:6) might mean in relation to other religions. Furthermore, with other conservative Christians, Pentecostals have been afraid of the dangers of recent "liberal" or pluralistic approaches to the issue.[43] A case in point is the recent warning from an official of the Assemblies of God, the largest predominantly white Pentecostal denomination in the United States. According to this statement, a pluralistic approach poses a threefold problem: (1) it is contrary to scripture; (2) it replaces the obligation for world evangelism; and (3) those who fail to fulfill the Great Commission are ultimately not living under the Lordship of Christ.[44]

An important impetus for prompting Pentecostals to begin engaging interfaith issues has come from ecumenical exchanges with older Christian traditions, beginning from the International Dialogue with Roman Catholics started in 1972.[45] There was a tentative discussion on the possibility of salvation for those not explicitly confessing faith in Christ during the second quinquennium (1978–82) of that dialogue, and no unanimity was reached. Not surprisingly, the Catholic and Pentecostal perspectives

---

[42] A quick survey of Pentecostal manuals shows this clearly: Ernest S. Williams, *Systematic Theology* (Springfield, MO: Gospel Publishing House, 1953), 3n15; Ned D. Sauls, *Pentecostal Doctrines: A Wesleyan Approach* (Dun, NC: The Heritage Press, 1979), 54; Guy P. Duffield and Nathaniel M. Van Cleave, *Foundations of Pentecostal Theology* (Los Angeles: L.I.F.E. Bible College, 1983), 268–70; Aaron M. Wilson, *Basic Bible Truth: A Doctrinal Study of the Pentecostal Church of God* (Joplin, MO: Messenger Publishing House, 1987), 115; Mark D. McLean, "The Holy Spirit," in *Systematic Theology: A Pentecostal Perspective*, ed. Stanley M. Horton (Springfield, MO: Logion Press, 1994), 392. For this bibliographical note I am indebted to Cecil M. Robeck, "A Pentecostal Assessment of 'Towards a Common Understanding and Vision' of the WCC," *Mid-Stream* 37/1 (1998): 31n40.

[43] For an important, comprehensive, and up-to-date discussion of the reasons Pentecostals have been very reserved about engaging the interfaith issues, see Tony Richie, *Speaking by the Spirit: A Pentecostal Model for Interreligious Dialogue* (Lexington, KY: Emeth Press, 2011), chap. 6. Richie briefly presents the main reasons for Pentecostals to reject interfaith engagement, including the dangers of compromised Christology, diminishing the value of the Bible, distorted soteriology, and undermining of mission and evangelization (pp. 26–29).

[44] Hardol Carpenter, "Tolerance or Irresponsibility: The Problem of Pluralism in Missions," *Advance* 31/2 (1995): 19.

[45] For a scrutiny of some relevant missiological and interfaith issues, see Veli-Matti Kärkkäinen, "'An Exercise on the Frontiers of Ecumenism': Almost Thirty Years of the Roman Catholic–Pentecostal Dialogue," *Exchange: Journal of Missiological and Ecumenical Research* 29/2 (2000): 156–71; *International Bulletin of Missionary Research* 25/1 (2001): 16–23; and "Culture, Contextualization, and Conversion: Missiological Reflections from the Catholic–Pentecostal Dialogue (1990–1997)," *Asian Journal of Mission* 2/2 (2000): 149–77.

diverged over the existence and/or meaning of salvific elements found in non-Christian religions.[46] Pentecostals insisted that there cannot be salvation outside the church.[47] Most Pentecostals wanted to limit the saving work of the Spirit to the church and its proclamation of the gospel, although they were willing to acknowledge the work of the Holy Spirit in the world convicting people of sin.[48] Furthermore, Pentecostals, like many of the early Christians, pointed out the demonic elements in other religions rather than common denominators.[49] It is yet to be seen what the still continuing important ecumenical discussions will bring about regarding this vital theme.

In recent years, differently from the past, some leading Pentecostal theologians have started a promising and groundbreaking inquiry into the matrix of interfaith encounters and the Spirit's role therein. In this endeavor American-Chinese-Malesian theologian Amos Yong stands in the forefront. His *Discerning the Spirit(s): A Pentecostal-Charismatic Contribution to Christian Theology of Religions*[50] and its sequel, *Beyond the Impasse: Toward a Pneumatological Theology of Religions,*[51] argue for a uniquely Pentecostal pneumatology that, while holding on to the uniqueness of Jesus Christ and trinitarian faith, would also be open to acknowledging the ministry of the Spirit outside the Christian church. His goal is to develop criteria for discerning the Spirit of God and distinguishing that ministry from the work of other spirits in the world.

In his important contribution to emerging Pentecostal systematic theology titled *The Spirit Poured Out on All Flesh: Pentecostalism and the Possibility of Global Theology,* Yong continues to hone a pneumatological approach to religions and "spirits" of religions. He issues a call to all Pentecostals to work toward a public theology by engaging Pentecostal pneumatology with interfaith dialogue. His thesis is that

> a pneumatologically driven theology is more conducive to engaging [interfaith issues] . . . in our time than previous approaches. . . . Religions are neither accidents of history nor encroachments on divine providence but are, in various ways, instruments of the Holy Spirit working out the divine purposes in the world and . . . the unevangelized, if saved at all, are saved through the work of Christ by the

---

[46] *Final Report 1991–1997,* #20. All the final reports are available on the Centro Pro Unione website.

[47] *Final Report 1978–1982,* #14.

[48] *Final Report 1991–1997,* #20.

[49] Ibid., #21.

[50] Amos Yong, *Discerning the Spirit(s): A Pentecostal-Charismatic Contribution to Christian Theology of Religions* (Sheffield: Sheffield University Press, 2000).

[51] Amos Yong, *Beyond the Impasse: Toward a Pneumatological Theology of Religions* (Grand Rapids, MI: Baker Academic, 2003).

Spirit (even if mediated through the religious beliefs and practices available to them).[52]

A major contribution to the developing Pentecostal theology of religions by Yong is *Hospitality and the Other: Pentecost, Christian Practices, and the Neighbor*.[53] Therein Yong taps into the theme of hospitality, enthusiastically embraced by much of contemporary interfaith conversations, as a way to help his movement engage the religious Other. Yong has also done groundbreaking work in pneumatological comparative theology with a focus on Buddhist-Christian topics.[54]

A significant recent contribution to emerging theology of religions by Pentecostals comes from Bishop Tony Richie (Church of God, Cleveland, Tennessee), whose monograph *Speaking by the Spirit: A Pentecostal Model for Interreligious Dialogue* (2011) considers carefully the typical objections posed by Pentecostals against the engagement of interfaith issues and also seeks to construct a viable approach to religions, building especially on the core Pentecostal practice of testimony. Richie considers it important to pursue this task in the matrix of Pentecostalism's "strong heritage of evangelism and missions, generally conservative ethical and theological history, and undeniable multicultural variety."[55] He also takes lessons from some Pentecostal pioneers in whose ethos he sees seeds of openness to religions while at the same time faithfully representing tradition.[56] A growing number of other Pentecostal theologians are currently engaging the topic of interfaith engagement.[57] My own work in the field of interfaith

[52] Amos Yong, *The Spirit Poured Out on All Flesh: Pentecostalism and the Possibility of Global Theology* (Grand Rapids, MI: Baker Academic, 2005), 235–36.

[53] Amos Yong, *Hospitality and the Other: Pentecost, Christian Practices, and the Neighbor* (Maryknoll, NY: Orbis Books, 2008).

[54] Amos Yong, *Pneumatology and the Christian-Buddhist Dialogue: Does the Spirit Blow through the Middle Way?* (Leiden: Brill, 2012); idem, *The Cosmic Breath: Spirit and Nature in the Christianity-Buddhism-Science Trialogue* (Leiden: Brill, 2012).

[55] Bishop Tony Richie, *Speaking by the Spirit: A Pentecostal Model for Interreligious Dialogue*, Asbury Theological Seminar Series in World Christian Revitalization Movements in Pentecostal and Charismatic Studies no. 6 (Lexington, KY: Emeth Press, 2011), 3.

[56] See also Tony Richie, "Azusa-Era Optimism: Bishop J. H. King's Pentecostal Theology of Religions as a Possible Paradigm for Today," *Journal of Pentecostal Tradition* 14/2 (April 2006): 247–60.

[57] For a recent collection of essays, several of them relevant to interfaith issues, by Pentecostal theologians widely representing global diversity, see *The Spirit in the World: Emerging Pentecostal Theologies in Global Contexts*, ed. Veli-Matti Kärkkäinen (Grand Rapids, MI: Eerdmans, 2009); and *Global Renewal, Religious Pluralism, and the Great Commission: Towards a Renewal Theology of Mission and Interreligious Encounter*, ed. Amos Yong and Clifton Clarke (Lexington, KY: Emeth Press, 2011). Some Pentecostal theologians have also participated in

studies has focused on developing a trinitarian understanding of the role of the Spirit in the world. In this pursuit the dialogue partners have been Protestant and Catholic colleagues outside Pentecostalism.[58]

Useful guidelines for the Pentecostal engagement of living faiths and religious pluralism are provided by Hispanic Pentecostal theologian Samuel Solivan. According to him, the following principles might help Pentecostals in this endeavor: (1) the fact that the Holy Spirit is the one who leads Christians to all truth; (2) the importance of identification with the poor of the world and the need to bring their distinctive voice into the dialogue; (3) the conviction of the prevenient workings of the Holy Spirit in every human being; (4) the empowerment of believers for witness by the Spirit; and (5) the diverse and pluralistic character of the Spirit's manifestations across racial, class, gender, language, and religious boundaries.[59] On this foundation, as a Pentecostal pastor and academic theologian, Solivan is led to "examine the diverse ways the Holy Spirit is at work among other people of faith."[60] Yet he does so critically since there are always pitfalls—such as relativization of the truth—in an approach to mission in which dialogue is the *main* vehicle.[61]

IN LIEU OF CONCLUSIONS: IMPORTANT TASKS AND CHALLENGES FOR PENTECOSTAL MISSION

Without repeating the themes and topics discussed above, all of which call for continuing discussion and collaboration, several other challenges await Pentecostal theologians in the area of mission and interfaith relations.

---

the continuing work of the WCC in its drafting of interfaith principles. For an important document on this, see "Christian Witness in a Multi-Religious World: Recommendations for Conduct" (Geneva: WCC, June 28, 2011).

[58] Veli-Matti Kärkkäinen, *The Trinity and Religious Pluralism: The Doctrine of the Trinity in Christian Theology of Religions* (Aldershot, UK: Ashgate, 2004); "'How to Speak of the Spirit among Religions': Trinitarian 'Rules' for a Pneumatological Theology of Religions," *International Bulletin of Missionary Research* 30/3 (July 2006): 121–27; "The Uniqueness of Christ and Trinitarian Faith," in *Christ the One and Only: A Global Affirmation of the Uniqueness of Jesus Christ*, ed. Sung Wook Chung (Exeter: Paternoster, 2005), 111–35; "Trinity and Religions: On the Way to a Trinitarian Theology of Religions for Evangelicals," *Missiology* 33/2 (2005): 159–74; "Trinitarian Rules for a Pneumatological Theology of Religions," in *The Work of the Spirit: Pneumatology and Pentecostalism*, ed. Michael Welker (Grand Rapids, MI: Eerdmans, 2006), 47–70.

[59] Samuel Solivan, "Interreligious Dialogue: An Hispanic American Pentecostal Perspective," in *Grounds for Understanding: Ecumenical Responses to Religious Pluralism*, ed. S. Mark Heim (Grand Rapids, MI: Eerdmans, 1998), 37–45.

[60] Ibid., 43.

[61] Ibid., 44.

For a movement with such great numerical success in missions work, another urgent theological task has to do with the issue of suffering.[62] Some leading global Pentecostal theologians from contexts as diverse as Africa[63] and Asia[64] have lamented the lack of theological reflection on the topic and called for a distinctively Pentecostal theology of suffering.[65] Canadian Martin William Mittelstadt's *The Spirit and Suffering in Luke-Acts*[66] makes a significant contribution in this regard. Promisingly, several other Pentecostals from various global contexts, including Puerto Rico[67] and Sudan,[68] have joined this common task.

Several other academic and practical tasks could be listed, crucial to the future of Pentecostal missions, including continuing reflection on the identity of Pentecostalism—"What makes Pentecostalism, Pentecostalism?"[69]— both in relation to "spiritual cousins," charismatics within the existing churches, and neocharismatics, and Pentecostal-type Christians among a bewildering number of independent movements in African Instituted Churches, in Chinese house churches, and so forth. Does Pentecostalism and its mission represent a distinctively unique manifestation in Christian history or is it rather an offshoot from a wider religious revival?[70]

A related issue has to do with the wider question of Christian unity, ecumenism. As mentioned above, a historically important dialogue pro-

---

[62] See Veli-Matti Kärkkäinen, "Theology of the Cross: A Stumbling Block to Pentecostal-Charismatic Spirituality," in *The Spirit and Spirituality: Essays in Honour of Russell P. Spittler*, ed. Wonsuk Ma and Robert P. Menzies (London: T & T Clark International, 2004), 150–63.

[63] See J. Kwabena Asamoah-Gyadu, *African Charismatics: Current Developments within Independent Indigenous Pentecostalism in Ghana* (Leiden: Brill, 2006), 218, 228–32.

[64] Gabriel Reuben Louis, "Response to Wonsuk Ma," paper presented to Asia Pacific Theological Association. This is a response to Wonsuk Ma, "Toward an Asian Pentecostal Theology," paper presented to Asia Pacific Theological Association, *Cyberjournal for Pentecostal-Charismatic Research*, January 2007.

[65] See William W. Menzies, "Reflections on Suffering: A Pentecostal Perspective," in Ma and Menzies, *The Spirit and Spirituality*, 141; Keith Warrington, "Healing and Suffering in the Bible," *International Review of Mission* 95/376/377 (2006): 154–64.

[66] Martin William Mittelstadt, *The Spirit and Suffering in Luke-Acts: Implications for a Pentecostal Pneumatology*, ed. John Christopher Thomas et al., Pentecostal Theology Supplement Series 26 (London: T & T Clark International, 2004).

[67] Samuel Solivan, *The Spirit, Pathos, and Liberation: Toward an Hispanic Pentecostal Theology* (Sheffield: Sheffield Academic Press, 1998).

[68] Isaiah Majo Dau, *Suffering and God: A Theological Reflection on the War in Sudan* (Nairobi, Kenya: Paulines Publications Africa, 2003).

[69] See Veli-Matti Kärkkäinen, "Identity and Plurality: A Pentecostal-Charismatic Perspective," *International Review of Mission* 91/363 (October 2002): 500–504.

[70] For some aspects, see Veli-Matti Kärkkäinen, "'The Re-Turn of Religion in the New Millennium': Pentecostalisms and Postmodernities," *Swedish Missiological Themes* 95/4 (Fall 2007): 469–96.

cess with Roman Catholics was started in 1972, and one of the topics taken up looked at missions and related concerns. A dialogue process was also started in the mid-1990s with the World Communion of Reformed Churches, and in 2016 with the Lutheran World Federation. In 2000, in the aftermath of the Harare General Assembly, an important Joint Consultative Work Group between the World Council of Churches and Pentecostals was founded. All of these more recent processes are ongoing and, similarly to the engagement with Catholics, are also considering the issues of mission, social concern, and other religions.

An urgent continuing challenge in these ecumenical talks has to do with evangelization and proselytism, a burning issue for any aggressively evangelizing body such as Pentecostals. Unbeknown to many, a whole quinquennium (1991–97) was devoted to that topic, alongside common witness and evangelization.[71] Whatever the direction global Pentecostalism will take with regard to other faith traditions, this challenge can no longer be ignored, and it will significantly shape and condition mission and evangelization in the third millennium.

---

[71] "Evangelization, Proselytism, and Common Witness: The Report from the Fourth Phase of the International Dialogue 1990–1997 between the Roman Catholic Church and Some Classical Pentecostal Churches and Leaders," available on the vatican website; for a theological analysis, see Veli-Matti Kärkkäinen, *Ad ultimum terrae: Evangelization, Proselytism, and Common Witness in the Roman Catholic–Pentecostal Dialogue 1990–1997* (Frankfurt: Peter Lang, 1999).

PART 2

CONTEXTUAL THEOLOGY

Chapter 6

Contexts and Theological Methods

Robert Schreiter

"I believe strongly that there is, in reality, no 'theology' as such—no 'universal' theologies—there are only contextual theologies." Stephen B. Bevans makes this statement at the beginning of *An Introduction to Theology in Global Perspective*.[1] To some, this may seem a truism. In a world keenly aware of cultural flows encountering one another, we assume that everything we say and do is influenced in some manner by the contexts in which ideas are born, shaped, and articulated. But embedded deeply within us is also a sense that those things most important to us somehow transcend space and time. We sense too that, if everything we say or do were utterly bounded by our contexts, then communication across those boundaries of contexts would be impossible, and we would all be locked into small enclosed worlds. We are deeply aware of how important it is to be able to cross those boundaries to foster the communion and solidarity necessary to make this a livable world.

In Christian faith we hold that God's revelation, though given "to our ancestors in many and various ways" (Heb 1:1), does indeed speak to every time and place, and that Jesus Christ is indeed "the way, the truth, and the life" (Jn 14:6) for all of humankind. Yet it falls to us, as finite beings, to craft that revelation into words. This poses a potential hazard for theology: in trying to speak of the transcendent and infinite God, we can fall into the trap of thinking that our speaking about God bears the same transcendence as its subject. Remembering that we must always use language (and there are over six thousand varieties of language on the planet today), and that we are finite beings, we must constantly remind ourselves that our utterings about God always bear the stamp of our finitude.

Most theologians have been at least somewhat aware of this limitation of theology. It has long been the custom to talk of two kinds of theology:

---

[1] Stephen B. Bevans, *Introduction to Theology in Global Perspective* (Maryknoll, NY: Orbis Books, 2007), 3–4.

101

cataphatic theology (what we are able to say about God), and apophatic theology (how God transcends the best human efforts to speak about God). It is especially in the mystical traditions that people become aware of how far human language falls short of speaking about God in any adequate way. Yet the urge to enter into the divine reality urges theologians on to draw near to God as closely as they can.

What has come to be called contextual theology is a way of doing theology that never loses sight of the fact that we speak out of distinctive contexts. This awareness began to coalesce in a special way in the middle of the twentieth century. Important social and cultural shifts going on in the world at that time led to a new sense that all theology was shaped by context: that is, not reduced to its context, but never free from its contexts either.

This chapter explores how theology came to be constructed and read more closely in terms of its contexts. It begins by tracing the history of how this awareness came about. Then it looks at how this awareness developed from the mid-twentieth century to the present time. In a third part it presents one of the significant ways found to show the varieties of interaction between theology and its contexts. And finally, it looks to the future of contextual theologies—the challenges such a way of doing theology will encounter.

HOW CONTEXTUAL THEOLOGIES DEVELOPED

There has long been awareness that the Christian message must be expressed in ways intelligible to specific contexts. This was already obvious in Paul's attempt to recast the Christian kerygma to the philosophers on the Areopagus in the Acts of the Apostles (Acts 17:16–32). Although terms like *context* and *culture* would not be used until much later, references to *custom* and *adaptation* captured some of the spirit of what would eventually come to be called contextual theology. Widely known too is Pope Gregory the Great's admonition to Augustine of Canterbury, as he began his mission to England at the turn of the seventh century: "The temples of the idols in that nation should not be destroyed, but let the idols that are in them be destroyed; let holy water be made and sprinkled in the said temples, let altars be erected, and relics placed."[2]

An even more distinctive moment in Christian history of awareness of context came with the missionary efforts of the East Syrian Church to China in the seventh and eighth centuries when, at the Christian center in Chang'an, there appears to have been close collaboration between Christian and Buddhist monks, so much so that "for the purpose of communicating the Christian Message, and for the deepening of their own faith-life in the

---

[2] Venerable Bede, *The Ecclesiastical History of the British Nation*, Bk. I, ch. xxx.

Messiah, they [the Christian monks] employed Buddhist terms, expressions, and symbols."[3] A remarkable document from that era gives an explanation of the Christian faith within the contextual framework of a Buddhist sutra.

With the voyages from Europe beginning in the late fifteenth century, the experience of Christians from that region encountering peoples whose languages and customs were utterly different from their own only intensified. The Office of the Propaganda Fide in Rome issued instructions in 1659 that showed a sensibility to context, even though the reasons behind it were not given conscious expression:

> Do not regard it as your task, and do not bring any pressure to bear on the peoples, to change their customs, manners and uses, unless they are evidently contrary to religion and sound morals. What could be more absurd than to transport France, Spain, Italy, or some other European country to China?[4]

But such advice was not always followed; indeed, it may have been honored more in the breach than in the application.

In the twentieth century a number of factors converged that laid the groundwork for doing theology with special attention to context. Four factors in particular may be singled out here.

First of all, what has come to be called the modern sense of culture emerged in the study of human societies.[5] This development began already in the second half of the eighteenth century. Before that time, *culture* referred to the highest artistic achievements of a people in their music, literature, and art. This is an understanding of culture that continues to this day and is often now referred to as the classical notion of culture. Alongside this older approach another meaning of *culture* arose within German Romanticism that saw culture as the genius of any given group of people. Johann Gottfried Herder captured the idea by seeing culture as a trinity of three things: the territory, language, and customs of a people. This modern sense of culture pointed to the fact that every people has culture—not just the elites of a given people. This meaning of *culture* as the combination of territory, language, and customs became the basis for the study of peoples in what was to become cultural anthropology and the other social sciences. As such, it became the place for analyzing the distinctive elements that make up a people's culture.

---

[3] John Kaserow, "Christian Evaluations of Buddhism" (doctoral dissertation, University of St. Michael's College, 1976), 716. Cited in Stephen B. Bevans and Roger P. Schroeder, *Constants in Context: A Theology of Mission for Today* (Maryknoll, NY: Orbis Books, 2004), 105f.

[4] *Sacra Congregatio de Propaganda Fide, Collectanea* 10/300 (Rome 1907), 103.

[5] On classical, modern, and postmodern senses of culture, see Kathryn Tanner, *Theories of Culture* (Minneapolis: Fortress Press, 1997).

The second factor in the development of contextual theologies was the appropriation of this modern understanding of culture by Christian missionaries and then, shortly after that, by the people to whom the missionaries had been sent. Rather than seeing the worldviews and customs of missionized peoples as either inspired by demons or other form of error, it became possible to articulate an appreciation for how local settings dealt with the problems of human existence and found ways of organizing their lives together. From the side of those who had been evangelized, this sense of culture became a basis for asserting their own human values and also for resistance to efforts to impose foreign cultural ways upon them. By the 1950s and 1960s, a new cultural sensitivity was making itself felt in missionary work. An important text that informed much of this early development was Divine Word Missionary anthropologist Louis B. Luzbetak's *The Church and Cultures: Applied Anthropology for the Religious Worker.*[6] With this and similar works, tools were becoming available to analyze the various dimensions of culture.

Raising questions about differences in context between Europe and colonized countries in Africa and Asia came not only from the missionaries but from the peoples themselves. In 1955, a group of young African scholars studying in Paris came together and posed serious questions about the theology they were being taught and how their own cultures were being ignored or depreciated by church leaders.[7] This sentiment would only increase in the subsequent decades, as decolonization got under way. By the 1970s the anticolonial voices of young theologians would gather as the Ecumenical Association of Third World Theologians (EATWOT), meeting first in Dar es Salaam in 1976 and then on a regular basis around the world in the years to follow.

In a similar sentiment in Protestant circles, Shoki Coe, a Taiwanese theologian who was to become the director of the Fund for Theological Education of the World Council of Churches, introduced the idea of theology as the interpretation of the scriptures in an ever-changing array of contexts. He called this contextual theology.[8]

A third factor leading to the rise of contextual theologies was the endorsement of the concept of culture by the fathers at the Second Vatican Council. Chapter 2 of the Second Part of the *Pastoral Constitution on the Church in the Modern World (Gaudium et spes)* is devoted to the concept of culture, and in other documents of the council—especially the *Declaration of Missionary Activity (Ad gentes)*—attention to culture in the formation of missionaries and others is encouraged. The understanding of culture used

---

[6] Louis B. Luzbetak, *The Church and Cultures: Applied Anthropology for the Religious Worker* (Techny, IL: Divine Word Publications, 1963). This classic book is still in print and available from the William Carey Library in Pasadena, California.

[7] *Des Pretres noirs s'interrogent* (Paris: Editions du Cerf, 1956).

[8] See "Text and Context: Keynote Address at NEAATS Inauguration," *Northeastern Asian Journal of Theology* 1 (1968): 127–38.

in these documents is a combination of classical and modern concepts of culture. In *Gaudium et spes, culture* is defined initially as referring to "all those things which go to the refining and developing of diverse mental and physical endowments" (GS 53). But right after that the constitution acknowledges that "culture necessarily has historical and social overtones, and the word 'culture' often carries with it sociological and ethnological connotations; in this sense one can speak of a plurality of cultures" (ibid.). In relation to this plurality of cultures the document states that "the Church has been sent to all ages and nations and, therefore, is not tied exclusively and indissolubly to any race or nation, to any one particular way of life, or to any customary practices, ancient or modern. . . . It can, then, enter into communion with different forms of culture, thereby enriching both itself and the cultures themselves" (GS 58). Put another way, this means that the good news of Jesus Christ can in principle find a home in any culture and is not beholden to any single culture. In *Ad gentes* the implication of this for education for ministry is made clear: "Therefore, the minds of students must be opened and refined so that they will better understand and appreciate the culture of their own people; in philosophy and theology they should examine the relationship between the traditions and religion of their homeland and Christianity" (AG 16).

Pope Paul VI carried these assertions of the council documents further in his travels and in his pronouncements.[9] In his Apostolic Letter *Africae terrarum* in 1967 and his address in Kampala in 1969 he said that the people there should be both truly Christian and genuinely African. The 1974 Synod of Bishops addressed the question of evangelization in the modern world. The Apostolic Exhortation *Evangelii nuntiandi* that followed in 1975 gave a firm foundation for considering culture and context in theology. As British theologian Aylward Shorter has said, "It offers an advanced theology of a multicultural church that has probably not been surpassed by any other official document. . . . As a basic statement of the issues involved, it is unrivalled. Subsequent papal and synodal documents have been no more than additions or corrections."[10] *Evangelii nuntiandi* recognizes the complexity of cultural settings and the many dimensions of the reception of the gospel message in those cultures. Important too is the fact that it does not focus on the role of the missionary as evangelizer as much as on the role of those receiving the message and how they give it shape within their own ways of thinking.

With Pope John Paul II, the word *inculturation* became part of official Vatican vocabulary. The term was first used in Jesuit circles in 1973 and carried with it an implicit theology of how gospel and context interact. The gospel message enters into culture just as the Second Person of the Trinity,

---

[9] An excellent overview of the Catholic Church's developing understanding of contextual theology at the official level may be found in Aylward Shorter, *Toward a Theology of Inculturation* (Maryknoll, NY: Orbis Books, 1988), 177–238.

[10] Ibid., 215.

the Word, entered into human existence: "And the Word was made flesh and dwelt among us" (Jn 1:14). The term *inculturation* is intended to carry echoes of the theological concept of incarnation. *Inculturation* has been the preferred term in Roman Catholic documents. Among theologians and missionaries it is used more or less interchangeably with *contextual theology*.

Pope John Paul II first used the term in 1979, in the Apostolic Exhortation *Catechesi tradendae*, which followed the Synod of Bishops' 1978 meeting on catechesis. This pope was deeply committed to an explicit appreciation of the role culture plays in transmitting the gospel. This grew, no doubt, from his experience of how the Polish church carried and sustained Polish culture for the more than 120 years when there was no Polish state itself and rival powers in Germany, Austria, and Russia tried to extinguish Polish identity. In 1982 he established the Pontifical Council for Culture. Although this Pontifical Council has been more concerned with preserving culture in its classical sense, its interest in the consequences of secularization in European cultures clearly intersects with the interests of contextual theology.

A fourth factor was greater attention among Catholics to the social and urban context. In the 1920s, Joseph Cardijn, a Belgian priest, led efforts to engage young factory workers in responding to their respective situations from the perspective of the gospel. He developed a methodology based on three moments: see-judge-act. People needed first to observe their situation closely, then make a judgment about what was going on in the light of the Gospel, and then act on that judgment. This simple method provided the basis for Catholic social action, in which the social problems facing people could be named, analyzed, and acted upon. As time progressed, that "seeing" came to be known as reading the signs of the times, echoing Jesus's words in Matthew's Gospel (16:3) where he berates his listeners for not knowing how to read the weather and, by extension, what is going on. The concept of signs of the times was taken up in Pope John XXIII's encyclical *Pacem in terris* in 1963 and introduced also into *Gaudium et spes* in 1965.

European missionaries who volunteered for work in Latin America starting in the 1950s took this methodology with them, where it melded with parallel efforts being developed in parts of the church there. The social problems facing Latin America—widespread poverty and inequality, oppressive military regimes that replaced democratic government, economic colonization by the United States, and other things—proved to be a fertile ground for the see-judge-act methodology. This came fully into the picture in 1968, when the Bishops' Conferences of Latin America (CELAM) met in Medellín in Colombia to reflect on the meaning of the Second Vatican Council for Latin America. During the council the pastoral agenda had been dominated by European problems, especially atheism and Communism. Latin American bishops tried to draw attention to the problems of poverty and social and economic oppression. They did get a hearing from many sympathetic ears, but the "more urgent problems" treated in the second part of *Gaudium et spes* reflected more on North Atlantic issues.

What the Medellín Conference became, in effect, was the inculturation of the thinking of the Second Vatican Council in the Latin American context. Here the cries of the poor and the need for liberation from all the forms of oppression took center stage. Both Catholic and Protestant theologians had begun working on this before Medellín, but it was that conference that set the tone for an inculturated theology that could grapple with the challenges of social change. Shortly after Medellín Peruvian theologian Gustavo Gutiérrez wrote *A Theology of Liberation.*[11] This landmark publication caught the tenor of the forces of social change in Latin America. It quickly became clear that it captured the imagination of theologians and church workers everywhere who were dealing with problems of poverty, oppression and, exclusion.

These four factors, then, set the stage for the development of contextual theologies, beginning in the 1970s.

THE DEVELOPMENT OF CONTEXTUAL THEOLOGIES FROM THE MID-TWENTIETH CENTURY

In the 1970s and 1980s contextual theologies developed along two tracks that often intersected: seeking a genuine Christian *identity* in the cultural context, and responding to *social change* from the perspective of the gospel.

Contextual Theologies as Seeking Christian Identity

One the one hand, there were contextual theologies that focused especially on issues of *identity.* This was a response to one of the defining features that drew attention to context in the first place. As was seen earlier, there was a strong sense in the churches in Latin America, Africa, Asia, and the South Pacific that the theology that was coming out of Europe did not speak to their concerns. This European theology either provided answers to questions no one was asking, or failed to address the pressing issues that local churches had. This was especially the case in countries that were gaining their independence from European colonization in this same period. The theology that had been given them was rooted in Western cultures. Those same Western cultures, as colonizers, had denigrated their local cultures, implying that to become Christian one had to relinquish

---

[11] Gustavo Gutiérrez, *A Theology of Liberation: History, Politics, and Salvation* (Maryknoll, NY: Orbis Books, 1973). The Spanish-language original was published in 1971.

those cultures and adopt European ways of thinking. Likewise, with independence many of these countries (especially in Africa and parts of Asia) wanted to steer a political path between liberal capitalism, on the one hand, and communism, on the other, which at that time defined geopolitics. Many sought a "third way" between capitalism and communism, echoing the "third-world" vision that had marked the conference of "non-aligned" nations held in Bandung, Indonesia, in 1955. In Tanzania, for example, President Julius Nyerere spoke of *ujamaa* as such a third way, while Leopold Senghor in Senegal spoke of *negritude*. Theologies that followed this call tried to build an interpretation of the Christian message using local cultural and social categories. Examples of such efforts in Africa would include the work of Ugandan theologian John Mbiti, Congolese theologian Benezet Bujo, and Japanese theologian (working in Thailand) Kosuke Koyama.[12] Alongside such efforts, books appeared that worked with the anthropological and sociological categories that could help shape a theology in its cultural context.[13]

Contextual theologies in postcolonial contexts were not the only kinds of theologies of identity that were emerging at this time. Especially in the United States, feminist theologies began to appear, appealing to women's experiences as the basis for doing theology beyond the male, patriarchal perspective. These theologies addressed not only cultural issues of how gender was understood, but issues of needed social change in line with the liberation theologies of Latin America.[14]

Also in the United States at this time theologies focusing on race and liberation appeared among Protestant African American theologians. A leader throughout this period has been James Cone, whose publications span half a century.[15] In turn, the work of Cone and other US African American theologians influenced the "black theology" that developed in South Africa that focused upon the struggle against apartheid in that country.

The voices of Hispanic/Latinx theologians in the United States began to be heard in the 1970s as well. The leading figure on the Catholic side was certainly Virgilio Elizondo, whose work on *mestizaje* (the mixing of

[12] John Mbiti, *African Religions and Philosophy* (Nairobi: Heinemann, 1969); Benezet Bujo, *African Theology in Its Social Contexts* (Maryknoll, NY: Orbis Books, 1992); Kosuke Koyama, *Waterbuffalo Theology* (Maryknoll, NY: Orbis Books, 1974).

[13] On the Protestant side, see especially Charles H. Kraft, *Christianity in Culture: A Study in Dynamic Biblical Theologizing in Cross-Cultural Perspective* (Maryknoll, NY: Orbis Books, 1979); on the Catholic side, see Robert Schreiter, *Constructing Local Theologies* (Maryknoll, NY: Orbis Books, 1985).

[14] An important figure throughout this period was Rosemary Radford Ruether. Among her many works, see especially *Sexism and God-Talk: Toward a Feminist Theology* (Boston: Beacon Press, 1983).

[15] James Cone, *A Black Theology of Liberation* (Philadelphia: Lippincott, 1970) has remained a classic work in African American theologies.

Spanish and indigenous identities) and popular religion set the stage for a flourishing of theologies from that period on into the present.[16]

Later, in the early part of the 2000s, queer theologies followed a similar trajectory, focusing on issues of identity and distinctness as well as themes of liberation from discrimination and exclusion.[17]

Notable in all of these theologies of identity—feminist, black, latinx, and queer—is that themes of identity and social change or liberation merge. We will return to this theme later. But for now, we need to look at contextual theologies that focus on social change.

Contextual Theologies Seeking Social Change: The Theologies of Liberation

As we have already seen, the see-judge-act methodology of the Young Christian Workers helped launch a new approach to the question of social action based on a reading of the context and a reading of the gospel. This methodology found a fertile location in the turmoil of Latin America in the 1960s and 1970s. What was needed was a way to look at all the dimensions of social change; a way of analyzing persistent social issues such a grinding poverty, discrimination, exclusion, and misuse of power; how the scriptures throw light upon these realities; and what would be Christian responses to these challenges. What became obvious is that all these social forces could not be looked at in isolation from one another; one needed a comprehensive analytic method or tool to lay bare the patterns of power and oppression behind these social realities. The early focus was especially on economic and social factors: What were the causes of poverty? What made poverty persist? How did the use of economic and social power twist human relationships to create and sustain unjust patterns in society? Of the comprehensive critiques of society that had emerged since the Industrial Revolution in Europe, the work of Karl Marx stood out in an important way for its keen analysis of the exploitation of workers in the new industrial arrangements that emerged in the nineteenth century. Other models—such as those of Max Weber in Germany or sociological models such as those developed by Talcott Parsons in the United States—did not exhibit the same incisive power. Marx's early work in the 1840s, prior to his 1848 *Communist Manifesto*, about the dehumanizing features of the emergent capitalism was of special interest to those seeking a vision of a more humane existence under what capitalism had become. To be sure, the social projects based on Marxian analysis that were attempted in the

---

[16] See, for example, Virgilio Elizondo, *The Future Is Mestizo: Life Where Cultures Meet* (Oak Park, IL: Meyer-Stone Books, 1988). This has been an influential work.

[17] For example, Marcella Althaus-Reid, *Indecent Theology: Theological Perversions in Sex, Gender, and Politics* (London: Routledge, 2000).

twentieth century (Soviet Communism, Maoism in China, smaller social-
ist movements elsewhere) raised legitimate questions about the adequacy
of his analysis. Latin American scholars were more interested in Marx's
analysis of worker oppression than the prescriptions for a new society that
people like Lenin or Stalin or Mao had drawn from them. Theologians
also heard behind Marx's analysis the voices of the great Hebrew prophets
who had spoken out against the oppression of the poor by the rich and
the powerful. (Marx's father had converted to Christianity from Judaism
as part of a strategy of assimilation found in the German-speaking world
of the early nineteenth century.) Some scholars have found the general
shape of Marx's thought to be a kind of secularized version of Jewish and
Christian eschatology. The privileging of the perspective of the poor and
the oppressed (in the scriptures, as especially beloved of God) certainly had
biblical resonance, as Gutiérrez pointed out in A Theology of Liberation.
Jesus's own charter for his ministry, as recounted in the synagogue incident
in Nazareth in Luke 4, carries these same resonances. While a few Latin
American theologians utterly embraced Marx, the great majority found
in his work its actual antecedents in the prophetic traditions of the Bible.

Thus, a focus on the sufferings of the poor and oppressed peoples, and
what might count as liberation from this oppression into the fullness of
human life, shaped the methodology of contextual theologies that focused
especially on social change. From these origins in Latin America, theologies of liberation spread rapidly to South Africa, among the low-caste and
no-caste peoples of India (where it came to be known as *dalit* theology),
and in the struggles for democracy in South Korea (the *minjung* theologies). Indeed, the theologies of liberation in all their different forms and
locations were perhaps the most prominent forms of contextual theologies
through the rest of the twentieth century. Efforts were made to develop
liberation theologies in Europe and the United States as well, and many
theologians, students, and church workers closely identified with the
struggles of their counterparts in Latin America, Africa, and Asia. These
attempts gave voice to oppressive situations in those parts of the world
but never gained the cachet that they experienced in what would come
to be called the "two-thirds world" (that is, where two-thirds of world's
population lived) or the "global South" (as opposed to the global North,
the home of capitalism and empire).

Theologies of liberation experienced two sets of distinctive challenges
in the 1980s and the 1990s. When these theologies had begun in Latin
America in the 1960s and 1970s, nearly every country in Latin America
was under some form of military rule, where political power had been
seized from democratically elected leadership. This provided a powerful
context for theology as a site of resistance to these violent and often ruthless
juntas. By the end of the 1980s nearly all of these countries had returned
to some form of democratic rule. Democracy came after more than two
decades of dictatorship in South Korea in the 1980s. Apartheid (at least

as a political reality) ended in South Africa in 1994. While poverty and forms of social oppression still remained, the loss of such concrete objects of resistance made maintaining the struggle in its original form more difficult. In the grassroots communities which in many countries had been powerful sources of resistance, people turned their attention from political struggle to other ways of bettering their lot. Not coincidentally, Pentecostal forms of faith began spreading rapidly in parts of Latin America and coastal regions of Africa at that time. The rapid economic growth in South Korea seemed to muffle the militant voices of the *minjung* movement. All of these events showed how deeply context shapes these theologies of social change. When social change does indeed come (however imperfectly, for much poverty, alienation, and oppression still remain), the shape of these theologies has to change.

The second set of challenges to the theologies of liberation came from within the churches, especially the Roman Catholic Church as regards Latin America. Before that time the church was often closely allied with the wealthy sector of society, an arrangement that went back to colonial times when colonization and Christianization often went hand in hand. The "irruption of the poor," as it was so graphically called in Latin America, challenged those social arrangements and alarmed those holding ecclesiastical power. Although there were bishops who stood in solidarity with the poor, the Vatican under Pope John Paul II and his Prefect of the Congregation of the Faith, Cardinal Joseph Ratzinger (who would succeed Pope John Paul II as Benedict XVI in 2005) worked to stop theologies of liberation. The concern was not just a shift in ecclesiastical power; there were theological concerns as well. It was felt that the prophetic dimensions of liberation theology owed more to Marxist revolutionary thinking than the prophetic tradition of the Bible; that liberation theology sought too much salvation in this-worldly change; that the anthropology at the basis of liberation theologies was built on antagonism between the classes rather than a vision of *koinonia* or communion. All of these points would be debated by those for or against the theologies of liberation, but it gave the church authorities the basis for action against this kind of contextual theology. Bishops were named who took a strong anti-liberationist stand. The major theologians of liberation all came under scrutiny and in some cases were silenced. Institutions teaching theology from the perspective of liberation theology were shut down.

In the 1990s and the first decade of the twenty-first century efforts were undertaken to reorient theologies of liberation, especially in Latin America. Theologians there reexamined their work and made some important adjustments. Most notably, the plight of indigenous peoples on the continent had never received the attention that working-class people and peasants had received. This was now righted, as a *teologia india* or *teologia indigena* was developed to complement what liberation theologies had been doing. In Africa, theologians such as Charles Villa-Vicencio in

South Africa and Kenyan theologian Jesse Mugambi proposed theologies of reconstruction. Both tried to maintain the prophetic energies of the theologies of liberation but suggested that the efforts required a new focus on what kind of social change was needed. In the case of South Africa, now that apartheid was being overcome, the guiding biblical metaphor for theology would no longer be the Exodus story, where God led the Hebrews out of slavery, but rather would be the story of the return from Exile and the need to rebuild the Temple and Jerusalem. Mugambi suggested that the focus of social change should be shifted away from apartheid to Africa's current problems, such as corruption, lack of democracy, and alleviation of poverty.[18] In a somewhat similar manner Francophone theologians of Western Africa had been doing this combination of cultural identity and social change for quite some time.[19]

A significant part of the energy that once guided theologies of liberation found a new focus in anti-globalization movements. Globalization appeared to many as the successor to the colonial empires that had shaped the previous generation of theologies of cultural identity and social change—and there are great continuities. Some of this theology has been given voice in a second generation of postcolonial theologies. The first generation, as we have seen, worked to find a "third way" between Cold War ideologies. This second generation mapped out more clearly the enduring effects of the colonization that continues in what might be called a "colonization of the mind" that continues to haunt the life and theology of formerly colonized peoples today. That analysis is enriched also by race and gender studies that have grown since the 1970s.[20]

The voices of the theologies of liberation continue to be heard in venues such as the World Social Forum, founded in 2001 as an alternative to the World Economic Forum, which meets in Davos, Switzerland. The World Social Forum is a space where anti-globalization movements, initiatives in social and ecological justice, and other alternative movements seek to show that another world is possible, that is, one in which the vision of social change found in the contextual theologies of liberation might be realized.

---

[18] Charles Villa-Vincencio, *Toward a Theology of Reconstruction: Human Rights and Nation Building* (Cambridge: Cambridge University Press, 1992); J. N. K. Mugambi, *Christian Theology and Social Reconstruction* (Nairobi: Acton Publishers, 2003).

[19] Among the most widely known of these in English were the Cameroonian theologians Engelbert Mveng and Jean-Marc Ela. The political dimensions of their theologies were costly to them; Mveng was assassinated, and Ela ended his years in exile.

[20] See, for example, the work of Susan Abraham, *Identity, Ethics, and Non-Violence in Post-Colonial Theory: A Rahnerian Assessment* (New York: Palgrave Macmillan, 2007).

MAPPING CONTEXTUAL THEOLOGIES:
THE WORK OF STEPHEN B. BEVANS

Is there a way of making sense of, or ordering, the many different approaches to contextual theology that have developed since the 1970s? A book by US theologian Stephen Bevans in 1992 provided a way of mapping the array of contextual theologies that had grown up in the world up to that time. In 2002 he published an expanded and revised edition of the book that reflected developments since the first edition. It remains one of the most widely used sources for understanding the various contextual theologies that have been mentioned so far and how they relate to one another.

Models of Contextual Theology provides six models of how theology and context have been related since the rise of contextual theologies in the 1970s.[21] Bevans uses *model* in a sense similar to that of Avery Dulles, whose book *Models of the Church* brought this way of thinking into theology, defining a model as "a relatively simple, artificially constructed case which is found to be useful and illuminating for dealing with realities that are more complex and differentiated."[22] A little earlier, anthropologist Clifford Geertz had made a distinction between "models of" and "models for": "models of" provides a framework of describing a phenomenon, and "models for" offers also implicit guidelines for evaluating a given phenomenon in light of similar phenomena.[23] Bevans explicitly moves between these two meanings of models and notes too that the use of one model does not preclude working with other models as well. Models, as Dulles had put it, are artificial constructions; they do not exist in pure form in reality. But they help us guide our thinking and make differentiations in a more responsible way.

The first of Bevans's six models is called the *translation model*. Here attempts are made to translate the divine revelation into terms intelligible to one's interlocutors. Paul's speech in Athens on the Areopagus (Acts 17:16–32), in which Paul tried to communicate Hebrew realities into Hellenistic terms, is an example of this. A translation-model approach lay behind many of the early attempts at contextual theology in the twentieth century. It was especially strong in Protestant circles, where the missionary task was seen first of all as a translation of the Bible into the local language. Indeed, that was behind the earliest usage of the term *contextual theology;* it was a translation of the (biblical) text into a new con-text. This seldom meant a literal word-for-word translation. Rather, following the

---

[21] Stephen B. Bevans, *Models of Contextual Theology* (Maryknoll, NY: Orbis Books, 1992; revised edition, 2002). For his most recent thought on the models, see Bevans, *Introduction to Theology in Global Perspective*, 167–88.

[22] Avery Dulles, *Models of the Church* (Garden City, NY: Doubleday, 1974), 30.

[23] Clifford Geertz, *The Interpretation of Cultures: Selected Essays* (New York: Basic Books, 1973), 87–125.

growing sophistication of translation in linguistic circles, it was an attempt at "dynamic equivalence," that is, a translation that captured the wider resonances of the original text inside the world of the hearer. A translation model approach to contextual theology is often still the first attempt at a contextual theology that is plied by the outsider to a culture trying to make sense of the biblical message in a new setting.

The *anthropological model* is a second approach to contextual theology. Here one tries to correct or somehow overcome the shortcomings of the translation model by shifting the emphasis away from the speaker to the hearer. The emphasis is on the cultural integrity of the one receiving the message, which may mean that the message being communicated may in the first instance end up looking very different from what the speaker had intended. An early example of this is Justin Martyr, who in the second century spoke of the "seeds of the word" being planted in different soil. The seed is the authentic revelation, but the shape it takes as it grows will be shaped by the soil in which it has been planted. The anthropological model was used especially by theologians who wanted to use the language and thought categories and patterns of a local people to bring forth a new yet authentic presentation of the Gospel. Theologians such as José de Mesa in the Philippines, Diego Irarrázaval in Peru, and Laurenti Magesa in Tanzania are examples of how to use the anthropological model.[24]

The *praxis model* is the third model that Bevans presents. If the anthropological model focuses especially on issues of cultural identity and authenticity, the praxis model tries to capture the dynamics of cultural change. The word *praxis* has different meanings, but here it is most often meant to represent the dynamic of action and thought in tandem. Action is always informed by some existing pattern of thinking. When action is analyzed, these patterns of thought should come to fore and, in turn, be changed by the experience of action itself. Hence, action and thought mutually qualify, challenge, and develop each other. The theologies of liberation discussed earlier are perhaps the best examples of this. The prophetic Christian message demands action. And that action returns us also to reflecting once again on that message. This approach to contextual theology is, then, in constant dialogue with the changing social situation in which Christians find themselves.

Bevans's fourth model, the *synthetic model*, might be considered an attempt to keep the dynamics of the previous three models in constant relation with one another. The emphases of each of these models—the integrity of the gospel message, the dignity and authenticity of the culture to which the gospel message is addressed, and the need to confront the social

---

[24] José de Mesa, *Doing Theology: Basic Realities and Processes* (Quezon City: Claretian Publications, 1990); Diego Irarrázaval, *Inculturation: New Dawn of the Church in Latin America* (Maryknoll, NY: Orbis Books, 2000; Laurenti Magesa, *Anatomy of Inculturation: Transforming the Church in Africa* (Maryknoll, NY: Orbis Books, 2004).

environment with the message of the gospel—can, by themselves, become one-sided and miss the important emphases of the other approaches. Bevans suggests that another name for the synthetic model might be a "dialogical model," since it emphasizes holding the values of all three of these models together. US theologian David Tracy's understanding of theology as conversation would be an example of this approach, working toward what he calls "mutual critical correlation" of revelation and human experience.[25]

The fifth model Bevans presents is the *transcendental model*. At first sight this may sound confusing, in that calling something transcendental implies that it rises above or beyond context. In his later reflections Bevans has suggested that it might also be called a *subjective model,* that is, it strives to refine and express the subjectivity and the authenticity of the one doing theology.[26] The use of the philosophical vocabulary of the transcendental can be traced back to Kant, who sought to have the human subject be the sole agent of genuine thinking, unencumbered by other influences. One might question whether this model really can travel out of its own cultural confines—a Western and Kantian heritage. Nonetheless, the theology that has flowed from this concentration on human subjectivity has been immensely influential in Roman Catholic circles, with thinkers such as the German Karl Rahner and the Canadian Bernard Lonergan among its users. Whether human subjectivity sorts itself out in transcendental reduction in the same way across cultures remains a contested point. Nonetheless, the widespread use of such an approach needs to be taken into any consideration of contemporary theology.

The sixth model Bevans proposes is called the *countercultural model*, something he first proposed in the second edition of his book on models. This model acknowledges the importance of the cultural context in which theology is being done, but unlike the previous ones, is highly critical of the context in which it finds itself and wonders whether such a culture can be a partner to the theological process without substantial revision. This model can be seen in theologies that are highly critical of Western modernity (such as Radical Orthodoxy), or what is perceived as the church's "Constantinian compromise" with European civilization that has blunted the true message of the gospel about "the world."[27] In its highly critical stance toward European modernity, it is somewhat reminiscent of the legacy of Karl Barth, but it genuinely engages the world it criticizes rather than simply dismissing it.

---

[25] David Tracy, *Plurality and Ambiguity: Hermeneutics, Religion, Hope* (San Francisco: HarperSanFrancisco, 1987).

[26] Bevans, *Introduction to Theology in Global Perspective*, 182.

[27] See, for example, the charter text of the Radical Orthodoxy movement, John Milbank, *Theology and Social Theory: Beyond Secular Reason* (Oxford: Basil Blackwell, 1990). The Gospel and Our Culture Network is an important resource for this countercultural approach (www.gocn.org).

Bevans's models are extremely helpful in sorting out some of the methodological issues of contextual theologies, regarding the relative weight to be
given to the partners in the theological enterprise: revelation and tradition,
culture, experience, identity, and social change. They are not intended to
be the final word on any of the attendant issues, but they do offer a way
of seeing the range of potential interactions of these important elements.

THE FUTURE OF CONTEXTUAL THEOLOGIES

In his study of contextual theologies Stephen Bevans not only asserts
that every theology is contextual (as we have seen). He goes on to say that
doing theology from a contextual perspective is a "theological imperative."
That is the guiding message of his *Introduction to Theology in Global
Perspective*. Contextual theologies, in all of their many forms, have been
with us as a conscious project for nearly half a century. What might be
said here in conclusion about the future of contextual methods?

First of all, as a global church or world Christianity comes more and
more into focus, we are constantly confronted with the unity and plurality
of the Christian reality. How are we to affirm unity and plurality at the
same time? Here the theological understanding of the incarnation plays an
important role. The Word Made Flesh did not assume a generic humanity
but took on flesh and blood in a certain time and place. But even within
the limits of such an incarnation, the fullness of divinity can be revealed.
That should say to us that culture and context are not simply an acciden-
tal envelope for a greater substance, but that accident and substance are
always given together. A human being utterly devoid of culture is no longer
a human being. Likewise, cultures are fluid, changing realities—perhaps
even more so in a time of nearly instantaneous communication and connection. We live in a "liquid" reality, as the Polish sociologist Zygmunt
Bauman has said.[28] Thus, social change—and social issues—impinge upon
the contextual nature of theology ever more.

What has been said thus far shows how changing contexts call for shifting approaches to understanding and engaging contexts and, therefore, how
theology is done. The theologies of liberation have undergone significant
change as the social contexts they wished to address have changed. The
same could be said for theologies focusing on cultural identity. After the
early attempts to ascertain Christian identity in non-Western contexts,
Europe discovered the possibility of doing contextual theology as a means
of revitalization of the churches facing secularization there. At the turn of
the twenty-first century, countries in Europe that had been under Soviet occupation turned to contextual theologies to reconstruct a public theology

---

[28] Zygmunt Bauman, *Liquid Modernity* (London: Polity, 2000).

where religion had been brutally suppressed.[29] So changing contexts will always call forth new efforts in contextual theology.

Contextual theologies have already been grappling with the phenomenon of globalization and all of its many consequences, both positive and negative. From a perspective focusing upon Christian heritage, "catholicity" has become a renewed effort to deal with this issue of the global reality in which we find ourselves.[30] The theologies growing out of the World Social Forum and among postcolonial writers keep on the track of the profoundly negative effects of globalization in the world today. Within that, themes such as migration, multicultural societies, growing economic inequality, discrimination, trafficking, consequences for the environment, and other spin-offs from the tide of globalization will continue to need theological attention. As the contexts and the issues within and among contexts change, so too will the lenses focused upon the Christian message. And as we have seen in the case of some of the North American theologies and also in post-apartheid South Africa, focus on cultural identity and social change is more commonly undertaken together. This is a point that has been made recently by Henning Wrogemann.[31]

A second front for contextual theologies is the interaction of Christianity with other religious traditions. Tensions both among and within religious traditions need a closer attunement to context. The world, it appears, is more religious than it was a quarter-century ago, with positive and negative extremes of religiosity and religious belonging making themselves felt. The interaction of the intercultural and the interreligious will need greater attention.

One final point may be made. Contextual theologies often began in local contexts, local communities. The local has been attenuated by the global, and their interaction must continue to engage our attention. One new form of the local has emerged as of this writing. This is the local becoming identified with populism. This kind of local tries to cut itself off from the larger social realities around it. If history proves any guide here, the recrudescence of such militancy will betray the basic Christian message. We have seen this most recently among the so-called German Christians in Germany in the 1930s.

To reiterate Stephen Bevans here, contextual theologies are a theological imperative for Christians in our time. Not to attend to this is to not take the incarnation seriously as our theological premise and to underestimate the breadth and depth of a genuine Catholicity.

---

[29] These are reflected in the introduction to the German translation of *Constructing Local Theologies* in the case of church revitalization, and in the introduction to the Russian translation of the same work for the former Soviet bloc countries.

[30] See Bevans, *Introduction to Theology in Global Perspective*, chap. 9.

[31] Henning Wrogemann, *Intercultural Hermeneutics* (Downers Grove, IL: InterVarsity Press, 2016).

Chapter 7

From Ecclesiology in Europe to Contextual Theology for the World

Thomas F. O'Meara, OP

After a century marked by two horrendous world wars and by constant social alteration and scientific discovery, Christian reflection and community are still called to live in the midst of change. Despite an absence of ecclesiastical direction, Roman Catholics continue to draw currents of contemporary culture into theology, ecclesiology, social ethics, and liturgy.

WORLD AS SUBJECTIVE AND CULTURAL REALITY

Modern thought changed the meaning of the term *world*. A world was not just unfettered nature or a monarchical realm but the existence and milieu of the person. Reflection creates subjectivity: the subject has its world. Around 1800, Friedrich Schlegel said that the new modern world revolved around three things: the structures of the knowing self, freedom, and history. The self fashions, interprets, and expands the reality it knows. Walter Kasper writes: "European thought is determined by two basic possibilities. The first is a thinking proceeding from being, essence, nature, fact; the second begins with freedom understood as an activity disclosing the world."[1] Not an assembly of objects like trees and bears but the forms of the human spirit, a world influences how people think and live through natural science, styles of art, psychology, and religions in history. Martin Heidegger wrote: "World is not the mere collection of things at hand that are either calculable or not, known or unknown.

---

[1] Walter Kasper, "Verständnis der Geschichte in der Theologie," *Theologie im Wandel* (Munich: Wewel, 1967), 112.

119

World is never an object that just stands before to be looked at. . . . World
is always the non-objectifiable before which we stand."[2]

After 1790, the Roman Catholic Church saw itself threatened by what
was modern, such as analytic psychology, democratic society, and the
theory of evolution. Nonetheless, in the first half of the nineteenth century
there were Catholic theologians who developed theologies from the ideas
of Friedrich Schelling, G. W. F. Hegel, and others.[3] These, for instance,
restored Pauline and patristic perspectives of the Christian community
as a charismatic and ministerial organism. And too, Romantic Idealism
accepted a positive history of human religions before and outside Christianity. If in the nineteenth century the Vatican began to repress Catholic
usages of what was modern and worked to have neo-Scholasticism replace
every philosophy and theology with neo-Aristotelian metaphysics, Catholic thinkers like French Dominicans and German Jesuits still pursued a
dialogue with modern thought ranging from economics to sculpture.[4] In
the 1950s, however, ecumenism, modern mosaics in churches, liturgical
renewal, and movements to aid the working class emerged to offer new
directions, although most found censorship from Vatican bureaucrats.
Vatican II brought two new dynamics together: Christianity outside of
Europe and history. Looking at the council Yves Congar—his life work
was to research and present the historical forms of the church—summarized as follows:

> Everything is absolutely historical including the person of Jesus
> Christ. The Gospel is historical. Thomas Aquinas is historical, Pope
> Paul VI is historical. Historical does not mean just that Jesus came
> at a certain point in time but that one must draw the consequences
> of this fact: he is thoroughly conditioned by the time in which he

---

[2] Martin Heidegger, *Der Ursprung des Kunstwerkes* (Stuttgart: Reclam, 1960),
44, 56.

[3] See Thomas F. O'Meara, *Romantic Idealism and Roman Catholicism: Schelling
and the Theologians* (Notre Dame, IN: University of Notre Dame Press, 1982);
Church and Culture: German Catholic Theology, 1860 to 1914 (Notre Dame, IN:
University of Notre Dame Press, 1991). Bevans's historical sections pay attention
to modern periods.

[4] See Paul Philibert and Thomas O'Meara, *Scanning the Signs of the Times:
French Dominicans in the Twentieth Century* (Adelaide: ATF Theology, 2013).
M.-D. Chenu's book on the theological school developed by the French Dominicans around a study of Thomas Aquinas and other theologians in their historical
periods—*Une École de théologie: Le Saulchoir* (Étiolles: Le Saulchoir, 1937)—was
condemned by the Vatican in 1942 precisely because it saw cultural history as the
context of a particular theology of an age and not as a perennial scholasticism
(see Paul Philibert, "M.-D. Chenu," in Philibert and O'Meara, *Scanning the Signs
of the Times,* 23–24).

lives. He develops like every other man; his consciousness grows, his knowledge expands.[5]

The dynamic self is subjectivity as world-creating through new forms within a cultural history.

Today's expressions of Christian revelatory grace employ approaches from modern thinkers.[6] Goethe said: "Each person in his or her interior experience is an entire world history."[7] Today's theologians would expand that, to say that each person shares in the religious history of the human race through the cultures of the globe. Transcendental analysis and historicity illumine the realms of grace and faith. The underlying and active ground of the Holy Spirit is at work in ministries, liturgies, and in the expression of the Christ-event in languages quite removed from Aramaic, Greek, and Latin.

Contemporary theology has set goals that are variously local and daringly universal. It sees beyond the past ethos of seminaries and ecclesiastical institutions and faces challenges created by continents of peoples, for in feudal or exclusivist forms the church is not credible, and in a provincial or xenophobic community it is not seen and heard. The starting points (either stated or implicit) of vital currents in Christian theology in the West are ways of expressing experience or analyzing existence in life and in society.

THE CONTEXTUAL THEOLOGY OF STEPHEN B. BEVANS

Stephen Bevans has pursued a contemporary theology of a world church that begins with a view of Christianity as a global missionary enterprise. His subject is the world, not the world of mental forms or of nature but the global world, expanding, disclosing. His book *An Introduction to Theology in Global Perspective*[8] provides a fundamental theology for this project; it interprets the gospel in different cultures through contextual theologies treating revelation and religion, faith and theology, and Catholic

---

[5] Jean Puyo, *Jean Puyo interroge le Père Congar: Une vie pour la vérité* (Paris: Le Centurion, 1975), 43.

[6] See Martin Heidegger, "Zeit und Sein," *Zur Sache des Denkens* (Tübingen: Niemeyer, 1969); see also O'Meara, "The History of Being and the History of Doctrine: An Influence of Heidegger on Theology," *American Catholic Philosophical Quarterly* 69 (1995): 351–74.

[7] Cited in Gerhart Baumann, ed., *Goethe, Lektüre für Augenblicke* (Frankfurt am Main: Insel, 1982), 63.

[8] Stephen B. Bevans, *An Introduction to Theology in Global Perspective* (Maryknoll, NY: Orbis Books, 2009). A global theology in today's words is treated in Bevans, "What Has Contextual Theology to Offer the Church of the Twenty-First Century?" in *Contextual Theology for the Twenty-First Century*, ed. Stephen Bevans and Katalina Tahaafe-Williams (Cambridge, UK: James Clarke, 2012), 3–17.

perspectives. This theology begins not with God or Jesus but with the local and global church. Global theology has its own historical course, from the New Testament and the patristic and medieval periods through the nineteenth century to Catholic life after Vatican II.[9] It has brought together Eastern Christian, Protestant, and Modern European approaches.

This fundamental theology leads to the perspective of *Models of Contextual Theology*.[10] Models come from philosophical and structural forms; they come from representative people like monks, foreign missionaries, or founders of caritative societies; they come from cultural periods. Here particular attention is given to contemporary models like translation, anthropological focus, praxis, and transcendental realization. For instance, the model of translation shows some necessity but also its limitations in presenting the gospel message in a new language with a few new concepts and words. All cultures do not have the same structure as each receives the gospel into a grammar. Sacrament and word are not simply transposed into a further language; they need to enter that language and pass to its depth born of the life and community of others. A second model, anthropological focus, recognizes the value of the human person amid relationships and meanings where God is already present, offering guidance and life. Paul teaches out of several cultures and models and presumes that this teaching will illumine and not reject peoples' histories. *Constants in Context: A Theology of Mission for Today* goes beyond abstract models to look at church in mission.[11] Constants can be ecclesiology, eschatology, and Christology, while the contexts are cultural, historical, and political. Theologies go beyond past devotional types like saving souls to new (or sometimes, ancient) ones of discovering the truth and commitment in liberation and transformation. Different emphases express seminal themes like the missions of the Trinity, liberating service for the reign of God, and the proclamation of Jesus as savior. These writings of a late-modern, global theology are born of historical analysis but with a contemporary missionary imagination.

To complement a fundamental theology and an analysis of models Bevans organized a *summa, A Century of Catholic Mission*.[12] It is not a

---

[9] Andrew Walls summed up: "Christianity began the twentieth century as a Western religion, and indeed *the* Western religion; it ended the century as a non-Western religion, on track to become progressively more so" ("From Christendom to World Christianity" [March 31, 2001], cited in Bevans and Tahaafe-Williams, *Contextual Theology for the Twenty-First Century*, 64).

[10] Stephen B. Bevans, *Models of Contextual Theology* (Maryknoll, NY: Orbis Books, 1992). A frequent exposition of statistics in religions and populations serves a global theology.

[11] Stephen B. Bevans and Roger Schroeder, *Constants in Context: A Theology of Mission for Today* (Maryknoll, NY: Orbis Books, 2004).

[12] Stephen B. Bevans, *A Century of Catholic Mission* (Oxford: Regnum Edinburgh Centenary, 2015).

collection of past citations but an assembly of contemporary experts from every continent and several generations. Informed by meetings on church and mission around the world, the authors have original, distinctive views of mission as local church in theory, and praxis. This collection, although ecumenical in wide senses, stresses Catholic identity seeking God's presence in cultures. For instance, Christianity has been present in Africa for almost two millennia. Efforts toward African theologies have been focused on Jesus Christ and liberation, but now Africa is showing its own ethical and ecclesial forms. "The church in Africa is faced with different problems from those which face most churches in Europe, America or elsewhere. . . . Africans are attempting to grapple with these problems, and to relate the Gospel to the practical issues, whether social and political, or cultural and liturgical, which confront them."[13] Other essays turn to Asia with perspectives and programs drawn from the conferences of Asian bishops. They seek to go beyond the "dialogue–mission conundrum."[14] These writings and this theology are resources for the church not as legislator but as learner. They are not first scholarly research into a biblical theme but a study of people and social forms in the present time. This is a recognition of the approaches of social forms and stages of education. Education and learning is life, existence, encounter with the world.[15]

Cultural contexts, theological constants, and new models are the frameworks for developing a theology of mission and local church. The past Roman Catholic predilection for administration has evolved into a spectrum of cultures, and the scholastic insistence on a single language has yielded to families of languages and ritual systems. The theological library has become a resource center with active perspectives. A previous ecclesiastical rejection of all ideological rivals has become a dialogue with (and an incarnation of) currents in human religions.[16]

THE CHURCH IN LATE MODERNITY

Contextual theologies from around the world are assisting churches immersed in their cultures. Is this a postmodern development?

It is not clear what *postmodern* means. That term began with architecture, where it is clearly seen in color and decoration going beyond

---

[13] Ibid., 22.

[14] Ibid., 222. See Edmund K. Chia, *Edward Schillebeeckx and Interreligious Dialogue: Perspectives from Asian Theology* (Eugene, OR: Pickwick Publications, 2012).

[15] See Thomas Krobath, "Kirche als lernendes System im Veränderungsprozess der Organisationsgesellschaft," in *Kirche: Lernfähig in die Zukunft?* ed. Thomas Krobath et al. (Innsbruck: Tyrolia, 1998), 131–40.

[16] See Bevans, "Introduction," in *An Introduction to Theology in Global Perspective,* 1–8.

rectangles of glass and chrome set upon a barren square of concrete, the secular palaces of modernity. In other areas, however, from philosophy to music, the postmodern turns out to be the intensification of the modern already present for decades. Mark Taylor's influential books on postmodern art and religion draw on the same sources (Nietzsche, Heidegger) to offer the same abstractions, the same termination in linguistics, and the same drive to be radical.[17] Roman Catholicism can hardly be entering a postmodern period, because it has accepted modern dynamics into its thinking and life for only fifty to eighty years. The struggle in that church for participation in political life and religious reflection, themes from the mid-eighteenth century, are still in their beginning stages. Today's cultural milieu is, at best, late modernity: a more intense or parodist expression of recent forms. Postmodernity, whether in the analysis of a poem or installation art, focuses on the piece, the fragment, the segment. It is critical of influential historical periods and of what is inclusive and systematic. Broad narratives inevitably meet a revisionist limitation or dissection.

A comprehensive and yet multicultural church-of-mission holds themes of historical unfolding, cultural variety, and creative thought forms that are congenial to Catholicism, rooted in sacramentality, communion, and ongoing incarnation.[18] Contemporary Catholic thinking is still pondering historical shifts of intensity. For instance, the ministerial structure of the church is moving from the Baroque and medieval to the contemporary diversity that resembles the church of the first centuries. The institution of the papacy, reluctant or not, is undergoing several highly influential changes in its social structure fashioned through the dynamics of democracy and media. A global theology in its dialogues meets large forms of religion and liturgy; it needs not to revise the past but to move beyond it into new

---

[17] Mark Taylor, *Disfiguring: Art, Architecture, Religion* (Chicago: University of Chicago Press, 1992); idem, *Erring: A Postmodern A/Theology* (Chicago: University of Chicago Press, 1984).

[18] John Paul II and Benedict XVI expended considerable effort to halt the presence of modern forms like participation in teaching and the expansion of ministry. Despite a rhetoric supporting Vatican II, they sought to return to the church of their boyhoods and seminary education. One sees the past and its limitations in Joseph Ratzinger's words: "There is no way back to the spiritual situation which existed before the results of European thought spread to the whole world" (*The Ratzinger Report: An Exclusive Interview on the State of the Church* [San Francisco: Ignatius Press, 1985], 193). The "new evangelization" is provincial, aiming at conversions amid middle-class and middle-aged laity in the secular urban West (see Stephen B. Bevans, "Beyond the New Evangelization towards a Missionary Ecclesiology for the Twenty-First Century," in *A Church with Open Doors*, ed. Richard Gaillardetz and Edward Hahnenberg [Collegeville, MN: Liturgical Press, 2015], 12–21); on papal documents impeding theological dialogue with religions and bemoaning relativism, seminal religion, and so on, see Bevans, "Pope John Paul II," "Pope Benedict XVI," in *International Bulletin of Missionary Research* 29 (2005): 140–41.

cultural worlds. It cannot afford to cultivate a cluster of focused analyses before it develops new perspectives on the large themes of Christian faith and the directions of the immediate future. Nonetheless, when Western theologies, traditional or innovative, meet African and Asian sociologies and psychologies in cultures that are experiential and open to the transcendent, late variations on the modern may emerge. The incipient directions of a late modernity are bringing some perspectives that are new, or newly found.[19]

LOCATING THE CHRISTIAN FAITH

In the enterprise of global theologies grace and revelation are not simply "out there." A subject, a community, and a salvation history are their living locations.

First, the *subject* remains important—subject as community as well as individual. The dynamics of knowing and insight ponder the world and not just modernity's anxiety. The Christian faith is not exclusively located in a solitary believing subject or an ecclesiastical authority. Transcendental capabilities and thought forms flow from the ground of all that is known, and the subject expresses revelation and grace through the forms and themes of new cultural worlds. The Christian *ecclesia* is the social place of religion and faith. Theology is not mainly about individual justification or mysticism but about the church in a wide sense. Revelation is ongoing; history is salvation history. Word and grace are more than a Middle Eastern text, for revelation is an unfolding of the Spirit's presence in the lives of people. The theologian attempts "to conceptualize or bring to speech his or her experience of God in a particular spatial-temporal or cultural milieu."[20]

Second, the church is not a library or a basilica in Western Christendom but a creation of the Holy Spirit calling the *community* to live in the kingdom of God fully. The Spirit equips the church by empowering its members to be ministers for the times, and thereby the church becomes a community of Pentecost here and now.

---

[19] Themes that Bevans finds emerging with global theologies are not infrequently found in Terrence Tilley's survey, *Postmodern Theologies: The Challenge of Religious Diversity* (Maryknoll, NY: Orbis Books, 1995).

[20] Bevans, *Models of Contextual Theology*, 101. This is the human being described by Aquinas as one who "exists in a kind of horizon between time and eternity" (*Summa contra gentes*, 2, 81). Martin Grabmann wrote in the early twentieth century of Aquinas's relationship to his world: "Thomas stands in a vital sympathy with his culture, with the scientific and social directions and streams of his age. His cultural philosophy is not a conceptual apriorism but is oriented to living reality" (*Die Kulturphilosophie des Hl. Thomas von Aquinas* [Augsburg: B. Filser, 1925], 20); see Thomas F. O'Meara, "Thomas Aquinas and Modernity," in *Thomas Aquinas and Contemporary Thought,* ed. Richard Woods (Chicago: Dominican Publications, 1989), 1–23.

The church's presence, if it is participating in God's mission authentically, is always in a particular context, a particular culture, in a particular language with the advantages and limitations of a particular age....Christians today must recognize that first and foremost they share God's mission and recognize their service of the reign of God as constitutive of their identity as church.[21]

Ecclesiologies advocate the panoply of ministry and the participation of the baptized in decision making—activities, ancient as well as new, of increasing importance. A variety of futures offers a "rich world of Christianity with its resulting wealth of contextual theologies" and suggests "new agendas, new methods, new voices, and a new dialogue."[22]

Third, there is the *salvation history* of Christianity. Based on Enlightenment ideas of Western superiority, earlier theologies of mission from both Protestant and Catholic perspectives in the nineteenth and early twentieth centuries led to a disdain for local cultures and a demonizing of religions. Toward the end of the nineteenth century in colonial realms, however, a few European priests, diplomats, and scholars gave birth to a perspective free of elitist disdain. Louis Massignon (1883–1962) made known Islamic mystics who had marked similarities to some Christian contemplatives. Jules Monchanin (1894–1957), a priest of the diocese of Lyons, founded a monastery in the style of a Hindu Sanyassi; he was joined by Henri Le Saux (1910–73) and Bede Griffiths (1906–93). Hugo (Enomiya) La Salle (1898–1990) a German Jesuit, brought a similar approach of discipleship and dialogue to the milieu of Japanese Buddhism through Christian-Zen retreat and meditation.[23] Spirituality and mysticism, not Christology, introduced dialogue to religion. To journey with time is to enter a wider world, encountering faith, spirituality, and church in the languages of cultures. Positive directions from the past fifty years bestowed by theologies of inculturation and cultural dynamics have nourished ecclesial-cultural theologies moving forward into futures other than that of Europe. They go beyond themes like faith's doubt, God's knowledge, the problem of evil, the historicity of Jesus, or religious linguistics prominent in American universities, modern liberal Protestant theologies, and phenomenological religious studies. Liturgy, social action, personal witness, ethics including environmental issues and consumerism, and spirituality in the sense of a cultural or mystical

---

[21] Bevans and Schroeder, *Constants in Context*, 396–97.

[22] Bevans, "What Has Contextual Theology to Offer the Church of the Twenty-first Century?" 5; see also, Bevans "The Church as Creation for the Spirit," *Missiology: An International Review* 35 (2007): 6.

[23] See Thomas F. O'Meara, "Exploring the Depths," in *In Verantwortung für den Glauben* [Festschrift Heinrich Fries], ed. Peter Neuner and Harald Wagner (Freiburg: Herder, 1992), 375–90.

approach with its distinctive incarnation of grace in a psychology are prominent.[24]

Global meetings have changed and expanded the nature of interreligious dialogue. It is more than conceptual or verbal comparison, more than searching in foreign texts for a theodicy acceptable to the Christian West or for the natural law obeyed. Christians confess the uniqueness of Jesus Christ along with the Spirit's presence within the traditions and practices of other religious ways. The religious history of a continent over millennia holds not only religious truths but human realities touched by grace. Liturgies display a transcendent search made concrete in the faith and worship of many.[25] In global theology time is not a sacral antiquity but the cultural future, moving forward not simply through comparison but through imagination. The church's path, its healthy and graced journey, is within history. Yves Congar took as one of his themes the effort of Vatican II to bring back history as the vision and the communal dynamic of the church, a church long sunk in timelessness during recent centuries.[26] Central to a Catholic view of religions is that dialogue is about the presence of grace, not about the ideas of theodicy. In these dialogues local churches are important because they know their contexts and milieus.

THE GLOBAL FUTURE OF MODERN CHRISTIANITY

Reflections on a contemporary theology conceived on a global scale reveal the theme of *beginning*. Mission and missions, evangelists and ministers live in the atmosphere and energy of a beginning. "Our time calls forth a church that moves beyond what has been called the new evangelization to the formation of a community of missionary disciples. Ecclesiology for our time has to reflect that community's life and practice as it participates

---

[24] James Keenan's writings and symposia support the churches of Asia, Africa, and Latin America in pondering the shift in moral theology from axioms and conclusions for confessors to the Christian gospel realized in life and society: *Catholic Theological Ethics in the World Church: The Plenary Papers from the First Cross-Cultural Conference on Catholic Theological Ethics* (New York: Continuum, 2009); *Catholic Theological Ethics, Past, Present, and Future: The Trento Conference* (Maryknoll, NY: Orbis Books, 2011).

[25] Karl Rahner wrote that a self-revelation of God as a free, gracious event is given at all times. God's self-communication permeates human existence, being encountered and accepted by men and women in different ways so that everywhere, history is the history of salvation and of revelation (see "Revelation," *Theological Dictionary* [New York: Herder and Herder, 1965], 410–11).

[26] Yves Congar, "Situation ecclésiologique au moment de 'Ecclesiam Suam' et passage à une église dans l'itinéraire des hommes," in *Le Concile de Vatican II: Son Église, Peuple de Dieu et corps du Christ,* ed. René Rémond (Paris: Beauchesne, 1984), 27.

in the mission of God."[27] Karl Rahner wrote of the incipient nature of trans-European ecclesiologies and spiritualities. "Admittedly we have only weak and indistinct ideas of how a community formed by the new Spirit of love of God and love of neighbor will appear in the concrete . . . , how it will express communal worship and be neither a department store of holiness or a cosy sect rejecting the world."[28] The arrow of time discloses itself on earth and in the cosmos only as going forward.

Inculturation and expansion vitalize the body of Christ so that it can be the community and voice of the kingdom of God. For the sake of its future the church is summoned now into an ecclesiology and format that is more than modern and incipiently global.

---

[27] Bevans, "Beyond the New Evangelization towards a Missionary Ecclesiology for the Twenty-First Century," 21–22.

[28] Karl Rahner, "The New Image of the Church," *Theological Investigations*, vol. 10 (New York: Seabury, 1977), 26–27.

Chapter 8

Christian Theology, Empire, and Race in North America

Leo D. Lefebure

The work of Stephen Bevans is a model of compassionate discernment and reflection on the contextual challenges of proclaiming Christian faith. Bevans properly insists that theologians attend to the specific details of a particular local context while also being aware of the global horizon of our reflection: "Theology today needs to be done in a dialogue with one's own contextual perspective and the broad and deep tradition of the Christian church, and in a dialogue as well with the results of this interaction and the perspectives of Christians from every part of our world."[1] Bevans notes a paradox that challenges all theologians today: "To do theology from a global perspective, ironically, is to look to the local."[2] Bevans proposes a model for doing theology that draws upon the strengths of various approaches, listening carefully to the many voices of the Christian tradition in a local situation while remaining aware of the global horizon. This essay seeks to honor the many contributions of Stephen Bevans by reflecting on the paradoxes and problems of the history of Christian faith, empire, and race in the context of North America.

In North America, as in many places around the globe, Christian theology inherits a tragic history of involvement in empires and racial discrimination that brought unspeakable suffering to countless persons. Often persons claiming to follow Jesus Christ combined the proclamation of the gospel with the conquest, domination, and enslavement of other peoples. In North America as elsewhere, some Christian leaders supported the brutal imposition of imperial and racial domination, with the result

---

[1] Stephen B. Bevans, *An Introduction to Theology in Global Perspective* (Maryknoll, NY: Orbis Books, 2011), 4.

[2] Ibid., 187.

that the credibility of the gospel message was put in jeopardy. Nonetheless, subaltern populations in North America learned to distinguish the emancipating message of Jesus Christ from the unjust practices of their oppressors. One of the greatest paradoxes in the history of Christian thought is that marginalized and oppressed peoples frequently understood the liberating message of the gospel better than the dominant powers that brought Christianity to their region. The newly evangelized often had much to teach the evangelizers. This ambiguous heritage continues to shape our contemporary horizon, offering both challenge and encouragement to Christian faith and practice today.

NEW WORLDS, NEW CHALLENGES

While there were many forms of imperial domination in antiquity, the ancient world did not have a conception of race or a practice of racial discrimination in the modern sense of these words; racial categories and discriminatory practices based on them emerged in the late medieval and early modern period of European imperial expansion in the context of the conquest, domination, and enslavement of peoples around the world. George M. Frederickson locates the birth and development of modern racism in the expansion of European colonial powers beginning in the fifteenth century. He finds difference and power at the core of racism: "It originates from a mind-set that regards 'them' as different from 'us' in ways that are permanent and unbridgeable. This sense of difference provides a motive or rationale for using our power advantage to treat the ethnoracial Other in ways that we would regard as cruel or unjust if applied to members of our own group."[3]

For centuries the Spanish and Portuguese had viewed the Reconquista of the Iberian Peninsula as a just war, since the Muslims had invaded the Iberian Peninsula at an earlier time. They believed that prisoners captured in a just war, especially those viewed as infidels, like the Muslims, could be legally enslaved. After the Spanish had driven the Moors out of Spain, the voyages to the Caribbean changed history dramatically and posed new theological challenges. Many Spanish believed that divine providence was guiding their discoveries and conquests. As the Spanish brought their traditional combative mentality to the New World,[4] there were fierce debates concerning the justice of their treatment of the indigenous peoples. To justify the mistreatment and enslavement of indigenous peoples, many Spaniards viewed the inhabitants of the Americas as lazy idolaters who had no rights. As Gonzalo Fernández de Oviedo y Valdés explained:

---

[3] George M. Frederickson, *Racism: A Short History* (Princeton, NJ: Princeton University Press, 2003), 9.

[4] Luis N. Rivera, *A Violent Evangelism: The Political and Religious Conquest of the Americas* (Louisville, KY: Westminster/John Knox Press, 1992).

They are naturally lazy and vicious, melancholic, cowardly, and in general a lying, shiftless people. Their marriages are not a sacrament but a sacrilege. They are idolatrous, libidinous, and commit sodomy. Their chief desire is to eat, drink, worship heathen idols, and commit bestial obscenities.[5]

However, not all were persuaded. On the last Sunday of Advent in 1511, Dominican friar Antonio Montesino preached a sermon denouncing the Spanish abuses:

Tell me, by what right or justice do you keep these Indians in such cruel and horrible servitude? . . . Why do you keep them so oppressed and weary, not giving them enough to eat, nor taking care of them in their illnesses? For with the excessive work you demand of them, they fall ill and die, or rather you kill them with your desire to extract and acquire gold every day. . . . Are these not men? Have they not rational souls? Are you not bound to love them as you love yourselves? Be certain that in such a state as this, you can no more be saved than the Moors or Turks.[6]

Gustavo Gutiérrez notes that Montesino weaved together themes from the Law of Nations and the gospel of Jesus Christ: "The various questions of Montesino's homily are interconnected, of course. But the one that recalls the Indian's quality as 'neighbor' to the Spaniards, which the missioners see as entailing a duty to love, is the furthest-reaching question, and the one that gives meaning to the others."[7] Bartolomé de Las Casas tells us that many were astonished at Montesino's message but "no one, so far as I have heard, converted."[8] However, Las Casas himself began to reflect in new ways on the *encomienda* system, and by the time of the Spanish conquest of Cuba in 1513 he became a strong critic of its violence, continuing and developing the concerns of Montesino.

In 1550–51, Las Casas famously defended the full humanity of the Indians against Ginés de Sepúlveda in a major theological debate over the humanity of the Indians of the Americas. Walter D. Mignolo comments that the debate concerning "'rights of the people' was the first legal attempt (theological in nature) to write down a canon of international law, that was reformulated in a secular discourse in the eighteenth century as

---

[5] Cited by Stephen Neill, *A History of Christian Missions,* revised for the second edition by Owen Chadwick (New York: Penguin Books, 1990), 146.

[6] Cited in ibid., 145; see also Gustavo Gutiérrez, *Las Casas: In Search of the Poor of Jesus Christ,* trans. Robert R. Barr (Maryknoll, NY: Orbis Books, 1993), 28–31.

[7] Gutiérrez, *Las Casas,* 31.

[8] Cited by Gutiérrez, *Las Casas,* 31.

the 'rights of men and of the citizen.'"[9] Tragically, this debate concerned only Amerindians, not enslaved Africans: "Amerindians were considered vassals of the king and servants of God; as such they, theoretically, could not be enslaved. They were supposed to be educated and converted to Christianity. African slaves were not in the same category: they were part of the Atlantic 'commerce.'"[10] While Emperor Charles V had decreed the debates, there was no formal decision, but Sepúlveda's side lost support in the subsequent years. Stanley L. Robe comments on the result: "The Indian was no longer a Wild Man in the official view. No other colonial power undertook such an examination of the relationship of the conqueror to the conquered in its overseas territories."[11] However, Luis N. Rivera notes that even though Las Casas sharply criticized the abuse of the American Indians, he did not advocate for their full independence but rather for a more benevolent but still paternalistic care over them: "The relationship of these free peoples with the Crown should be similar to that of the free cities of Europe and Spain, which recognize the emperor as their ultimate sovereign, without such an authority canceling their autonomy and powers for self-determination."[12]

Las Casas had definite flaws. One of the most controversial aspects of his career is that for a time he tragically approved of importing enslaved Africans to the Americas to replace Indians as workers in the mines and elsewhere. Lawrence A. Clayton comments that "Las Casas was thinking of African slavery as he knew it from his childhood, growing up in Seville and its environs. It was not the degrading form of plantation slavery later developed by European planters in other parts of the Americas."[13] Clayton notes that Las Casas later turned sharply against slavery, "long before the morality of the slave trade—and African slavery in the Americas itself—was challenged by abolitionists almost two hundred years later."[14] Gustavo Gutiérrez notes that in about 1547 Las Casas read reports about the actual conditions of enslaving persons in Africa, and this turned his attitude sharply against the slave trade, leading him to become the first leader of his time to denounce slavery: "What Las Casas perceives around the middle of the sixteenth century is that the injustice

[9] Walter D. Mignolo, *Local Histories/Global Designs: Coloniality, Subaltern Knowledges, and Border Thinking* (Princeton, NJ: Princeton University Press, 2012), 29.

[10] Ibid., 30.

[11] Stanley L. Robe, "Wild Men and Spain's Brave New World," in *The Wild Man Within: An Image in Western Thought from the Renaissance to Romanticism,* ed. Edward Dudley and Maximillian E. Novak (Pittsburgh: University of Pittsburgh Press, 1972), 47.

[12] Rivera, *A Violent Evangelism,* 65.

[13] Lawrence A. Clayton, *Bartolomé de las Casas and the Conquest of the Americas* (Malden, MA: Wiley-Blackwell, 2011), 138.

[14] Ibid.

committed against the Africans is of the same nature as that suffered by the Indians. There is no justification for enslaving these peoples."[15] By 1550, Las Casas had become the prototype of the abolitionist. Despite his tragic flaws and limitations, the example of Las Casas stands as a protest against the horrors that were done to the Indian populations; Gustavo Gutiérrez has interpreted Las Casas as a Christian "in search of the poor of Jesus Christ."[16]

THE DEVELOPMENT OF RACIAL DISCRIMINATION IN THE COLONIAL PERIOD IN NORTH AMERICA

In the centuries that followed the establishment of the Spanish and Portuguese empires, a number of other European countries along the Atlantic Ocean successively conquered and ruled much of the remainder of the world. The global course of empire continued to be accompanied by both Christian missionaries and the development of modern racist assumptions. Christian faith came to play multiple and conflicting roles in the tortured history of racial relations in colonial North America and the United States of America. In principle, Christian faith calls its followers to respect every human life as created in the image and likeness of God (Gen 1:26–27), and Jesus's parable of the Good Samaritan makes clear that the command to love one's neighbor applies to members of communities that are disrespected or despised (Lk 10:25–37). Yet from colonial times to the present, Christians of European descent in North America all too often embraced racist perspectives and engaged in forms of racial injustice. While the dominant powers often failed to see the contradiction between these practices and Christian faith, American Indians and African Americans frequently did.

In the British colonies in North America, Europeans, Africans, and American Indians encountered one another in an unprecedented situation, often marked by conflict and violence. As a result of the new contacts, countless American Indians died of unfamiliar diseases brought by European settlers, including smallpox, measles, mumps, chicken pox, and influenza.[17] In the wake of the demographic collapse, Europeans imported enslaved Africans to provide needed labor.[18] Earlier generations of American historians traditionally highlighted the contributions of English settlers who came to Virginia and New England and downplayed the roles of American

---

[15] Gutiérrez, *Las Casas,* 329.

[16] Ibid.

[17] Daniel K. Richter, *Before the Revolution: America's Ancient Pasts* (Cambridge, MA: Belknap Press of Harvard University Press, 2011), 143–47.

[18] Hugh Thomas, *The Slave Trade: The Story of the Atlantic Slave Trade: 1440–1870* (New York: Simon and Schuster, 1997).

Indians and enslaved Africans in shaping the new society. More recently, historians have recognized the vital importance of what happened to the Indian and African populations.[19]

Historian Alan Taylor comments on the crucial role that race played in shaping identities in colonial America: "Over time, race loomed larger— primarily in British America—as the fundamental prism for rearranging the identities and the relative power of the many peoples in the colonial encounters. A racialized sorting of peoples by skin color into white, red, and black was primarily a product, rather than a precondition of colonization."[20] He stresses the unimaginable scale of the suffering of the victims of this process: "More than minor aberrations, American Indian deaths and African slaves were fundamental to colonization. The historian John Murrin concludes that 'losers far outnumbered winners' in 'a tragedy of such huge proportions that no one's imagination can easily encompass it all.'"[21]

Racialized slavery developed in North America during the period from 1650 to 1700. Before this time the Spanish and Portuguese had enslaved Africans on plantations in the Caribbean and Latin America. The rationale for slavery during the Reconquista of the Iberian Peninsula from the Moors was that it was just to enslave captives who were not Christian and who were captured in a just war. As Spanish and Portuguese forces defeated Muslim armies, they enslaved some of the population. However, it was much harder to claim the conquest of populations in the New World was a just war.

While some Spanish monarchs tried to end slavery in the Americas, their decrees were never fully enforced, and forced labor continued throughout the Spanish colonies. For a while some English opposed this practice, and Sir Francis Drake tried to free enslaved Africans in Central America in the 1570s and 1580s. Drake hoped to bring enslaved Africans from Spanish-ruled Santo Domingo and Cartagena to the new foundation at Roanoke, invite them to become Protestant Christians, and treat them better than the Spanish had done. Drake hoped to establish a beacon of English-sponsored liberty to attract others from Spanish-ruled areas. The Africans appear to have been lost in a storm at sea, the colony at Roanoke was deprived of supplies from England because of the threat of the Spanish Armada, and so the colony disappeared by 1590. While Drake's effort offers an intriguing window onto "what might have been," greed would later render English

---

[19] Ronald Takaki, *A Different Mirror: History of Multicultural America* (Boston: Little, Brown and Co., 1993); Roxanne Dunbar-Ortiz, *An Indigenous Peoples' History of the United States,* ReVisioning American History Series (Boston: Beacon Press, 2014).

[20] Alan Taylor, *American Colonies,* The Penguin History of the United States, ed. Eric Foner (New York: Penguin Books, 2001), xii.

[21] Ibid., xi.

slavery even worse than the Spanish forms.[22] In time, the English and the Dutch began using enslaved Africans in the Caribbean to produce sugar, because this was highly profitable.[23]

At first much of the labor in the North American English colonies was supplied by indentured servants from England who came under a contract to labor for a set period of time; at the end of this time they would be free and often were promised tools or land to start independent living. However, in the middle and later part of the seventeenth century, it became more difficult to recruit indentured servants because England endured the great Civil War (1642–51), which killed large numbers of people, and then the Great Fire in London in 1666, which killed many more and also created the need for labor to rebuild the city. To supply the needed labor to North America, some began the new practice of "kidnapping," that is, seizing young men and forcing them to go to the colonies as indentured servants; however, English authorities prescribed strict penalties for this. The English tried to enslave Indians, but they could escape more easily and this practice made relations with Indian nations more difficult.

To resolve the difficulty, the English began importing Africans. Between 1600 and 1670, the status of Africans in North America was fluid. After King Charles II returned to the throne of England in 1660, he authorized the Royal African Company to ship enslaved Africans to his colonies; he also authorized the establishment of Carolina in order to challenge the Spanish in Florida and the Caribbean. After 1670, English settlers came to North America from Barbados with enslaved Africans.

As we have seen, the earlier justification for enslaving people was based not on racial theory but on the principles for a just war against infidels. North Americans developed a new race-based rationale for slavery between 1650 and 1700 in what Peter Wood has called "the terrible transformation." Wood identifies three main causes. First, the lower classes began allying across color lines since they had common grievances. Those in forced labor often outnumbered the wealthy and possessed arms. There was an uprising in Virginia in 1676 that dramatically demonstrated this threat. Authorities realized that they needed to divide the lower-class labor force of whites from Indians and Africans, and racialized slavery fit the need.

Second, there was negative feedback if the wealthy mistreated English indentured servants; word would get back to England, and abusive masters would have difficulty finding new laborers. Mistreated Indians could run away or find a way to tell other Indians. But Africans had no possibility of establishing a feedback loop. White sailors would not carry messages for Africans, and so they had no way of communicating with their family and friends in Africa. As a result, Africans were much more vulnerable to mistreatment than whites or Indians.

---

[22] Peter H. Wood, *Strange New Land: Africans in Colonial America* (Oxford: Oxford University Press, 2003), 16–18.

[23] Ibid., 25–27.

The third factor involved a shift from basing the right to enslave on religion to the claim to be enslaving an inferior race. Wood comments: "Increasingly, the dominant English came to view Africans not as 'heathen people' but as 'black people.' They began, for the first time, to describe themselves not as Christians but as whites. And they gradually wrote this shift into their colonial laws."[24] Thus, instead of English viewing themselves as Christians and Africans as "heathen," there developed a color-coded system of identity: people were now identified as white, red, or black.

During this same period there was a shift in the status of children born to a parent who was a slave. According to English common law, a child born to a slave followed the status of the father. This was followed in the case of Elizabeth Key in Virginia in 1655: "By the Comon Law the Child of a woman slave begot by a freeman ought to bee free."[25] Seven years later the Virginia Assembly reversed the Common Law of England, ruling that a child born to an enslaved woman would follow the status of the mother. This ruling set a precedent that was imitated elsewhere and had a massive impact on the entire later history of slavery in North America.

As British settlers constructed new forms of identity at a distance from the class system of their homeland, they increasingly turned to racial discrimination to justify their domination over American Indians and Africans. This resulted in greater equality for lower-class whites, but it condemned generations of American Indian and African Americans to a systematically subordinate position: "British colonial elites gradually accepted a white racial solidarity based upon subordinating 'blacks' and 'reds.' Once race, instead of class, became the primary marker of privilege, colonial elites had to concede greater social respect and political rights to common white men."[26] As British colonists developed the rhetoric of freedom and equality, they intended it to apply to free white males, not to American Indians or enslaved Africans; nonetheless, the claims of universal human freedom and equality for all would remain a challenge for all later generations, down to the present. This development is part of a broader pattern in modern European political philosophy. In the nineteenth century John Stuart Mill would write very influentially on liberty; he also followed closely the British activities in India. Mill divided humans into those who could govern themselves and those who could not. He believed that those with lighter skin color could govern themselves and those with darker skin color, whether from Africa or India, could not; this claim justified representative government for the English and colonial domination of the non-European world.[27]

---

[24] Wood, *Strange New Land,* 32.

[25] Ibid., 32.

[26] Taylor, *American Colonies*, xiii.

[27] Lisa Lowe, *The Intimacies of Four Continents* (Durham, NC: Duke University Press, 2015), 111–18.

CHRISTIAN FAITH AND RACIAL RELATIONS

As a racialized society developed in North America, Christian faith came to play a variety of often contradictory roles. Many European Christians viewed American Indians as following abominable religious practices. Puritans in New England saw the indigenous inhabitants as barbarous savages practicing cannibalism, lacking humanity, and thus having no legal claim to the land they in which they had always lived.[28] Puritans saw themselves as the new Israelites on an "errand in the wilderness," and thus viewed New England as their Promised Land, with the American Indians cast in the role of the Canaanites. While they sought to evangelize the American Indians, Puritans also wanted to be rid of them, which on occasion led to massacres of civilian populations: "The pressure of demographic expansion, coupled with the psychological fear of acculturation, moved the Puritans toward a policy of exterminating the Indians or, at best, reducing them to a semicaptive status on strictly and narrowly delimited reservations (called, at that time, praying towns)."[29]

While some abused Christian faith to justify coercion in colonial America, Roger Williams from the beginning dissented from the Puritan approach and challenged such oppressive practices. Surveying the bitter history of religious conflicts in Europe since the time of Constantine, he concluded that imposing religious loyalties was a violation of the Gospel of Jesus Christ. Williams interpreted Jesus's parable of the wheat and the weeds (Mt 13:24–30) as forbidding Christians to attack those with whom they disagreed.[30] Williams daringly judged Emperor Constantine, who legalized Christianity in the Roman Empire, to have been more of a danger than his predecessor Nero, who had persecuted Christians. Under Nero, Christians had heroically suffered and died; with Constantine, Christians took power, became corrupted, and began to impose Christianity by governmental authority.[31] Williams argued that it was unjust for the king of England to pretend to have the right to give away lands where American Indians had lived for centuries. For Williams, the fact that Native Americans had different religious practices did not deprive them of their right to their homeland.[32] After the Puritans banished Williams from Massachusetts as a dissenter in 1635, he moved south, where he purchased land from American Indians and established a new community, Rhode Island, as a

---

[28] Richard Slotkin, *Regeneration through Violence: The Mythology of the American Frontier, 1600–1860* (Norman: University of Oklahoma Press, 1973), 38.

[29] Ibid., 42.

[30] James P. Byrd Jr., *The Challenges of Roger Williams: Religious Liberty, Violent Persecution, and the Bible* (Macon, GA: Mercer University Press, 2002), 9.

[31] Ibid., 114–15.

[32] Edwin S. Gaustad, *Roger Williams*, Lives and Legacies (Oxford: Oxford University Press, 2005), 24–26.

"haven for the cause of conscience," founded on the principle of religious liberty for all. Even though the Puritans strongly opposed his establishment of religious freedom or, in his phrase, "soul liberty," his example would stand as an inspiration for later Americans.[33]

To support the development of racialized slavery in the New World, many Christians interpreted the so-called curse of Ham in the Book of Genesis as a basis for the enslavement and subordination of all persons of African descent (Gen 9:20–27).[34] According to Genesis, after the great flood Noah planted a vineyard, made wine, drank too much, and lay down naked in his tent, apparently in a drunken stupor. His son Ham reportedly looked upon him and then told his brothers Japheth and Shem about the situation. Respecting their father, Japheth and Shem took a garment and walked backward into the tent to cover their father without looking upon him in his naked, shameful state. When Noah recovered and learned of what happened, he cursed, not Ham, but rather Canaan, the son of Ham: "'Cursed be Canaan; lowest of slaves shall he be to his brothers.' He also said, 'Blessed by the Lord my God be Shem; and let Canaan be his slave. May God make space for Japheth, and let him live in the tents of Shem; and let Canaan be his slave" (Gen 9:25–27). Later generations identified Shem as the ancestor of Semitic peoples in the Middle East, Ham as the ancestor of Africans, and Japheth as the ancestor of Europeans.

In the text of Genesis there is no stated reason for Canaan to be cursed for the misconduct of his father, Ham. More important, the passage does not explicitly authorize what white Americans interpreted it to mean: there is no indication that all the descendants of either Ham or Canaan were to be enslaved for centuries to come. Moreover, Canaan is just one of Ham's four sons; another son, Cush, was traditionally viewed as the ancestor of black Africans, while Canaan was thought to be the ancestor of the Canaanites; and there is no indication in Genesis that the other sons of Ham or their descendants were to be enslaved. Nonetheless, white Americans repeatedly identified themselves as the descendants of Japheth and cited the alleged curse of Ham as justification for them to enslave any person of African descent.[35]

Not all American Christians agreed with this interpretation. In 1700, Samuel Sewall, a Boston lawyer, noted that Noah's curse did not fall on

[33] Edmund S. Morgan, *The Church and the State*, 2nd ed. (New York: W. W. Norton, 2007).

[34] There was enslavement of American Indians as well, though the large majority of enslaved persons were of African descent. See Andrés Reséndez, *The Other Slavery: The Uncovered Story of Indian Enslavement in America* (Boston: Houghton, Mifflin, Harcourt, 2016).

[35] E. Brooks Holifield, *Theology in America: Christian Thought from the Age of the Puritans to the Civil War* (New Haven, CT: Yale University Press, 2003), 496; Stephen R. Haynes, *Noah's Curse: The Biblical Justification of American Slavery* (Oxford: Oxford University Press, 2002).

Ham but rather on Canaan. Sewall argued that Canaan was not the an-cestor of Africans at all but rather, as his name suggests, of the ancient Canaanites. Moreover, Sewall stressed the decisive authority of the golden rule of Jesus as forbidding slavery.[36] In response, another Boston lawyer, John Saffin, cited precedents for slavery in the Hebrew Bible as alleged proof of its legitimacy. Saffin insisted that enslavement gave Africans the benefit of hearing the truth of Christian faith and accepting it.[37] This debate did not receive much attention for the next seventy years, but by the late eighteenth century it was vigorously renewed and continued until the American Civil War, with evangelical Protestants in particular prob-ing questions of biblical hermeneutics and arguing over the principles for deciding which biblical texts had greater authority.[38]

AMERICAN INDIAN AND AFRICAN AMERICAN CHRISTIAN LEADERS

The racist attitudes and practices of many white Christians severely hindered the proclamation of the gospel in North America. Nonetheless, a number of American Indians and African Americans came to embrace Christian faith. The First Great Awakening beginning in the 1730s was the decisive moment when Christian faith began to appear as a liberating, live option for these populations. The preaching of Jonathan Edwards, George Whitefield, and many other Protestant leaders presented Christian faith as a vivid personal experience of recognition of sin and grace, preaching that all humans are caught in sin and all are freed by God's grace apart from any merit of their own. In contrast to Europe, where established state churches were the norm, in North America the numerous Protestant dissenting movements were the dominant forces shaping society. The Great Awakening encouraged a focus on strong personal experience and a distrust of long-established hierarchies. The challenge to established hi-erarchies was one factor shaping the context of the American Revolution against Great Britain.

Protestant preaching based on what Mark Noll calls the "imperial Bible," that is, "the sacred book of an expanding Protestant Britain," had multiple effects. Preachers in the First Great Awakening could quote the imperial Bible to support Protestant Christendom against French Catholics, but Noll emphasizes that the biblical rhetoric of liberty was unpredictable: "By giving a scriptural sanction to ideals of liberty and virtue against the

---

[36] Holifield, *Theology in America*, 495.
[37] Ibid.
[38] Mark A. Noll, *The Civil War as a Theological Crisis* (Chapel Hill: University of North Carolina Press), 50. See also idem, *In the Beginning Was the Word: The Bible in American Public Life, 1492–1783* (Oxford: Oxford University Press, 2016), 248–54.

French, it [the imperial Bible] anticipated a soon-coming day when Scripture would sanction ideals of liberty and virtue against the British."[39] Of great importance was the liberating potential for oppressed groups: "The decline of Protestant Christendom also had the revolutionary effect of liberating Scripture for populations exploited, enslaved, or marginalized by the very structures of Christendom."[40]

The newfound religious enthusiasm was very appealing to the American Indian and African American populations that had traditionally been marginalized. American Indians came to participate in Christian worship services in unprecedented numbers. When American Indians accepted Christianity, they did not completely leave behind their earlier views and practices. Linford D. Fisher comments that "Indians had long incorporated new ideas and practical skills alongside old ones, often without intending to drop, remove, or alter the existing ones. This would strongly suggest that Native Americans, whether individually or communally, rarely 'converted' in some sort of totalizing way, as is often assumed."[41]

The vivid emotions of the revival meetings appealed to enslaved Africans, who could find a resonance with their African heritage. Albert J. Raboteau comments: "Drawing upon the worship traditions of Africa, as well as those of revivalistic Christianity, the slaves created services that resembled the spirit-empowered ceremonies of their African ancestors. Both traditions assumed that authentic worship required an observable experience of the divine presence."[42] American Indians and African Americans could emerge as preachers inspired by their own religious experience. By the end of the eighteenth century a tradition of African American Christianity was taking root. Often Christian communities were the only place in society where African Americans could challenge racial prejudices and exercise roles of leadership.

CONFLICTING PERSPECTIVES
IN THE NINETEENTH CENTURY

Many European Americans in the eighteenth and nineteenth centuries saw their nation as uniquely blessed by God with a divine mandate to spread freedom and democracy around the world. Many Americans went so far as to claim a millennial role for the United States as a "redeemer nation," destined to bring freedom, democracy, and liberty to the entire

---

[39] Noll, *In the Beginning Was the Word*, 204.

[40] Ibid.

[41] Linford D. Fisher, *The Indian Great Awakening: Religion and the Shaping of Native Cultures in Early America* (Oxford: Oxford University Press, 2012), 88.

[42] Albert J. Raboteau, *Canaan Land: A Religious History of African Americans* (Oxford: Oxford University Press, 2001), 45.

world.[43] The vision of peace, however, would sometimes require might of arms to establish and defend it.

In the nineteenth century American Indian and African American leaders pointed out that this exalted self-understanding was based on the oppression of other peoples, and they forcefully challenged the combination of white racism and Christian faith. In 1831, Maria Stewart, an African American Christian leader who was an eloquent spokesperson for the rights of all, especially African American women, linked Christianity to the cause of freedom and challenged white Americans:

> America, foul and indelible is thy stain! Dark and dismal is the cloud that hangs over thee, for thy cruel wrongs and injuries to the fallen sons of Africa. The blood of her murdered ones cries to heaven for vengeance against Thee. . . . You may kill, tyrannize, and oppress as much as you choose, until our cry shall come up before the throne of God; for I am firmly persuaded, that he will not suffer you to quell the proud, fearless and undaunted spirits of the Africans forever; for in his own time, he is able to plead our cause against you, and to pour out upon you the ten plagues of Egypt.[44]

Two years later, in New England in 1833 Methodist minister and theologian William Apess from the Pequot nation issued an analogous challenge to the racist assumptions of the white churches:

> Now let me ask you, white man, if it is a disgrace for to eat, drink, and sleep with the image of God, or sit, or walk and talk with them. Or have you the folly to think that the white man, being one in fifteen or sixteen, are the only beloved images of God? Assemble all nations together in your imagination, and then let the whites be seated among them. . . . Now suppose these skins were put together, and each skin had its national crimes written upon it—which skin do you think would have the greatest? I will ask one question more. Can you charge the Indians with robbing a nation almost of their whole continent, and murdering their women and children, and then depriving the remainder of their lawful rights, that nature and God require them to have?[45]

---

[43] Ernest Lee Tuveson, *Redeemer Nation: The Idea of America's Millennial Role* (Chicago: University of Chicago Press, 1968).

[44] Maria W. Stewart, *Maria W. Stewart: America's First Black Woman Political Writer: Essays and Speeches,* ed. and intro. Marilyn Richardson (Bloomington: Indiana University Press, 1987), 39–40.

[45] William Apess, *On Our Own Ground: The Complete Writings of William Apess, a Pequot,* ed. and intro. Barry O'Connell (Amherst: University of Massachusetts Press, 1992), xiii; see also Philip F. Gura, *The Life of William Apess, Pequot* (Chapel Hill: University of North Carolina Press, 2015).

Even though most enslaved African Americans were not allowed to receive formal education, they expressed a lively and perceptive grasp of Christian faith in the spirituals. Often they sang of biblical images such as the freeing of the slaves in the Exodus or the crossing of the River Jordan as figures of liberation from slavery in America. The great twentieth-century African American theologian Howard Thurman describes the unshakable fundamental confidence of the spirituals: "God was the deliverer. . . . Daring to believe that God cared for them despite the cruel vicissitudes of life meant the giving of wings to life that nothing could destroy."[46] The spirituals expressed faith in a God of freedom: "In God's presence at least there would be freedom; slavery is no part of the purpose or the plan of God. Man, therefore is the great enemy of man."[47] Often the spirituals expressed a double meaning, one that would be apparent to the slaveholder and the other that would be recognized by those in chains. In the spirituals African Americans expressed their awareness that God was on their side: "They know from cruel experience that the Christian ethic has not been sufficiently effective in the life of the Caucasian or the institutions he controls to compel him to treat the Negro as a fellow human being. . . . The Christian ethic and segregation must forever be at war with each other."[48]

Many American Indians and African Americans made a sharp distinction between authentic Christianity and what was being promoted by the white racist leaders of the time. After completing the narrative of his life, noted African American leader Frederick Douglass worried that readers might think he was rejecting religion altogether, and so he offered a clarification in an appendix:

What I have said respecting and against religion, I mean strictly to apply to the *slaveholding religion* of this land, and with no possible reference to Christianity proper; for, between the Christianity of this land, and the Christianity of Christ, I recognize the widest possible difference—so wide, that to receive the one as good, pure, and holy, is of necessity to reject the other as bad, corrupt, and wicked. To be the friend of the one, is of necessity to be the enemy of the other.[49]

Similarly, Dakota Sioux leader Charles Alexander Eastman, known also by his Indian name Ohiyesa ("winner"), challenged the illusion that the United States was a modern Christian civilized nation and maintained that Christian faith was much closer to the indigenous American Indian

[46] Howard Thurman, *Deep River and the Negro Spiritual Speaks of Life and Death* (1975; reprint, Richmond, IN: Friends United Press, 1990), 15.

[47] Ibid., 44.

[48] Ibid., 49–50.

[49] Frederick Douglass, *Narrative of the Life of Frederick Douglass, an American Slave,* and Harriet Jacobs, *Incidents in the Life of a Slave Girl, Written by Herself* (New York: Modern Library, 2000), 107.

religious traditions than to so-called modern civilization: "It is my personal belief, after thirty-five years' experience of it, that there is no such thing as 'Christian civilization.' I believe that Christianity and modern civilization are opposed and irreconcilable, and the spirit of Christianity and of our ancient religion is essentially the same."[50] On one occasion Eastman encountered an older Indian who identified Jesus as an American Indian:

> I have come to the conclusion that this Jesus was an Indian. He was opposed to material acquirement and to great possessions. He was inclined to peace. He was as unpractical as any Indian and set no price upon his labor of love. These are not the principles upon which the white man has founded his civilization. It is strange that he could not rise to these simple principles which were commonly observed among our people.[51]

In presenting Christianity to other Indians, Eastman insisted on the distinction between authentic Christian faith and what the white Americans were doing: "My effort was to make the Indian feel that Christianity is not at fault for the white man's sins, but rather the lack of it, and I freely admitted that this nation is not Christian, but declared that the Christians in it are trying to make it so."[52]

As white Protestant Christians variously defended and attacked slavery during the early nineteenth century, these bitter controversies divided many white American Protestant churches into northern and southern branches.[53] Meanwhile, Catholic bishops did not play a decisive role in the debate. Pope Gregory XVI condemned the slave trade in 1839 in his apostolic letter *In supremo apostolatus fastigio*, but many American Catholic bishops and institutions owned slaves. Most American Catholic leaders stayed on the sidelines of the raging debates.[54] Some Catholic bishops in the South defended the institution of slavery. Bishop Auguste Martin of Natchitoches, Louisiana, issued a pastoral letter that justified slavery, referring to both the curse upon Canaan and the allegedly degraded status of Africans. The Congregation of the Index delegated Vicenzo Gatti, OP, to respond to the pastoral letter. Gatti pointedly rejected Martin's claim that

---

[50] Charles Alexander Eastman (Ohiyesa), *The Soul of the Indian* (1911; reprint, Mineola, NY: Dover Publications, 2003), 6; see also David Martínez, *Dakota Philosopher: Charles Eastman and American Indian Thought* (St. Paul, MN: Minnesota Historical Society Press, 2009).

[51] Charles Alexander Eastman (Ohiyesa), *From the Deep Woods to Civilization* (1916; reprint, Mineola, NY: Dover Publications, 2003), 81.

[52] Ibid., 84.

[53] Manisha Sinha, *The Slave's Cause: A History of Abolition* (New Haven, CT: Yale University Press, 2016).

[54] Cyprian Davis, *The History of Black Catholics in the United States* (New York: Crossroad, 1996), 39–66.

African Americans shared the curse of Canaan; Gatti questioned first of all whether they were actually Canaan's descendants, but he went on to insist that even if such a curse did exist, the redemption offered by Jesus Christ would have ended it. Gatti also chided Bishop Martin for claiming that blacks suffered from an "original degradation" from which whites were supposedly immune; Gatti reminded the bishop that original sin is strictly universal and argued that with education blacks could become equal to whites.[55] On December 17, 1864, Pope Pius IX approved Gatti's recommendation that Martin's pastoral letter on slavery be placed on the Index of Forbidden Books. By this time the American Civil War was nearly ended, and the papal ruling made little difference to the outcome of the struggle.

Some American Catholics, such as Orestes Brownson, criticized slavery while also expressing racist attitudes. Brownson, a firm opponent of slavery, spoke for many Catholics in both the North and the South in asserting:

> The inferior races, the yellow, the red, or the black, nearly all savage, barbarous, or semi-barbarous, are not . . . types of the primitive man. . . . They mark rather so many stages or degrees in human degeneracy. . . . The African negro is not the primitive man . . . but the degenerate man.[56]

European American Catholics generally shared the racism of American society at large, viewing African Americans and American Indians as inherently inferior.

The biblical debate over the legitimacy of slavery was resolved only on the battlefields of the American Civil War, which involved a strong theological dimension.[57] White racist attitudes survived the Civil War and the abolition of slavery, shaping the institution of the notorious Jim Crow laws, which systematically discriminated against African Americans throughout the South. White racism also led to the establishment of a reign of terror through the lynching of African Americans. White Christians often combined their interpretation of Christian faith with discriminatory beliefs and practices; but even in the period of widespread lynching during the late nineteenth and early twentieth centuries, African Americans continued to distinguish between Christian faith and the actions of European Americans who called themselves Christian. Like the authors of the spirituals, African American artists during this period interpreted the Bible in relation to the experiences of African Americans; European American Christian leaders, however, were generally oblivious to the parallel between the crucifixion

[55] Ibid., 56.

[56] Orestes Brownson, "Abolition and Negro Equality," cited in Davis, *The History of Black Catholics in the United States*, 61.

[57] Noll, *Civil War as a Theological Crisis*; Harry S. Stout, *Upon the Altar of the Nation: A Moral History of the American Civil War* (New York: Viking, 2006).

of Jesus Christ and the repeated lynching of African Americans. James H. Cone notes the irony that African American artists saw so clearly what European American Christian leaders could not:

> What enabled artists to see what Christian theologians and ministers would not? What prevented these theologians and ministers, who should have been the first to see God's revelation in black suffering, from recognizing the obvious gospel truth? Did it require such a leap of imagination to recognize the visual and symbolic overtones between the cross and the lynching tree, both places of execution in the ancient and modern worlds?[58]

Cone comments that singing, dancing, and shouting vividly expressed the paradoxical combination of "both the wretchedness and the transcendent spirit of empowerment that kept blacks from going under, as they struggled, against great odds, to acknowledge humanity denied."[59] The challenge was daunting: "On the one hand, faith spoke to their suffering, making it bearable, while, on the other hand, suffering contradicted their faith, making it unbearable."[60] While many whites in this period interpreted Christianity as supporting racist practices and perspectives, African Americans and American Indians repeatedly found support and hope in the promises of the gospel.

THE CIVIL RIGHTS MOVEMENT
AND THE CONTEMPORARY SITUATION

Ever since the eighteenth century, Christian communities had offered areas where African Americans could develop and exercise leadership and communication skills. So it is not surprising that in the twentieth century much of the leadership of the Civil Rights movement came from Christian pastors. As African American leaders looked for strategies of resistance to the dominant racism of their society, the influence of Mahatma Gandhi's practice of *satyagraha* ("grasping truth," that is, nonviolent resistance, stubbornness) was of great importance. In 1937, Howard Thurman led a delegation of African American leaders to India to meet Mahatma Gandhi. Thurman learned that Gandhi, like many African Americans and American Indians, made a distinction between the religion of Jesus and what British Christians were doing in India: "I close this section of my discussion with the rather striking words of Mahatma Gandhi to me: 'The greatest enemy

---

[58] James H. Cone, *The Cross and the Lynching Tree* (Maryknoll, NY: Orbis Books, 2011), 94.
[59] Ibid., 124.
[60] Ibid.

that the religion of Jesus has in India is Christianity in India.'"[61] Thurman and other African Americans studied Gandhi's practice of *satyagraha* and pondered its relevance for addressing racial discrimination in the United States. Thurman was a friend of Martin Luther King Sr., and the young Martin Luther King Jr. studied Thurman's work carefully. Paradoxically, it was a Hindu who opened the eyes of many Christians to the significance of Jesus's teaching for nonviolent resistance to social evil.[62]

Martin Luther King Jr. eloquently and powerfully combined a strong affirmation of the founding ideals of the United States with a biblical faith rooted in the tradition of African American Christianity. He spoke in a way that engaged the entire national community, delivering his most famous speech, "I Have a Dream," on August 28, 1963, to a large civil rights assembly in front of the Lincoln Memorial in Washington, DC.

The Civil Rights movement led to many victories, including the 1964 Civil Rights Act and the Voting Rights Act in 1965. Tragically, many whites continued to resist the call for racial justice, and Dr. King was assassinated in April 1968. While the Civil Rights movement profoundly transformed racial relations in the United States for the better, the events of recent years make clear that many challenges remain. More than fifty years after the signing of the Civil Rights and Voting Rights Acts, the United States is again in the midst of a major reassessment of racial relations on many levels. Many voices are challenging the judicial and policing practices that have led to the imprisonment or death of numerous African Americans. In the last few years the nation as a whole has become more aware of the practices of police officers toward African Americans, with many instances of injustice coming to public attention in a new way.

The Black Lives Matter movement organized demonstrations in many cities to protest racial injustice. On the evening of July 7, 2016, one such peaceful protest was under way in Dallas, Texas, when shots rang out, killing five police officers and wounding a number of other persons. The shooter was an African American military veteran who was enraged over the police shootings of African Americans and who wanted to kill white police officers in revenge. President Barack Obama spoke in Dallas after this particularly tragic shooting of police officers who were protecting an otherwise peaceful demonstration. Obama began by recalling a biblical perspective: "Scripture tells us that in our sufferings there is glory, because we know that suffering produces perseverance; perseverance, character; and character, hope. Sometimes the truths of these words are hard to see.

---

[61] Howard Thurman, "What We May Learn from India," in *American Religions: A Documentary History,* ed. R. Marie Griffith (Oxford: Oxford University Press, 2008), 496.

[62] Terrence J. Rynne, *Gandhi and Jesus: The Saving Power of Nonviolence* (Maryknoll, NY: Orbis Books, 2008).

Right now, those words test us."[63] Obama mentioned each of the slain police officers, praising their sense of commitment and duty to protect lives. Obama noted the deep concern felt by many Americans:

> "Faced with this violence, we wonder if the divides of race in America can ever be bridged. We wonder if an African American community that feels unfairly targeted by police, and police departments that feel unfairly maligned for doing their jobs, can ever understand each other's experience. [Nonetheless, the president sought to move beyond the seeming impasse:] I understand. I understand how Americans are feeling. But, Dallas, I'm here to say we must reject such despair. I'm here to insist that we are not as divided as we seem. And I know that because I know America. I know how far we've come against impossible odds."[64]

Americans of European descent are beneficiaries of an often invisible prejudice known as white privilege. While whites are frequently oblivious to the workings of this bias, they enjoy unearned gifts of credibility, trustworthiness, and access to resources that are all too often denied to persons of color and recent immigrants to the United States. As Jim Wallis comments, "Whether we or our families or our ancestors had anything to do with the racial sins of America's establishment, *all white people* have benefited from them. . . . *You can never escape white privilege in America if you are white.*"[65] Wallis challenges white Americans to work with persons of all backgrounds to cross a bridge to a more just America: "In the end, we can and must shed ourselves of our racial idols and divisions that have bound and separated us, and find our dignity together as the children of God all made in the image of the One who loves us all."[66]

The history of the European Christian empires established racism as a global problem, but racism always manifests itself in a particular manner in a specific local context. The history of Christianity in North America demonstrates many ways in which Christian faith has been abused in order to justify imperial domination, oppressive systems, and discriminatory racial practices; but this history also reveals how Christians, particularly those from oppressed communities, have repeatedly found hope and support in the gospel message of freedom and respect for all persons. Christian faith continues to offer a forceful critique that challenges Americans to reject the racial injustice that has so often marred their society. Through its call

---

[63] Barack Obama, "Remarks by the President at Memorial Service for Fallen Dallas Police Officers," July 12, 2016.

[64] Ibid.

[65] Jim Wallis, *America's Original Sin: Racism, White Privilege, and the Bridge to a New America* (Grand Rapids, MI: Brazos Press, 2016), 34–35.

[66] Ibid., 219.

to recognize the dignity and rights of all human beings and also through its proclamation of hope for reconciliation, Christian faith offers a stimulus to further reflection and social transformation.

In this challenging situation the dialogical method of Stephen Bevans of attending to both the global horizon and the local context offers needed guidance to Christians seeking to overcome the legacy of racism both in the United States and around the world. Bevans's careful attention to the details of a particular situation challenges us to note and resist the contours of racist attitudes and practices; his thoughtful retrieval of the social teaching of the Christian tradition calls our attention to resources for opposing racism; his commitment to intercultural and interreligious understanding offers a model of working with others of diverse backgrounds to overcome prejudices of all kinds. In facing these daunting challenges, we can be grateful for the many contributions of Stephen Bevans to this undertaking.

Chapter 9

Doing Theology in World Christianity: New Paths, Different Themes, Strange Locations

Peter C. Phan

One of the volumes, and one of the best sellers in the Theology in Global Perspective series published by Orbis Books, of which I am the general editor, is Stephen Bevans's *An Introduction to Theology in Global Perspective*.[1] Its introduction offers a succinct and lucid explanation, complete with a graphic, of what it means to be (1) *doing* theology, (2) doing *Catholic* theology, (3) doing Catholic *systematic* theology, and (4) doing Catholic systematic theology in *global* perspective.[2] What Bevans writes there can serve as the best programmatic statement I wish I had at my disposal when I was conceptualizing the nature and aims of the series.

Bevans's conception of the task of theology, as outlined above, was a gradual process. In his autobiographical reflections, aptly titled "Becoming a Global Theologian: A Personal Journey," Bevans traced the long and tortuous intellectual development—from Rome (Italy) to Ilocos Sur (the Philippines), Notre Dame (Indiana), Chicago (Illinois), and many other parts of the *oikumene*—at the end of which he came to the triple conviction that, as he puts it, there is no such thing as "theology" but only contextual theology; that theology can only be adequately done with a "missiological imagination"; and that theology can only be adequately done from a "global perspective."

These three features of theology—contextual, missiological, and global—are not, of course, disparate but are intrinsically interconnected, with one aspect implying the other two. The one thread that binds them together is, I submit, the ecclesial reality that is now referred to as world

---

[1] Stephen B. Bevans, *An Introduction to Theology in Global Perspective* (Maryknoll, NY: Orbis Books, 2009).

[2] Ibid., 1–5.

Christianity. In this chapter I extend Bevans's reflections on theological methodology by exploring the implications of world Christianity for doing theology today.

The immediate impact of the concept of world Christianity is on the discipline of church history, or more accurately, history of Christianity, as evidenced by *The Cambridge History of Christianity*.[3] Another academic discipline that has been significantly affected by this view of world Christianity is missiology. Works by renowned missiologists such as David Bosch, Andrew Walls, Dana L. Robert, Lamin Sanneh, Robert Schreiter, and Bevans himself, to cite only a few, have shifted the focus of mission from evangelization by foreign missionaries to the building of the local churches by native Christians, thereby contributing to the indigeneity and variety of Christianities.

In their comprehensive survey of world Christianity, Sebastian Kim and Kirsteen Kim spell out six aspects in which Christianity as a world religion can be studied. Topographically, the mapping of Christianity will take into account its local varieties and types throughout the globe. Theologically, Christianity's claim to be both universally applicable and locally inclusive will need to be taken seriously. Geographically, its presence and impact in all parts of the globe must be recognized. Sociopolitically, its diversities and multiplicities will be seen mainly as the result of attempts by indigenous and grassroots communities and not by expatriate missionaries to contextualize the Christian faith. Historically, Christianity's global expansion was never carried out by and from a single geographical and ecclesiastical center, exporting and imposing a homogeneous and identical form; rather, Christianity was polycentric from its very beginnings, expanded in different directions and in diffuse fashion, and adapted itself to each locale and context. Last, structurally, Christianity is shown to be a transnational and transcontinental movement constituted by complex networks of diverse kinds.[4]

A parallel focus on the impact of world Christianity on systematic theology is also emerging, especially on the way theology should be done (methodology) and on how the various *loci theologici* are to be reformulated (systematics). Regrettably, theology has not yet dealt with the concept of world Christianity with the same vigor and intensity as the history of

---

[3] On the distinction between "church history" and "history of Christianity," see Peter C. Phan, "World Christianity: Its Implications for History, Religious Studies, and Theology," *Horizons* 39/2 (2012): 171–88. On how the concept of world Christianity demands new ways of doing church history, see the insightful and challenging work by Justo L. González, *The Changing Shape of Church History* (St. Louis: Chalice Press, 2002), and Paul V. Kollman, "After Church History? Writing the History of Christianity from a Global Perspective," *Horizons* 31/2 (2004): 322–42.

[4] See Sebastian Kim and Kirsteen Kim, *Christianity as a World Religion* (London: Bloomsbury, 2013).

Christianity and missiology. One reason for this relative paucity of interest is that systematic theologians, whose field is doctrine, generally tend to be more concerned with permanence and less sensitive to historical changes than their colleagues in history and missiology. Furthermore, it comes as no surprise that most of the theological effort to respond to the challenges of world Christianity has so far taken place in the so-called Third World (or Two-Thirds or Majority World), that is, Africa, Asia, and Latin America, where new types and forms of Christianity are proliferating. However, third-world theologians generally do not enjoy the same academic status as their Western colleagues, and their writings are for the most part unknown—unless they come under scrutiny and censure by ecclesiastical authorities, especially in the Catholic Church. Stephen Bevans is the rare exception among Western theologians who has intentionally tried to become a "global theologian," as his prolific writings amply testify.[5]

In what follows I focus on the challenges of world Christianity to the theological enterprise, and more specifically to dogmatic/systematic/constructive theology, leaving to others the task of reflecting on its implications for other sub-disciplines such as biblical, historical, moral, and practical theologies. I first examine the new methods in which theology is being performed in world Christianity. Next, to flesh out this methodological section, I illustrate these new ways of doing theology with concrete examples on some key *loci theologici* taken from different parts of the Christian world. Finally, I indicate how the emergence of world Christianity in strange places poses extraordinary challenges for doing systematic theology.[6]

THEOLOGY IN WORLD CHRISTIANITY: NEW PATHS

Theology as faith seeking understanding—*fides quaerens intellectum*, to use Anselm's celebrated definition—is as ancient as Christianity, but this old task is carried out in ever novel ways and on new paths throughout the course of Christian history, searching for understandings and practices of the faith that would be appropriate to different sociopolitical, economic, cultural, and religious contexts, as any historical survey of Christian theology readily shows. All theologies, without exception, just as rationality itself, are unavoidably context-dependent, and any theology's pretensions to universal applicability and permanent validity can easily be unmasked

---

[5] One recent work that explores the implications of world Christianity on theology as a whole is *World Christianity: Perspectives and Insights*, ed. Jonathan Y. Tan and Anh Q. Tran (Maryknoll, NY: Orbis Books, 2016). Bevans contributes an important essay titled "Models of Contextual Theologizing in World Christianity," 146–60.

[6] For a more extensive explanation of the concept of world Christianity, see Phan, "World Christianity," 171–88; and Dale T. Irvin, "What Is World Christianity?" in Tan and Tran, *World Christianity*, 3–26.

as symptoms of either intellectual naivete or hegemonic ambition. The question, then, is not whether world Christianity can or should shape theological method, but rather *how* it actually does so. To see the impact of world Christianity on theology in recent decades one convenient way is to examine how it has affected the deployment of the six sources, or to use John Macquarrie's expression, "formative factors," of theology. Let us briefly consider each.

Experience

Since theology is, to use Gustavo Gutiérrez's celebrated phrase, "critical reflection on praxis" that "rises only at sundown,"[7] its matrix must be the various concrete contexts in which world Christianity is located. In the West, at least since the eighteenth century, the primary experience for theology consists of such cultural shibboleths as secularism, atheism, agnosticism, and relativism, against which Christian thinkers have devised a whole array of philosophical arguments in defense of theism and objective truth. No doubt these Enlightenment-inspired ideologies are also present outside the West, but in these non-Western countries the pervasive reality from which theology arises is not centered upon these epistemological and metaphysical issues but upon massive and dehumanizing material poverty and oppression bolstered by economic and political structures. Elsewhere, in Africa and Asia, the destructive legacy of Western colonialism has been enormous, and now insidious and manifold forms of neocolonialist capitalism, with its Western models of economic development through monetization and technological modernization, are reducing millions of people who used to live on subsistence economy to abject poverty because they have no role and are of no use in a global-market economy. These new forms of economic domination challenge world Christianity to find new ways to speak about God and things pertaining to God.

Beside poverty, other forms of oppression such as racism, classism, and patriarchalism confront theology in as well as outside the West. Ecological degradation is another pressing worldwide issue. Other problems of global character include stateless terrorism, violence, and national and international migrations. By contrast, some problems are peculiar to certain countries, such as the caste system, tribalism, and communalism. In light of these very diverse contemporary experiences many theologians in non-Western Christianity have abandoned introspective, spiritualistic, and individualistic conceptions of experience as the context for theology. Instead, they expand the nature of theology as *sapientia* (wisdom) and *sacra scientia* (rational knowledge) by doing theology as critical reflection on praxis that is animated by the "option for the poor" *(orthopraxis)*. The

---

[7] Gustavo Gutiérrez, *A Theology of Liberation*, trans. Sister Caridad Inda and John Eagleson (Maryknoll, NY: Orbis Books, 1991), 9.

basic questions for theology in world Christianity are therefore about *which* and *whose* experiences should be both its source and its hermeneutical lens.

Revelation

God's self-communication in the history of Israel and supremely in Jesus of Nazareth remains of course the definitive norm *(norma normans)* for Christian theology. However, more than ever world Christianity is encountering other religions that also claim to be recipients of divine revelation. such as Hinduism with its *sruti* (that which is heard), Islam with its Qur'an, and the Church of the Latter Day Saints with its *Book of Mormon*, not to mention a host of other recent religious movements and sects with their respective founders' religious experiences and recorded utterances (for example, the Unification Church or the Moonies with its *Divine Principle*). Whereas Christian theology has until recently limited itself to considering divine revelation exclusively in Israel and in Christianity, especially in the context of Jewish-Christian dialogue, theologians in world Christianity are today challenged to consider the possibility of divine revelation as the in-breaking and disclosure of Holy Mystery in religions other than Judaism and Christianity and relate it to God's self-gift in Jesus Christ. This, in turn, leads to a systematic reconceptualization of God, Christ, the Holy Spirit, church, and other *loci theologici.*

Scripture

Intimately connected with the possibility of divine revelation outside Judaism and Christianity is scripture. Many religions other than Judaism and Christianity possess scriptures whose origins also are attributed to divine communication and that are venerated as the inspired word of God. Furthermore, even religions that do not claim divine origin have sacred texts, such as Buddhism (the Tripitaka), Jainism (the *Agamas*), Sikhism (the *Guru Granth Sahib*), Zoroastrianism (the *Avesta*), Confucianism (the Four Books and Five Classics), and Daoism (the *Daodejing*). In world Christianity, particularly in Asia, where Christians regularly encounter the followers of other religious traditions, it is imperative to reexamine the Christian doctrine of biblical inspiration and canonicity in light of the existence of non-Christian scriptures and sacred texts, especially in interreligious dialogue and shared religious rituals and prayer services.

In this connection the issue of biblical hermeneutics often comes up for discussion. Whereas in the West biblical scholars for the most part have adopted the historical-critical method and interpret the Bible as a self-standing text, and in some cases, only intratextually, theologians in world Christianity are urged to practice an intertextual and, more sig-

nificantly, interreligious reading of the sacred texts. This is the project of
the emerging disciplines of cross-cultural and interreligious hermeneutics
and comparative theology. However, an almost opposite hermeneutical
approach is widespread in several parts of world Christianity, particularly
those associated with Pentecostalism, the fastest-growing Christian Church
in Africa, Latin America, and in some Asian countries such as China. It
privileges biblical elements that are largely dismissed in mainline churches,
such as prophecy, exorcism, glossolalia, and miraculous healing.[8] Thus,
theologians in world Christianity can no longer assume the historical-
critical method that is regnant in the Western academy as the standard or
limit themselves to practicing an exclusively intratextual hermeneutics.

Tradition

Also under intense debate in world Christianity is the nature of tradition and, above all, what should count as tradition. Rejection of tradition
does take the form of *sola scriptura*, especially in Pentecostal churches
of world Christianity. By and large, however, the necessity of tradition
is readily acknowledged, particularly in cultures, such as those of Asian
societies, where tradition is generally given a normative role. Rather, the
debate centers on what should count as normative tradition. Ironically,
Vincent of Lérins's triple canon formulated in his celebrated dictum: "That
which has been believed everywhere *(ubique)*, always *(semper)*, and by all
(ab omnibus)," which is commonly appealed to in conservative circles in
defense of tradition, is given a new and surprising twist in light of world
Christianity.[9] Geographical ubiquity, temporal antiquity, and numerical
universality, which are often attributed to Western tradition as proof of its
universality and normativity, are now turned on their heads. For the first
time, it is argued, these three Vincentian criteria of Christian orthodoxy
have been met—albeit never perfectly and unambiguously—by world
Christianity. Only in world Christianity are the criteria of "everywhere"
found, "always" instantiated, and "by all" realized. In world Christianity,
Western tradition of the past as well as of the present is not given a privileged, much less normative, status. Western Christianity is not related to
world Christianity as center to periphery with all the privileges attendant
to the center; rather, it is only one Christianity among other Christianities,
no more, no less, and its traditions, often maintained through power and

---

[8] This point is strongly made by Philip Jenkins in *The New Faces of Christianity:
Believing the Bible in the Global South* (Oxford: Oxford University Press, 2006).
[9] The best critical edition of Vincent of Lérins's *Commonitorium* is by Roland
Demeulenaere in *Corpus Christianorum Series Latina* 64 (1985), 127–95. An older
edition, with a very informative introduction, is Reginald Stewart Moxon, *The
Commonitorium of Vincent of Lérins* (Cambridge: Cambridge University Press,
1915).

imposed by force, legal and otherwise, must be seen for what they really are: local, context-dependent, and culture-bound historical particularities.

Needless to say, it is in local traditions that world Christianity embodies its specific differences and peculiarities. These traditions embrace each and every aspect of church life: Bible translation, liturgical language, sacramental celebration, worship, prayer, sacred object, art and architecture, music, dance, canon law, organizational structure, theology, spirituality, and so on. In world Christianity variety in tradition is not simply the result of adapting previously existing—mainly Western—traditions to different local contexts through the process of translation, linguistic and cultural, though admittedly this did happen extensively thanks to the work of expatriate missionaries. Rather, in world Christianity new traditions are constantly "manufactured," especially in Pentecostal and Independent churches, with staggering variety and dazzling ingenuity, in a process of "globalization from below." This independent and unrestrained proliferation of traditions, often the work of charismatic leaders and without local, national, and international consultation and agreement, poses a serious threat to faithfulness to the Christian faith and church unity. How to achieve this faithfulness and unity without falling into uniformity and fostering "the tradition of the dead" is one of the most difficult tasks for theology in world Christianity.[10]

Culture

Nothing is more conspicuous in world Christianity than the fact that the gospel is expressed in a mind-boggling variety of languages and cultures, at times even within the same country, such as Indonesia with its more than seven hundred spoken languages.[11] Beneath the language lies a worldview or a common pattern of thought and behavior into which the Christian faith is contextualized, indigenized, or inculturated. Culture, in contrast to nature, is a human construction, and in the process of cultural creation the powerful often arrogate for themselves the right to determine what belongs to culture and what does not, what is true and normal and what is false and deviant. Thus, only what serves their interest is acceptable as culture. Furthermore, even where there is no conscious attempt at domination, certain cultural achievements by the elite are elevated to the status of classical or high culture that alone deserves propagation and preservation. As a result, popular culture and the cultures of minority and tribal groups are neglected and even marginalized.

---

[10] See *Christian Worship Worldwide: Expanding Horizons, Deepening Practices*, ed. Charles Farhadian (Grand Rapids, MI: Eerdmans, 2007).

[11] For Christianity in Indonesia, see the over 1,000–page *A History of Christianity in Indonesia*, ed. Jan Sihar Aritonang and Karel E. Steenbrink (Leiden: Brill, 2008).

In inculturation, that is, the encounter between Christianity and local cultures, the same dynamic is at work. In the past, cultural indigenization was conducted between official Christianity and "world religions," with their canonical classics, hierarchical leaders, and approved theologians (for the most part, expatriate missionaries). This was the case, for instance, with Matteo Ricci and the Confucian literati in China and Roberto de Nobili and the Hindu Brahmins in India. In contemporary world Christianity, however, the dialogue between Christianity and cultures (note the plural) has eschewed this elitist bias, and much attention is now being paid to the local, regional, ethnic, and tribal "subaltern" or "small traditions." For instance, in India local Christianity is made up largely of Dalits and tribals, and in China, Catholic, Protestant, and Pentecostal churches gain the largest following in rural areas where Chinese folk religion is widely practiced. In Africa, African Independent/Initiated Churches (AICs) whose membership increased from fifty thousand in 1900 to ninety-nine million in 2010, have incorporated many beliefs and practices of African Traditional Religion.[12] In general, it is the adoption of these "small traditions" that is the distinguishing mark of Christianity in the Third World.[13]

---

[12] On African Christianity in general, see Adrian Hastings, *The Church in Africa 1450–1950* (Oxford: Clarendon Press, 1994). Hastings's book should be brought up to date with his own *A History of African Christianity 1950–1975* (Cambridge: Cambridge University Press, 1979); Elizabeth Isichei, *A History of Christianity in Africa: From Antiquity to the Present* (Grand Rapids, MI: Eerdmans,1995); and Kwame Bediako, *Christianity in Africa: The Renewal of a Non-Western Religion* (Maryknoll, NY: Orbis Books, 1995). On African Independent/Initiated Churches (AICs) and their bewildering varieties and multiplicities, the literature is growing rapidly. See David Barrett, *Schism and Renewal in Africa: An Analysis of Six Thousand Contemporary Religious Movements* (Nairobi: Oxford University Press, 1968); Bengt Sundkler, *Bantu Prophets in South Africa* (London: International African Institute, 1961); Allan Anderson, *Zion and Pentecost: The Spirituality and Experience of Pentecostal and Apostolic/Zionist Churches in South Africa* (Pretoria: University of South Africa Press, 2000); idem, *African Reformation: African Initiated Christianity in the Twentieth Century* (Trenton, NJ: Africa World Press, 2000); Martin L. Daneel, *Quest for Belonging: Introduction to a Study of African Independent Churches* (Gweru: Mambo, 1987); John S. Pobee and Gabriel Ositelu II, *African Initiatives in Christianity* (Geneva: WCC Publications, 1988). It is extremely difficult to obtain the exact number of the members of the AICs, According to a report of the WCC, in 1981 AICs constituted 15 percent of the total Christian population in sub-Saharan Africa. Assuming a growth estimated at more than two million per year, their adherents probably numbered close to 100 million in 2010, thus constituting a significant section of African Christian demography.

[13] With this statement I am only making a historical and phenomenological observation on the way third-world churches have dealt with local cultures, not a value judgment on their ecclesial character, that is, whether they are more, or less, authentic than mainline churches. Such a doctrinal judgment is of course predicated upon a set of mutually agreed criteria for orthodoxy, which may not be available.

In this context an issue that is being hotly debated is popular religiosity or popular devotions. In the past a good number of these popular devotions were condemned as superstition, idolatry, and magic, and conversion to Christianity required a total renunciation of these practices. Witness the repeated proscription of ancestor worship by Roman authorities in the Catholic Church until 1939 (the so-called Chinese Rites Controversy). In world Christianity, especially in the Catholic Church, there has been a vibrant renaissance of popular piety, especially devotion to Mary and the saints, veneration of ancestors, and pious practices such as novenas, processions, and pilgrimages, particularly in Christianity influenced by Iberian spirituality, such as those in Latin America, the Philippines, and Vietnam. Furthermore, "popular Catholicism" has become an important source for Catholic theology. In general, the relation between Christianity and local cultures has been widely discussed in contemporary theology, especially in missiology, and an abundant literature has been produced on the issue known under various names such as contextualization, indigenization, localization, or inculturation of the Christian faith.

Reason

The last formative factor in theology in Macquarrie's list is reason. Though originated from divine revelation and thus not rational in the sense of being derived from pure philosophy or autonomous reason, Christianity claims to be reasonable, not merely in the sense that it is not absurd and contrary to reason (*pace* Tertullian) but also in the sense that at a minimum it must give a justification for its hope. This is done not by appeal to divine authority and authorized tradition but by means of reasoned arguments with publicly available criteria of truth (apologetics and fundamental theology). Moreover, beyond this apologetical task, Christian theology has engaged in conversation—at times in friendly alliance, at other times in hostile confrontation—with various philosophies and other human sciences such as history, anthropology, psychology, sociology, and natural sciences. This, of course, has been the main way in which Western Christianity has interacted with reason.

In other parts of world Christianity, however, the dialogue between Christian faith and reason takes on unfamiliar forms. In many countries— India, China, Japan, Korea, Tibet, and others, just to cite a few Asian

---

With regard to AICs in particular, they no doubt had strong connections with Pentecostal missionary movements from the West, but they have consciously severed these connections by their attitude—by no means uniformly positive—toward African Traditional Religion and culture. Motivations for ecclesial independence are varied and include considerations that are political (freedom from Western imperialism), denominational (the Protestant tendency to divide and separate in situations of conflict), and cultural (adoption of the African worldview).

countries—there are centuries-old and well-developed philosophies. Here, Hindu, Buddhist, Confucian, Daoist, and Islamic philosophical systems are in full vigor, expressed in sophisticated conceptual frameworks and in a huge number of multilingual writings, such that no one scholar can claim mastery of even one philosophical tradition.[14] Interestingly, many Asian philosophers are well versed in Western philosophy, which may facilitate the dialogue between Asian philosophy and Christianity, but the same cannot be said of Western theologians, for the majority of whom Asian philosophy still remains a closed book.

Furthermore, for the majority of people in world Christianity outside the West, where orality is predominant, philosophical worldviews are expressed not in philosophical texts but in myths, stories, proverbs, koans, songs, dances, rituals, festivals, and dramas. Here the dialogue between Christianity and these forms of rationality is no less theologically complicated and pastorally even more urgent.

Thus far I have shown through a cursory examination of the six formative factors in theology how in world Christianity doing theology has been made highly complex, much more in non-Western countries than in the West. Both the resources of theology and their deployment have changed and multiplied as Christianity becomes global, requiring widely divergent approaches and methodologies and entailing new and different articulations of the basic Christian beliefs. Next I highlight some of the ways in which the main *loci theologici* have been reconceptualized in world Christianity.

THEOLOGY IN WORLD CHRISTIANITY: DIFFERENT THEMES

New contexts, new experiences, new resources, new methodologies, and a new generation of theologians inevitably bring forth new theological insights, and this is especially true of Christianity in the non-Western world. A rapid survey of theological developments since the second half of the twentieth century shows that apart from some significant trends in Germany and France, and to a lesser extent, Britain and the United States, the most challenging, and even revolutionary innovations in theology have taken place in Latin America, Africa, and Asia.[15] In the Catholic Church this general assessment is confirmed by the fact that under the leadership of then-cardinal Joseph Ratzinger as prefect of the Congregation for the

---

[14] A helpful one-volume guide to Asian philosophies is *Companion Encyclopedia of Asian Philosophies*, ed. Brian Carr and Indira Mahalingam (London: Routledge, 1997).

[15] Bevans's magisterial account of the theological developments in world Christianity is a veritable tour de force and represents a pioneering effort of privileging the non-Western theologies (*An Introduction to Theology in the Global Perspective*, 205–324).

Doctrine of the Faith, and later as Pope Benedict XVI, the two theologies that were attacked, and their key proponents censured, were liberation theology and theology of religious pluralism, both of which originated in the Third World, the former in Latin America and the latter in Asia.

This does not at all mean that these two and other theological trends developed by themselves, in isolation, without extensive dialogue with and learning from Western theologies. On the contrary, in recent decades there has been an extensive and constant contact and exchange among various parts of world Christianity. The Catholic Church with the Second Vatican Council (1962–65), the World Council of Churches with its numerous general assemblies and committees, and the World Evangelical Fellowship have greatly fostered communication and collaboration among theologians in all parts of the world. In addition, the Ecumenical Association of Third World Theologians (EATWOT), founded at Dar es Salaam, Tanzania, in 1976, has been a fertile venue for worldwide theological exchange. Furthermore, thanks to innumerable academic conferences, church gatherings, international networks, and online communications, theological ideas and movements circulate the globe with a speed unimaginable only a couple of decades ago.

Theologies in world Christianity have been given different names in which the relation between Christianity and culture is described by various prefixes. If culture is deemed positive, these theologies are said to be *trans*cultural, *multi*cultural, *cross*cultural, and *inter*cultural, each denoting a particular aspect of the dynamics of the encounter between faith and culture.[16] The theologian's task is to mediate between faith and culture, and the goal is to express the contents of the faith in categories understandable to the people of a particular place and time, and if necessary, to jettison the traditional, even ecclesiastically sanctioned, formulations of the Christian beliefs and practices to meet the needs of the age. On the other hand, theologies are dubbed *counter*cultural and *anti*cultural if a particular culture is judged godless and hostile to the gospel ("culture" standing in for "world" in the Johannine sense of being opposed to God). In the latter case the main task of theology is to critique and, when necessary, resist and reject cultural trends that are judged to be inimical to the Christian faith rather than seeking ways to accommodate the Christian faith to culture.

By and large, however, the terms *intercultural* and *contextual* as well as the underlying positive perceptions of culture are more common in world Christianity. *Intercultural* highlights the fact that contemporary theology is inevitably a culture-dependent and culture-bound intellectual production arising out of and at the same time shaping the encounter between the gospel and a particular culture. *Intercultural* makes it clear that this encounter

---

[16] See Volker Küster, *Einführung in die Interkulturelle Theologie* (Göttingen: Vanderhoeck and Ruprecht, 2011), 16–17. See also *Intercultural Theology: Approaches and Themes*, ed. Mark J. Cartledge and David Cheetham (London: SCM Press, 2011).

is not between a culture-free, "pure" gospel and another culture—which the words *inculturation* or *incarnation*, commonly used in Catholic circles, might misleadingly suggest—but always between an already culture-laden gospel (Jewish and Hellenistic) and a particular culture or more likely cultures in a given place that usually contain both values and disvalues. *Contextual*, on the other hand, accentuates the fact that the cultural context is not a neutral geographical venue in which world Christianity is implanted but rather that which conditions and influences the very way theology is constructed.[17] Let us now review the main rearticulations of the Christian beliefs in world Christianity, in terms of *God, Christ, religious pluralism and interreligious Christology*, and the *Holy Spirit*.

God

Whereas most third-world theologians emphasize the need to start from an accurate social analysis of concrete sociopolitical, economic, cultural, and religious contexts in which theology is done—the first moment of the three-stage process of see-judge-act—the primary object of their theologies is not human experience as such but God and all things insofar as they pertain to God. This should be said in response to the criticism, often voiced by conservative theologians, especially those under the sway of Karl Barth, that third-world theologies, allegedly heirs of modernity and liberal theology, are anthropocentric and immanentist in orientation and have lost sight of the real object or rather subject of theology, namely, God as the Absolute Transcendent and the Totally Other.[18] On the contrary, it must be acknowledged that God remains the central focus of many currents of theology in world Christianity, and therefore it is appropriate to begin the discussion of theology in world Christianity with God. However, what is new and distinctive of these theologies is that they take the vastly different experiences in world Christianity, as outlined above, and not the Bible and church teachings as the starting point, perspective, and hermeneutical lens for a reconstruction of the traditional understanding of God. Broadly speaking, their method is more inductive than deductive.

Interestingly, this critique of the doctrine of God was undertaken first in Western Christianity, where it took the form of a wholesale rejection of what is termed classical theism. By this is meant a philosophy and theology of God in which under the legacy of Hellenism, God's perfection is

---

[17] This connotation of *context* is implied in the subtitle of Timothy C. Tennent, *Theology in the Context of World Christianity: How the Global Church Is Influencing the Way We Think about and Discuss Theology* (Grand Rapids, MI: Zondervan, 2007).

[18] This criticism is often voiced by the proponents, especially John Milbank, of the so-called Radical Orthodoxy.

understood to imply aseity, self-sufficiency, immutability, impassibility, and total detachment from the change, pain, and suffering of the world. Leading this charge are Process philosophers and theologians such as Alfred North Whitehead, Charles Hartshorne, John Cobb Jr., Joseph Bracken, and a host of others. Akin to Process theology, in evangelical theology, proponents of Open Theism, such as Clark Pinnock, argue for a view of God that presents God as freely and intimately involved in a dynamic relationship of love with human beings that makes God vulnerable to temporality, change, and suffering and in which God affects creatures and creatures affect God.[19]

Third-world theologies of God would resonate sympathetically with the basic understanding of God proposed by Process theology, especially its concept of a suffering God, However, their starting point, resources, and methodology, and hence their resulting theology of God, are substantially different. As mentioned above, their immediate context is not dissatisfaction with "classical theism," and their goal is not an elaboration of a speculative metaphysics in which God as, to use Process thought's expression, "responsive love" (God's "consequent nature") is subject to change, and as a "fellow-sufferer who understands," acts in the world by persuasion and lure, and not by coercive power. By contrast, the context of third-world Christianity is, as has been alluded to above, massive systemic impoverishment and exploitation. Seen in this context, and from the Bible read through this hermeneutical lens, God is understood primarily as liberator of the oppressed who has made an option for the poor, and because of this option, "has shown strength with his arm; has scattered the proud in the thoughts of their hearts; has brought down the powerful from their thrones and lifted the lowly; has filled the hungry with good things, and sent the rich away empty" (Lk 1:51–53).

For liberation theologies it is these acts of God in "lifting the lowly" and "filling the hungry with good things" that define the nature of God. What and who God is, is known in and through what God does, not in generic actions in the world such as creation, providence, and consummation (the customary categories in Western theology to describe God's activities in the world) but in specific, highly partial, and politically charged interventions to liberate those who are treated as nonpersons by the rich and the powerful, and in this way overturning the social order. Thus there has been

---

[19] See Charles Pinnock et al., *The Openness of God: A Biblical Challenge to the Traditional Understanding of God* (Downers Grove, IL: InterVarsity Press, 1994); and John Sanders, *The God Who Risks*, rev. ed. (Downers Grove, IL: InterVarsity Press, 2007). In its early phase, from the 1930s to the 1960s, process theology focuses on God. After the 1970s it turns to other topics such as liberation (Schubert Ogden), feminism (Marjorie Suchocki), science (Ian Barbour, Philip Clayton, Ann Pederson), interreligious dialogue (John Cobb Jr., David Ray Griffin, Clark Williamson, Joseph Bracken), evil (Griffin, Suchocki, Bracken), and ecology (Jay McDaniel).

in third-world theologies of God a shift not merely from the immanent Trinity to the economic Trinity, as the two paragons of first-world theology, Karl Barth and Karl Rahner, have done. There is also a shift from a concept of the economic Trinity as the self-actualization of the immanent Trinity in human history in general to a concept of the economic Trinity as the self-actualization of the immanent Trinity precisely in God's identification and solidarity with a specific group of people designated with the umbrella term *the poor.*

Needless to say, these poor in turn reconceptualize God from their particular form of oppression, not because, as a black woman in Sue Monk Kidd's novel *The Secret Life of Bees* tells a white girl who wonders why there is a black Madonna: "Everybody needs a God who looks like them."[20] Rather, it is because it is precisely in these people with their specific forms of oppression that God has revealed what and who God is and for whom God "has shown strength with his arm." Thus, there is black theology (against racism), African theology (against cultural colonialism), Latin American theology (against economic oppression), feminist theology in its various forms (against patriarchy and androcentrism), *dalit* theology (against the caste system), tribal theology (against marginalization and exploitation of minorities), *minjung* theology (against dictatorship and capitalism), theology of struggle (against state security ideology), ecological theology (against environmental degradation), and so forth. Because of their focus on particular forms of human oppression, these theologies run the risk of being perceived as anthropocentric and being accused of reducing salvation to the sociopolitical and economic dimensions.

Furthermore, because these theologies are critical reflection on praxis, they may be liable to the charge that they foment class struggle and even violent revolution. In light of these misunderstandings, it is necessary to point out that when these theologians articulate their theologies of God, they are not indulging their "need to have a God who looks like them" (Feuerbachian and Marxian theories of projection) but are seeking to reveal the real face of God as God has truly appeared in the world (the economic Trinity) and the specific ways in which God saves humanity and the cosmos (grace as freedom, salvation as liberation). In sum, in world Christianity God is world relational, all inclusive, co-suffering, and saving by liberating.[21]

---

[20] Sue Monk Kidd, *The Secret Life of Bees* (New York: Penguin Books, 2002), 141.

[21] An example of this theology of God can be found in the works of the Taiwanese Presbyterian theologian Choan-Seng Song. Among his many writings, see *The Compassionate God: An Exercise in the Theology of Transposition* (Maryknoll, NY: Orbis Books, 1982). Of course this theology of God is not exclusive to third-world theologians. Among first-world theologians Jürgen Moltmann must be counted as the foremost proponent of it.

Christ

Because Jesus is the human face of God, it is in Christology that the distinctiveness of third-world theologies is most evident. Indeed, it is in Christology that the effort by world Christianity to contextualize the Christian faith has produced the largest amount of literature. Again, as in the theology of God, though the Bible still functions as the *norma normans*, it is the context that serves as the starting point, the perspective, and the hermeneutical lens for christological construction. As K. K. Yeo puts it concisely,

> Global Christologies seek creative dialogues toward: (1) a *catholic* faith based on biblical Christologies that honor multiple and inter-acting worldviews; (2) a global theology that respects cross-cultural and shifting contexts in which faithful communities embody real-life issues; (3) a translatability of the Scripture that upholds various dynamic vernaculars and hermeneutics; and (4) a round-table symposium of proclaiming and worshiping a biblical Christ portrayed in varied Christologies.[22]

Add to Yeo's list of missiological (proclaiming) and doxological (worshiping) goals the praxiological dimension (overturning and transformation of oppressive societal structures) of third-world theology, and we thus have a glimpse of the dazzling variety of non-Western Christologies. Within this framework it is possible to classify Christology in world Christianity according to the various concerns relating to race (black), ethnicity (Chinese, Indian, Latin Americans, and so forth), gender (white, womanist, mujerista, and so on), class *(dalit),* tribe (American Indian, tribals in northeast India), geography (continents and countries), culture, and religion.

My point here is not to offer a bibliographical survey of these Christologies; any competent overview of contemporary Christologies will present their significant trends, their guiding concepts, and the writings of their prominent proponents. Rather, I would like to examine the basic ideas that provoke, challenge, and shape the bewildering variety of christological reflections in world Christianity. One helpful way to understand their basic orientations is to group them under the three major concerns of world Christianity, namely, liberation, inculturation, and interreligious dialogue. It is, however, most important to remember that these three tasks are not distinct and unrelated; rather, they are deeply intertwined and overlap

---

[22] K. K. Yeo, "Biblical Christologies of the Global Church: Beyond Chalcedon? Toward a Fully Christian and Fully Cultural Theology," in *Jesus without Borders: Christology in the Majority World*, ed. Gene L. Green, Stephen T. Pardue, and K. K. Yeo (Grand Rapids, MI: Eerdmans, 2014), 168.

with one another so that one task cannot be fully achieved without the other two, though each can be given a particular emphasis depending on the local context.

Under the first category, that is, liberation, which was developed first and foremost in Latin America, the focus is on the historical Jesus as liberator with his message of the reign of God as reported primarily in the Synoptic Gospels. Jesus's words and deeds during his ministry, death, and resurrection are mined to highlight Jesus's preferential option for the poor and the liberative force of his actions against all kinds of oppression in all aspects of life, including the earth. Here lie the major contributions of Latin American, black, feminist, and ecological Christologies.

The second category includes inculturation Christologies, which find a congenial home in Africa, where colonialism has wrought extensive cultural pauperization. They center on the retrieval and adoption of certain elements of indigenous cultures to present Christ as a universal person, "without borders" and cross-cultural, and precisely for that reason, capable of being "African." Here the images that emphasize kinship and community obtain pride of place and are used to present Jesus as mother, elder brother, ancestor, chief, and healer. Again, the Synoptic Gospels as well as the other writings of the New Testament, especially the Pauline letters, provide ample materials for inculturated Christologies.

Religious Pluralism and Interreligious Christology

The third category of Christology, which falls within the ambit of interreligious dialogue, is so complex, vast, and controversial that it merits discussion under a separate heading. Of all the Christologies developed in world Christianity, interreligious Christology has the potential to be the most revolutionary trend, shaking Christianity to its foundations. Interreligious encounter is not new, of course, as Western theologians from the earliest times had to present Christ in relation to—more precisely, *over against*—Judaism, pagan religions, and Islam.

What is novel and is causing deep reverberations in Christology in world Christianity is that, first, interreligious dialogue is now taking place across Christianity, but for obvious reasons, particularly in Asia, the cradle of all world religions. Thanks to globalization and migration, religious pluralism is now a global phenomenon, with large and complex sociopolitical, economic, cultural, and religious implications, calling for interreligious dialogue, not least for the sake of world peace and harmony. Second, the encounter between Christianity and other religions is now conceived, at least by the majority of Christians, no longer as confrontation but *dialogue*, requiring a set of virtues, intellectual and moral, that make mutual understanding and cooperation among believers of different faiths possible.[23] Third, this interreligious dialogue now involves new partners, not only Judaism and Islam, with which Christianity has family resemblances and a common heritage, but religions with which Christianity has few or no connections, such as Hinduism (nonpersonal theism), Buddhism (non-theism), Confucianism and Daoism (immanentism and humanism), and a host of other no less global religious traditions, such as Jainism, Sikhism, and primal religions. Fourth, this dialogue has led to a radical and thorough reexamination of all the major Christian *loci theologici*; indeed, none of the reputed nonnegotiables of the Christian faith has been left undisturbed. These include not only Christology but also the doctrine of God and the Trinity, pneumatology, revelation, inspiration, biblical hermeneutics, church, worship, spirituality, and ethics, and of course, as mentioned above, the six formative factors in theology.

Again, it is not my intention to provide here an overview of how Christian theology has been challenged by religious pluralism; informative surveys of interreligious dialogue are plentiful.[24] What I would like to do is outline the various challenges that religious pluralism poses to Christology and the two main types of interreligious Christology in world Christianity.

First, regarding theological challenges, the very foundation of traditional Christology has been shaken. With regard to Judaism, one major issue concerns supersessionism, that is, the doctrine that Christ, and hence Christianity, have "fulfilled" Judaism, and therefore the covenant or testament that God has made with the Jews has become obsolete, replaced by the "new" Christian covenant. This anti-Jewish and anti-Judaic "teaching of contempt" is widespread in Christian tradition and is said to be based on a number of statements in the New Testament, especially the Gospels of Matthew and John and the Letter to the Hebrews. It is now asked, with deep moral anguish, especially in light of the Holocaust, whether this supersessionism is biblically grounded in view of God's eternal faithfulness to his word and of what Paul says about the Jewish covenant (see

---

[23] This is not to say that dialogue occurs everywhere in world Christianity. Conflicts with, violence against, and persecutions of Christians in countries such as China, India, Sudan, Nigeria, and many Middle Eastern countries have been widely reported. What I intend to say is that even in these situations of conflict the only means to achieve peace, justice, and reconciliation is dialogue, especially in its fourfold mode, namely, common life, practical collaboration, interreligious conversation, and sharing of spiritual experiences.

[24] See, for instance, *The Wiley-Blackwell Companion to Inter-religious Dialogue*, ed. Catherine Cornille (Oxford: Wiley-Blackwell, 2013); *Understanding Interreligious Relations*, ed. David Cheetham, Douglas Pratt, and David Thomas (Oxford: Oxford University Press, 20013); and *Catholic Engagement with World Religions: A Comprehensive Study*, ed. Karl Becker and Ilaria Morali (Maryknoll, NY: Orbis Books, 2010).

Rom 9—11). If this supersessionism is rejected, and in my judgment it must be, disturbing questions are raised about the number of covenants and "peoples of God" (note the plural!) outside the historical Jesus and Christianity and their mutual relation, and about the appropriateness of Christian mission to "convert" the Jews.

Furthermore, traditional claims regarding Jesus as the unique, universal, and eschatological revealer and savior have been challenged. Troubling questions are raised regarding the salvific function of non-Christian religions: Are they, as missionaries of generations past and in our time, Karl Barth, have held, merely human, mostly superstitious, idolatrous, and vain attempts at self-salvation or, on the contrary, are they God-intended and God-initiated "ways of salvation" in themselves? And if the latter, how do they relate to Christ and Christianity? Are they parallel and independent ways, or mutually complementary? Contemporary theologies of religions— commonly categorized as exclusivism, inclusivism, pluralism, and a variety of combinations thereof—are too well known to require exposition here.[25]

Connected with this christological issue are biblical hermeneutics and the role of the sacred books of non-Christian religions. It is not merely a question of how to interpret (critics would say: interpret away) exclusive-sounding texts that categorically affirm the uniqueness of Christ such as Acts 4:12; 1 Timothy 2:5; and John 14:6. It has been suggested that their seeming exclusiveness can be overcome by contextualizing them within an all-inclusive and universalistic orientation of the whole biblical tradition, expressed powerfully, for example, in John 1:9. However, the more challenging task is how to interpret the Bible in light of non-Christian sacred scriptures. It is here that third-world biblical scholars and theologians such as Samuel Ryan, George Soares-Prabhu, R. S. Sugirtharajah, Archie C. C. Lee, and Kwok Pui-lan, just to mention a few, have made innovative contributions to interreligious hermeneutics. Furthermore, in some places, for example in India, experiments have been made to include selected texts from these non-Christian scriptures into worship and prayer. Implicit in this hermeneutical practice and liturgical usage is a theology of revelation and inspiration that acknowledges the activity of the Holy Spirit (in-*spiration*) in the origination and composition of these sacred texts.

Second, concerning its basic approaches, contemporary interreligious Christology has pursued two lines of research. The first explores how Christ and Christianity have historically been viewed in non-Christian sacred texts and by non-Christian thinkers themselves. This task is somewhat straightforward in the case of Judaism and Islam, given the fact that they and Christianity are "religions of the Book" and given the long history of encounter among theologians of the three faiths. The Qur'an contains narratives about Abraham, the prophets, the Jews, Jesus, and Mary; the Christian Bible includes the Tanak; and there has been a lively conversation

---

[25] A very helpful introduction to these issues is Paul Knitter, *Introducing Theologies of Religion* (Maryknoll, NY: Orbis Books, 2002).

among Jews, Christians, and Muslims concerning their common theological heritage. The challenge is how to remove mutual misunderstandings, suspicions, and hostility embodied in these texts and to bring to full flowering the common heritage and shared convictions among these three Abrahamic religions.

The second line of research in interreligious Christology is much more arduous and controversial than the first. It seeks to relate the figure of Jesus to other religious founders and moral teachers such as the Buddha and Confucius, and to read the Bible in the light of the sacred texts that have little historical and literary commonality with it, such as the Vedas, the Upanishads, the Tripitaka, the *Guru Granth Sahib*, and the Chinese classics. Fortunately, Christian theologians are neither the first nor the only ones to embark upon this task. Not a few Hindu, Buddhist, and Confucian thinkers have attempted this comparative work, often out of a sincere admiration for Jesus's life and teaching, but without converting to Christianity. Thus, in this type of Christology, similarities as well as differences between Jesus and the other religious figures are highlighted, allowing Jesus to be spoken of as the Sage, the Way, the Guru, the Avatara, the Bodhisattva, the Satyagrahi, the Servant, the Compassionate, the Dancer, and the Pilgrim.[26] Obviously these new christological titles, notwithstanding their linguistic strangeness, resonate with those ascribed to Jesus in the New Testament, but clearly they also expand and enrich our traditional understanding of Jesus and speak meaningfully to third-world Christians. At the same time, this interreligious Christology causes much anxiety among guardians of orthodoxy for its alleged downplaying of the uniqueness of Jesus and its syncretistic tendency.[27]

The Holy Spirit

Another momentous development in contemporary theology in world Christianity is the emergence of a vigorous and vibrant pneumatology, thanks in part to theological attempts to account for the activity of God outside of Jesus and Christianity. Appealing to Irenaeus's arresting metaphor of God the Father's "two hands" working in the world, namely, the Word of God and the Holy Spirit, a number of theologies of religion

---

[26] See Martien E. Brinkman, *The Non-Western Jesus: Jesus as Bodhisattva, Avatara, Guru, Prophet, Ancestor or Healer?* (London: Equinox, 2007); Gregory A. Barker, ed., *Jesus in the World's Faiths: Leading Thinkers from Five Religions Reflect on His Meaning* (Maryknoll, NY: Orbis Books, 2005); and Michael Amaladoss, *The Asian Jesus* (Maryknoll, NY: Orbis Books, 2006).

[27] Within the Roman Catholic Church this anxiety is well known, especially in the Congregation for the Doctrine of the Faith and its attempts to censure writings by theologians such as Jacques Dupuis, Jon Sobrino, Roger Haight, Michael Amaladoss, and a host of others, which have been well chronicled.

invoke the activities of the Holy Spirit before, during, and after the incarnation of the Word of God in Jesus of Nazareth. The Holy Spirit, it is argued, functions not independently from (much less in opposition to) but in collaboration and harmony first with the Logos-not-yet-made-flesh *(Logos asarkikos)* and then the Logos-made-flesh *(Logos sarkikos)*. But this collaboration between the Spirit and the Word of God should not be understood as dependence of the former on the latter, which the traditional Western theology of the Trinity, with its conception of the linear procession of the Spirit from the Father and the Son *(Filioque)*, might misleadingly suggest. On the contrary, as the "two hands" metaphor implies, the Son and the Spirit work autonomously, single-handedly, albeit in mutual collaboration, in different places and times, in diverse modalities, and with varying degrees of impact.

The venue in which the Spirit is actively present outside the historical Jesus and Christianity is preeminently non-Christian religions, with their beliefs and practices. In interreligious dialogue there have been attempts at finding analogues for the Spirit in the teachings of non-Christian religions similar to those made in Christology mentioned above. Again, this task is relatively straightforward in the case of Judaism and Islam, though the challenge to express the "personality" of the Spirit remains considerable. The task is much more complex in the case of Asian religions, given the great differences in conceptual frameworks. Contemporary research has singled out the concepts of *prana* (Hinduism) and *Qi/Chi* (Chinese thought), the energy or life force circulating in all things, as particularly illuminating analogues for the Spirit as immanent grace and life-giving power.[28]

However, the main catalyst for the current resurgence of pneumatology in world Christianity is not interreligious dialogue but the phenomenal growth of evangelicalism/Pentecostalism—a new Pentecost—in third-world Christianity, especially in Africa, Asia (especially South Korea, India, and China), and Latin America (especially Brazil and Guatemala). As a result, a different type of Christianity, quite different from the mainline churches of the First World, is spreading like wildfire, with a more literal understanding of the Bible and an exuberant panoply of the gifts of the Spirit.[29]

---

[28] See, for instance, Kirsteen Kim, *The Holy Spirit in the World: A Global Conversation* (Maryknoll, NY: Orbis Books, 2007); Grace Ji-Sun Kim, *The Holy Spirit, Chi, and the Other: A Model of Global and Intercultural Pneumatology* (New York: Palgrave Macmillan, 2011); and Hyo-Dong Lee, *Spirit, Qi, and the Multitude: A Comparative Theology for the Democracy of Creation* (New York: Fordham University Press, 2014).

[29] See Donald E. Miller, Kimon H. Sargeant, and Richard Flory, eds., *Spirit and Power: The Growth and Global Impact of Pentecostalism* (Oxford: Oxford University Press, 2013). Philip Jenkins has drawn the contrasts between the Christianity of the global North and that of the global South in *The Next Christendom: The Coming of Global Christianity*, 3rd ed. (Oxford: Oxford University Press, 2011). Jenkins has at times overdrawn these contrasts, but his general point about the difference between these two types of Christianity is well taken.

THEOLOGY IN WORLD CHRISTIANITY: STRANGE LOCATIONS

This mention of the astounding global expansion of Pentecostal churches is the natural transition point to the last part of my chapter. With all the developments in world Christianity hinted at above, what is aborning is not a new Christendom but a new Christianity, better, the birth of Christianities in strange and unexpected places. This will make the kind of theology that Bevans rightly and eloquently advocates—contextual, missiological, and global—much more complex and unpredictable, one that no contemporary theologian, Bevans included, can fathom, let alone design.

It is well known that, according to some demographic projections, by 2050 four out of five Christians will live in the global South, namely, Africa, Asia, and Latin America.[30] One of the possible developments in this future world Christianity is the enormous challenge it poses to the construction of a recognizable Christian theology. How should we do *Christian*, and more specifically *Catholic*, systematic theology in a contextual, missiological, and global way if the reality out of which and for which theology is done, namely the church, is so diverse that its Christian identity is severely threatened? As far as church unity is concerned, it is possible that there will be no center that holds, at least in the way it did when divisions occurred during the sixteenth-century Reformation. The dividing lines now run not merely among churches, but in the midst of each church and denomination, especially where there is no central authority, or recognized authoritative interchurch bodies. Possibly there will not be a checklist of universally agreed-upon doctrinal nonnegotiables that can serve as a litmus test for Christian identity, such as a commonly formulated creed. Furthermore, relations with other religions will enter into discussions on intra-church matters, especially where Christians are but a minority, such as Asia and North Africa, since it is impossible to be religious without being interreligious in these parts of the world. Last, political factors such as government intervention will play a more invasive role, especially where religious freedom is severely curtailed.

Lest it be thought that the above rumination is an alarmist doomsday scenario, let us consider the case of Pentecostal Christianity, especially in China. In his informative study of Chinese Christianity *Redeemed by*

---

[30] Whereas in 1900 over 80 percent of all Christians lived in Europe and North America, by 2005 this proportion had fallen to under 40 percent; it is likely to fall below 30 percent before 2050. Philip Jenkins, on the basis of various statistical projections, notes that in 2015, 60 percent of the estimated two billion Christians in the world lived in Africa, Asia, or Latin America. By 2050, there will be an estimated three billion Christians, 75 percent of whom will live in the global South (Jenkins, *The New Faces of Christianity*). The two most helpful statistical studies of global Christianity are Todd M. Johnson and Kenneth R. Ross, eds., *Atlas of Global Christianity 1910–2019* (Edinburgh: Edinburgh University Press, 2009); and Patrick Johnstone, *The Future of the Global Church: History, Trends, and Possibilities* (Downers Grove, IL: InterVarsity Press, 2011).

Fire,[31] Lian Xi, professor of world Christianity at Duke University, focuses on what he terms Chinese "popular Christianity," that is, the Christian movements that developed in China outside of mainline Protestant Christianity and the Catholic Church since the Taiping Uprising (1850–64) and continue today in the explosive and bewildering mushrooming of unregistered "house churches." "Popular Christianity" is an attempt by Chinese Protestants to indigenize Christianity by drawing inspiration from anti-foreign nationalism, Pentecostal revivalism, Chinese rural and grassroots utopian millenarianism, and beliefs and practices of Chinese popular religion to form an indigenous Christianity.

Lian Xi traces the roots of popular Christianity back to the Christian-inspired millenarian and utopian Taiping Heavenly Kingdom with its founder Hong Xiuquan (1814–64). Other charismatic leaders of attempts at autonomous, self-supporting churches in late-Qing coastal China include Xi Zichi, known as Xi the Overcomer of Demons, founder of the opium-refuge churches; Xie Honglai, organizer of the Chinese Christian Union; Yu Guozhen, founder of the China Christian Independent Church; Cheng Jingyi, who eloquently urged nondenominational Christianity at the 1910 Edinburgh World Missionary Conference; Ding Limei, founder of the Chinese Student Volunteer Movement for the Ministry; Yu Cidu, a Methodist revivalist itinerant preacher. In the post–Boxer Uprising these Chinese Christians felt that the survival and growth of Christian communities in China appeared to hinge on their ability to separate themselves from Western missions. However, due to lack of personnel and financial resources, these movements toward autonomy succeeded only in fulfilling the missionary vision of a native church safely within the limits of mainline Western Protestantism.

What was still required for successful and lasting independent Protestant churches to arise was a millenarian vision of an impending end of the world and of the imminence of the second coming of Christ. Lian Xi traces the origins and chronicles the development of six such churches with their founders: the True Jesus Church (Wei Enbo, 1876?–1919); the Jesus Family (Jing Dianying, 1890–1957); the Shandong Revival and the Spiritual Gifts Society (Ma Zhaorui, Yang Rulin, and Sun Zhanyao); the Christian Tabernacle (Wang Mingdao, 1900–91); the Bethel Worldwide Evangelical Band (John Sung/Song Shangjie, 1901–44); and the Little Flock (Watchman Nee/Ni Tuosheng, 1903–72). In the two decades 1930–50 these churches experienced unprecedented growth. However, as the Communist government orchestrated the Three Self movement to unify the Protestant churches in China, their phenomenal growth came to an abrupt end. However, their apocalyptic, premillenarian fire was smoldering and waited for the right time to burst into new Pentecostal flames.

---

[31] Lian Xi, *Redeemed by Fire: The Rise of Popular Christianity in Modern China* (New Haven, CT: Yale University Press, 2010).

Lian Xi ends his study with a survey of the stupendous explosion of unregistered, independent house churches after the Cultural Revolution (1966–76). It is, in his assessment, "in the unofficial churches where one would find the heartbeat of the Christianity of China's masses and glimpse the future of Chinese Protestantism, which, at the turn of the twenty-first century, was already poised to rival the CCP [Chinese Communist Party] in total membership."[32] These house churches mostly grew out of the six pre-1949 churches mentioned above and have taken on lives of their own, spinning off dizzying numbers of idiosyncratic and uncontrollable sects under charismatic leaders. True to their Pentecostal origins, these churches prize glossolalia, visions, trances, miracles, and exorcisms.

There is no doubt that Christianity in its apocalyptic, premillenarian form is experiencing an explosive revival in China, so much so that some Western observers, such as David Aikman, have breathlessly predicted a "Christianized China" that will, together with Christian America, promote global evangelism and contribute to world peace. Lian Xi is rightly skeptical of the likelihood of such a scenario: "Persecuted by the state, fractured by its own sectarianism, and diminished by its contempt for formal education (theological or otherwise), it [Chinese contemporary popular Christianity] will probably also remain, as sectarian religious groups in the past, in the state of 'intellectual decapitation.'"[33] Lian Xi also astutely notes that as long as Chinese politics, Chinese society, and Chinese life in general evolve toward the rule of law, stability, greater equality, and harmony, Chinese Christianity is unlikely to foment popular uprising, and that, even if it does, it is unlikely to succeed, "given the historical tendency of messianic movements in China toward utopian radicalism, internal strife, a plebeian estrangement of the elite, and, ultimately, political incompetence."[34]

Of course, contemporary Chinese Christianity is *sui generis,* and many of its features, especially those related to its cultural and political contexts, are not found outside China. But its basic ecclesial characteristics are derived from the evangelical/Pentecostal movement and are common to innumerable communities throughout the globe, including Africa, Latin America, and the United States. Together they form the fastest-growing Christian group today, with an estimated membership of more than a half billion. There is no doubt that most of these Independent churches, though they have some common networks among themselves, do not have a central authority and lack many of the essential attributes that traditional ecclesiology considers constitutive of "church."[35]

---

[32] Ibid., 206.

[33] Ibid., 242.

[34] Ibid., 247.

[35] Though AICs have formed ecumenical organizations among themselves, and some are members of National Councils of Churches and of the WCC, most lack some of the features, such as apostolic succession and the Eucharist, that are considered essential to authentic "ecclesiality" by historic mainline churches.

I mention the case of evangelical/Pentecostal churches in China precisely to stress that the only way to do theology responsibly today is the way advocated by Bevans. By the same token, we should be alert to the enormous challenges that this kind of theology will face. In sum, from what has been said above about the formative factors of theology, the rearticulations of fundamental *loci theologici*, and the emergence of world Christianity in strange locations, it is clear that there are enormous challenges as well as rich opportunities for doing Catholic systematic theology today. We are just beginning to espy the complex contours of such a theology, but we must try to discern the forward movement to respond to what God is saying to the churches. And we are deeply grateful to Stephen B. Bevans for being our trailblazing pioneer and sure guide.

PART 3

PROPHETIC DIALOGUE

Chapter 10

Christianity Interrupted: Liberation Theology's Past, Present, and Future through the Lens of Rupture

Gemma Tulud Cruz

THE RISE OF LATIN AMERICAN LIBERATION THEOLOGY

Liberation theology is undoubtedly one of the most significant theological developments of the twentieth century. While it has many varieties, the Latin American version is arguably the most widely known. It has been described as revolutionary theology, especially in its early years, as it offered a new way of doing theology.[1] Stephen Bevans, for example, points to how this new method that is "critical reflection on praxis" is built on a "new way of knowing" that seeks not so much intellectual understanding as an understanding that is built on reflective activity.[2] However, like most pioneering theologies, liberation theology was plagued with criticisms and controversies. Many found fault with it,[3] just as numerous people sang its praises. While its advocates and practitioners trumpet it as theology in a new key, its critics argue against its Marxist social analysis and its assumption that liberation is equivalent to revolution.[4] Other criticisms

---

[1] Gustavo Gutiérrez, *A Theology of Liberation: History, Politics and Salvation* (Maryknoll, NY: Orbis Books, 1988), 3–10.

[2] Stephen B. Bevans, *An Introduction to Theology in a Global Perspective* (Maryknoll, NY: Orbis Books, 2009), 137.

[3] For a good survey of the criticisms, see Arthur McGovern, *Liberation Theology and Its Critics: Toward an Assessment* (Eugene, OR: Wipf and Stock, 2009), 47–61.

[4] One of the well-known critics is Colombian bishop Alfonso López Trujillo. See, for example, Bishop Alfonso López Trujillo, *Liberation or Revolution?* (Huntington, IN: Our Sunday Visitor, 1977), 39.

relate to the perception that liberation theology politicizes the faith,[5] pits the hierarchy against the laity, and dissociates sins that are personal from those that are social.

The fact that Latin American liberation theology remains relevant and arguably helped (further) develop or, at the very least, put the spotlight on other forms or varieties of liberationist theologies in the public and global consciousness means that classical Latin American liberation theology provided a valuable contribution to Christian life and theology. It is to this contribution this essay now turns.

RUPTURES AND
CLASSICAL LATIN AMERICAN LIBERATION THEOLOGY

Beginning to think in a different way requires us to take different positions on the subject of knowing: to open up spaces for new ways of thinking and to consider our own thinking in terms of how our goals affect our perceptions. In many ways opening up spaces is what classical Latin American liberation theology did. It is a contribution that, despite criticism from various sectors, has kept liberation theology alive until today.[6] Three kinds of spaces were opened, which I consider here as "ruptures." First, there is the rupture between faith and lived experience. Prior to Vatican II and the CELAM meeting in Medellín, Colombia, in 1968, the Latin American hierarchy had not openly engaged the concrete sociopolitical and economic conditions of the people in regard to the direction they wanted the Latin American church to take. In the historic meeting in Medellín, however, the hierarchy spoke strongly against the economic oppression plaguing the majority of Latin Americans. It also spoke of the failure of developmentalism and Latin America's consequent need for liberation from economic dependency.[7] Most important, it was at this historic meeting that the bishops asserted that the Latin American church should have an option for the poor: "The Lord's distinct commandment to 'evangelize the poor'

---

[5] See, for example, Congregation for the Doctrine of the Faith, *Instruction on Certain Aspects of the Theology of Liberation* (1984); this document carried López Trujillo's criticism further (see, in particular, Parts VII–VIII).

[6] Three more recent developments attest to this. The first is the Vatican doctrinal office's green light to proceed with the cause for the sainthood of the late Óscar Romero. The second is the meeting between Pope Francis and Gustavo Gutiérrez. Last but not least is the book co-authored by Gustavo Gutiérrez with Gerhard Müller, the former secretary of the Congregation for the Doctrine of the Faith. See Gustavo Gutiérrez and Gerhard Müller, *On the Side of the Poor: The Theology of Liberation*, trans. Robert Krieg and James Nickoloff (Maryknoll, NY: Orbis Books, 2015). See also Joshua McElwee, "Pope Meets with Liberation Theology Pioneer," *National Catholic Reporter*, September 25, 2013.

[7] José Miguez Bonino, *Doing Theology in a Revolutionary Situation* (Philadelphia: Fortress Press, 1975), 27.

ought to bring us to a distribution of resources and apostolic personnel that effectively gives preference to the poorest and most needy sectors."[8]

In putting the poor at the center, including advocacy on behalf of the poor, the Latin American church also bridged the rupture between faith and politics. The bishops eloquently sent the message that faith is personal but never private, as theologians, missionaries, and the late Archbishop Óscar Romero himself gave witness, in word and in deed, that the gospel has sociopolitical implications. At their meeting in Puebla, Mexico, in 1979, the bishops also arguably bridged the rupture between faith and culture. Taking inspiration from Paul VI's *Evangelii nuntiandi* (1975), which links the church's abiding concern for social justice with the evangelization of cultures, the Latin American church drove home the point that culture is a mediating element between socioeconomic realities and religious consciousness. In fact, some of the earliest articulations on the liberating potential of popular religion date back to the meeting in Puebla.[9]

These developments galvanized Latin American Christians, who took their cue from the religious leadership, and encouraged those who were already actively engaged in the work for liberation. They became even more aware that Christian life is not just about piety, prayer, and charity and that they are not just expected to pray, pay, and obey but also to speak and advocate for and with the poor. For the millions of poor people in the continent, the pivot of the Latin American church to be a church of the poor provided an energizing vision and inspiration to their struggle for justice and peace and consequently in their active participation in the process of liberation. Thousands of small groups of dispossessed and creative Christians collectively sought to engage the Christian faith and to relate it not only to their own struggle against various forms of injustice but also to their daily life experiences. Moreover, these small Christian communities took on the task of integral and liberating evangelization themselves. In "The Use of the Bible in Christian Communities of the Common People," for example, Carlos Mesters points to how the common people in Latin America make up their own version of the "Bible of the poor" by resorting to songs and stories, pictures, and little plays not only because these are the cultural forms and expressions they can most relate to, but primarily because many of them do not know how to read.[10] Mesters says that thanks to songs, many people who have never read the Bible know almost every story in it.

---

[8] Second General Conference of Latin American Bishops, *The Church in the Present-Day Transformation of Latin America in the Light of the Council* (Division for Latin America, 1973), no. 175.

[9] See, for example, Norbert Greinacher and Norbert Mette, "Editorial," *Concilium* 186 (1986): ix–x.

[10] Carlos Mesters, "The Use of the Bible in Christian Communities of the Common People," in *Liberation Theology: An Introductory Guide*, ed. Curt Cadorette et al. (Maryknoll, NY: Orbis Books, 1992): 45–46.

Here we see another rupture that Latin American Christians exposed and bridged, that is, the rupture between history and agency, particularly among people on the periphery. Enrique Dussel, a prominent liberation theology historian, insists that prior to the rise of liberationist thinking Latin Americans were always outside their own history. With liberation theology, however, they started to rewrite their own and their continent's history, thus making liberation theology truly a theology from the underside of history. The small Christian communities, in particular, became the poor in action and, consequently, an icon of the voiceless and powerless actively participating in their own liberation. This potent combination of a pastoral clergy and a courageous laity significantly accounts for the birth and rise of this critical and prophetic theology we now know as liberation theology.

No theological expression arises or exists in isolation. It has a context of its own that is heavily dictated by the present; it arises from another context that forms part (but not all) of its past; and its future partly depends upon the critical, constructive, and creative weaving of these two.[11] This situation applies to liberation theology insofar as more recent liberationist theologies are partly a result of the critical, constructive, and creative approach to classical (Latin American) liberation theology. One could also argue that contemporary liberation theologies carry on the same spirit of exposing and bridging ruptures within Christianity that characterized classical Latin American liberation theology. It is to these ruptures within the rupture that this essay now turns.

IDENTITY THEOLOGIES: BRIDGING THE RUPTURE BETWEEN ECONOMIC AND CULTURAL CONTEXTS

Toward the end of the twentieth century, particularly in the Ecumenical Association of Third World Theologians (EATWOT) conferences since the 1980s, Latin American liberation theologians were criticized for focusing too much on class or economic poverty.[12] Georges De Schrijver contends that a methodological shift within liberation theology from economic

---

[11] Stephen Bevans's contribution in understanding the role and importance of context in doing theology is widely acknowledged, particularly with his book *Models of Contextual Theology* (Maryknoll, NY: Orbis Books, 2002).

[12] Georges De Schrijver, "Paradigm Shift in Third World Theologies of Liberation: From Socio-economic Analysis to Cultural Analysis?" in *Liberation Theologies on Shifting Grounds: A Clash of Socio-economic and Cultural Paradigms*, ed. G. De Schrijver (Leuven: Leuven University Press, 1998), 3. De Schrijver also points to the presence of this shift in the Latin American bishops' conferences from 1968 to 1992. De Schrijver particularly points to how Medellín (1968) focused on the option for the poor, while Puebla (1979) emphasized the evangelization of culture that he surmised to be due to Vatican pressure to rescue the spiritual

analysis to cultural analysis started around this time, particularly when African and Asian liberation theologians proposed that the class-based analysis should be complemented with culture-based analysis. Sergio Torres and John Eagleson, for example, point to how the cultures of the Indians and the blacks in Latin America seem to have been ignored by Latin American theologians[13] and to black theologians' suspicions of Latin American theologians' white European bias because the latter's emphasis on class struggle seems to make no mention of race oppression.[14] Moreover, women from inside and outside of Latin America began to criticize how the concept *poor* fails to take into account women's experience and perspective. Elina Vuola insists that the generic term *poor* is problematic as it totalizes the "subject" and does not necessarily integrate poverty's female face.[15] Thus Ivone Gebara proposes the articulation of an option for the poor as specifically an option for poor women.[16] Women members of EATWOT also revolted against their marginalization within EATWOT, resulting in what postcolonial biblical critic R. S. Sugirtharajah calls the "irruption within the irruption"[17] with the creation of women's groups such as the Circle of Concerned African Women Theologians, which was founded by Mercy Amba Oduyoye in 1989. The lament of Filipina feminist theologian Mary John Mananzan, in an EATWOT gathering on gender dialogue, reveals classical liberation theology's deficiency when it comes to the integration of women's experience and perspectives. Mananzan shares: "My own impression of the dialogue we had with our male colleagues in the Philippines, was that although they seemed to understand the women's perspective as we explained to them, they have not actually taken it into consideration in their own theologizing. They consider it as primarily the business of the Women's Commission."[18] These irruptions within the irruption put the spotlight on liberationist theologies in the context of cultural identities.

---

dimension, as distinguished from the socioeconomic and political preoccupations of the liberation movement that was the primary focus in Medellín.

[13] Sergio Torres and John Eagleson, eds., *The Challenge of Basic Christian Communities* (Maryknoll, NY: Orbis Books, 1981), 258.

[14] Ibid., 266.

[15] Elina Vuola, *Limits of Liberation: Feminist Theology and the Ethics of Poverty and Reproduction* (New York: Sheffield Academic Press, 2002).

[16] Ivone Gebara, "Option for the Poor as an Option for Poor Women," in *The Power of Naming: A Concilium Reader in Feminist Liberation Theology*, ed. Elisabeth Schüssler Fiorenza (Maryknoll, NY: Orbis Books, 1996), 142–49.

[17] This is a description for a particular type of liberation discourse that is started by those subjects of liberation discourses who feel that their voices are being marginalized in the liberation discourses themselves. R. S. Sugirtharajah, *The Bible and the Third World: Precolonial, Colonial, and Postcolonial Encounters* (Cambridge: Cambridge University Press, 2001), 222.

[18] Mary John Mananzan, "Gender Dialogue in EATWOT: An Asian Perspective," *Voices from the Third World* 19/2 (June 1996): 76.

So what concretely are these identity theologies? In Asia these include *dalit* theology, which articulates the struggle of the untouchables in India;[19] *minjung* theology, which tackles the plight of the ordinary oppressed people of South Korea; and *burakumin* theology, which embodies the struggle of the Burakumins, a group of indigenous people in Japan.[20] In the Middle East there is the Palestinian theology of liberation, primarily fashioned by Naim Stifan Ateek, who insists that a Christian theology of liberation that attends to the Palestinian context would have to speak about justice in relation to the use and interpretation of the Bible. Ateek argues that "strangely—shockingly . . . the Bible has been used by some Western Christians and Jews in a way that has supported *in*justice rather than justice"[21] toward Palestinians. Filipinos, in the meantime, became known for a theology of struggle that drew attention to how faith is lived in the context of a process of working out or working toward full humanity and liberation. Struggle marks and characterizes Filipino lives. The revolutionary point is that their struggle cannot be viewed in isolation from a living and embodied faith. It is a struggle that is at once personal, political, historical, and sacred. This interpretation of liberation, I submit, shares some similarities with *mujerista* theology, a form of liberationist theological reflections of Latinas in the United States. This resonance could be discerned from an oft-repeated phrase by its main proponent, Cuban American theologian Ada María Isasi-Díaz: "la vida es la lucha" (to live is to struggle).[22] Other forms of theologies of liberation in Asia are either explicitly political, like the homeland theology in Taiwan,[23] or directly cultural, like the waterbuffalo theology that Kosuke Koyama fashioned with Thailand in mind.

Having mentioned *burakumin* theology, it is also noteworthy to mention here indigenous Christian theologies as generally belonging to identity theologies or theologies of struggle. In the United States, George Tinker, particularly in *Spirit and Resistance*, serves as an example.[24]

---

[19] See Arvind P. Nirmal, "Toward a Christian Dalit Theology," in *Frontiers in Asian Christian Theology: Emerging Trends,* ed. R. S. Sugirtharajah (Maryknoll, NY: Orbis Books, 1994), 27–40.

[20] See Kuribayashi Teruo, "Recovering Jesus for Outcasts in Japan," in Sugirtharajah, *Frontiers in Asian Christian Theology,* 11–26.

[21] Naim Stifan Ateek, *Justice and Only Justice: A Palestinian Theology of Liberation* (Maryknoll, NY: Orbis Books, 1989), 75.

[22] See Ada María Isasi-Díaz, "Mujerista Theology: A Challenge to Traditional Theology," in *Introduction to Christian Theology: Contemporary North American Perspectives,* ed. Roger A. Badham (Louisville, KY: WJK Press, 1998), 237–52.

[23] For an example of theological reflections on this theme, see Wang Hsien Chih, "Some Perspectives on Homeland Theology in the Taiwanese Context," in Sugirtharajah, *Frontiers in Asian Christian Theology,* 185–95.

[24] See George Tinker, *Spirit and Resistance: Political Theology and American-Indian Liberation* (Minneapolis: Fortress Press, 2004).

Theologies that reflect on multiple or hybrid identities also form part of identity theologies. Among Asian Americans, for instance, Jung Young Lee talks about a theology of marginality.[25] Rita Nakashima Brock proposes a theology on interstitial integrity, especially for Asian Pacific American women.[26] While the two are grounded in paradoxical "both-and" thinking and construct Asian Pacific American identity in its relationship to the hegemony of the dominant culture, Nakashima Brock posits that interstitial integrity draws more faithfully from Asian Pacific Americans' fluid, multilayered, transversal experiences as well as their Asian religio-cultural roots which are embedded in nondualistic metaphysics and religions.[27] While there is more to Asian Pacific American liberationist theologies than identity politics and cultural retrieval, theo-ethical discourse is certainly predicated on identity and difference whereby disruptive wholeness and unruly identity are valued. In a sense the Latino/a theology known as *mestizaje* theology has parallels to Asian Pacific American theologies insofar as its hermeneutical category, that is, *mestizaje*, attends to hybrid, contested identities that have been forged and continue to be recreated in the fire of history.[28]

Somewhat related to identity theologies are two liberation-oriented theologies that are worth mentioning here. The first is postcolonial theologies, which emerged from the theological exploration of the social, political, economic, cultural, and religious practices that arose in resistance to colonialism. Postcolonial theologies typically critique the notion of the "West as center" and engage in a symbolic overhaul and reshaping of dominant meanings within and beyond the Christian world. Romney Moseley provides an example of this in his unmasking of the European Christ or the colonizer's Christ as a symbol of oppression and his proposal for a kenotic Christology, that is, one that does not divorce the glorified Christ—the colonizers' predominant Christ—from the crucified Christ.[29]

The second emerging theology in identity theologies is queer theology, which the late Marcella Althaus-Reid prefers to call "indecent theology." Althaus-Reid maintains that at the heart of the problem that indecent theologies face is the theological construction of normality and the fact

---

[25] See Jung Young Lee, *Marginality: The Key to Multicultural Theology* (Minneapolis: Fortress Press, 1995).

[26] Rita Nakashima Brock, "Interstitial Integrity: Reflections toward an Asian-American Woman's Theology," in Badham, *Introduction to Christian Theology*, 187.

[27] Ibid., 187–88.

[28] Ruy Suárez Rivero, "US Latino/a Theology: A View from the Outside," in *From the Heart of Our People: Latino/a Explorations in Catholic Systematic Theology*, ed. Orlando Espín and Miguel Díaz (Maryknoll, NY: Orbis Books, 1999), 241–42.

[29] Romney Moseley, "Decolonizing Theology in the Caribbean: Prospects for Hermeneutical Reconstruction," in *Constructive Christian Theology in the Worldwide Church*, ed. William R. Barr (Grand Rapids, MI: Eerdmans, 1997), 77–78.

that sexuality in the church is an object of redemption, not dialogue. The tragedy, according to Althaus-Reid, is that Latin American liberation theology has not taken seriously the rich traditions of the sexually different in Latin America, like the Las Locainas (mad festivities) in Venezuela where some men become cross dressers while others are traditionally dressed as priests, and the whole community engages in acts of defiance of a gendered and sacred order.[30]

THEOLOGIES OF DIALOGUE: BRIDGING THE RUPTURE BETWEEN CULTURES AND RELIGIONS

Another cluster of contemporary liberation theologies are the so-called theologies of dialogue, which expose and try to bridge the rupture between cultures and religions. I tackle two of these here, namely, theologies on interreligious dialogue and intercultural theology.

Let us take the case of theologies of interreligious dialogue. Since the 1980s Asian theologians have pointed out to Latin American liberation theologians that the irruption of the non-Christian world challenges liberation theology to expand the existing boundaries of orthodoxy. For example: Aloysius Pieris, who publicly drew attention to this lacuna in liberation theology in one EATWOT general assembly, criticized some Latin American liberation theologians, particularly Jon Sobrino, for promoting a Christology that pits Christ against other religions. Pieris suggests a "Christ of religions" approach in which persons of all religious traditions might unite in a quest for liberation from all forms of oppression.[31] Today, we would have to expand this even further by taking into account that the poor in our midst may not necessarily be believers or adherents of any religion.

In any case the majority of Christian theologians of religions in the First World echo this liberationist approach to religions, also known as the soteriocentric model of religious pluralism. This is true in the case of Paul Knitter. In "Toward a Liberation Theology of Religions," for example, Knitter comments that the hermeneutical privilege that liberation theology gives to the poor could provide a common approach or a common context with which the religions could begin a dialogue. Knitter contends:

---

[30] Marcella Althaus-Reid, "From Liberation Theology to Indecent Theology: The Trouble with Normality in Theology," in *Latin American Liberation Theology: The Next Generation*, ed. Ivan Petrella (Maryknoll, NY: Orbis Books, 2005), 30–33.

[31] See Aloysius Pieris, "Towards an Asian Theology of Liberation: Some Religio-Cultural Guidelines," in *Asia's Struggle for Full Humanity*, ed. Virginia Fabella (Maryknoll, NY: Orbis Books, 1980), 75–96.

Because of its hermeneutical priority and potency, therefore, the preferential option for the oppressed (at least in the world as it exists today) serves as an effective condition for the possibility of dialogue. . . . If the religions of the world, in other words, can recognize poverty and oppression as a common problem, if they can share a common commitment (expressed in different forms) to remove such evils, they will have the basis for reaching across their incommensurabilities and differences in order to hear and understand each other and possibly be transformed in the process.[32]

It is no secret that in the West or in first-world countries the irruption of the non-Christian world is largely due to migration and the imbrication of religion with violence, particularly through acts of terrorism. But when people move they not only bring their religions but also their customs and traditions, which become both gift and challenge to many host societies. Hence, Christian theologies nowadays talk not only of interreligious dialogue but also intercultural dialogue. One theology that has recently emerged from the latter form of dialogue is intercultural theology. Intercultural theology, according to Frans Wijsen, is "the theological reflection on the localization and globalization of contexts and/or the interaction between cultures. . . . In a word, it is the theological reflection on the "intercultural encounter."[33] Traditionally, we talk of multicultural theology which may not be sufficient as it does not fully capture and attend to "the interaction and juxtaposition, as well as [the] tension and resistance when two or more cultures are brought together sometimes organically and sometimes through violent means."[34] Asian American theologian Kwok Pui-lan clarifies this in the case of feminist theology by saying "feminist theology is not only multicultural or rooted in multiple communities and cultural contexts, but is also intercultural because different cultures are not isolated but intertwined with one another."[35] In the United States one can see this in the shifting discourse and images of multiculturalism from the melting pot to the salad bowl to the quilt.

---

[32] Paul Knitter, "Toward a Liberation Theology of Religions," in *The Myth of Christian Uniqueness: Toward a Pluralistic Theology of Religions*, ed. John Hick and Paul Knitter (Maryknoll, NY: Orbis Books, 1992), 186. For profiles of other prominent theologians who take a liberationist approach to religions, see Alfred Hennelly, *Liberation Theologies: The Global Pursuit of Justice* (Mystic, CT: Twenty-Third Publications, 1997), 300–333.

[33] Frans Wijsen, "Intercultural Theology and the Mission of the Church," https://sedosmission.org/old/eng/wijsen.htm.

[34] Kwok Pui-lan, "Feminist Theology as Intercultural Discourse," in *The Cambridge Companion to Feminist Theology*, ed. Susan Frank Parsons (Cambridge: Cambridge University Press, 2002), 25.

[35] Ibid., 24–25.

THEOLOGY OF TRIPLE DIALOGUE:
AN ASIAN PERSPECTIVE ON LIBERATION

One contemporary liberationist theology that takes dialogue as a heuristic lens and means for liberation and is, therefore, treated separately in this section, is the Asian church's theology of triple dialogue. Asia is home not only to the world's great religions and an immense diversity of cultures, but also to more than half of the world's poor. This is the reality that the Federation of Asian Bishops' Conferences (FABC) has seriously taken into consideration, with its concept of dialogue as triple dialogue—dialogue as liberation, dialogue as inculturation, and interreligious dialogue.

According to FABC, the essential mode in which evangelization is carried out in Asia today must be dialogue, more precisely through a more resolute, more creative, and yet truly discerning and responsible inculturation; through interreligious dialogue undertaken in all seriousness; through solidarity and sharing with the poor and the advocacy of human rights.[36]

With regard to dialogue as inculturation, the Asian bishops are convinced that the dialogical encounter between the local churches and Asia's living traditions and cultures is critical in building a church *of* Asia and not so much a church *in* Asia. The bishops reckon that an inculturated church "seeks to share in whatever truly belongs to the people: its meanings and its values, its aspirations, its thoughts, and its language, its songs and its artistry."[37] They maintain that true inculturation, far from being a means for the propagation of the faith, "belongs to the very core of evangelization, for it is the continuation in time and space of the dialogue of salvation initiated by God and brought to a culmination when he uttered his Word in a very concrete historical situation."[38]

This stance is firmly rooted in FABC's recognition of the gifts and richness that Asia's diverse cultures have to offer. This is the same attitude that the Asian bishops have assumed in relation to Asia's various religions. Noted Indian Jesuit theologian Sebastian Painadath, in his exposition of FABC's theology of dialogue, underscores the bishops' fundamental commitment to interreligious dialogue, drawing attention to the promise that they made in their first meeting in Manila in 1970: "We pledge to an open, sincere and continuing dialogue with our brothers and sisters of other great religions of Asia that we may learn from one another how to enrich ourselves spiritually and how to work more effectively together

---

[36] For a fairly comprehensive look into FABC theology, see *For All the Peoples of Asia*, 5 vols. (Manila: Claretian Publications, 1997–2014). Volume 1 is edited by Gaudencio Rosales and Catalino Arevalo; volume 2 by Franz-Josef Eilers.

[37] Jonathan Tan, "Local Churches and the Task of Christian Mission in Asia," in *Dialogue: Resource Manual for Catholics in Asia*, ed. Edmund Chia (Bangkok: Federation of Asian Bishops' Conferences-OEIA, 2001), 106.

[38] Rosales and Arevalo, *For All the Peoples of Asia,* 1:94.

on our common task of human development."[39] The pledge suggests that
the work of human development depends upon a sustained commitment
to dialogue.

Dialogue as liberation, in the meantime, is born out of the Asian bishops'
conviction that Christ is calling the churches of Asia to address the material
deprivation of poor people.[40] The FABC believes that because millions in
Asia are poor, "the Church in Asia must be the Church of the poor."[41] The
practice of justice is a commitment made very explicit during the bishops'
sixth plenary assembly, which centered on the theme "Christian Discipleship in Asia Today: Service to Life." The bishops declare:

> Like Jesus, we have to "pitch our tents" in the midst of all humanity
> building a better world, but especially among the suffering and the
> poor, the marginalized and the downtrodden of Asia. In profound
> "solidarity with suffering humanity" and led by the Spirit of life, we
> need to immerse ourselves in Asia's cultures of poverty and depriva-
> tion, from whose depths the aspirations for love and life are the most
> poignant and compelling. Serving life demands communion with
> every woman and man seeking and struggling for life, in the way of
> Jesus' solidarity with humanity.[42]

In the mind of the bishops this dialogue with the poor toward liberation addresses one crucial goal of the Asian church, that is, "total human
development" or "integral human development." In fact, one point repeatedly stressed by the FABC is that human development and progress in all
aspects—political, social, economic, technological, and cultural—form an
intrinsic and constitutive dimension of the church's evangelizing mission.
This integral human development, also expressed by FABC in terms of
"holistic life," is understood in three senses. First, it embraces all the dimensions of the human person as a unity of body-psyche-spirit and rejects the
reduction of human development to economic and technological progress.
Second, it means that all resources and means, not only technological and
material ones, should be pressed into service. Third, it must go hand in
hand with the other two components of the Asian concept of dialogue,
that is, inculturation and interreligious dialogue. Indeed, the three forms
of dialogue are closely linked, with dialogue as liberation often making up
the hub. Drawing from the bishops' thoughts, Painadath asserts:

> Hence, when believers of various religions work together to bring
> about integral human liberation and environmental harmony, they

---

[39] Sebastian Painadath, SJ, "Federation of Asian Bishops' Conferences Theology
of Dialogue," in Chia, *Dialogue: Resource Manual for Catholics in Asia*, 102.

[40] Rosales and Arevalo, *For All the Peoples of Asia*, 1:16.

[41] Ibid., 23.

[42] Eilers, *For All the Peoples of Asia*, 2:8.

discover the creative and redemptive forces in each religion and
articulate the liberative and unifying potential of each religion. . . .
Concern for the poor, therefore, is the meeting point of religions;
compassion is the hallmark of a religious person.[43]

Painadath as well as Peter Phan commend this inseparable linkage
among the three as part of the originality and depth of FABC's theology
of dialogue. Phan, in particular, highlights the importance of making interreligious dialogue and inculturation necessary phases of the church's work
for liberation, avoiding possible distortions of a one-sided emphasis on the
material and political aspects of salvation. Phan states that by combining
these three aspects of the church's ministry, FABC has improved upon
papal teachings on human development and most Western theologies of
inculturation and interreligious dialogue.[44]

To achieve or, at the very least, to work toward integral human development, the FABC's Bishops' Institute for Social Action came up with a
methodology called the pastoral cycle. Designed to help persons engaged
in programs of human development arrive at appropriate policies and
effective courses of action, the pastoral cycle has four steps. The first is
exposure-immersion by the agents of human development to the concrete
situation of the poor, with whom and for whom they work. The second is
social analysis, where the social, economic, political, cultural, and religious
systems of society, as well as the signs of the times, the events of history,
and the needs and aspirations of the people are investigated. The third step
is the "integration of social analysis with the [Asian] religio-cultural reality,
discerning not only its negative and enslaving aspects but also its positive,
prophetic aspects that can inspire genuine spirituality."[45] Aloysius Pieris
calls this step *introspection.* He contends that a "liberation-theopraxis" in
Asia that uses only the Marxist tools of social analysis will remain un-Asian
and ineffective until it integrates the psychological tools of introspection
that Asian sages have discovered.[46] The fourth step is *pastoral planning,*
or the formulation of practical and realistic policies, strategies, and plans
of action toward integral human development. As the plans of action are
implemented, they are continuously submitted to evaluation by a review
of the first three steps of the pastoral cycle.

The Asian notion of liberation, Pieris observes further, is a modified and
significantly enriched version of papal social teaching and Latin American

[43] Painadath himself speaks of the poor as meeting point in FABC's three forms
of dialogue. See Painadath, "Federation of Asian Bishops' Conferences Theology
of Dialogue," 104.

[44] Peter Phan, *Christianity with an Asian Face: Asian-American Theology in the
Making* (Maryknoll, NY: Orbis Books, 2003), 199.

[45] Rosales and Arevalo, *For All the Peoples of Asia,* 1:231.

[46] Aloysius Pieris, *An Asian Theology of Liberation* (Maryknoll, NY: Orbis
Books, 1988), 80.

liberation theology. This can be seen in how contemplation or introspection is added to social analysis as part of the theological method. Most important, this can be seen in how interreligious dialogue and inculturation are made necessary phases of the church's work for liberation. Pieris regards this "double baptism," that is, baptism in the Jordan of Asian religions and the Calvary of Asian poverty, as "the way toward ecclesiological revolution."[47]

ENVIRONMENTAL THEOLOGIES: BRIDGING THE RUPTURE BETWEEN HUMANITY AND THE CREATED WORLD

Whether it is creation theology, ecological theology, planetary theology, or theology on the cosmos, ecology has also become a hermeneutical category in contemporary liberationist discourse. One group of theologians who attend to this issue and make an explicit connection to liberation theology are those who argue that environmental exploitation and destruction contribute to or worsen poor people's oppression. The late Sr. Dorothy Stang exemplifies this.[48] Another group makes a direct link between environmental injustice and racism. Steven Bouma-Prediger, for example, points to a study that concluded that although socioeconomic status plays an important role, race is the best predictor in identifying communities most likely to be locations for toxic waste sites.[49]

The growth of environmental theologies is notable in the past decade with the release of theological works[50] as well as pastoral statements from various parts of the world[51] relating to the care for the environment or a cosmological perspective on human life. To be sure, there are various strands within these theologies. Thomas Massaro, for example, points out four categories: dominion model, stewardship model, creation-centered approach, and deep ecology.[52] A liberationist perspective is discernible in Pope Francis's encyclical *Laudato si'*, which relates integral development

---

[47] Ibid., 45–50.

[48] See Roseanne Murphy, *Martyr of the Amazon: The Life of Sister Dorothy Stang* (Maryknoll, NY: Orbis Books, 2007).

[49] Steven Bouma-Prediger, "Environmental Racism," in *Handbook of US Theologies of Liberation*, ed. Miguel De La Torre (St. Louis: Chalice Press, 2004), 283.

[50] See, for example, Elizabeth Johnson, *Ask the Beasts: Darwin and the God of Love* (London: Bloomsbury, 2014), esp. 260–86.

[51] Pope Francis mentions and footnotes seventeen of these pastoral letters, the majority of which are from the global South, for example, Bolivia and the Philippines, in his 2015 encyclical *Laudato si' (On Care for Our Common Home)*. See, for example, footnotes 22–27.

[52] Thomas Massaro, SJ, *Living Justice: Catholic Social Teaching in Action* (Lanham, MD: Rowman and Littlefield, 2015), 181.

with integral ecology by seeking a sustainable development that clearly respects the human and social dimensions and is inextricably linked to the environmental question.

RUPTURES FOR THE SAKE OF THE FUTURE?
CHALLENGES FOR CONTEMPORARY
LIBERATION THEOLOGIES

So what does the future hold for contemporary forms of liberation theology? What are some of the problems they face, according to critics? Let me offer two. One has to do with the question of which analytical category should be prioritized. Ivan Petrella, for instance, insists that material deprivation based on class remains the most important form of oppression—but that the upsurge of race, ethnicity, gender, sexuality, and ecology as the organizing axis for liberation theology has blurred its critical role. Petrella contends that the most egregious assaults on human dignity most commonly occur not because one is brown or black or because one is female, but because one is poor. To be a person of color and/or female and poor increases the risk, he says, that is grounded in class.[53] I wonder, however, if it is really simply a case of going back or reemphasizing the original category of analysis, that is, class. Does one category of analysis really have to take prominence, or would it have to be based on context? And if we really have to emphasize class over color or gender, who are the poor that we are talking about here?

The other tension within contemporary liberation theologies is the struggle between the universal and the particular. Elisabeth Schüssler Fiorenza articulates this in relation to feminist theologies in the United States. Schüssler Fiorenza posits that "feminist discourses in religion have for the most part not yet critically problematized American capitalist nationalism as a structure of domination" and challenges American feminists, whether black, white, Asian, *mujerista*, or Latina, to theologize critically on their "Americanness" or, more concretely, on how their Americanness shapes their discourses. She asks, "Is it sufficient to name and reflect critically on our racial, sexual, gender, and class social-religious locations while at the same time leaving out our nationalist determinedness?"[54] Schüssler Fiorenza also argues for a critical consideration of nationalism, insofar as discourses of feminist theology and religious studies tend to define and construct identity in terms of continents—Asian, African, South American,

---

[53] Ivan Petrella, "Globalizing Liberation Theology: The American Context, and Coda," in *The Cambridge Companion to Liberation Theology*, 2nd ed., ed. Christopher Rowland (Cambridge: Cambridge University Press, 2007), 284.

[54] Elisabeth Schüssler Fiorenza, "Feminist Studies in Religion and Theology In-Between Nationalism and Globalization," *Journal of Feminist Studies in Religion* 21/1 (Spring 2005): 115.

African American, or Euro-American feminist theology—and tend to reinscribe nationalistic tendencies. Korean American theologian Anselm Min echoes this by suggesting that it is time for ethnic theologies to move forward from regional theology to a concretely universal theology, proposing a new paradigm called "solidarity of Others."[55]

The questions, therefore, are these: Has liberation theology's vision been reduced because of tribalism? Have contemporary liberation theologies, particularly identity theologies, become insular and parochial? Is there really too much focus on particular concerns and identities such that more universal concerns and realities, like world hunger, are not getting a much needed and equally important place?

CONCLUSION

Rupture ordinarily connotes a broken state, a breaking in, or a breaking apart of something. It also refers to a breach in relations or a breakdown in a friendly or peaceful relationship. While most of us would probably prefer an "un-ruptured" world, this is not always the best case for theology. Theological ethics, for example, cannot be done in a closed setting. As Clemens Sedmak writes:

It has to be open to disruptions . . . [whereby] established points of reference for identity are being called into question. Disruptions stop the status quo. Disruptive processes change the coordinates of the unquestionable, of what is simply accepted. . . . Disruptions change the "structures of relevance" (Alfred Schuetz) so much so that the relevance of relevance becomes an issue. Disruptions change the "systems of acceptance" (Keith Lehrer) so much so that the very idea of acceptability becomes questionable.[56]

Classic liberation theology clearly constitutes a disruption, a rupture to Christian theology. Accordingly, contemporary liberation theologies insofar as they are a rethinking, reimagination, and critique of classic liberation theology could be regarded as ruptures within the rupture or the disruptions within the disruption. The same is true with the criticisms leveled at the contemporary forms of liberation theology. Insofar as the criticisms are constructive and transformative, they are a much welcome disruption. "Disruptions shatter the foundations of our life plans and life

---

[55] Anselm Min, "From Autobiography to Fellowship of Others: Reflections on Doing Ethnic Theology Today," in *Journeys at the Margin: Towards an Autobiographical Theology in Asian-American Perspective*, ed. Peter Phan and Jung Young Lee (Collegeville, MN: Liturgical Press, 1999), 135–60.

[56] Oliver Davies et al., *Transformation Theology: Church in the World* (London: T & T Clark, 2007), 119.

forms. Disruptions call for a new reading of our life, a new life plan, a new quest for identity, a new way of being in the world. . . . Disruptions are fundamental invitations to begin yet again, to make a fresh start,"[57] to do theology in a new key—and the extent to which we are able to do this will be the extent to which we will able to say we have listened to the groaning of the Spirit in our midst.

---

[57] Ibid., 120.

Chapter 11

Contextual Theology
from a Cultural Perspective

José M. de Mesa

The influential Society of the Divine Word missionary anthropologist Louis Luzbetak tells a story about a group of foreign missionaries listening to the lament of a Christian in Asia about how the gospel is communicated in his country: "You say that you are bringing Jesus and a new humanity to us. But what is this 'new humanity' which you are referring to? We want to see, touch, taste, feel what this is. Jesus cannot just be a name to us; he needs to become real to us. You must be able to describe Jesus as a fellow human being." Luzbetak's comment on this incident is pertinent: "All human beings are *cultural* beings. Jesus must be culturally relevant if he is really to be understood and appreciated. This is *a most obvious fact unfortunately only too often ignored*" (emphasis added).[1]

RECOVERY OF EXPERIENCE AND CULTURE
IN THEOLOGIZING

There have been a number of developments in theology that responded to the neglect of culture in doing theology. One is renewed attention to experience. Experience is not only essential because it is what gives theology its relevance, but also constitutive because theology is precisely reflection arising from and speaking to experience. The elements of reality and interpretation permeate all experiences.

Experience has always been a part of the theological process, but there were times when it seemed to have been eclipsed by doctrine. This was the case with neo-Scholasticism, which dominated the theological scene in

---

[1] Louis J. Luzbetak, SVD, *The Church and Cultures: New Perspectives in Missiological Anthropology* (Maryknoll, NY: Orbis Books, 1988), 374.

the nineteenth and early twentieth centuries. Developed to respond mainly
to the challenges hurled at the church's doctrine by rationalism, it made
doctrine the beginning and the end of theological reflection.[2] Typical of
its methodology was presentation of the doctrine, proofs of the doctrine
from scripture and tradition, and speculative elaboration and application
of the doctrine to the situation. True knowledge, especially supernatural
knowledge, known as truths, was its foremost concern. Human experience
was virtually absent in its consideration, even though it was actually the
experience of rationalism that brought it to existence.

Experience is necessarily interpreted experience. When we speak of
experience we mean contact with reality and interpretation. There is no
experience bereft of interpretation.[3] Interpretation does not begin only
when questions are asked about the significance of what one has experienced; interpretative identification is already an intrinsic element of the
experience itself, first unexpressed and then deliberately reflected on. This
process of identification is unavoidably a speech event as well. There are
interpretative elements in an experience that find their foundation and
source directly in what is actually experienced. Some of these may be
implicit, while others are explicit.

One of Asia's famous didactic tales illustrates this conviction. It is the
story of blind men trying to figure out what an elephant is. The tale has
many versions. At its core, however, is that each of the men feels a different
part of the elephant, but only one part. When they start comparing what
they think the elephant is, they realize that each one's experience of the
elephant is different. They are in complete disagreement. Variations of the
story deal with how the elephant's body parts are described.

However, there are also interpretative elements that come to us from
elsewhere, at least from outside an experience. It is never possible to draw a
clear distinction between these elements and those that come directly from
a particular experience. Such is culture. Culture is "shared gut feeling,"[4]
the set of basic dispositions toward reality and meanings that people create, and that create people, as members of societies. Upon inquiring as
to where many of us get most of our interpretations of reality, we find
ourselves turning to culture. We can, of course, make sense of the reality
we encounter with interpretations from previous experience, knowledge
gained through education, personal philosophy, or any other meaningful
perspective. But we all have a cultural community to which we belong.
Having been socialized into it, we have grown accustomed to its ways. This
is why I regard inculturation, with its focus on culture, as an important
aspect of doing contextual theology.

---

[2] See Donald K. McKim, *Westminster Dictionary of Theological Terms* (Louisville, KY: Westminster John Knox Press, 1996), 185.

[3] *Rashomon* is a film by the Japanese director Akira Kurosawa that demonstrates
the importance of interpretation.

[4] Shared with me in a conversation with anthropologist and theologian Gerald
Arbuckle.

People spontaneously express themselves through their culture, a collective tradition of experiences and manner of living that becomes second nature to them. It is through this dynamic and integrated system of feeling, behaving, and thinking that they instinctively tend to make sense of any given reality. This insight is not new. The Scholastics recognized the power of such an inclination in their dictum "whatever is perceived is perceived by the mode of perception of the perceiver."[5]

The Shift from a Classical to an Empirical Understanding of Culture

Adding to the recovery of experience and interpretation in theology is the significant change in viewing culture. Before the important shift around the 1950s from a classical to an empirical understanding of culture, the Euro-American West widely regarded itself as superior for being the only cultured people in the world. Presupposing possession of the only culture in existence, the other peoples were to follow its ways en route to civilization.[6] Through colonization, often in tandem with evangelization,

---

[5] See also Stephen B. Bevans, *Models of Contextual Theology* (Maryknoll, NY: Orbis Books, 2002), xix.

[6] Cf. Bernard Lonergan, *Method in Theology* (New York: Herder and Herder, 1972), 124, 301, 326–30, 362–63. A classicist, writes Lonergan, "would feel it was perfectly legitimate for him to impose his culture on others. For he conceives culture normatively, and he conceives his own to be the norm. Accordingly, for him to preach both the gospel and his own culture, is for him to confer the double benefit of both true religion and the true culture" (363).

Western thought and practice were propagated from the sixteenth to the twentieth centuries among peoples of the Third World.

The missionaries who were part of the venture to spread Christianity were in general unaware of its cultural underpinnings. Western theological thought, its content and methods, became known and dominant in the churches they initiated and guided. The peoples so instructed were made to believe they were getting the best there was and that they had nothing of their own to offer. This phenomenon frequently led to a feeling of "anthropological poverty,"[7] whereby communities struggled to find their own cultural voice; this forms part of the long-term effects of a time of cultural debasement.[8]

Oftentimes the native language was marginalized by the colonizer's mother tongue, as in the case of the Philippines. Among Filipinos today, American English is the language of preference if one wants to be considered thoughtful, intelligent, and cultured. English rather than the Filipino language, not surprisingly, is the *lingua franca* of the local theological enterprise. It tends to control and dominate indigenous thought in theological matters, making it difficult to theologize in Filipino.[9] And so one of the main tasks in inculturation is the re-appropriation of the faith through culture and language.[10]

---

[7] Stephen Bevans, "Letting Go and Speaking Out: Prophetic Dialogue and the Spirituality of Inculturation," in *Prophetic Dialogue: Reflections on Christian Mission Today*, ed. Stephen B. Bevans and Roger P. Schroeder (Maryknoll, NY: Orbis Books, 2011), 96.

[8] José Rizal, the national hero of the Philippines, describes the effects of the Spanish colonial rule as "little by little [the Filipinos] lost their old traditions, the mementos of their past; they gave up their writing, their songs, their poems, their laws. . . . Then they declined, degrading themselves in their own eyes; they became ashamed of what was their own; they began to admire and praise whatever was foreign and incomprehensible; their spirit was dismayed and it surrendered." Quoted in Teodoro A. Agoncillo, *History of the Filipino People* (Quezon City: Garotech Publishing, 1990), 100.

[9] See Stephen B. Bevans, *An Introduction to Theology in Global Perspective* (Maryknoll, NY: Orbis Books, 2009), 24–25. Aloysius Pieris thinks a people's native tongue is like its "cultural DNA-code," and that "stubborn refusal to consult each other's linguistic idioms, or even to be familiar with one's own cultural heritage, will remain one major obstacle to the discovery of a truly Asian Theology." See "The New Quest for Asian Christian Identity," in *Viele Weg-ein Ziel: Herausforderungen im Dialog der Religionen und Kulturen,* ed. Ludwig Bertsch, SJ, Martin Evers, and Marco Moerschbacher (Freiburg: Herder, 2006), 28.

[10] This endeavor, which has also been called vernacular hermeneutics, "privileges (the) indigenous culture as an authentic site for doing theology" and "focuses on native characteristics and ideas." See R. S. Sugirtharajah, "Vernacular Resurrections: An Introduction," in *Vernacular Hermeneutics*, ed. R. S. Sugirtharajah (Sheffield: Sheffield Academic Press, 1999), 13.

The myth that there was only one culture for all peoples, namely, the Euro-American civilization, was debunked with the discovery and recognition of different cultures. The West's claim to cultural superiority was negated in the context of cultural plurality and the rise of collective self-identity. Local, pluriform cultures are now, rightfully, clamoring for more recognition of their self-definition in this postcolonial period. As is just, the Euro-American West will be seen increasingly as only one—though still important—among the many cultures of the world, not only in theory but also in actual practice.[11]

Toward a World Church and Local Theologies: The Impetus Set by Vatican II

Stimulated by this change, Christian churches on a global level, both Catholic and Protestant, have seen the need to review their understanding of culture and of mission. The Catholic Church, after holding the groundbreaking Second Vatican Council (1962–65),[12] stopped talking about "transplanting" the European church in other lands as the aim of disseminating Catholicism. The announcement of the gospel, rather than being seen in terms of translation into the local idiom, came to be viewed as a re-appropriation of it by the people themselves. With the council the Catholic Church began speaking of the importance of culture in the life and practice of the church (*Gaudium et spes*, 53).

Theologian Karl Rahner, in the context of change in both cultural perception and ecclesial understanding, gave a most instructive interpretation of Vatican II. From his viewpoint there are three cultural epochs of Christianity: Jewish, Greco-Roman, and today the many different third-world cultures. With the third kind of expression, the church was on its way to birthing a "world church."[13] Just as the Council of Jerusalem had made it possible for the church to go beyond Jewish Christianity in the first century, so the Second Vatican Council in the twentieth century enabled the community to translate Greco-Roman Christianity into different cultural forms of ecclesiality. Inculturation—the re-appropriation of the gospel in terms of constantly changing systems of cultural feelings, practices, and beliefs of a people—is being realized in different localities. In other words, just as the Jewish Christians used their culture to express their faith in Jesus Christ, and the Greeks and the Romans employed theirs to embody

---

[11] Shaji George Kochuthara, "Christianity in Asia Today: Attempts to Re-discover Its Heritage and Identity," *Asian Horizons* 10/3 (September 2016): 577–95.

[12] Walter M. Abbott, SJ, *The Documents of Vatican II* (New York: Guild Press, 1966). All quotations from the council's documents are from this source.

[13] Karl Rahner, "Towards a Fundamental Interpretation of Vatican II," *Theological Studies* 40/4 (1979): 716–27.

their allegiance to the Gospel, the peoples of today are articulating new cultural expressions of the Christian faith.[14]

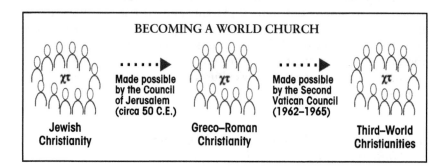

Vatican II is calling us to do our very own theologies in the context of our cultures. It explains why in *Gaudium et spes* (GS). Overall, the Second Vatican Council has emphasized the importance of culture and inculturation for making the gospel meaningful. First, it reminds us that the cultural is part of humanity's total well-being. Human flourishing as cultural identity and integrity is part of the soteriological intent of the church. We read, "It is a fact bearing on the very person of man that he can come to an authentic and full humanity only through culture" (GS 53). Then, citing the incarnation, it affirms that revelation reached its fullness through the cultural medium and we know that God "has spoken according to the culture proper to different ages" (GS 58). God speaks through people's cultural idiom.

Accordingly, the document sketches a historical panorama of the church in cultural terms. "Living in various circumstances during the course of time, the Church, too, has used in her preaching the discoveries of different cultures to spread and explain the message of Christ to all nations, to probe it and more deeply understand it, and to give it better expression in liturgical celebrations and in the life of the diversified community of the faithful" (GS 58).

It is only right then that a development of "local churches" rooted in their respective cultural contexts would be pursued, considering that each local culture has the capability of expressing the gospel in its own terms (GS 44). Roman Catholicism began to be seen as only one of the

---

[14] A shift in attitude toward culture, from an obstacle to an important reality in announcing the gospel, has also occurred in evangelical missionary circles. See, for instance, the *LOP 2—The Willowbank Report: Consultation on Gospel and Culture*. Lausanne Occasional Paper 2 of Lausanne Committee for World Evangelization (1978).

many expressions of the Christian faith. Other churches should not be deterred because "the Church, sent to all peoples of every time and place, is not bound exclusively and indissolubly to any race or nation, not to any particular way of life or any customary pattern of living, ancient or recent. Faithful to her own tradition and at the same time conscious of her universal mission, she can enter into communion with various cultural modes, to her own enrichment and theirs too" (GS 58).

We turn to inculturated theologies to illustrate this. Instead of imagining God's communication with humanity only in the form of the neo-Scholastic category of revealing supernatural truths that were absolute and immutable, and human beings assenting to those truths, Vatican II re-envisioned it in terms of the Jewish and biblical notion of the "Word of God." "The Word of God," that is, God, "speaks" with humanity as friends, offering them life and love, and people express their faith by "hearing" *(obedire)*. This change in the understanding of revelation-faith by the council served as an impetus in the West for comprehending the relationship in personalist I-Thou terms. It is a *traditio personae*, God giving God's total Self to other selves. Filipinos, for their part, can now view revelation-faith in terms of *loób*. *Loób*, a local concept rich in meaning, refers to one's most authentic relational self and the source of all feelings, behavior, and thought. Metaphorically, God makes us *feel (dama)*, that is, experience God's *loób*, and we in turn internalize this *loób* of God *(pagsasa-loób)* by faith. This description has traces of Eastern theology's notion of *deification (theosis)*.[15]

CHANGED ATTITUDE TOWARD CULTURES AFTER VATICAN II

Significantly, the church's attitude toward culture changed after the Second Vatican Council. Previously considered pagan and full of superstitions, culture was regarded by Vatican II as generally positive. It incorporated this stance in its theologizing. *Ad gentes (Decree on the Missionary Activity of the Church)* states what inculturation implies—it is to follow Christ in his dealings with culture, first in general and second in particular. *Ad gentes* (AG) notes, "Christ Himself searched the hearts of men, and led them to divine light. . . . So also His disciples, profoundly penetrated by the Spirit of Christ, should show the people among whom they live, and should converse with them" (AG 11). Then centering on the dialogical posture of Jesus, the decree states, "Thus they themselves can *learn by sincere and patient dialogue* what *treasures* a bountiful God has distributed among the nations of the earth. But at the same time, let them try to illumine

---

[15] "Communicating 'Revelation-Faith' with Culture in Mind," in *José M. de Mesa: A Theological Reader* (Manila: De La Salle University Publishing House, 2016), 315–28.

these treasures with the light of the gospel, to set them free, and to bring them under the dominion of God their Savior" (AG 11, emphasis added).

Creation-centered Approach to Inculturation

One can consider two major and distinct approaches to inculturation in theology.[16] Before Vatican II, a redemption-centered approach predominated. Its focal point was the redemption brought about through Jesus Christ. People had souls to be redeemed. Their culture, which was outside the ambit of God's grace, had to be snatched from the snares of the devil. The church's task was to win back everything for God. Understandably, from this perspective, culture was in the shadow of darkness. Preferably, one's culture would be abandoned upon conversion. This had caused many cultures in Asia to think that to be a Christian was to be a traitor to one's people.

Another approach to inculturation is creation centered. It highlights, according to Paul, "whatever is true, whatever is honorable, whatever is just, whatever is pure, whatever is pleasing, whatever is commendable, if there is any excellence and if there is anything worthy of praise, think about these things" (Phil 4:8). Its starting point focused on original blessings rather than original sin and its consequences. We start from the creation belief that humanity and all of creation was good, indeed "very good" (Gen 1:31). The highlighting of "treasures" suggests giving a certain priority to the hermeneutics of appreciation,[17] where cultural elements that are positive are foregrounded before tending to what is negative in the culture. The inculturation process does not deny death-dealing elements in the culture. But it gives space to the wisdom and genius of the culture, lest what is detrimental in human life gain primary attention in our theologizing.[18]

This shift suggests also the re-evaluation of cultures before the advent of Christianity. "Pagan" cultures were considered non-salvific and the people who subscribed to them were in danger of getting lost. Assuming that outside the church there was no salvation, they had to be converted to Christianity in order to be saved. But if, as *Ad gentes* suggests, every culture has "treasures a bountiful God has distributed among the nations of the earth," then it is a reminder to us that God was at work from the very beginning of our cultural history. Every embodied sentiment, practice, belief, and institution bears traces of God accompanying us and active in our culture long before Christianity reached our shores. After all, we believe that the Holy Spirit "hovered over the waters" of chaos. God as

---

[16] Bevans, *Models of Contextual Theology,* 21–22.

[17] "Hermeneutics of Appreciation: Approach and Methodology," in *José M. de Mesa: A Theological Reader*, 102–95.

[18] Bevans comments on this in what he calls "the spirituality of the insider." See Bevans and Schroeder, *Prophetic Dialogue*, 95–99.

Spirit was already offering salvation in God's work from the time of creation. Truly, "the beginning of the history of human liberation coincides with the beginning of creation."[19]

The change of attitude toward culture does not mean accepting everything in it as commendatory. Like any human endeavor, culture is a mix of both the life giving and the death dealing, at times the former more than the latter, and at other times the negative prevails. What tends to life must be fostered, and what tends toward death must be resisted and challenged.

Highlighting Cultural Energies

Together with the change in attitude toward culture and cultures is the revision of how we describe culture itself. This has implications for doing theology as "inculturation," a term used by the Asian bishops as early as 1971. *Inculturation* is another word for *contextualization,* but with a nuance. It privileges culture in its broadest sense, meaning the whole of humanly interpreted human existence. Culture affects the whole of life, but it is not the whole of life. *Inculturation,* which means the re-appropriation of the gospel in a particular vibrant culture, wants to highlight the use of specifically cultural interpretations to express the good news, while being aware of the other elements of context such as the personal, gender, social, economic, political, ecological, and global realities. Drawing primarily from the traditional set of feelings, practices, and thought, and renewing them, inculturation tries to make sense of contemporary situations and experiences.

The turn to the culture did not mean concentration solely on the traditional culture, but rather on worthwhile communal living at the present time. Traditional culture precisely embodied experience-tested and time-tested traditions that a community found valuable for living life together. We are not to undervalue or overvalue the traditional. We appreciate and honor the ways of our predecessors by sustaining and renewing our traditions. By their effort and creativity they were able to create a way of life worthy of human beings. We remind ourselves that just because we come after them, we are not therefore necessarily better than they in every way.

The culture of traditions is better viewed as a repository of cultural energies.[20] Knowing that our ancestors have labored, through trial and error, trial and success, to what we have today as the present state of our culture is to realize our huge indebtedness to them. Rather than seeing our traditions as artifacts, as a petrified, embedded inventory of knowledge,

---

[19] Edward Schillebeeckx, *Interim Report on the Books "Jesus" and "Christ"* (New York: Crossroad, 1981), 119.

[20] Albert Alejo, SJ, suggests the term *cultural energies* in narrating the Manobos experience. See *Generating Energies in Mt. Apo: Cultural Politics in a Contested Environment* (Quezon City: Ateneo de Manila University Press, 2000), 80–121.

we view them as stored energies. They are a valuable stock of knowledge containing important lessons for living life together. As cultural energies, cultures are prepared, therefore, for new eventualities. Let me give an example from an indigenous tribe in the Philippines that faced the nightmare of globalization.

Serving as a parable in response to this outlook is a study on the Tuddok (Pillars), a movement for cultural regeneration among the Obo Manobo tribe.[21] It pinpoints key concerns with which indigenous people are preoccupied: land, cultural identity and integrity, and ancestry. The tribe lived in an area that was affected by a 250–megawatt geothermal power plant set up by the Philippine National Oil Corporation in the southernmost part of the Philippines in Mt. Apo, Mindanao. The place was an ecologically sensitive and politically explosive site, besides being a recognized heritage site in Southeast Asia because of its rich biodiversity. More important, it is home to several thousand people who consider the mountain sacred. Apart from being a shelter for armed insurgents, there were the deleterious intrusions of business, the military, and the government in the area. Interventions made by church groups and nongovernmental organizations on behalf of the tribe were of no real benefit. The conflicting interests and actions simply made the Manobos passive to what was going on. In the midst of all these troubles, the most unfortunate and perhaps fundamental affliction that visited the Obo Manobos was the absence of the will to survive and the consequent nonchalance regarding the permanent loss of their land due to the establishment of the power plant.

This dispirited outlook was articulated by the Manobos themselves when they said to an anthropologist researcher who wanted to study their situation, "Why do you still want to study us? We have no more culture here." The response implied a number of things: a feeling of inferiority, a sense of embarrassment in the hunters who were unable to catch prey in their disturbed forest, awkwardness at having to borrow old gongs so that they could dance, the pain of being fired from jobs because they did not have the necessary technical skills, shame that arose from being scolded by nurses in municipal clinics and from being accused of having sold their souls to the "development aggressor."

Perhaps out of a combined sense of desperation and a pining for the familiar, the Manobos thought it best to work for what is called cultural regeneration. This meant a whole cluster of missing and interrelated things: The retrieval of traditional values like family closeness and resource sharing. The revival of old rituals and of epic songs as well as the relishing of the interaction when singing such songs. Experiencing once again their dances and the wearing of their traditional bright red costumes with the ornamental sequins and beads during their self-chosen tribal festivals.

---

[21] Ibid. This is a summary of the outlook, the actions that flowed from this frame of mind, and its overall outcome.

The giving back to the *datu* (leader) the honor of being the village strong man and wise man, and acknowledging his capacity to settle disputes. The recovery of the ancient ways of healing through the use of herbs and barks according to the instructions of spirits communicated in dreams. The renewed desire to learn and speak their own language and possibly produce literature in it. No doubt the unspoken wish was the recovery of their collective self-confidence and self-determination.

From this deep desire for cultural regeneration was born a very specific plan of action: the holding of a family reunion that would last three days and three nights. This was surprising given the chaotic and turbulent condition the tribe was experiencing. But it was their idea, not one imposed on them from the outside, and it would not only address their situation the way they saw it, but would also touch on land as it was tightly bound to their culture and future. Considering the amount of time needed to raise the funds for the big event and the necessary arrangements to be made, the tribe calculated it would require two years of preparation.

But as the Manobos mobilized themselves for the event, they became so enthused by the whole plan that resources and contributions quickly flowed in. As a result, the projected preparation of two years was reduced to three months. An immediate and fortunate consequence of the process was that old people became important again. Families, inquiring after their ancestry, turned to the elderly for answers. For the dancing that was essential to the reunion, musical instruments had to be borrowed from another tribe. Theirs had been sold earlier to pay bills and to respond to other necessities.

The celebration was held as planned. In this coming together ties were strengthened, cultural traditions were revived, and the tribe's spirit was emboldened. The concerns of the community began to get organized attention. Finally, the tribe faced the most important issue of ancestral domain claims. From the cultural rejuvenation, which included a critical discernment of what was sustainable and what was not, arose energies to tackle economic and political issues confronting the community. It was as if the Manobos were asking, "How can we continue to dance if we are not secure on our land?"

Thus, a seemingly harmless cultural celebration had shown itself to be a powerful source of energy for the determination to continue as a people and became the preparatory step to legally filing their ancestral domain claim. At the end of the anthropological study the Obo Manobos had organized themselves to credibly prove their rights over their ancestral domain and, as a result, were readying themselves to receive back at least twenty thousand hectares of their land that was occupied by the Philippine National Oil Corporation. What was originally a simple cultural activity, "apolitical dancing," was transformed into an engagement with political forces.

Inculturation Is for Human Flourishing

On the other hand, we are not to overvalue our cultures as defining achievements, as though after our predecessors there is to be no more creativity and improvement. Rather, the focus on the traditional for some was mainly, perhaps, the result of previous neglect. Adaptation and indigenization as theological methodologies explored in post–Vatican II discussions exemplified this. Almost at the same time, theologians were becoming aware that culture as a context was a dynamic rather than a static reality. The approaches of inculturation and contextualization embodied this thought. Anyone reflecting on cultural realities must consider not only what has been traditionally achieved by that culture, but also the changes experienced by the tradition in the present-day situation. It is worth remembering that the present-day realities impinging on the present tradition and transforming it will be, in their own turn, tomorrow's traditions. Both the traditional and the new are aimed toward the well-being of the community. Might it be better, then, to reimagine these as cultural energies equipping us to face challenges that concern cosmic well-being?

The Theological Education Fund of the World Council of Churches in the 1970s suggested *contextualization* for this development. It acknowledged the importance of indigenization, but it sought to press beyond it by also taking into account "the process of secularity, technology, and the struggle for human justice, which characterize the historical moment of nations in the Third World."[22] The word *context*, which depicted the conditions of a reality one was to focus on in general, increasingly became part of theological methodology. This was admirably described by Stephen Bevans in *Models of Contextual Theology*. Attention to culture does not intend to detract from mindfulness of other dimensions of context. Focusing on the culture means using it as a primary frame of reference in seeing reality and as an entry point to the other dimensions or contexts of human experience.

DOING (CONTEXTUAL) THEOLOGY AS INCULTURATION

Culture is, as a whole, a people's shared model of interpretation for life. The Digger Indians describe it beautifully: "In the beginning God gave to every people a cup, a cup of clay, and from this cup they drank their life. They all dipped in the water, but their cups were different."[23] A human

---

[22] TEF Staff, *Ministry in the Context: The Third Mandate Programme of the Theological Education Fund (1970–1977)* (Bromley: The Theological Education Fund, 1972), 20.

[23] R. Benedict, *Patterns of Culture* (Boston: Houghton Mifflin Co., 1934), 21–22.

community's culture embodies, learns, and communicates its energies in singular beliefs, values, and ways of doing things. Hence, it is vital to take seriously the culture of a people in communicating the realities of faith to them.

This has not escaped the notice of Vatican II's *Ad gentes.* Without reducing culture to its communicative dimension, it speaks of the church utilizing the way of life of people to enhance their faith and their grasp of it: "From the customs and traditions of their people, from their wisdom and their learning, from their arts and sciences, these Churches borrow all those things which can contribute to the glory of their Creator, the revelation of the Savior's grace, or the proper arrangement of Christian life" (AG 22). Soon after, Paul VI, who considered the evangelization of cultures to be of prime importance, wrote that "evangelization loses much of its force and effectiveness if it does not take into consideration the actual people to whom it is addressed, if it does not use their language, their signs and symbols, if it does not answer the questions they ask" (*Evangelii nuntiandi,* 63).

Mutual Interaction between the Judeo-Christian Tradition and Cultural Experience

In describing theologizing when it dealt with contemporary human experiences, Vatican II said that the people's present needs, which go to the roots of the human race and which characterize the present age, must be considered "in the light of the gospel and of human experience" (GS 46). It is here that the basic principle of theologizing must be recognized: the mutual interaction of the two poles of theology, which are the Judeo-Christian *tradition* and the human cultural *experience.* Both poles are essential and constitutive in articulating any understanding of the faith. Together, they suggest the need of any given theology to be rooted in the culture and to be faithful to the tradition.

In this principle, the two poles mutually interact with each other. The tradition throws light on human experience, as human experience sheds light on the tradition. In doing contextual theology we grasp the meaning of the tradition precisely through the lens of human experience, and we comprehend our human experience from the vantage point of the tradition. It is important, to my mind, to insist on the *mutual interaction* of the two poles in order to avoid the imposition of the tradition understood in a particular cultural way on the pole of experience, as well as to prevent the pole of cultural experience from merely using the tradition to justify its perspective. By this process an inculturated interpretation of faith in Jesus as the Christ is made possible, a reading which is faithful not only to the tradition but to the culture as well.

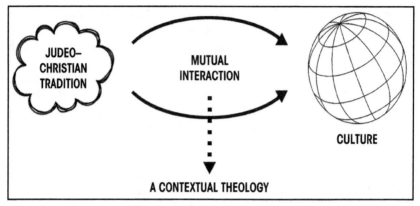

Judeo-Christian tradition, gospel, tradition, faith heritage, and *faith* all refer broadly to the same thing. The Judeo-Christian tradition, which is centered on Jesus the Christ, is one that started with the person of Jesus as interpreted by his first disciples. Based on him and around him grew a tradition of energizing beliefs, values, and customs, as well as institutions that actualize his spirit and legacy at different times and different places. It arose from the Jewish tradition of faith and blended into the Christian reinterpretation of it. It is constituted by the communally recognized, discerned, and accepted experiences of believers, past and present, which collectively represent this community's life and acquired wisdom, and which serve as a continuing source of guidance and inspiration. This tradition enables us to discern ambiguous situations in the light of faith and to see the divinely charged depths of our experiences today. Seen in this way, we ask: how do we make sense of Jesus, his spirit and legacy, given our situation? Mind you, "translating" this core message is a contextualization, an interpretation of sorts.

But when we consider the other pole, that is, experience or culture, and start with that, a question of hermeneutics arises. When we consider our culture, our history, our personal and communal experiences, our sociopolitical situation, and our ecological concerns, what does our faith in Jesus the Christ have to say to us? Contemporary experiences equally matter not only because they make up life today, but also because they throw light on the meaning and importance of the tradition, providing for the continuing relevance of this tradition for our times. Realizing that the Judeo-Christian tradition comes to us mediated by a culture, we must take care that we interact with the "inner meaning" of the gospel rather than with the present cultural interpretation of it.

Through the mutual interaction of the Judeo-Christian tradition and our present-day experiences or culture, we interpret our relationship with God through the instrumentality of our culture, and our culture in the light of this relationship. This results in an indigenous interpretation of the faith; the faith is interpreted, to be sure, but with indigenous categories. Conversely, the culture is interpreted, but in the light of the faith tradition.

What our present-day experiences mean to us as Christians will also be dependent on interpretative elements we utilize from the tradition.

Allow me to make a distinction between *starting principle* and *starting point*. It is the awareness of the two poles as a starting principle that makes it difficult for me to answer the question of which comes first, the pole of the tradition or the pole of experience/culture. Basing it on the starting principle, I would say, both the Judeo-Christian tradition and culture, though there are those who would prefer one or the other as their starting point for doing theology. I say both because, almost simultaneously, awareness of one pole requires awareness of the other pole. Remember, theology is faith seeking understanding. For instance, when I am attending to a facet of the tradition, I am implicitly led to at least take notice of the aspect of cultural experience that is related to or that I am trying to relate to the tradition. On the other hand, when I am attending to a cultural experience, in understanding and analyzing that experience, I am tacitly trying to associate it to the relevant feature of the tradition. This interaction is not only mutual but also dynamic. As the interaction progresses, so does the understanding of each of the poles.

As for the starting point, whether Judeo-Christian tradition or cultural experience, I consciously start with the pole that I know more about or am more conversant with. To me, this is a practical decision that one must make in theologizing. Sometimes, I am more acquainted with a specific issue or situation than I am with the corresponding aspect of the tradition. But it might be the case that I commence with resources I am more at ease with in the tradition. I begin simply with what I am more informed about in one of the poles. But that is the catch. I *merely* start knowing that the pole I am preoccupied with must be correlated with the other pole. I recognize that if doing theology proceeds from the pole of cultural experience, it must nevertheless complete the cycle by seeing the pole of experience from the perspective of the tradition.

Theologizing with Themes

In inculturation the mutual interaction may use themes. Since these two poles are in constant mutual interaction, it is possible to draw themes from either source to start the hermeneutical process. Without thematizing, one would be overwhelmed by an abundance of data and, maybe, fail to make sense of all of it. Constructing themes is a fruitful way of organizing such data. Here individual or related ideas converge into a cluster, throw light on one another, and form distinct yet integrated wholes.

Thematizing, to be sure, is limiting. But it does provide a feasible way of understanding and appreciating the tradition and the culture. Any manner of looking at reality is necessarily a limited way of looking at it. Interpretation, which is an intrinsic part of experience, in one way or another selects, limits, and demarcates our grasp of reality. Because we interpret, no one has a grasp of the total reality. Besides, comprehensive analysis is not really necessary for the theological task to move ahead. Hans Küng writes, "Our contemporary world of experience must be reflected in theology but not necessarily in the form of comprehensive economic, political, sociological or philosophic analysis, but rather as a recurrent theme touching upon our contemporary experience and sense of life and current concern."[24]

Themes, which provide starting points for inquiry, can be drawn either from the culture itself or from the gospel. Themes from the culture may revolve around important aspects of the indigenous worldview. Hence, key dimensions as well as elements involved in those dimensions or main ideas around which other ideas cluster can be the springboard of the investigation. Bear in mind that it is the issue, concern, or question that guides us to a particular theme or even a set of themes. It sensitizes or alerts us to the relevant cultural themes that must be analyzed.

Likewise, the issue, concern, or question may indicate for us which theme in the gospel is meaningful. The usefulness of this manner of proceeding arises from the fact that there are times or occasions when we (at least, initially) may be more familiar with the gospel theme related to the human situation than with a cultural one. In this case, we let the Gospel theme sensitize us, in turn, to one that is cultural. This evangelical theme alerts or leads us inevitably to a cultural one because reality is culturally interpreted if we remember how inextricably cultural we all are.

An Example of Thematic Theologizing:
Soteriology and Ginhawa[25]

We believe that in Jesus we find salvation. We announce the message of salvation to people and engage in works of salvation. Salvation is a key theme in the Judeo-Christian tradition and, in many ways, brings together several theological elements. How does one articulate this in a way that resonates with Filipinos?

Starting from a more familiar grasp of the tradition's notion of "salvation" (in English!), my attention was then set on the Filipino language and culture. Having learned about a neo-Scholastic understanding of salvation (saving souls), I scrutinized different equivalent cultural models. Then, veering away from a direct translation of heavenly salvation as *kaligtasan* (safe, delivered from), there was the earthly oriented general

---

[24] Hans Küng, "Toward a New Consensus in Catholic (and Ecumenical) Theology," *Journal of Ecumenical Studies* 17/1 (Winter 1980): 15.

[25] José M. de Mesa, "The *Ginhawa* Which Jesus Brings," in *José M. de Mesa: A Theological Reader*, 329–53.

term *kapakanan* (welfare). Although it conformed to what I wanted to say about historical well-being, it did not sit well with the Filipino in me on the experiential level.

But there is an experience and a word very close to the gut feel of the Filipino and likewise oriented to earthly well-being: *ginhawa*. It is an everyday word, very ordinary, and is included in the saying, "Kung may hirap, may ginhawa" (If there is hardship and suffering, there is relief and well-being). Its noteworthiness may be gleaned from its inclusion in the cultural pledge of marital fidelity in bad and good times: "sa hirap at ginhawa" (for better and for worse). *Ginhawa* refers to the over-all sense of well-being. It covers the experience of relief from pain, sickness, and straits; rest; satisfaction; freedom from want; and comfort; more in the inner world of the self than in the outer world of the senses. *Ginhawa* intimates *shalom*.

Knowing that its main orientation is historical, I wondered how it could express the eschatological aspect—the "more"—of salvation. When I realized that the cultural words for *salvation* in the tradition were all earth bound—*yasha* (Jewish), *soteria* (Greek), *salus* (Roman), *salvation* (Anglo), *liberación* (Latin American)—but capable of expressing the eschatological element of the faith, I thought it worthwhile to propose *ginhawa* as the indigenous appellation for the reality we call "salvation" in English.

Further reflection brought me to deeper understanding of the experience of *ginhawa* as *ginhawa* of the *loób* (the most authentic relational self) and *ginhawa* of the *katawan* (the body as symbolizing the outer world of relationships). These and the other cultural characteristics of *ginhawa* I then used as an interpretative model to make sense of *ginhawa* in and from Jesus Christ.

CONCLUSION

I started from a story calling for the consideration of cultural dimensions in theologizing. After discussing the development of neo-Scholasticism, in which the categories of experience and interpretation were downplayed, I cited the resurgence of cultural experience made possible by a significant shift in viewing culture and by the impetus of church renewal by Vatican II.

Defining experience as contact with reality together with an interpretation, I focused on cultural perspectives. Culture is a communally shared interpretation of reality in which people have been inculturated. Admittedly, culture is but one of the conditioning life contexts in society. But it is one that shapes us existentially as we give shape to it. As a tested tradition of experiences contributing to the well-being of the community, it is better viewed as a repository of energies. It is characterized by openness and dynamism in being adaptive to new challenges. This pole of experience is one of the poles of theology.

The other pole, the Judeo-Christian tradition, is a tradition of faith experiences as people live their relationship with God in varying cultural contexts. Embodied and expressed in cultural terms, people encounter the God of life. Saying that God works in and through human cultural experiences is an essential part of the tradition itself. For Christians, this is particularly true in Jesus Christ.

The two poles, which interact mutually, are necessary to form a theological reflection on a theme. One can begin the reflection either from the pole of (cultural) experience or the pole of the tradition, since beginning with one necessarily and inevitably leads to the other. Theologically considered, the pole of the Judeo-Christian can only be meaningful if the pole of cultural experience sheds light on it. And the pole of cultural experience only yields its Christian significance if it is seen from the light of the Judeo-Christian tradition. The two poles must be held together in mutual interaction to create a contextual theology worthy of a believer.

Chapter 12

Experience Seeking Faith: From Theology of Religions to Interreligious Theology

Anh Q. Tran, SJ

This chapter attempts to further the conversation on contextual theology, a method advocated by missiologist theologian Stephen Bevans.[1] In a world where Christianity is no longer the dominant voice of the major world religions, Christian thinkers are compelled to reexamine the role of theology in a context where the church is facing, on one hand, secularism and materialism in the Western world, and on the other, the increasing competition of Islam and, to a lesser extent, Hinduism and Buddhism in the global South. This new situation requires contemporary theologians to rethink how theology can and should be done in an interreligious context.

Since the beginning of Scholasticism in the Middle Ages, theology has been regarded as an academic explanation of the faith. Anselm of Canterbury's *fides quaerens intellectum* (faith seeking understanding) has become the standard definition of God-talk (theology).[2] Most European Christian theologians—from Thomas Aquinas to Joseph Ratzinger—have assumed

---

[1] Stephen B. Bevans, *Models of Contextual Theology*, rev. and exp. ed. (Maryknoll, NY: Orbis Books, 2002). See also idem, *An Introduction to Theology in Global Perspective* (Maryknoll, NY: Orbis Books, 2009), esp. chap. 8. Bevans is not the first theologian to discuss contextual theology. The credit belongs to Taiwanese Presbyterian theologian Shoki Coe (Ng Chiong-hui/Hwang Chang-hui, 1914–88), who proposed the idea of a "contextual theology" in his article "In Search of Renewal in Theological Education," *Theological Education* 9 (Summer 1973): 233–43. Bevans, however, has popularized the concept in Catholic circles through his writings.

[2] Anselm further explains the relation between faith and understanding: "Neque enim quaero intelligere ut credam, sed credo ut intelligam" (I do not seek to understand in order that I may believe, but rather, I believe in order that I may understand) (*Proslogium*, 1). See *St. Anselm Basic Writings: Proslogium, Monologium, Cur Deus Homo, and Gaunilo's on Behalf of the Fool*, 2nd ed., trans. S. N. Deane (Chicago: Open Court, 1962), 53.

that the main task of theology is limited to exploring and defending the doctrines of the church through the arguments and counter-arguments of various propositions. The task of theologizing "from above" requires a prior acceptance of the Christian faith and is carried out by drawing on biblical revelation and Christian tradition. In such theology religious thought by other religions is often not accepted, although, in reality, there have been numerous borrowings by Christian theologians from other religions, as evidenced in the medieval exchanges among Jewish, Muslim, and Christian theologians.

Today a homogeneous understanding of faith, or even of God, no longer exists. As Christianity expanded outside the Western world, the task of theology has also changed, moving from a Eurocentric concern to a global perspective. In their encounters with devout, intelligent, and holy men and women of other religious traditions, Christian missionaries and theologians have been confronted with many profound questions that challenge the traditional understanding of the task of theologizing.

The task of rethinking and reformulating Christian doctrines and practices in this new setting is not a twentieth-century innovation. After all, as Stephen Bevans has emphatically declared, "There is no such thing as 'theology'; there is only *contextual* theology."[3] For Bevans, doing theology contextually is not an option, nor is it the task of only theologians from the global South. It is really "a theological imperative," "a process that is part of the very nature of theology itself."[4] This theology "from below" necessarily takes into account the context of one's life—both as individuals and as members of a community—and its linguistic, cultural, socioeconomic, and religious elements.

If theology today must begin not from a dogmatic starting point but from the human experience of the transcendent Other, then it may be conceived of as *experience seeking understanding that leads to faith.* One might say that human experience as a starting point of theological reflection is not a new endeavor; in fact, it is as old as the story of biblical narratives themselves. Before Sacred Scriptures—both the Old and New Testaments—were written down, there were the individual experiences of God by such figures as Abraham, Moses, David, the prophets, and the early Christian disciples. They were only later retold, collected, and passed on as collective memories forming the Christian tradition. If one believes that the Holy Spirit underwrites the whole process of reception and transmission of the individual experience of the Holy One, the shift from a "theology from above" to a "theology from below" in our times is an inevitable development.

---

[3] Bevans, *Models of Contextual Theology*, 3.
[4] Ibid.

Today, we can no longer ignore the presence and the positive contributions of other religions in public discourse, religious exchanges, and even in theology. Encountering the religious others will often result in profound questions and, in many cases a change of heart and an alteration in the way one studies and teaches theology.[5] Since the early twentieth century the movement toward Christian unity has helped Christian theologians approach theological disciplines ecumenically. Today, interreligious exchanges, from the practical to the spiritual and doctrinal levels, have made it easier for Christian thinkers to do their theology *interreligiously*. This is in line with the Vatican II's *Decree on the Missionary Activity of the Church (Ad gentes),* which exhorts the faithful to discover the seeds of the Word that lie hidden in other religious traditions (AG 11). The fresh spirit of Vatican II opens the door for Catholic theologians to examine the use of the experiences, sacred writings, beliefs, and practices of the religious others as sources for theological reflection.

In delineating the nature of interreligious theology, I first discuss how interreligious exchanges contributed to Vatican II's change of mind on the values and roles of non-Christian religions and how the encounter with the religious others have altered the way some Christian thinkers did their theology. Second, I trace the development of the theology of religions as evidence of the rethinking of important Christian doctrines such as revelation and salvation. Next, I discuss how interreligious studies have given rise to the field of comparative theology. Finally, I lay out some principles for doing theology interreligiously.

FROM CONFRONTATION
TO DIALOGUE

The affirmation of the intrinsic values of other religions in Vatican II's *Declaration on the Relation of the Church to Non-Christian Religions (Nostra aetate)* rang true fifty years ago among Catholics in the global South and still does today. For many faithful of the church in Asia and Africa, this text is a breath of fresh air, signifying a change of direction in how Catholics should relate to their non-Christian neighbors. The council

---

[5] Paul Knitter, for example, describes how he has changed his mind on a number of Christian beliefs as a result of his relationships with members of other religions. See his autobiographical introduction in Paul Knitter, *One Earth Many Religions: Multifaith Dialogue and Global Responsibility* (Maryknoll, NY: Orbis Books, 1995), 1–22. Other theologians who went through a similar transformation include Jacques Dupuis, Raimon Panikkar, Aloysius Pieris, Michael Amaladoss, Francis Clooney, James Fredericks, John P. Keenan, Leo Lefebure, Peter C. Phan, and Stephen Bevans himself.

fathers urge members of the church to dialogue and collaborate with the followers of other religions: "Let Christians, while witnessing to their own faith and way of life, acknowledge, preserve, and encourage the spiritual and moral truths found among non-Christians, together with their social life and culture" (NA 2).[6]

The original schema of *Nostra aetate*—one of the most debated documents at the council—was originally conceived to reconcile Jewish-Christian relations. After several rounds of discussion and at the request of first the bishops of the Middle East and then of the rest of Asia, the sections on Islam and Asian religions were added to the document to expand it beyond a narrow Jewish-Christian concern. These additions, especially what eventually became paragraph 2 of *Nostra aetate*, signify a new direction in the church's engagement with the world—this time the religious world of humankind. For the first time in church official statements, Asian religions receive positive appreciation. This part of the text, which represents a 180-degree turn from the church's previous attitude of prejudice and condemnation against non-Christian religions, deserves to be quoted in full:

> In Hinduism, men explore the divine mystery and express it both in the limitless riches of myth and the accurately defined insights of philosophy. They seek release from the trials of the present life by ascetical practices, profound meditation and recourse to God in confidence and love. Buddhism in its various forms testifies to the essential inadequacy of this changing world. It proposes a way of life by which men can, with confidence and trust, attain a state of perfect liberation and reach supreme illumination either through their own efforts or by the aid of divine help. So, too, other religions which are found throughout the world attempt in their own ways to calm the human heart by outlining a program of life covering doctrine, moral precepts and sacred rites. (NA 2)

The document goes on to say that "the Catholic Church rejects nothing that is true and holy in these religions. She has a high regard for the manner of life and conduct, the precepts and doctrines which, although differing in many ways from her own teaching, nevertheless often reflect a ray of that truth which enlightens all men" (NA 2). These statements show a radical change in the church's relation with other religions, which must be marked by sincere respect and admiration. No longer can one speak of Asian and African religious traditions as wholesale "idolatries" and "superstitions."

---

[6] Translation of Vatican II documents follows Austin Flannery, ed., *Vatican Council II: The Conciliar and Post-Conciliar Documents*, vol. 1, new rev. ed. (Grand Rapids, MI: Eerdmans, 1992), 739.

In the aftermath of Vatican II, Eugene Hillman proposed that interreligious or interfaith activities be considered as the "wider ecumenism."[7] In the context of religious pluralism of Asia, Asian theologians—those who are of Asian origin or those who work in Asian cultural and religious contexts—have begun to integrate Asia's cultural and religious contexts into their theology. Since 1974, the Federation of Asian Bishops' Conferences (FABC) has embraced interreligious dialogue as one of the three pillars of Christian mission (the other two being dialogue with the Asian poor and dialogue with Asia's cultures). The reason is straightforward. Asia is the home of the major world religions, and Christianity is only one among them. Given this reality of religious pluralism, dialogue is the preferred mode of evangelization and theological reflection.

Interreligious dialogue has become a constitutive aspect of the church's missionary activities and self-understanding. In dialogue one is not to vanquish the partners or to impose one's view on them, but to respect the differences of opinion. Respect for differences, however, does not mean there can be no meaningful exchange of opinions or even conversion to the other person's view. On the contrary, a genuine interreligious dialogue includes the possibility of conversion, a change of heart in the biblical meaning of *metanoia*.

For the vast majority of Asians, dialogue does not primarily take the form of intellectual exchange between experts of various religions, as is often done in the West. Rather, of the four models of interreligious dialogue suggested by the Pontifical Council for Interreligious Dialogue in *Dialogue and Proclamation* in 1991, the dialogues of *shared life* (common living as good neighbors) and of *common action* (collaboration for development and liberation) take precedence over the other two, namely, dialogue of *theological exchanges* and dialogue of sharing *religious experiences*, because the latter two dialogues are effective only if there is a prior shared common life and common work (see DP 42–46). In seeking a deeper understanding and appreciation of other religious traditions, the challenge for Asian Christians is to find an appropriate way to proclaim Jesus Christ to the Asian people without denying the Christian fundamental belief that "Christ is the way and truth and life" (Jn 14:16).

INTERPRETING RELIGIONS:
PARADIGMS OF THEOLOGY OF RELIGION

It may be helpful to give a brief overview here of the theologies of religion and interreligious dialogue that have been formulated in the past

---

[7] See Eugene Hillman, *The Wider Ecumenism* (London: Burns and Oats, 1968); and *Christianity and the Wider Ecumenism*, ed. Peter C. Phan (New York: Paragon House, 1990).

fifty years or so. What are the theological frameworks for understanding the relationship between Christianity and other religions?

The theology of religion is a recent development. In the past it was treated as part of *missiology* when discussing the evangelization of non-Christians; *ecclesiology* in exploring the relationship between the church and non-Christians; and *soteriology* in treating the possibility of the salvation of non-Christians. As a new theological treatise, contemporary theology of religion asks what religion is and seeks to interpret the universal religious experience of humankind in light of the Christian faith. The theology of religion studies the dynamic and mutual relationships between Christianity and the other religions and the Christian understanding of the values and places of the world religions according to missiological, ecclesiological, or soteriological concerns.

At the risk of oversimplification, it may be stated that a number of theologians have proposed a threefold or fourfold classification of the Christian attitude toward the religious others. Alan Race is largely responsible for the oft-quoted, threefold paradigm of exclusivism, inclusivism, and pluralism.[8] Other theologians offer a similar taxonomy. Aloysius Pieris discusses the tripartite division of Christ against religions, Christ of religions, and Christ among religions.[9] Jacques Dupuis names ecclesiocentrism, Christocentrism, and theocentrism.[10] Paul Knitter renames the three categories as replacement, fulfillment, and mutuality, and adds a fourth, acceptance.[11] The different paradigms of the theology of religions can be briefly, perhaps simplistically, summarized as follows:

- *Religious exclusivism or replacement model,* maintained, for instance, by medieval Catholicism, Protestant fundamentalism, and Islamic fundamentalism. My religion is the *only true way* to God/salvation; other paths are false.

---

[8] Alan Race, *Christians and Religious Pluralism: Patterns in the Christian Theology of Religions* (London: SCM Press, 1983). For an early assessment and critique of this classification, see Perry Schmidt-Leukel, "Exclusivism, Inclusivism, Pluralism: The Tripolar Typology—Clarified and Reaffirmed," in *The Myth of Religious Superiority: A Multifaith Exploration*, ed. Paul Knitter (Maryknoll, NY: Orbis Books, 2005), 13–27.

[9] Aloysius Pieris, "Speaking of the Son of God in Non-Christian Cultures," in *Jesus, Son of God, Concilium* 153 (London: SCM Press, 1982), 65–72.

[10] Jacques Dupuis, *Toward a Christian Theology of Religious Pluralism* (Maryknoll, NY: Orbis Books, 1997); and idem, *Christianity and the Religions: From Confrontation to Dialogue* (Maryknoll, NY: Orbis Books, 2002). Veli-Matti Kärkkäinen follows a similar classification in *An Introduction to the Theology of Religions* (Downers Grove, IL: InterVarsity Press, 2003). Note that Dupuis also offers other paradigms beyond the triple category, such as regnocentrism, soteriocentrism, logocentrism, and pneumatocentrism.

[11] See Paul Knitter, *Introducing Theologies of Religions* (Maryknoll, NY: Orbis Books, 2002).

- *Religious inclusivism or fulfillment model,* maintained, for example, by modern Catholicism, mainline Protestantism, Judaism, Buddhism, and others. My religion/way is the *true way* to God/salvation, but not necessarily the only way; other paths may lead to God/salvation but are inferior or incomplete.
- *Religious pluralism or mutuality model,* as espoused by John Hick and Paul Knitter: My religion/way is *one among many ways* to God/salvation; other paths are equally valid.

The biblical data on the relationship between Israel and other nations, and later between Jesus and the Gentiles, are ambiguous. There seems to be both acceptance and rejection of the religious others. On the one hand, non-Jews were ridiculed as aliens, pagans, or "dogs."[12] On the other, a Samaritan was praised as "exemplary"; a Roman centurion as "believing"; and a Syro-phoenician woman as "humble." Their faith and charity are said to exceed those of Jesus's contemporaries. In assessing the attitude of Jews and early Christians toward Gentiles, it is important to note that the biblical writers were not confronted with our present-day issues and concerns with religious pluralism. Their concern was maintaining Israel as God's chosen people and the church as the realization of God's plan to enlighten all nations. At worst, the religions of the Ancient Near East were seen as idolatry; at best, as preparation for the eventual acceptance of God's reign through the witness of Israel or the church.

The Christian exclusivist and inclusivist attitudes toward other faiths have a long history. The superiority complex of ancient Israelites toward the neighboring nations and their religions, later inherited by the Christian church, colored their attitude toward its competitors. The Israelites took pride in knowing the true God, and their covenant with God was used as the standard to judge others. Some early Christian missionaries to Asia have pointed to the story of Babel in Genesis 11 as evidence for the deterioration of the true religion after the great deluge.[13] As the successor and fulfillment of Israel's covenant with God, Christians see themselves in the same exclusive light.

---

[12] This refers to Jesus's encounter with a Syro-phoenician woman (Mk 7:25–30).

[13] See, for example, the arguments put forth by Matteo Ricci (1552–1610) and Alexandre de Rhodes (1591–1660) regarding the origin of Chinese "sects" in their respective catechisms: *The True Meaning of the Lord of Heaven* (Beijing, 1603) and the *Catechism for Those Who Want to Be Baptized in Eight Days* (Rome, 1651). For English translations of these texts, see Matteo Ricci, *The True Meaning of the Lord of Heaven*, trans. Douglas Lancashire and Peter Hu Kuo-chen, rev. ed. by Thierry Meynard (Boston: Institute of Jesuit Source, 2016); de Rhodes's catechism is translated by Peter C. Phan in Peter C. Phan, *Mission and Cathechesis: Alexandre de Rhodes and Inculturation in Seventeenth-Century Vietnam* (Maryknoll, NY: Orbis Books, 1998), 211–315.

Only Christianity is the true way to God, and from this it is con-cluded that *extra ecclesiam nulla salus* (there is no salvation outside the church). While this notion was first formulated in the early church con-troversy about the validity of baptism performed by schismatic groups, its ecclesiocentric sense arose in the High Middle Ages, when salvation was restricted to those who submitted themselves to the jurisdiction of the papacy. At the time of the Western mission and colonial expansion beginning in the 1500s, it was taught that salvation is only available within the church.[14] Although this exclusivist attitude may sound of-fensive and narrow-minded to the religious others, nevertheless it is still alive and embraced by present-day fundamentalists in both Protestant and Catholic circles.

When ecclesiocentrism gives way to Christocentrism, the role of the church fades into the background, but Christ still remains definitive. There are a variety of ways to nuance this Christocentrism by using such adjectives as *constitutive, definitive, normative, complete, full, universal,* or *unique* to describe the salvific role of Christ. One can grant the pos-sibility of salvation outside the Christian sheepfold, but it can happen only through the salvific work of Christ. Salvation is understood to be possible *extra ecclesiam* (outside the church), but it is possible *propter Christum* (because of Christ). This position, often called inclusivism, puts Christ as the norm of all norms *(norma normans)*, against which the mer-its of other religious founders and their ways of life are measured. Karl Rahner's notion of non-Christian believers as "anonymous Christians" is an example of this type of theology.[15] Protestant theologians such as Paul Tillich and Wolfhart Pannenberg adopt more or less similar posi-tions, ready to find God's presence in the world, but at the same time, they insist on the commitment to the uniqueness of Jesus. They maintain that salvation comes *only* from Christ—the promised One of God—and that other religions do not provide that particular promise.[16]

Still, there are theologians who struggle with this kind of normative or uniqueness language. Jacques Dupuis, for one, argues that Christo-centrism is only applicable to Christians. In an attempt to make room for Christianity within the pluralism of India, he wants to shift from Christ's "normative exclusiveness" to his "relational distinctiveness."

---

[14] For a good summary of the development of this formula, see Francis A. Sul-livan, *Salvation Outside the Church?* (New York: Paulist Press, 1992).

[15] Some people might object to the term *anonymous Christian* because it does not maintain the difference between Christians and non-Christians. I personally prefer to use the term *analogous Christian* to indicate a similarity and yet differ-ence between a Christian and a member of another faith.

[16] Wolfhart Pannenberg, "Religious Pluralism and Conflicting Truth Claims," in *Christian Uniqueness Reconsidered: The Myth of a Pluralistic Theology of Religions,* ed. Gavin D'Costa (Maryknoll, NY: Orbis Books, 1990), 96–106.

Dupuis stresses a personal commitment to Christ by Christians but re-fuses to make a judgment on the merits of other religions in the salvation process.[17] Worried that this might relativize the normative role of Christ, the Vatican Congregation for the Doctrine of the Faith upholds against Dupuis that Jesus is the "sole and universal mediator of salvation for all humanity."[18] In this sense Jesus is said to be the fulfillment and complete-ness of God's self-manifestation; there is no other truth apart from him.

Before moving on to describe the pluralist position, it is important to note that both exclusivism and inclusivism also exist in other faiths, for example, within the conservative Muslims of Saudi Arabia or among the fundamentalist Hindus of India. These positions, different in degrees but not in kind, make their dominant religion the standard against which others are judged. The minority faiths and their members are often mar-ginalized in the interfaith dialogue, and thus a fruitful dialogue does not take place. At best, some form of religious tolerance is allowed; at worst, members of other faiths are ridiculed, harassed, or denied religious liberty.

The pluralist attitude toward the religious others recognizes the plu-rality and diversity of religious faiths. It began with the study of "world religions" in the middle of the nineteenth century and gave birth to other disciplines such as the sociology and anthropology of religion, as well as comparative religion. These religious studies have challenged Christian thinkers to reconceive the relationship between Christianity in a world of religious pluralism. A growing fascination with the so-called Oriental religions—the Indian and Chinese traditions—prompted both religious scholars and theologians to examine these religions on their own merits and not only through a Christian lens.[19] The serious study of Muslim, Hindu, Buddhist, Confucian, and Daoist sacred texts reveals their deep sense of the presence of the divine. Furthermore, the encounter with religious practices such as Zen meditation, Daoist introspection, or Sufi dance opens the Christian believers to a new experience of the

---

[17] See Dupuis, *Toward a Christian Theology of Religious Pluralism*, chap. 11; and idem, *Christianity and the Religions*, chaps. 6–7.

[18] "It must be firmly believed that Jesus Christ, the Son of God, made man, crucified and risen, is the sole and universal mediator of salvation for all humanity. . . . It is consistent with the Catholic Church to hold that the seeds of truth and goodness that exists in other religions are a certain participation contained in the revelation of Christ. However, it is erroneous to hold that such elements of truth and goodness, or some of them, do not derive ultimately from the source-mediation of Jesus Christ." Congregation for the Doctrine of the Faith, "Notification on the Book *Toward a Christian Theology of Religious Pluralism*," January 24, 2001, nos. 1, 4.

[19] There are also interpreters of non-Christian religions through Christian categories, notably in the work of Jean Danielou, *The Salvation of the Nations* (Notre Dame, IN: University of Notre Dame Press, 1962).

divine, comparable to Christian spiritual practices.[20] In addition, various collaborations and dialogues between Christians and the adherents of other faiths break down Christians' centuries-long prejudices and biases. Jews are not unrepentant Christ-killers,[21] Muslims are not heretics and imposters,[22] and members of the Asian religions are not idolaters.[23]

As the study of religion progresses, more and more Christians begin to recognize that non-Christian religions are not poor replicas of Christianity; they are not just human efforts to reach God. Furthermore, it is widely recognized that all religions, including Christianity, lose their absoluteness as they encounter the Ultimate Mystery. Instead of Christ occupying the center as in the exclusivist and inclusivist paradigms, in the pluralist vision God takes center stage. John Hick, one of the early proponents of this position, calls this shift the "Copernican turn" in the theology of religions.[24] He and others have questioned the uniqueness and universality of Christ, and by implication, the superiority of the Christian faith. Their argument runs as follows: If God desires to save all people, and Jesus Christ is but a historical embodiment of God's plan, then it is possible that God communicates Godself with humanity in other concrete ways and thus allow

---

[20] Not all people are open to this type of interreligious exchange. For example, the Congregation for the Doctrine of the Faith has warned against the use of other religious writings in Christian liturgy (see *Dominus Iesus,* June 16, 2000, no. 8) or incorporation of Eastern meditation techniques to supplement Christian prayer (see *Letter to the Bishops of the Catholic Church on Some Aspects of Christian Meditation,* October 15, 1989, nos. 1, 12, 27–28).

[21] Many church fathers, from Augustine to John Chrysostom, considered Jews to be a cursed people because they killed Christ.

[22] St. John Damascene (c. 675–749), for one, thinks that Islam is a variation of Arianism. In *Against the Heresy of the Ishmaelites* he wrote: "From that time to the present a false prophet named Mohammed has appeared in their midst. This man, after having chanced upon the Old and New Testaments and likewise, it seems, having conversed with an Arian monk, devised his own heresy. Then, having insinuated himself into the good graces of the people by a show of seeming piety, he gave out that a certain book had been sent down to him from heaven. He had set down some ridiculous compositions in this book of his and he gave it to them as an object of veneration." See *John of Damascus: Writings,* trans. Frederic H. Chase Jr., Fathers of the Church Patristic Series (Washington, DC: Catholic University of America Press, 1958), 153.

[23] Missionary writings on the religions of China before the Second World War tend to characterize these religions in terms of superstition and idolatry. See, for example, Henri Doré, *Recherches sur les supersitions en Chine,* 18 vols. (original, Shanghai: T'ou-se-we, 1911–1938; reissued, Paris: Librarie You-Feng, 1995).

[24] For Hick's position, see John Hick, *God Has Many Names* (Philadelphia: Westminster Press, 1982); idem, *An Interpretation of Religion: Human Responses to the Transcendent* (New Haven, CT: Yale University Press, 1989/2004); and idem, *A Christian Theology of Religions* (Louisville, KY: Westminster John Knox Press, 1995).

humankind to be saved in other religions. The inclusivist position, they say, is still an attempt to retain the universal claim of Christianity.

The pluralist theology of religion seeks to build bridges between Christians and persons of other religions, allowing for an authentic dialogue to take place with benefits to both sides. The pluralist theologians want to meet the religious others on their own ground as potential dialogue partners. For this to be a relationship of mutuality—where each side can listen and learn from the other—requires the creation of a level playing field, allowing the other faiths to have their own space and merit. The assumption is that there is only One Reality, and the religions are manifestations of, or diverse paths toward, this Oneness. All roads will eventually lead to the same mountaintop. This move effectively reduces Christianity to being one among the many religions of the world.

The various pluralist approaches to other religions are summarized by Paul Knitter in three categories: philosophical-historical, religious-mystical, and ethical-practical. The first recognizes the historical limitations of all religions and the probability that there is a divine Reality behind and within them all. The second acknowledges the limitations of language and concept in describing the Mystery in all religions, and that this Divine Mystery can be experienced in all of them. The third stays away from metaphysical or religious concerns and instead focuses on alleviating the concrete problems and sufferings afflicting humanity and the earth.[25]

The pluralist theology of religion reminds Christians that they do not have a monopoly on Truth, nor is their way the only way to God. Reactions to the pluralist paradigm, understandably, are multiple. Progressive Christians generally espouse this view, while conservatives strenuously oppose it. For the latter, it seems to lead to religious indifferentism and relativism. Furthermore, it is impossible to assume that all paths to the Divine are valid without examining their historical, cultural, and religious contexts. If all religions are potentially equal, how does one distinguish between the life-affirming one and the destructive one? If there are both positive and negative aspects within each religious tradition, what would be the litmus test to judge their merit? In addition, by overemphasizing the similarity among the religions and glossing over their real, incompatible differences, would one be dishonest with oneself and the other religious partners in dialogue? Even in global ethics there are fundamental differences in how one understands the ethical imperatives of justice, peace, harmony, and so on.

So far, the chief concerns of various Christian theologies of religions are twofold: revelation and salvation. The first asks whether one can find God or the Divine outside the Christian revelation. More and more people today tend to answer yes rather than a flat no. They point to the sacred writings and mystical experiences in all religions that show the divine Presence.

---

[25] Knitter, *Introducing Theologies of Religions*, 109–49.

Still, the official teaching of the Catholic Church only acknowledges that "rays of Truth" or "elements of goodness and grace" can be found in other religions and in the lives of their members, but not the fullness of truth and grace. Other sacred writings cannot be considered inspired scripture, like the Bible, even though they can be of benefit for their followers.[26]

The second concern is the possibility of the salvation of non-Christians apart from Christianity and, more important, whether non-Christian religions can be considered as ways of salvation in themselves. The answers to these questions divide the exclusivist and inclusivist camp, on the one hand, and the pluralist camp, on the other. Understandably, the eternal fate of the unbaptized has been the main motivation for missionary activities for centuries. The challenge for theologians is to affirm two seemingly contradictory principles: (1) salvation is available to all humans through the Christ event, and (2) God desires the salvation of all and therefore has the freedom to save individuals in whatever way God desires. How to balance between the "universality of God's love" and the "particularity of God's love in Jesus Christ" is tricky. Exclusivists and inclusivists lean toward the first principle, whereas pluralists embrace the second.

BEYOND SOTERIOLOGICAL CONCERNS
TO OPEN HERMENEUTICS

A growing dissatisfaction with the soteriological focus gives rise to the fourth position in the theology of religion—the so-called *particularism*, or, in Knitter's terminology, the "acceptance model."[27] It is coupled with the postmodern understanding of religions: religions have different concerns and agendas, different goals and priorities. They have different religious ends and cannot be reduced to a mega-religion that will be acceptable to all. Mark Heim has called for attention to the real and different goals and fulfillments of religions.[28] Religious traditions are like languages; they have different syntax, vocabularies, and concepts that cannot be reduced into one. Just like in any human language, translations are approximations; they can never get into the soul of the languages, as evident in the translations of poetry. The differences between religious concepts and ideas can become contradictory if one insists that they describe the same Reality. In some cases it might be possible, but in other cases it can be like trying to square a circle. While one can hold that Allah is another name of God, YHWH cannot be reduced to the impersonal Dao. The different

---

[26] "The Church's tradition, however, reserves the designation of *inspired texts* to the canonical books of the Old and the New Testament, since they are inspired by the Holy Spirit" (*Dominus Iesus*, 8).

[27] Knitter, *Introducing Theologies of Religions*, chaps. 10–12.

[28] S. Mark Heim, *Salvations: Truth and Difference in Religions* (Maryknoll, NY: Orbis Books, 1995).

understandings of the Divine make any attempt to come up with one supra-religion impossible.

Religions, as Heim points out, have different religious ends, or "salvation*s*"—it is crucial to note the plural here. They actually are fulfillments of different specific realities. What counts as important and essential in one tradition might not exist in other traditions. The impersonal state of extinction *(nirvana)* as the goal of final Buddhist liberation *(moksha)* from the cycle of birth and death is not what Hindus mean by union between *atman* and *Brahman*, and clearly it is far from the Christian understanding of the beatific vision of God or from life in paradise as conceived by Muslims. Zen Buddhists reach enlightenment *(satori)* and Christians arrive at the kingdom of God *(regnum Dei)*. Both *salvations* bring happiness to their proponents. What Heim advocates is the unity of the human quests for meanings that can be found on diverse paths. The model of unity-in-diversity, grounded in trinitarian theology, can perhaps give Christians a way forward to accepting religious pluralism.[29]

Other theologians such as Frank Clooney and James Fredericks want to push the particularist model further. A contemporary theology of religion should move beyond the concerns of salvation for the members of other religions or even the role of those religious traditions in the salvation of their members. Instead of starting with Christian scriptures and tradition and considering the salvation of the religious others, as Heim has done, they want to start from the other side.[30] They propose that Christians theologize in comparison with the other faiths' categories. Moving from soteriological concerns to an open hermeneutic, these theologians have pioneered what is known as *comparative theology*.[31] The comparative study of religion, of course, did not originate with Clooney or Fredericks,

---

[29] Heim further develops this idea in *The Depth of Riches: A Trinitarian Theology of Religious Ends* (Grand Rapids, MI: Eerdmans, 2001).

[30] Francis X. Clooney, *Theology after Vedanta: An Experiment in Comparative Theology* (Albany: State University of New York Press, 1993). Also James L. Fredericks, "A Universal Religious Experience? Comparative Theology as an Alternative to a Theology of Religions," *Horizon* 22 (1996): 67–87; idem, *Faith among Faiths: Christian Theology and Non-Christian Religions* (New York: Paulist Press, 1999); and idem, *Buddhists and Christians: Through Comparative Theology to Solidarity* (Maryknoll, NY: Orbis Books, 2004).

[31] David Tracy, "Comparative Theology," in *Encyclopedia of Religion* (original 1986), ed. Lindsay Jones, 2nd ed. (Detroit: Macmillan References USA, 2005), vol. 13: 9125–34; John Renard, "Comparative Theology: Definition and Method," *Religious Studies and Theology* 17 (1998): 3–18; Stephen J. Duffy, "A Theology of Religions and/or a Comparative Theology?" *Horizon* 22 (1996): 67–87. Francis Clooney is quite active in promoting the field of comparative theology in academic professional organizations. Among his recent books on the subject are *Comparative Theology: Deep Learning across Religious Borders* (West Sussex: Wiley-Blackwell, 2010) and an edited volume, *The New Comparative Theology: Interreligious Insights from the Next Generation* (London: T & T Clark, 2010).

but with scholars in the philosophy or history of religion and comparative ethics.[32] In the area of theology, Clooney acknowledges the pioneering works of others such as Keith Ward[33] and Robert Neville.[34] The difference between Clooney and Fredericks and the others is that they compare particular texts, specific persons, concrete rituals, significant symbols, and geographical or historical contexts, not for the sake of finding similarities and differences among the religions but to illuminate Christian beliefs and encourage dialogue. In other words, they venture out into the deep waters of other faiths to come back and reflect as Christians, using the experience of the other religious traditions.

More than spectators of religious similarities and differences, comparative theologians also want to engage members of other faiths on their grounds. Working with their creed, code, cult, community, and concern, they address these believers standing in their midst, from within, not as outsiders. Comparative theologians seek to clarify and understand accurately what a Hindu, Buddhist, or Muslim might believe or do, and why. In that process they also try to validate their own beliefs and gain deeper insights into Christian doctrines and practices. Taken far enough, comparative theology might develop into an *interreligious theology* or theologizing interreligiously.[35]

TOWARD AN INTERRELIGIOUS THEOLOGY

If theology today is understood as the process of experience seeking understanding that leads to faith, as I suggested at the beginning of this

---

[32] See, for example, Wilfred Cantwell Smith, *What Is Scripture? A Comparative Approach* (Minneapolis: Fortress Press, 1993); Lee Yearley, *Mencius and Aquinas: Theories of Virtue and Conceptions of Courage* (Albany: State University of New York Press, 1990); Xinzhong Yao, *Confucianism and Christianity: A Comparative Study of Jen and Agape* (Brighton: Sussex Academic Press, 1997); and Aaron Stalnaker, *Overcoming Our Evil: Human Nature and Spiritual Exercises in Xunzi and Augustine* (Washington, DC: Georgetown University Press, 2006).

[33] Keith Ward, *Religion and Revelation* (Oxford: Clarendon Press, 1994); idem, *Religion and Creation* (Oxford: Clarendon Press, 1996); idem, *Religion and Human Nature* (Oxford: Clarendon Press, 1998); idem, *Religion and Community* (Oxford: Clarendon Press, 2000); and idem, *Religion and Human Fulfillment* (Oxford: Clarendon Press, 2008).

[34] Robert Neville led the comparative religious ideas project through a number of seminars at Boston University between 1995 and 1999. The result is a trilogy of volumes edited by Neville: *The Human Condition* (Albany: State University of New York Press, 2000), *Ultimate Realities* (Albany: State University of New York Press, 2000), and *Religious Truth* (Albany: State University of New York Press, 2000).

[35] Francis Clooney makes the distinction between comparative theology and interreligious theology, which for him means a theology that flows out of interreligious dialogue (*Comparative Theology*, 10–11).

chapter, then one should engage and use other religious ideas, concepts, symbols, metaphors, and methods of inquiry appropriately for Christian theological reflection. By interreligious theology I mean a process of theologizing from an interreligious perspective by employing the data from comparative studies and one's own interreligious experience. The goal is not to arrive at a syncretistic Christian theology but a theology that reflects the contemporary Christian experience of religious pluralism.

Interestingly enough, doing theology interreligiously already existed in the Middle Ages. One can find an example in Ramon Llull's *Book of the Gentile and the Three Wise Men* (ca. 1280)—an imagined trilogue among a Christian, a Jew, and a Muslim. This work evinces the remarkable ability of a medieval theologian to think outside his religious conviction.[36] Another example is Nicholas of Cusa's *De pace fidei—The Peace of Faith* (1454), an imaginative interreligious summit in heaven where the participants are seen as members of *una religio in rituum varietate* (one religion manifested in different rites). Cusa's work, however, is much more controversial than Ramon Llull's trilogue, because it seeks to find *una fide orthodoxa* (one right faith) among the religions.[37] The same can be said of early Jesuit missionaries to India and China in the sixteenth and seventeenth centuries, especially Roberto de Nobili (1579–1656) and Matteo Ricci (1552–1610). Not all interreligious studies began with Christians, however. In India, Hindu thinkers have been actively engaged since the nineteenth century in reading and interpreting the Christian Gospels and doctrines from the Hindu perspectives.[38]

Today, as a result of interreligious dialogue and collaboration, an interreligious theology seems possible. Together with comparative theology and going beyond it, interreligious theology can be considered a form of contextual theology in the contemporary multi-religious world. Theological questions are answered not only on the basis of one's own religious tradition but also on the basis of other religious traditions. An interreligious theology can be developed on three principles.

Principle of Mutual Trust

First, we need to be grounded in our own religion but at the same time remain open to learning from the religious others. I call this the *principle*

[36] For an English translation, see *Selected Works of Ramon Llull (1232–1316)*, 2 vols., ed. and trans. Anthony Bonner (Princeton, NJ: Princeton University Press, 1985), 1:93–305.

[37] For an English translation of Cusa's work, see William F. Wertz, trans. and ed., *Toward a New Council of Florence: 'On the Peace of Faith' and Other Works by Nicolaus of Cusa* (Washington, DC: Schiller Institute, 1993).

[38] For example, Raja Ram Mohan Roy (1774–1833), Ramakrishna Paramahamsa (1836–86), Swami Vivekananda (1863–1902), and Mahatma Gandhi (1869–1948).

of mutual trust—trust in ourselves and in the others. Before attempting an interfaith inquiry, one must have confidence in one's own tradition. It is no use for us and for our interreligious interlocutors if we are ignorant of our own tradition. Knowing our own strengths and limitations allows us to be honest in our interreligious pursuit. Interreligious learning begins with our desire to approach the Mystery in humility and allows God to lead the way and illuminate our experience of the Divine through the encounter with the religious others. After all, God is always greater than our effort to pigeon-hole God into our own texts, traditions, and religious practice. In reading the others' sacred writings, participating in their worship and festivals, conversing with their teachers, and working with their members on a common cause, we trust that all these interreligious activities will help us experience God and do God-talk (theology) in a different light. We trust that there is a unity of experience that is common to humanity. Our theories and doctrines, beliefs and practices may be different and even contradictory, but all religions still have to face the fundamental questions and concerns of human life and its place within the cosmos. Making sense of blessings and misfortunes, good and evil, life and death, and the meaning of life itself is the perennial concern of humanity.

Principle of Focused Inquiry

The second principle involves the analysis of the issues and concerns that inform one's faith. I call this the *principle of focused inquiry*. No individual theologian can theologize on every issue or synthesize all religious perspectives. Rather, we might need to narrow down to a particular area of theology or concern for interreligious learning. We can ask, for instance, which particular doctrines emerge most clearly in the context of interreligious dialogue and which doctrines need to be stressed. Here, Perry Schmidt-Leukel offers us four methodological approaches that can be helpful in our learning and theologizing with the others: *perspectival*, *imaginative*, *comparative*, and *constructive*.[39] By *perspectival* Schmidt-Leukel means that one should start from a confessional stand. Interreligious theologians do not bracket their religious convictions. But this does not mean that their beliefs are a fixed set of irreformable propositions. The challenge of an interreligious hermeneutic is being vulnerable to new information and methods of inquiry that might lead to a disruption of their previously conceived notions of faith. They should be prepared to be proved wrong and to revise their beliefs when necessary.

The *imaginative* approach allows the inquirer to see through the eyes of the other. Theologians can gain more insight if they understand and articulate the other's belief or practice and the reasons behind it. They do

---

[39] Perry Schmidt-Leukel, *Religious Pluralism and Interreligious Theology* (Maryknoll, NY: Orbis Books, 2017), chap. 8, esp. 139–46.

not necessarily need to accept those reasons as their own, but they must be as fair and accurate as possible. There is nothing worse than misrepresenting the other in an interreligious dialogue. Just as Jewish scholars have written commentaries on the New Testament, Christian theologians in recent times have engaged in serious studies of the sacred texts of the Asian religions and have benefited from them.[40]

The *comparative* approach encourages seeking reciprocal illumination. It is a reversal of the previous approach. Here, we do not only look at an issue through the other's eyes but also allow the other to examine our own tradition from their perspective. In the mutual exchanges each side will learn to reimagine the issues not only from one's own tradition but also from that of one's dialogue partner. This process is one of reciprocal illumination and has been described as the process of "passing over" and "coming back."[41] During this process a change in one's perspective is also a transformation of the self, an intellectual and spiritual conversion.

The last approach is *constructive*. It aims at the mutual transformation. When we engage in serious dialogue, we grow into a deeper understanding of reality, are transformed by this experience, and then live accordingly.[42] Not only individuals but religious institutions are transformed. The history of religions provides many examples of this cross-fertilization of religions when their members work and live side by side in mutual aid and exchanges. Take, for instance, the Daoist influence on Neo-Confucianism, giving it a cosmological doctrine in the Supreme Ultimate concept. At the

---

[40] Comparative theologians who have contributed to this interreligious theology include Catherine Cornille, *Song Divine: Christian Commentaries on the* Bhagavad Gita (Grand Rapids, MI: Eerdmans, 2006); Daniel P. Sheridan, *Loving God: Krsna and Christ: A Christian Commentary on the* Ñarada Sutras (Grand Rapids, MI: Eerdmans, 2009); Francis X. Clooney, *The Truth, the Way, the Life: A Christian Commentary on the* Three Holy Mantras of the Sri Vaishnava Hindus (Grand Rapids, MI: Eerdmans, 2009); John P. Keenan and Linda K. Keenan, *I Am / No Self: A Christian Commentary on the* Heart Sutra (Grand Rapids, MI: Eerdmans, 2011); Leo Lefebure and Peter Feldmeier, *The Path of Wisdom: A Christian Commentary on the* Dhammapada (Grand Rapids, MI: Eerdmans, 2011); Reid P. Locklin, *Liturgy of Liberation: A Christian Commentary on Shankara's* Upadesasahasri (Grand Rapids, MI: Eerdmans, 2012).

[41] Raimon Panikkar describes his experience in these words: "I left Europe [for India] as a Christian, I discovered I was a Hindu and returned as a Buddhist without ever having ceased to be a Christian." (*The Intra-religious Dialogue* [New York: Paulist Press, 1978], 2); also see http://www.raimon-panikkar.org/english/biography-3.html. Paul Knitter also discussed this "crossing boundaries experience" in *Without Buddha I Could Not Be a Christian* (Oxford: Oneworld Publication, 2009).

[42] This is a paraphrase of Leonard Swilder's first principle in the Decalogue for Dialogue. See "The Dialogue Decalogue: Ground Rules for Interreligious Dialogue," *Journal of Ecumenical Studies* 20/1 (Winter 1983): 1–4.

same time medieval Daoism also absorbed Buddhist monasticism and accepted the importance of having a canon of sacred texts.[43]

Principle of Interreligious Friendship

The third principle of interreligious theology is of a more practical nature, and that is the *principle of interreligious friendship*.[44] Interreligious theology cannot be divorced from actual dialogue. The process of theologizing flows from two dialogues that happen simultaneously: (1) the *intra*-religious dialogue, which occurs within the individual theologian[45] as he or she appropriates and incorporates the religious experiences and concepts of other faiths into his or her own; and (2) the *inter*-religious exchange between the Christian theologian and the members of other religions. This theologizing is not only *of* dialogue but also *for* dialogue. Interreligious theology is not only about learning and theologizing for the benefit of one's own religion. The multilateral dimensions of theological discourses will also benefit the partners in dialogue. Eventually, such sustained conversations will form interreligious friendship that allows people to collaborate intellectually and socially for the betterment of this world. After all, the practical purpose of interreligious dialogue and theology is the shared concern for the flourishing of the human family.

CONCLUSION

In "Decree 5: Our Mission and Interreligious Dialogue," which emerged from the 34th General Congregation of the Society of Jesus, held in 1995, we find this description: "To be religious [or authentically Catholic] today is to be interreligious in the sense that a positive relationship with believers of other faiths is a requirement of a world of religious pluralism."[46] Maintaining a positive relationship with believers of other faiths is a good starting point but not the end product; it is not enough. We all need a deep *metanoia*, that is, conversion from prejudice, xenophobia, misappropria-

---

[43] Erik Zürcher, "Buddhist Influence on Early Taoism: A Survey of Scriptural Evidence," *T'oung Pao*, second series, 66–1/3 (1980): 84–147.

[44] James L. Fredericks is a pioneer in naming this category as a theological approach. See "Interreligious Friendship: A New Theological Virtue," *Journal of Ecumenical Studies* 35/2 (Spring 1998): 159–74; see also James L. Fredericks and Tracy Sayuki Tiemeier, *Interreligious Friendship after* Nostra Aetate (New York: Palgrave Macmillan, 2015).

[45] Here I borrow the term from the title of Raimon Panikkar's book *The Intrareligious Dialogue*.

[46] Thirty-fourth General Congregation of the Society of Jesus, "Decree 5: Our Mission and Interreligious Dialogue," no. 3 (1995).

tion, and demonization of those we perceive as the others. Without allow-ing the faith and the religious experiences and practices of other believers to make an impact on us, interreligious encounters are futile. It is easy to become a religious tourist, crossing borders for a new experience but eventually retreating back to our own ideological and theological camp, isolated from the others. The encounter with the religious others and their ways of life, no matter how significant, will fade if we do not allow it to be part of our theological reflection.

Just as ecumenism has changed the way Christians do theology, religious pluralism, the wider ecumenism, will affect how we Christians theologize as well. Interreligious theology as a new contextual form of theology is on the horizon. As a relatively new discipline it might take years before we can see its impact. In the course of doing theology interreligiously, critical ques-tions can be raised: Is interreligious theology a transgression of religious borders? Is it an interesting academic exercise with no real application? Could one distort the Christian revelation to the point that it is no longer a Christian but a syncretistic theology? Such questions are legitimate as we consider the impact and limits of interreligious theology. And yet, the task of doing theology interreligiously is a natural extension of doing theology ecumenically. Religious pluralism makes it nearly inevitable. Its goal of understanding God and the world in deeper ways makes it worthwhile. As theologians who engage in interfaith dialogue have discovered, this type of theological enterprise will always be an open-ended exercise, a work in progress. There will never be a *summa theologica interreligiosa*—nor is there a need for one. After all, the task of doing theology means taking one's experiences, including religious experiences, seriously, exploring them, and constructing them within an intelligible frame of reference—the divine-human relationship revealed by Jesus Christ and in other religions.

Chapter 13

The Church:
Mission-Led Ecclesiology for Today

Carolyn Chau

Mission is not tangential to church history. It is rather at the heart of the church's life.
—BEVANS AND SCHROEDER, *PROPHETIC DIALOGUE*

The church does not have a mission, but the mission has a church.
—BEVANS AND SCHROEDER, *PROPHETIC DIALOGUE*

It would seem that there is no better place to start, in an essay on the church in honor of Stephen Bevans, than the pithy statements above about the centrality of mission to the essence of the church. Bevans and Schroeder go on to state what every ecclesiologist would grant: "The church is not about the church. It is about what Jesus called the reign of God."[1] In this chapter we flesh out what it means to say that the church is about the reign of God, how the church strives to stay true to its reason for being, and how a mission-led ecclesiology for today might look.

ECCLESIOLOGY AS A THEOLOGICAL SUBJECT VS. LIVED ECCLESIOLOGY

Prior to elucidating the content of ecclesiology, let us comment on what the word *ecclesiology* itself signifies. While the study of the church as a technical sub-discipline within theology only truly emerged in the

---

[1] Stephen B. Bevans and Roger P. Schroeder, *Prophetic Dialogue: Reflections on Christian Mission Today* (Maryknoll, NY: Orbis Books, 2011), 16.

early 1300s,[2] lived ecclesiology has been practiced by the church since its inception. We see ecclesiology as a *lived* reality in the New Testament: in the four Gospels to greater and lesser degrees, in the Pauline and deutero-Pauline letters, and particularly in the Book of Acts. The Book of Acts details the growth of the church through the apostolic age, with Peter leading the charge.

What we understand today as the traditional marks of the church—oneness, holiness, catholicity, and apostolicity—are rooted in the lived ecclesiology that we find in scripture. Paul's hymn to the oneness of the body of Christ in the first letter to the Corinthians has long been ground for recognition that the church must be one body, with Christ as its head. The holiness of the church is called for by Christ himself—"Be perfect as your father in heaven is perfect" (Mt 5:48)—and by the many examples of holy people presented throughout the New Testament. Catholicity is prominent in the Gospels of Mark and Luke as they focus on spreading the gospel to a Gentile audience, and particularly the Gospel of Matthew, which contains the Great Commission: "Go, and make disciples of all nations" (Mt 28:19). Apostolicity has its roots in the scriptural passage of Matthew 16, the chapter in which Jesus renames Simon as Peter or Cephas, which is Hebrew for "rock," stating, "You are Peter, and upon this rock I will build my church," and in the pastoral epistles of Paul, wherein we see the expansion of the church providing incentive for finding an organizational structure for the church and its posterity.

As the church expanded and grew in influence and life span, it realized that it needed to articulate some parameters about its nature. Ecclesiology as the intellectual study and pursuit of theological knowledge about the church develops out of and alongside lived theology, because, as Bevans notes, the church is a believing community that seeks *understanding* of its faith.[3]

THE CHURCH AND SALVATION OR THE REIGN OF GOD

It has been a part of the church's self-understanding from the beginning that it is a unique instrument of healing and newness of life. *Salus*, the Latin term for "salvation," means, at its core, healing. The earliest Christians

---

[2] Eric Plumer, "The Development of Ecclesiology: Early Church to the Reformation," in *The Gift of the Church: A Textbook on Ecclesiology in Honor of Patrick Granfield, OSB,* ed. Peter C. Phan (Collegeville, MN: Michael Glazier, 2000), 23. Indeed, Peter Phan would assert that serious ecclesiology began only after the Protestant Reformation (see Peter C. Phan, "Doing Ecclesiology in the World Church," Third Annual Louis G. Vance Chair of Systematic Theology Lecture, Oblate University, October 17, 2017).

[3] Stephen B. Bevans, *An Introduction to Theology in Global Perspective* (Maryknoll, NY: Orbis Books, 2009), 61.

were moved to become followers of Christ because, in part, they witnessed the miraculous restoration of health and life performed by Jesus's closest friends, who viewed him as their teacher. The Book of Acts details this experience. The kind of healing that salvation signifies is, however, more global and profound than physical restoration alone. The depiction of the church as "the New Israel" in the Gospel of Luke indicates the way in which the church sees itself as playing a critical role in healing the history of the world, or what is called salvation history: God, through Christ and the church, brings about justice, redemption, and liberation from the oppression and brokenness of the world, which the Israelites experienced in an especially poignant way.

Salvation is the language used to express the human understanding of how the rift between God and humanity is healed. We understand Jesus to save humanity because Jesus becoming human and dying in obedience and love inaugurates the reign of God. God's reign is marked by true peace and true joy; it is the reign of total, self-giving love. Anselm of Canterbury, among others, provided a key account of how sin is healed in and through Jesus Christ. Known as a satisfaction theory of atonement, this account of salvation or soteriology describes how cosmic order broken by sin is restored, and humans thereby experience rehabilitation; on the cross, Jesus, the only just man, makes satisfaction or atones for our sins. Some would say that the concept of salvation as transformation[4]—in line perhaps with Lonergan's[5] notion of salvation—may be more intelligible and compelling for our age. Jesus's life, ministry, and death on the cross make true justice, true beauty, and true goodness possible for us. A new way of life is opened up for us through Jesus's powerful act of love that changes what dying can mean and what it can effect.[6]

The work of Christ is the work of salvation, and it is only through participation in Christ's work that the church is salvific. At one point in time, the church pronounced that "outside the church there is no salvation" *(extra ecclesiam nulla salus)*. However, the church did not always hold this view, and, moreover, today the position of the church on the salvation of non-Catholics and the salvation of non-Christians has changed. In other words, the view that outside the church there is no salvation is a historically particular and theologically nuanced view that requires unpacking. Specifically, and to expound briefly, this ecclesiological statement came at a time when key thinkers of the church, Cyprian of Carthage in particular, were deeply concerned with the issue of the unity of the church. To clear up any existing misunderstanding of the

---

[4] Ibid., 53.

[5] Theologian Bernard Lonergan's modern interpretation of Christ's salvific power is known as the law of the cross.

[6] For a good, straightforward account of Lonergan's soteriology, see Christopher McMahon, *Called Together: An Introduction to Ecclesiology* (Winona, MN: Anselm Academic, 2010).

importance of being in communion with the one true church, and this through obedience to the authority of the bishops of the church that had descended from the apostles, who received their authority from Christ, Cyprian drew the line starkly: one was either in communion with the church through faithfulness to the teachings of the church and participation in the sacraments, or one was not saved. Heresies threatening to divide the church as well as a climate of persecution of the church provided the context for such comments.

In light of the great event in the church's life in modern history, the Second Vatican Council, however, it is acknowledged now that God's saving grace, while working within and though the church, may indeed work outside of the church as well. In *Nostra aetate*, a summation of the council's serious reflection on other religions, the church states that it rejects nothing that is true and holy in other religions, and recognizes that these may have salvific value for its adherents. Nonetheless, the church maintains that it is through the person and work of Jesus Christ that salvation is actually effected. While the way in which the church has discussed *how* it is an instrument of salvation has changed over time, *that* it is intimately involved in salvation is a "constant" in the ongoing life of the church.[7]

BEING FAITHFUL TO ITS MISSION, BEING THE CHURCH OF CHRIST

So how does the church stay true to its mission to bring about the reign of God? First, it recognizes that it must stay close to Jesus in order to bring about the reign of God, as this man, whom Christianity understands to be the Son of God, was the one to inaugurate this reign, this path to peace, this way of love and joy. Continuing the mission of God, *missio Dei*, constitutes the church's own mission and task.

Images abound in scripture of the church and its relationship to Christ, the Savior. Whether it is the body of Christ in 1 Corinthians, of which Christ is the head, or Christ as the vine and his disciples, or the church, as the branches, or the spousal imagery of the church as the bride to Christ's bridegroom in the Book of Revelation, it is clear from the holy scriptures of the Christian tradition that the church receives its very identity and reason for being from Christ. Some would add that it is the mission of the triune self-giving God that gives rise to the church, and so the church is constituted not only by the person of Christ but also by the mission of the triune God. Indeed, Pope Francis has noted that when the church is self-referential, not realizing that its basic identity is that it exists in Christ and that it is thus sent into the world—called to move beyond itself—it

---

[7] Stephen B. Bevans and Roger P. Schroeder, *Constants in Context: A Theology of Mission for Today* (Maryknoll, NY: Orbis Books, 2004).

is sick.[8] Theologian Walter Kasper has recently drawn attention anew to the centrality of the relationship between Christ and the church in order to have a proper understanding of the latter.[9]

If the church is about the reign of God and the church is also understood to be one, holy, catholic, and apostolic, then something about each of these aspects of the church is necessary for ushering in the reign of God. So we approach an account of the marks of the church in this manner.

Oneness

The church, although meant to be one, became "a house divided" due to several events over time, two of which stand out: (1) the controversy over the origin of the Holy Spirit and the jurisdiction of the papacy, which led to schism in 1054 between the Eastern and Western wings of the church; and (2) the Reformation, attributed officially to Martin Luther and his 95 theses criticizing the church, in 1517. Today we might say that a significant division exists between the more "progressive" and the more "conservative" groups in the church, though it has not expressed itself in formal schism.

Nonetheless, we can see how oneness is necessary to promote the reign of God; that is, if the reign of God is about the power of love to heal the world, and love is unity, the triumph of love can never be attained or attested to by a divided body.

Holiness

There is a sanctifying process that takes place as the church gathers all of humanity together and as the church goes out together to build unity. In addition, holiness is essential to the process of reaching out to others and bringing them into a community that praises, reverences, and serves God. The self-emptying God reigns only when he reigns in his people, who show that they are committed to the God who is Love as they themselves embody a self-emptying love for those around them for the sanctification of the whole world.

Catholicity

Catholicity, which is often understood to signify the universality of the church's faith, has been recognized as meaning wholeness as well. Indeed,

---

[8] Jorge Mario Bergoglio, handwritten notes prior to conclave in which he was elected pope: "The evils that, over time, happen in ecclesial institutions have their root in self-reference and a kind of theological narcissism." Reported in Beth Griffin, "Evangelization, Mercy, Encounter Mark Pope's First Four Years, Nuncio Says," *America* (March 16, 2017).

[9] Walter Kasper, *The Catholic Church: Nature, Reality, and Mission* (New York: T & T Clark, 2015).

the reign of God cannot be for one part of the world only or for some people or some part of a people; rather, the reign of God is about God being all in all, about God reigning in the whole cosmos in and through every human heart. It is the nature of God's reign, the reign of love, to be shared. The mission of the church is tied, then, to the catholicity of the church. Related to this is the notion that the truth of the church is not an arbitrary truth that holds for some people but not others, but that love is the deepest reality of all that exists.

Apostolicity

The reign of God is exercised in time as well in space. The reign of God in and through time can only be effected through unity across time. The name we give to the process that enables unity across time is tradition, which comes from the Latin word *tradere*, which means, literally, "handing on." Historically, the church claims to be authoritative in its teachings because of its origins, that is, the Roman Catholic Church claims the apostles of Jesus Christ were the first heads of the church. Through them, and through the ordination of bishops through the ages, the teachings of the church have been passed on. Thus, it is the structures of authority in the church, and particularly the Petrine office, that maintain the unity and stability of the church across time.

MISSION-LED ECCLESIOLOGY FOR TODAY: ENGAGING THE PLURALITY AND SECULARITY OF TODAY'S CONTEXT

Vatican II

The Second Vatican Council, which took place in the 1960s, was the attempt by the church to understand and open itself to the encounter with modernity. Key documents of Vatican II include *Lumen gentium (Dogmatic Constitution on the Church), Gaudium et spes (Pastoral Constitution on the Church in the Modern World), Sacrosanctum concilium (Constitution on the Sacred Liturgy),* and *Dei verbum (Dogmatic Constitution on Divine Revelation).* From its prefatory remarks, the council might be said to pay particular attention to the catholicity of the gospel and the need to share the good news with the world: "We are entering a period that might be called one of universal mission . . . and we need to recognize the 'signs of the times' . . . and to discern amid such great darkness the many indications that give good cause for hope." While much conflict has ensued since Vatican II over the council's meaning and significance, it is also widely thought to be a rich source of new life in the church.

Unique to Vatican II was its expansive approach to its audience. While the council was convoked to give the church an opportunity for serious self-reflection and attention to the unfolding context of modernity around it, many of its documents, particularly *Gaudium et spes*, are addressed to all people of good will. Notably, this is a church that understands itself not as isolated from the wider world but as part of the world, even as it remains a distinctive presence within the world. The positive tone toward the world and toward all manner of difference—religious others, non-Catholic others, and the Catholic "other" (the laity)—indicated that the council was aiming to be truly pastoral and engaged. It was a gathering marked by much positivity and hopefulness. Non-Catholics were invited to participate as expert observers, and the issues considered were vast. The scope of the council was expansive in every way. Twenty-four hundred council fathers from all over the world met over a period of four years. Hallmark concepts of the council included a desire to bring the church up to date, described by the Italian neologism *aggiornamento,* while remaining true to the tradition, termed *ressourcement,* a French-derived word to signify returning to the deep sources of the Christian tradition for grounding in truth. Other key concepts of renewal and retrieval associated with the council include communion, collegiality, and dialogue. Now, contextualization of the church's understanding of God and God's reign is "traditional."[10] Nonetheless, the church came to realize that theology is truly contextual at Vatican II.[11]

Oneness Today

Authority and office. Some distinctive terms that arise in a Catholic discussion of authority are *magisterium, sensus fidelium, infallibility, reception,* and *dissent.* Perhaps the most contentious of these, and also the most misunderstood, is the concept of infallibility. Most often referring to the authority of the pope and his teaching authority, as it was decreed at the First Vatican Council, there is a tendency to overlook that infallibility of belief refers to that of the entire church, insofar as it follows the light of the Holy Spirit. As Bevans notes, both magisterium and infallibility refer not only to the hierarchy or particular members of the hierarchy, but to the whole church. One of the key points from the council on understanding the relationship between theology and church is that theology is the

---

[10] Stephen B. Bevans, *Models of Contextual Theology* (Maryknoll, NY: Orbis Books, 2002), 8. Bevans shows this in referring to the early church fathers who tried to assimilate Greek categories into their understanding of Jewish Christianity, and Aquinas, whose synthesis of Aristotle profoundly shaped the foundational understanding of the church.

[11] Bevans, *An Introduction to Theology in Global Perspective,* 165.

task of the whole church and the whole church is authorized, therefore, by virtue of membership in the one body of Christ[12] to lead, to witness, and to be missionary, priest, prophet, and king, though not literally in the case of priesthood.

Ecclesiality. Pope Francis underscores this meaning of infallibility, showing that the power of his office, as pope, arises from being a representative member of the whole church:

> The people itself constitutes a subject. And the church is the people of God on the journey through history, with joys and sorrows. Thinking with the church, therefore, is my way of being part of this people. And all the faithful, considered as a whole, are infallible in matters of belief, and the people display this *infallibilitas in credendo*, this infallibility in believing, through a supernatural sense of the faith of all the people walking together. . . . When the dialogue among the people and the bishops and the pope goes down this road and is genuine, then it is assisted by the Holy Spirit. . . . And, of course, we must be very careful not to think that this *infallibilitas* of all the faithful I am talking about in light of Vatican II is a form of populism. No; it is the experience of "holy mother the hierarchical church," as St. Ignatius called it, the church as the people of God, pastors and people together. The church is the totality of God's people.[13]

Indeed, one of the most important ways of understanding the unity of the church is through the image of the people of God, which highlights the manner in which the church is a community rooted in the person of Christ and inspired by the Holy Spirit. The Holy Spirit is the One who gathers people together, which is one way of describing the church's mission: to gather all of humanity back into the One who is Love. Notably, Francis highlights that the church as people of God need not stand in opposition to the church as hierarchical or as holy mother, even though there may be a healthy tension among those images and models of church. Some would also suggest the formulation that the church's communion is found in the carrying out of mission.[14]

Ecumenism. Officially, the great development in church unity over the past century, and the name given to all efforts to promote unity among the divided Christian churches, is ecumenism. In *Lumen gentium* a key phrase was added that indicated a remarkable change in the teaching of the church on the validity of churches of other Christian traditions: the church of Jesus Christ subsists in *(substitit in)* the Catholic Church. This indicated a step beyond what until then had been the traditional understanding that

---

[12] Ibid.

[13] Pope Francis, quoted in Antonio Spadaro, SJ, "A Big Heart Open to God: An Interview with Pope Francis," *America* (September 20, 2013).

[14] Bevans and Schroeder, *Constants in Context*, 286.

the church of Jesus Christ is identical with the Roman Catholic Church. With the acknowledgment that Christ's body may be found outside of the Catholic Church, the church recognized that the experience of the body of Christ on earth is one of division and that such division within the Christian family bears false witness to Christ and his Spirit. Many dialogues among churches sprouted from the recognition that building unity between the Christian churches is an ecclesiological imperative for truthful witness to Christ himself.

Catholicity Today

Catholicity is often translated as "universality," but this doesn't quite capture the richness of the word. Catholicity is certainly that "mark" or "dimension" of the church that insures that the church perseveres in the whole gospel and strives to live and flourish in every part of the world and in every cultural context. At the same time, however, catholicity is the dimension of the church that champions and preserves the local, the particular. Rather than a bland uniformity, Christianity is endowed with a dynamic that moves toward unity through a rich diversity, through conversation and even argument among people of particular personal, cultural, and historical experience. Only if every group in the church—Vietnamese, Laotian, Filipino, Salvadoran, European, North American, Ghanaian and so forth—is included in its particularity will the church truly be the church. Only as the church enters into serious dialogue with every culture can it be witness to the "Pleroma" that is Jesus Christ.[15]

Intercultural theology. One of the indisputable signs of the times that the church must increasingly recognize is the cultural diversity of its people. For a few decades now people have spoken of the reality of the world church.[16] Western theologians such as Karl Rahner and Bernard Lonergan offered rich foundations for a more geographically and historically contextualized approach to theology and, by extension, ecclesiology.[17] Over the past thirty years we have seen the birth and proliferation of theology—*contextual theology*—within such cultural and ethnic contexts as that of the African church, the African American church, the churches in Latin America, and

---

[15] Bevans, *Models of Contextual Theology,* 14–15.

[16] However, Bevans and others will note rightly that the church has always been a world church.

[17] Kevin Burke, among others, has underscored the gift of cultural diversity to theology in a fine essay on the topic: Kevin Burke, "Thinking about the Church: The Gift of Cultural Diversity to Theology," in *Many Faces, One Church: Cultural Diversity and the American Catholic Experience,* ed. Peter C. Phan and Diana Hayes (Lanham, MD: Sheed and Ward Books, 2005).

the churches in Asia. Thanks to the pioneering efforts of theologians such as Shawn Copeland (black theology), Gustavo Gutiérrez (Hispanic theology), and Peter Phan (Asian American theology), to name a few, we have come to recognize that Catholicism is not synonymous with *Romanitas*[18] but is something truly universal that touches down in unique and beautiful ways in every part of the world.

The past several decades have seen an increased awareness of Christianity's transition from being merely a European export and product of colonialism to something much more diverse and local around the globe. Robert Schreiter has expounded the need to recognize the church throughout the whole world, as it is embedded within cultures that differ significantly from one other, through the act of communication.[19] As theologians have explored the variety of Christian churches throughout the South and the East in particular, Dana Robert highlights and echoes how each global/local instantiation of church should be understood according to its own particularity.[20]

Inculturation is the process by which the message of the gospel is planted in a local culture. Inculturation is the interaction of multiple cultural orientations, not a single interaction between the gospel and a culture. Intercultural theology is, then, theological reflection upon the process of interculturation. Some say that we need to move from inculturation to *inter*culturation.

This perspective and approach to mission is based on several developments: the "discovery" of being a world church at Vatican II (Rahner); recognition of the presumption of European theology from within and outside of Christianity, for example, secularism; and the reality that two-thirds of the church in the twenty-first century lies in the global South. The

---

[18] One should observe that it would be unproductive simply to assume criticism of Romanness, however, and that recently, some have made a provocative attempt to claim that Rome is in fact the source of the diversity and richness of Western civilization. See Remi Brague, "Athens—Jerusalem—Rome," *Communio* (Spring 2013): 35.

[19] Robert Schreiter, *The New Catholicity: Theology between the Global and the Local* (Maryknoll, NY: Orbis Books, 1997).

[20] "As historians work within the tensions between the global and the local that characterize indigenous world Christianities today, we should recognize that each form of twenty-first century Christianity represents a synthesis of global and local elements that has its own integrity" (Dana Robert, "Shifting Southward: Global Christianity since 1945," in *Landmark Essays in Mission and World Christianity,* ed. Robert L. Gallagher and Paul Hertig [Maryknoll, NY: Orbis Books, 2009], 60). Also: "As Christianity declines in Europe and grows in the South, historians need to recognize what the International Missionary Council saw in 1938: the future of world Christianity rests with the so-called younger churches and their daily struggles. . . . The challenge for historians lies in seeing beyond an extension of Western categories and into the hearts, minds, and contexts of Christ's living peoples in Asia, Africa, and Latin America" (ibid.).

issue of catholicity has thus raised questions: Have we been too European in our outlook? How do we account for and include the diversity of the cultures in which the church finds itself and remain one church? How do we receive the gift of interculturalism without falling prey to "church as multinational import firm," that is, third-world theologies seen as exotic complements to European theology?

It is all too easy, even in and as the church, to see the world from the lens of our clan, our ethnic group, and to forget that other groups, other races, other cultures, also have a claim to be honored as rich contributors to human flourishing. It is not enough, moreover, to acknowledge and even to celebrate the uniquely different and beautiful ways in which different parts of the body of Christ in Africa, Latin America, and Asia worship. We need to see that we are closest to being the world church when we allow the unity in Christ, which binds us to one another, to bear one another's burdens; and to learn from the struggle happening in all parts of the world, in all parts of Christ's body, by being in solidarity with the people in our local church who endure them.

To consider a couple of examples in greater detail: in fall 2007, Pope Francis, then Cardinal Jorge Bergoglio, was chair of the committee concluding the document of Benedict XVI on *Aparecida*. In this document three principles were named as key to understanding *Aparecida*: (1) from below upward; (2) liturgy and popular piety have a unifying and evangelizing force; and (3) fidelity to the Lord is "a blossoming." From below upward means that collegial harmony and collegiality are key ways of being church in Latin America. The principle regarding liturgy and popular piety indicates that popular religiosity is also a profound and legitimate way of being Christian. Both the Eucharist and popular Catholicism show that God is still active in history and in the small stories of faith and devotion that inspire culture. Fidelity is a "blossoming" means that believing faith is expressed always as a change, a going out, a growth.

Peter Phan names the various ways in which Christianity, and Asian Christianity especially, comprise a range of diversities—"geographic, linguistic, ethnic, economic, political, cultural and religious"[21]—and thus urges us to approach the topic of Asian Christianity with care and humility. In addition to being marked by great diversity, Phan helps us to see that the church in Asia experiences overwhelming poverty and that it values in a particular way universal harmony and dialogue. These are, then, some ways in which the experiences and values of the Asian church may enrich the universal church as it forges a path into the future.

Interreligious dialogue. Recognizing the need to participate in a universal mission, the years since Vatican II have crystallized the seeming paradox of dialogue with other religions and mission into an understanding

---

[21] Peter C. Phan, "Reception of Vatican II in Asia," *Theological Studies* 74/2 (June 2013).

that dialogue and mission in fact go hand in hand.[22] Moving from an affirmation of what is true and holy in other religions to the importance of finding ways to grow continually in mutual understanding of one another through theological exchange (dialogue of theological discourse), working together for justice (the dialogue of action), sharing religious experience together, and simply living side by side in the world (the dialogue of life), interreligious dialogue has grown from mere affirmation of the other to emphasizing that the church needs to bring itself to the table as well. While progressing in the conceptual work of interreligious dialogue may be challenging, some attitudes that help to foster interreligious dialogue have been established: openness and receptivity, strong convictions with respect for the other, openness to truth through a contemplative spirit, and patience and perseverance.

Apostolicity Today

Historically, when apostolicity was discussed, the issue of authority was never far ahead or behind. However, the question of authority is one that many today believe must be answered not by apostolicity in the traditional and literal sense—wherein it is possible to trace a historical connection between Christ and church—but by contemporary action with integrity. In other words, in a post-existentialist, post-phenomenological, post-pragmatist world, true apostolicity is discerned in the fruits of those who would call themselves Christian. What authorizes the church to offer the religious and moral teachings that it presents as true and universally valid? While those who have experience belonging to an ecclesial tradition may recognize that the question of authority hearkens back to the apostolic aspect of the Catholic Church's identity, many today challenge ecclesial authority on moral grounds: how is the church a credible source of moral teaching in areas that its decision makers do not experience personally? For example, many today find the church's claim of moral authority problematic, particularly in the realm of human sexuality. An answer regarding ecclesial authority today may lie in how the church is called to refigure holiness as well.

Apostolicity and Secular Culture

First, however, a word about the aspect of secularity in many cultures around the world today. Typically understood as the widespread decline in religious practice or belief, or the evacuation of religion from the public

---

[22] The Pontifical Council for Interreligious Dialogue, *Dialogue and Proclamation: Reflection and Orientations on Interreligious Dialogue and the Proclamation of the Gospel of Jesus Christ.*

sphere, the church had often in the latter half of the twentieth century decried the pervasiveness of secularism and relativism in contemporary Western cultures such as those of countries in Europe and North America.

The question of how the church might mediate the Catholic tradition for the secular cultures of the world today presents myriad avenues for exploration. The many possibilities of this question arise, first of all, due to the complex reality that we call culture. Cultural reality is not mono- lithic, as theologian Kathryn Tanner has pointed out. Tanner highlights the obsolescence of the notion of cultures as "self-contained and clearly bounded units, internally consistent and unified wholes."[23] She endorses in its place a postmodern anthropology of culture that underscores the particularities, multiplicities, and porous nature of culture. Indeed, cultures of peoples around the world today are a tapestry of cultures and subcul- tures, and multicultural belonging could well define the identity of every person living today. Julius-Kei Kato makes an argument for the existence of hybridity[24] in almost every part of the world today, despite a disquiet- ing homogeneity that is discernible in contemporary Western versions of secularism. Tanner shows that a shift in intellectually privileged norms calls, moreover, for reconsidered ecclesial theories of culture.[25]

If another meaning of apostolicity is how the teachings of the church are communicated or disseminated, we may consider some theoretical reflections on Christianity's discursive practices. Graham Ward asks:

> How do the discursive practices of Christianity fare, and why do they fare in that way rather than in any other way? Only by demonstrat- ing how this question might be answered can an account be given of the relationship between Christian living (and talking) and the implicit values of public consciousness. Only by being able to give an account of this relationship can a space be cleared for rethinking the gospel's specific transformative practices of hope in the new urban landscape. And so theology has to engage with social, political and cultural theory, cultural anthropology, philosophy, hermeneutics, con- textual accounts of epistemology, social semiotics and performative notions of gendered subjectivity (among a few of the contemporary "sciences") while remaining theological.[26]

Ward also indicates the complex challenge involved in attending to the normative dimension of Christian engagement with culture, particularly

---

[23] Kathryn Tanner, *Theories of Culture: A New Agenda for Theology* (Min- neapolis: Fortress Press, 1997), 38.

[24] Julius-Kei Kato, *Religious Language and Asian American Hybridity* (New York: Palgrave Macmillan, 2016).

[25] Tanner, *Theories of Culture.*

[26] Graham Ward, *Cultural Transformation and Religious Practice* (New York: Cambridge University Press, 2005), 2–3.

from within the horizon of the postmodern. On the one hand, a Christian voice in culture must recognize that its transformative task will be held accountable by a secular public on terms outside its own, and it must thus attempt to communicate across the religious and epistemological difference:

> The Christian critique, then, that issues from the examination of contemporary Christian *poiesis* will also have to defend itself against the charge of being arbitrary because its relevance lies in the relationship it bears to questions our contemporary culture is already asking about itself. But, in that defence, it appeals to other categories that it offers for public accreditation and provides an account of interrelationality that is not based in an essentialized and universalized humanism.[27]

On the other hand, Christianity must hold itself accountable to the gospel if it is to transform with integrity:

> As a standpoint-project, Christianity, then, approaches the world critically. The critique issues from both its ethical and its eschatological vision. By ethical I refer to Christianity's conceptions of God's goodness, beauty and justice, conceptions incarnated in Christ whom Christianity are called to imitate. The ethical vision provokes judgment with respect to distorted and distorting forms of social relation: that is, social relations that do not reflect God's goodness, beauty and justice, but rather manifest violent inequalities, exploitations and subjugations. The ethical vision also provokes the advocacy of new possibilities in Christ.[28]

Following Ward on the point of the need to cast broadly—"social, political and cultural theory, cultural anthropology, philosophy, hermeneutics, contextual accounts of epistemology, social semiotics and performative notions of gendered subjectivity (among a few of the contemporary 'sciences')"—for an engagement of and with contemporary cultural discourse, it seems all the more important for ecclesiology "from below" to ask how the church "does ethics" today in a way that helps or hinders those who consider themselves secular in encountering and experiencing receptivity to Christian faith.

It seems the church needs to employ narrative, intertextual and multilinguistic approaches to articulate its version of human personhood in a pluralistic and secular context. In particular, perhaps the underlying hermeneutical criterion for how the church does ethics today is the degree to which it embodies kenosis, that is, the donative and divinizing quality by which we know, hear, see, and experience love.

There must be recognition of the way in which the church and the world are similar and different, a naming of how the church and the world share points of compatibility and ways in which the church has something

---

[27] Ibid., 99–101.
[28] Ibid., 168.

unique and life-giving to offer the world. In the Catholic tradition these are sometimes described respectively as the sacramental and the prophetic dimensions of the church. In terms of prophetic dialogue, one might say that dialogue involves a sharing of how the church sees God in the goodness of all of creation; the prophetic is where the church calls the world to transform itself so that it may realize the reign of God, a reign of peace, justice, and love in all circumstances and among all people.

Arguably, there is a fruitfulness in raising the question of personhood as a point of prophetic dialogue between secular culture and the church: who speaks the truth about being human? According to the church, community, belonging, connectedness, and a larger horizon of love are the true horizons for the human person; beyond *ego* and *dasein*, there is the givenness of all experience, a law oriented to goodness that is written into our whole person, rational and pre-rational, larger stories and social frameworks that hold our rising and our falling, and communities and friendship that nurture us into growth. Despite attestations to community and horizons of love in secular culture, the latter is underwritten not by a liturgy oriented to self-opening and abiding with others but "liturgies" of individual choice and happiness, privately conceived and achieved.

Holiness Today

Holiness today may be the key inspiration for mission in a secular culture. However, this would be holiness understood not as perfection but as commitment to being one's true self, recognizing, however, that authenticity emerges only in community and not in self-authorizing originality. We may find that holiness today involves the church speaking prophetically about what it means to be human, that one cannot make oneself completely on one's own without assistance from anybody or anything, but that one finds one's true self in a community that witnesses to a Love that exceeds any merely human capacity. To that end, one may suggest that the mission of the church today calls for holiness to be expressed as a mission of accompaniment,[29] particularly of those whom sociologists of religion would designate "seekers" or "the nones."[30]

---

[29] For a fuller account of a mission-centered local ecclesiology imagined specifically for a secular cultural context such as that of contemporary North America and particularly Canada, see Carolyn Chau, *Solidarity with the World: Charles Taylor and Hans Urs von Balthasar on Faith, Modernity, and Catholic Mission* (Eugene, OR: Cascade Press, 2016). The author outlines the way in which authentic personhood may be a site of prophetic dialogue for contemporary Catholic mission in a secular age.

[30] Those who self-identify today as having no religion have been labeled by some as "the nones," and this group, along with the group known as "seekers," have by many accounts been shown to be growing more rapidly than other groups by sociologists of religion.

Lay ecclesial movements and secular institutes. When the church takes up the challenge of reaching out to lives that are seeking meaning without finding it, accompanying the lost, and binding up the broken, then it proclaims the reign of God in a way that may be recognized anew. In a post-Christian age, as some have designated this time, some have argued that it is the age of the laity, and, in particular, laity committed to live out the reign of God in a radical way.

Since the late twentieth century, there has been a blossoming of gospel living in the church in the form of what are known as lay ecclesial movements and secular institutes. These may be oriented to practicing the social justice teachings of the church in a thoroughgoing way, for example, the Catholic Worker movement in the United States; or emphasizing the use of the language of the liturgy in one's day-to-day encounters with one another, for example, the Focolare group greeting each other as brothers and sisters at all times. Others focus on the message of communion and liberation that lies at the heart of the reign of God and challenge one another to learn these lessons daily in striving to meet Jesus in their everyday lives (for example, Communion and Liberation, a Catholic lay ecclesial movement). Secular institutes are communities of lay persons who choose to live according to the evangelical counsels of poverty, chastity, and obedience in the midst of the world, witnessing to the radical and radiant love of the gospel with their lives.

Church as an agent of formation—returning to discipleship. At the heart of the church is mission, and it is mission that precedes the church. Mission is often understood as the church *ad extra* or the church in its orientation outward to the world. However, there is also an *ad intra* aspect to mission.[31] We might say that mission begins with the inner transformation of the church by the light of Christ and culminates in the sharing of that light with others.

CONCLUSION

In a world where it is all too easy to try to resolve moral, emotional, psychological, and intellectual distress on one's own, the church offers a profoundly effective alternative whose efficacy lies in the fact that it is true to the nature of humans: we are social beings. Arguably, in a time when individualistic notions of authenticity pervade our culture and our world, and there are such deep experiences of isolation and despair despite the proliferation of virtual and high-tech forms of community, the church, as a people gathered together to love and worship the One who loves all, stands as a witness to the power of belonging to community for forming

---

[31] Bevans and Schroeder, *Constants in Context*, 394.

one for authentic living. At the very least, it is honest about the fact that all people need accountability for their life stories.

In honing sociality, the church develops community and authenticity, and ultimately, it makes disciples. Taking discipleship seriously means taking mission seriously. Each of us in the body of Christ has a mission field. Propositionally, they may not cohere, but as we tend to our plot, we move and shift the imagination of the ones to whom we are sent. Mission cannot be preached univocally, particularly in our secular, pluralistic age.

PART 4

A PERSONAL REFLECTION FROM STEPHEN B. BEVANS, SVD

Chapter 14

Becoming a Global Theologian: A Personal Journey

Stephen B. Bevans, SVD

A LIFE-CHANGING QUESTION

My journey to becoming a global theologian began when an Indian confrere of mine in Rome challenged me on using the sun as an image of Advent brightness and warmth. In India, he said, the sun is something to be avoided; its warmth is dangerous and even destructive. It was from that moment that my education as a contextual and global theologian began, although I didn't fully know it at the time.

That realization began to be more fully developed, however, only about three years later, two or three days after I arrived in the Philippines in 1972, my first assignment after ordination and the completion of my STL degree in Rome. On that day I ran into fellow Society of the Divine Word (SVD) Leonardo Mercado, who was working on the PhD from the University of Santo Tomás in Manila, writing a dissertation on Filipino philosophy. I had met Lenny a year or so before in Rome, and when he saw me he welcomed me to the Philippines and asked me a question that I think changed my life: What kind of theology was I going to teach at the diocesan seminary to which I had been assigned—*Roman* theology or *Filipino* theology?

Lenny's question both confused and intrigued me. It confused me because I didn't think that I had learned "Roman theology" in Rome. I thought I had just learned "theology"—the only theology that there was. I had been taught by some great professors, most of whom had been members of commissions who had produced the documents of Vatican II.

This material was first presented in a breakout group on global solidarity at the Catholic Theological Society of America annual meeting, June 2017. A version of this essay will appear in the October 2018 issue of the *International Bulletin of Mission Research*.

I had memorized tons of material and had a pretty good handle on the history of theology and tradition. I was pretty sure that I knew the best theology of the day. On the other hand, Lenny's question intrigued me because I had heard rumors of efforts to develop theologies of liberation and revolution, of theologies rooted in the culture and customs of various peoples. I had vaguely heard of Medellín, and the Federation of Asian Bishops' Conferences had been formed barely a year before, when Paul VI had visited the Philippines. I had no idea that several years before, in 1969, that same pope had told the bishops of Uganda, "You may, you must have an African theology!" But the possibility of doing what would later be called contextual theology or inculturation was in the air. Lenny was to be one of its pioneers in the Philippines, and he was opening up a new horizon for me.

The next several months I immersed myself in learning Ilokano, the local language of the region in northern Luzon where I would work, and I read a good bit of Philippine history and culture—and any Filipino theology I could find. In my first semester teaching at the Archdiocesan Major Seminary in Vigan, Ilocos Sur, in June 1973, I offered a noncredit course in Filipino theology, and about ten students signed up. We were searching together, reading the small amount of literature that was appearing in the area of indigenous theology, as it was called then, and Filipino theology in particular. As a result of that seminar I wrote my first published article, very much rooted in Bernard Lonergan's transcendental method, entitled "Becoming a Filipino Theologian."[1] This was a first articulation of what later I would call the transcendental model of contextual theology. It was a call to do theology as honestly as possible—as a person of faith and a person aware of one's cultural identity.

MODELS OF CONTEXTUAL THEOLOGY

Two years later, in 1975, I team-taught a course on fundamental ethics in a summer session at Divine Word University in Tacloban, Leyte. My teaching partner (my classmate Jim Heiar) and I used Bernard Lonergan's *Insight*[2] and tried to integrate Lonergan's approach with Filipino values. Being an ethical person, we were convinced, meant being as authentic as possible, both personally and culturally. Jim had just published a short book entitled *Christian Filipino*. The title was important: not Filipino *Christian*, but Christian *Filipino*. Culture, as Pope Paul VI had said in *Evangelii nuntiandi*, was not a simple veneer but the very embodiment of Christian faith.

[1] Stephen Bevans, "Becoming a Filipino Theologian," *The Ilocos Review* (1973): 208–14.
[2] Bernard Lonergan, *Insight: A Study of Human Understanding* (London: Longmans, Green and Co., 1957).

The president of the university where we were teaching was none other than Lenny Mercado, who was also teaching a course in the university entitled "Towards a Filipino Theology." Lenny had finished and published his PhD thesis on Filipino philosophy and had just completed a manuscript on Filipino theology and was testing it out in his course. After teaching my own course, I attended Lenny's classes, read the manuscript, and learned a lot.

Lenny's approach was different from the one I had been developing. He saw Filipino theology as emerging from a close study of the culture and language of Filipinos, trusting that the Spirit was at work in the midst of Filipino life. His approach was different also from one of the most eminent theologians in the Philippines at the time, Catalino G. Arévalo, who had developed a "theology of the signs of the times," very much along the lines of the liberation theology that was beginning to emerge out of Latin America. I began to wonder which approach was right—Lenny's, Arévalo's, or my own more transcendental approach. To add to the confusion, at a conference that was held at our seminary earlier in 1975, a bishop who was present suggested that a Filipino theology was simply a matter of translating concepts like *homoousios*, person, and substance into the various Filipino languages. Who had discovered the right approach?

Then one day it hit me. All these approaches were right! They were just different approaches to the same question. This was the genesis of my *Models of Contextual Theology*,[3] although it would take me fifteen more years to conceive of, write, and publish the book. My insight would become more sophisticated. I would borrow my use of models from Avery Dulles's classic book *Models of the Church*,[4] and I would later realize the profound meaning of *context*, the discernment of which validates the use of a particular model. But the basic insight was here, in 1975. I was already well on my way to a global integration of theology.

THE MISSIONARY NATURE OF THE CHURCH

I tried as much as possible to integrate Filipino culture and values into my teaching of theology back at the seminary in Vigan, with some success and a good bit of failure as well. Another discovery, however, helped me to further develop some kind of global perspective in my teaching approach. This was the discovery of the radical missionary nature of the church, expressed in what was a rather neglected line in the Vatican II document on mission, *Ad gentes* (AG): "The pilgrim church is missionary by its very nature." The reason for this is that the church participates in the very mission of the triune God. I began to realize the importance of mission, and it radically changed my thinking about the church. I began to develop

---

[3] Stephen B. Bevans, *Models of Contextual Theology* (Maryknoll, NY: Orbis Books, 1992, 2002).

[4] Avery Dulles, *Models of the Church* (New York: Doubleday, 1974).

my course on ecclesiology from the perspective of its missionary nature. Vatican II had made the breakthrough from understanding the church as essentially an institution to understanding it as a communion, a community, the people of God. But at the same time it had understood the church as a community in mission, coming into existence for the sake of the reign of God, called to incarnate itself in every nation, every culture in the world.

It would take me a long time to fully understand this. A commentary on *Ad gentes* that I wrote in 2009 would deepen my appreciation of the document's depth despite its flaws and datedness, and an article for *Theological Studies* in 2013 helped me see even more clearly that Vatican II, from start to finish, was a missionary council.[5] I still have hopes of finishing a systematic ecclesiology that would work this out fully. But the discovery of the "missionary imagination" that needed to be at the heart of theology was a major step in my development, and one that would guide my global integration of my approach to theological education.

CATHOLIC THEOLOGICAL UNION

I really didn't understand this yet, though. In 1981 I left the Philippines to do the PhD in systematic theology at the University of Notre Dame. I wrote my dissertation, under the direction of the distinguished Dominican Thomas F. O'Meara, on the understanding of God's personal nature in the theology of the relatively obscure Presbyterian Scots theologian John Wood Oman. I interviewed and was hired at Catholic Theological Union (CTU) in Chicago to teach systematic theology, and I thought that I had left contextual theology and missiology behind.

But that was hardly the case. I had gotten my job at CTU precisely because of my missionary experience and my few publications on contextual theology in the Philippines and in the journal *Missiology* in 1984. CTU was a theological school that understood itself as having world mission at its very heart. My religious community, the Society of the Divine Word, had come to CTU in 1973 because it saw the opportunity of creating a curriculum there that would honor mission and global consciousness. Further, CTU's young dean, Robert Schreiter, had committed the school to developing such a curriculum.

When I joined the CTU faculty in 1986, Schreiter assigned me to teach courses in the "mission track" of the curriculum with titles like "Origins and Ends in Mythic Consciousness" (a course on creation and eschatology) and "Missionary Dynamics of the Church" (a course in ecclesiology). As

[5] Stephen B. Bevans and Jeffrey Gros, *Evangelization and Religious Freedom* (Mahwah, NJ: Paulist Press, 2009); Stephen B. Bevans, "Revisiting Mission at Vatican II: Theology and Practice for Today's Missionary Church," *Theological Studies* 74/2 (May 2013): 261–83.

I worked on these courses, some of my other courses, like the ones on the Trinity and an introduction to theology, began to reflect the same global and missionary consciousness and the same cultural and contextual sensitivity. It was in these years that I began to attend the annual meetings of the American Society of Missiology (ASM) as well as the Catholic Theological Society of America (CTSA). I became one of the associate editors of the ASM's journal, *Missiology: An International Review* (thanks to an invitation by its new editor, Darrell Whiteman), and for twelve years I refereed over fifty articles on mission a year. I was asked by my friend Bill Burrows at Orbis Books to co-edit, with the eminent missiologist James A. Scherer, a series on new directions in mission and evangelization, and I wrote my book *Models of Contextual Theology*. All of this was in the context of teaching students at CTU, who came from many different cultures and nations, and trying to gear my teaching toward their needs and questions.

The 1990s were exciting at CTU. The Association of Theological Schools was emphasizing the importance of a more global understanding of theological education, and members of our faculty were participating in a number of immersion programs that the association offered. In the early 1990s, CTU partnered with our neighbors, the Lutheran School of Theology at Chicago and McCormick Theological Seminary, to form the Chicago Center for Global Ministries, and I was asked to be its director, succeeding Robert Schreiter, the founding director, and Robert Marshall, an eminent Lutheran churchman and former bishop in the Lutheran Church of America. I served as director of the center for six years, trying to bring a global consciousness to our three faculties through faculty continuing education, annual world mission conferences on such topics as reconciliation, urbanization, and ecology, and offering immersion trips for students in Ghana, West Africa. At the same time, I was serving as editor of *Mission Studies*, the journal of the International Association for Mission Studies, and in that capacity I was in touch almost daily with scholars from every part of the world.

I began to be convinced of several things. First, there was no such thing as "theology"; there was only contextual theology. Second, theology could only be done adequately with a missiological imagination, as I tried to articulate in a plenary talk at the CTSA in 2001.[6] Third, theology could only be adequately done from a "global perspective," something that I worked out more clearly in my book *An Introduction to Theology in Global Perspective*, published in 2009.[7]

---

[6] Stephen B. Bevans, "Wisdom from the Margins: Systematic Theology and the Missiological Imagination," *CTSA Proceedings* 56 (2001): 21–42.

[7] The second edition of *Models of Contextual Theology* was published in 2002, and the opening words were about the contextual nature of all theology. See "Wisdom from the Margins: Systematic Theology and the Missiological Imagination," *CTSA Proceedings* (2001); and Stephen B. Bevans, *An Introduction to Theology in Global Perspective* (Maryknoll, NY: Orbis Books, 2009).

CONSTANTS IN CONTEXT

But I am getting ahead of myself. In 1997 the Overseas Ministries Study Center in New Haven, Connecticut, offered me the chance to be one of their scholars in residence, and I took the opportunity to invite my friend and colleague Roger Schroeder to come with me to begin work on a book that we had decided to write together. The book began as a simple introduction to the history and theology of mission but soon grew far beyond that. Roger had been involved as a consultant on a project authored by Scott Sunquist and Dale Irvin that would employ what came to be called the "new church history"[8]—the conceiving and writing of church history from a truly global perspective. This new perspective saw church history as really the history of the world Christian movement and began to incorporate the movement of Christianity eastward toward Asia in its first years, the movement southward to Africa, the role of women, and other subaltern perspectives. One of these perspectives is that the evangelization of Latin America in the sixteenth century was, in the long run, much more significant than the European Reformation, which took place at the same time. Roger and I were convinced that this was the perspective from which mission history needed to be written. Roger took the lead in writing the history chapters in the book; I would later write a short history of theology from the same perspective in my introduction to theology several years later.

At the same time, at the urging of Bill Burrows at Orbis Books, we began to see that a mission *theology* had to be developed in dialogue not just with Roman Catholic thinking, but with Protestant, evangelical, and Pentecostal thinking as well. The result of all this was *Constants in Context*, nine long years in the making, which was published in 2004.[9] In our book we tried to develop an insight from our SVD General Chapter in 2000—the idea that the best way to think about and engage in mission is in a practice and spirit of prophetic dialogue. This was an idea that Roger and I developed more fully in the following years. One fruit of these developments was the book *Prophetic Dialogue*, published in 2011.[10]

---

[8] See Wilbert R. Shenk, ed., *Enlarging the Story: Perspectives on Writing World Christian History* (Maryknoll, NY: Orbis Books, 2002); Dale T. Irvin, *Christian Histories, Christian Traditioning: Rendering Accounts* (Maryknoll, NY: Orbis Books, 1998); Justo L. González, *The Changing Shape of Church History* (St. Louis: Chalice Press, 2002). See also Dale T. Irvin and Scott W. Sunquist, *History of the World Christian Movement*, 2 vols. (Maryknoll, NY: Orbis Books, 2001, 2012).

[9] Stephen B. Bevans and Roger P. Schroeder, *Constants in Context: A Theology of Mission for Today* (Maryknoll, NY: Orbis Books, 2004).

[10] Stephen B. Bevans and Roger P. Schroeder, *Prophetic Dialogue: Reflections on Christian Mission Today* (Maryknoll, NY: Orbis Books, 2011).

ECUMENISM AND THE WORLD COUNCIL OF CHURCHES

The ecumenical approach to *Constants in Context* connects to another important aspect of my development in global integration—my involvement with the World Council of Churches' (WCC) Commission on World Mission and Evangelism (CWME). I began to develop this connection in about 2010 when I attended the 2010 Edinburgh Conference, commemorating the great 1910 World Mission Conference at Edinburgh. In 2012, I was invited to the pre-assembly of the CWME in Manila and served on the listening committee. The purpose of the pre-assembly was to test out a draft document on mission—the first one of the CWME in thirty years—that was eventually published as *Together towards Life: Mission and Evangelism in Changing Landscapes.*[11] An invitation from David Esterline, now president of Pittsburgh Theological Seminary, to join in the preparation for the Global Ecumenical Theological Institute led to a formal invitation from the WCC to join the international faculty of the institute at the Tenth Assembly of the WCC in Busan, Korea, in November 2013. I was also asked to offer a plenary address to introduce *Together towards Life* to the Assembly (the only Catholic to do so), and soon afterward I received a further invitation to be a commissioner on the CWME, one of three representatives of the Catholic Church on the commission. The experience has been challenging, but it is certainly one where I have learned to practice global theologizing in an ecumenical key. My life has been greatly enriched by this, and my teaching as well. Being a member of the CWME is one of the great honors of my life.

This ecumenical engagement has also led me to be among the founders of the Global Forum of Theological Educators, a group composed of six ecclesial traditions and from many countries around the world. The idea of the forum is to provide a space for exchange on an ecumenical and global level about theological education. Our first meeting, outside Frankfurt, Germany, numbered about eighty scholars and was basically a "get to know you" meeting. Our next meeting will be in May 2019 in Crete and will have about the same number of scholars, but forty will be new. The theme of the conference will be contextualization in theological education.

As I mentioned above, I published an introduction to theology in global perspective in 2009. The book was based on many years teaching the course "Introduction to Theology" in the Philippines and at CTU, but it became a more *global* book with an invitation by Peter Phan to locate it as a volume in his series on theology in global perspective. My work had been strongly influenced by contextual theologies and mission perspectives before, but

---

[11] Commission on World Mission and Evangelism, *Together Towards Life: Mission and Evangelism in Changing Landscapes* (World Council of Churches, 2012).

writing this book helped me to think even more broadly than I had up to this point. As I wrote this book, especially the history of theology in the last one hundred pages or so, I realized that doing contextual theology in local contexts was not enough. Theology needed to be done as well as a dialogue of contextual theologies, one with the other. In a chapter written for the Festschrift in honor of Peter Phan that was published in 2016, my thinking in this regard coalesced in an article on "Models of Doing Theology in World Christianity."[12] Here I speak about the "contextual theology model," the "neglected themes model" (for example, migration, Pentecostalism), the "global perspective model" (exemplified in Peter Phan's series), and "the comparative theology model," pioneered by experts in non-Christian religions like Francis X. Clooney and James Fredericks, and a model that I suggested could be used analogically in a mutual critical dialogue among contextual theologies.

In the last several years I have been fascinated by another aspect of theology that actually goes beyond the global to the cosmic. This is the theology being developed by such diverse thinkers as John Haught, Elizabeth Johnson, Denis Edwards, Ilia Delio, and Thomas O'Meara. To think theologically in terms of the new creation story, as Thomas Berry calls it, to think in terms of the vast amount of time, the 13.8 billion years since the Big Bang, to think of the vastness of space in this universe of billions of light years in diameter, to think in terms of the complexity of cosmic and biological evolution—all of this changes completely our understandings of doctrines like creation, redemption, Christology, ecclesiology, and mission itself. Contextual theology has been inspired by the turn to the subject that marked both modernity and postmodernity. Now theology needs to be marked by the turn to the cosmic. Theology needs not only to be contextual in the context of the local, or done in global dialogue, but also to be done in cosmic context and in cosmic perspective.

Before I conclude, let me reflect on one more thing I discovered that has helped me in a global integration of my teaching: using images in my classes that reflect the faces, the landscapes, and the theologies of the entire world. In a subtle but very clear way the projection of an African or an Asian Christ on the screen as I talk about the Council of Nicaea, or the depiction of Filipino *bayanihan* as I lecture on the communal nature of the church, or a female image of God as I mention the trinitarian roots of ministry has had an amazing effect. I think that the inclusion of images from every land and people has made me more globally conscious and has widened the horizons of my students as well.

I can only say in conclusion that my journey as a global theologian has been an amazing one and has given me a vision of theology that is so much bigger than the one that I brought to the Philippines in 1972,

---

[12] Stephen B. Bevans, "Models of Doing Theology in World Christianity," in *World Christianity: Perspectives and Insights*, ed. Jonathan Y. Tan and Anh Q. Tran (Maryknoll, NY: Orbis Books, 2016), 146–60.

certainly bigger than the one I had that Advent evening in Rome. As I have written these reflections I have become very conscious of the debt that I owe to important mentors and colleagues in my life: Lenny Mercado, Bob Schreiter, Larry Nemer, Claude Marie Barbour, James Scherer, Jack Boberg, Roger Schroeder, Peter Phan, my doctoral mentor Thomas O'Meara and my best friend, Bill Burrows. Perhaps even more I owe a debt of gratitude to my students in the Philippines, at CTU, in Australia. I dedicated my introduction to theology book to them with a line that a veteran Philippine missionary shared with me just after Lenny Mercado's life-changing challenge. "Father Bevans," he told me, "*docendo discimus*—we learn by teaching." If I have contributed anything to global integration in theological education, it is because I have learned by teaching. And I have learned a lot!

Bibliography
of Stephen B. Bevans, SVD

BOOKS

1992   *John Oman and His Doctrine of God*. Cambridge: Cambridge University Press.

1992   *Models of Contextual Theology*. Maryknoll, NY: Orbis Books. Translations in Spanish, Indonesian, and Korean.

2002   *Models of Contextual Theology*. Revised and Expanded Edition. Maryknoll, NY: Orbis Books.

2004   With Roger P. Schroeder. *Constants in Context: A Theology of Mission for Today*. Maryknoll, NY: Orbis Books. Translations in Spanish, Chinese, Indonesian, Italian, Korean, and Vietnamese.

2009   *An Introduction to Theology in Global Perspective*. Maryknoll, NY: Orbis Books. Translation in Indonesian.

2009   With Jeffrey Gros. *Evangelization and Religious Freedom:* Ad Gentes *and* Dignitatis Humanae. Mahwah, NJ: Paulist Press.

2011   With Roger P. Schroeder. *Prophetic Dialogue: Reflections on Mission Today*. Maryknoll, NY: Orbis Books. Translation in Indonesian, Italian, Portuguese.

2018   *Essays in Contextual Theology*. Leiden: Brill.

EDITED BOOKS

1992   With James A. Scherer. *New Directions in Mission and Evangelization I: Basic Statements 1974–1991*. Maryknoll, NY: Orbis Books.

1994   With James A. Scherer. *New Directions in Mission and Evangelization 2: Theological Foundations*. Maryknoll, NY: Orbis Books.

1997   With Karl Müller, Theo Sundermeier, and Richard H. Bliese. *Dictionary of Mission: Theology, History, Perspectives*. Maryknoll, NY: Orbis Books.

1997   With Roger Schroeder. *Word Remembered, Word Proclaimed: Selected Papers from Symposia Celebrating the SVD Centennial in North America.* Nettetal: Steyler Verlag.

1999   With James A. Scherer. *New Directions in Mission and Evangelization 3: Faith and Culture.* Maryknoll, NY: Orbis Books.

2000   With Eleanor Doidge and Robert J. Schreiter. *The Healing Circle: Essays in Honor of Claude Marie Barbour.* Chicago: CCGM Publications.

2001   With Roger Schroeder. *Mission for the Twenty-First Century.* Chicago: CCGM Publications.

2011   With Katalina Tahaafe Williams. *Contextual Theology for the Twenty-First Century.* Eugene, OR: Pickwick Books / Cambridge, UK: James Clarke & Co. (2014).

2012   *Mission and Culture: The Louis J. Luzbetak Lectures.* Maryknoll, NY: Orbis Books.

2013   *A Century of Catholic Mission: From 1910 to the Present.* Oxford: Regnum Books.

2015   With Cathy Ross. *Mission on the Road to Emmaus: Constants, Context, and Prophetic Dialogue.* London: SCM / Maryknoll, NY: Orbis Books.

2015   With Teresa Chai, Nelson Jennings, Knud Jørgensen, and Dietrich Werner. *Reflecting on and Equipping for Christian Mission.* Oxford: Regnum Books.

2018   With Robin Ryan. *Priesthood in Religious Life: Searching for New Ways Forward.* Collegeville: The Liturgical Press.

CHAPTERS IN BOOKS

1976   "Five Approaches to the Indigenization of Theology." In *The Kingdom of the Word: Philippine SVD Festschrift.* Manila: Catholic Trade School, 112–37.

1988/90 "The Good News of the Kingdom." In *Faith Alive: A New Presentation of the Catholic Faith*, edited by R. Pasco and J. Redford. London: Hodder and Stoughton, 87–88; Mystic, CT: Twenty-Third Publications, 89–90.

1991   "Reaching for Fidelity: Doing Catholic Theology Today." In *Doing Theology in Today's World*, edited by J. Woodbridge and T. McComiskey. Grand Rapids: Zondervan, 321–38.

1993   "The Biblical Basis of the Mission of the Church in *Redemptoris Missio.*" In *The Good News of the Kingdom,* edited by C. van Engen, D. S. Gilliland, and P. Pierson. Maryknoll, NY: Orbis Books, 37–44.

1993   "What Makes the 'Heart of the Church' Beat? Motives for Mission in Contemporary Church Teaching." In *Verbi Praecones: Festschrift für P. Karl Müller SVD zum 75. Geburtstag,* edited by K. Piskaty and H. Rzepkowski. Nettetal: Steyler Verlag, 51–70.

1997   "Unity and Diversity: Vision, Fact, Possibility." In *Word Remembered, Word Proclaimed: Selected Papers from Symposia Celebrating the SVD Centennial in North America,* edited by Stephen Bevans and Roger Schroeder. Nettetal: Steyler Verlag, 237–55.

1999   "Living between Gospel and Context: Models for a Missional Church in North America." In *Confident Witness—Changing World,* edited by C. van Gelder. Grand Rapids, MI: Eerdmans, 141–54.

1999   "Fundamentos Teológicos del Carisma para la Misión Ad Gentes." In *Misión para el Tercer Milenio: Memorias.* Mexico City: Misioneros de Guadalupe, 9–26.

2000   "Partner and Prophet: The Church and Globalization." In *Reflecting Mission, Practicing Mission: Divine Word Missionaries Commemorate 125 Years of Worldwide Commitment,* edited by Heribert Bettscheider. Nettetal: Steyler Verlag, 1:91–110.

2000   With Roger Schroeder. "Missionary by Its Very Nature: A Reading of the Acts of the Apostles." In Bettscheider, *Reflecting Mission, Practicing Mission,* 1:3–36.

2007   "Missione tra I Migranti, Missione dei Migranti: Missione della Chiesa." In *Missione con I Migranti, Missione della Chiesa,* edited by Gioacchino Campese and Daniel Groody. Rome: Urbaniana University Press, 83–104.

2008   "Mission *among* Migrants, Mission *of* Migrants: Mission of the Church." In *A Promised Land, A Perilous Journey: Theological Perspectives on Migration,* edited by Gioacchino Campese and Daniel Groody. Notre Dame, IN: University of Notre Dame, 89–106.

2009   "From Edinburgh to Edinburgh: Towards a Theology of Mission for Today." In *Mission After Christendom,* edited by Ogbu Kalu, Edmund Chia, and Peter Vethanayagamony. Nashville, TN: Westminster John Knox, 1–11.

2010   "From Roman Church to World Church: Catholic Theological Education 1910–2010." In *Handbook of Theological Education in World Christianity,* edited by Dietrich Werner, David Esterline, Namsoon Kang and Joshva Raja. Oxford: Regnum Books, 3–12.

2010   "A Ministry for Ministry: The Vocation of Ministerial Priesthood in the Church." In *Catholics on Call: Discerning a Life of Service in the Church*, edited by Robin Ryan. Collegeville, MN: Liturgical Press, 132–47.

2011   "The Mission Has a Church: Perspectives of a Roman Catholic Theologian." In *Edinburgh 2010: Mission Today and Tomorrow*, edited by Kirsteen Kim and Andrew Anderson. Oxford: Regnum Books, 201–7.

2011   "La Rete del Vangelo: Teologia per la Missione." In *Antologia del Novecento Teologico*, edited by Rosino Gibellini. Brescia: Queriniana, 332–35.

2011   "Reflections." In Gibellini, *Antologia del Novecento Teologico*, 337–38.

2012   "Kicking the Hornet's Nest: Conversion, Church, and Culture." In *Konversion zwischen empirischer Forschung und theologisicher Reflexion*, edited by Martin Reppenhagen. Göttingen: Neukirchener Theologie, 185–204.

2013   "The Gift of Mission: A Synthesis." In *The Gift of Mission: Yesterday, Today, Tomorrow: Maryknoll Centennial Symposium*, edited by James H. Kroeger. Maryknoll, NY: Orbis Books, 226–29.

2013   "Migration and Mission: Pastoral Challenges, Theological Insights." In *Contemporary Issues in Migration and Theology*, edited by Elaine Padilla and Peter C. Phan. New York: Palgrave Macmillan, 157–77.

2013   "'Scholar among Scholars; Hispanic among Hispanics': Justo's Legacy to the Church at Large" In *A Legacy of Fifty Years: The Life and Work of Justo González*, edited by Stan Perea. Nashville, TN: Abingdon Press, 35–46.

2013   "Revisiting Mission at Vatican II: Theology and Practice for Today's Missionary Church." *Theological Studies* 74/2 (May): 261–83. Reprinted in *50 Years On: Probing the Riches of Vatican II*, edited by David G. Scholtenover. Collegeville, MN: Liturgical Press, 2015.

2013   "Introduction" and "Mission at the Second Vatican Council." In *A Century of Catholic Mission: From 1910 to the Present*, edited by Stephen B. Bevans. Oxford: Regnum Books, 1–7; 101–11.

2013   "Foreword." In Leonardo N. Mercado. *Power as the Holy Spirit and Grace*. Manila: Logos Publications, vii–viii.

2013   "Kumppanuuteen Jumalan kanassa—Lähetystyön uudelleen-ariointia." In *Uskonto ja Valta: Näkökulmia Kirdon Missioon*, edited by Mari-Anna Pöntinen. Helsinki: Suomen Lähatysseura, 43–54.

2013   "Foreword." In Danielle Achikian, Peter Gates, and Lana Turvey. *The Francis Effect: The Joy of the Gospel.* Sydney: Catholic Mission and Catholic Relgious Australia, 5–6.

2013   "Inculturation and the Church's Mission: Theological and Trinitarian Foundations." In *Communities of Faith in Africa and the African Diaspora. In Honor of Dr. Tite Tienou with Additional Essays on World Christianity*, edited by Casely B. Essamuah and David K. Ngaruiya. Eugene, OR: Pickwick Books, 214–33.

2014   "Contextual Theology as Practical Theology." In *Opening the Field of Practical Theology: An Introduction*, edited by Kathleen A. Cahalan and Gordon S. Mikoski. Lanham, MD: Rowan and Littlefield, 45–59.

2014   "Doing Mission Today: Where We Do It, How We Do It, What We Do." In *Creating a Welcoming Space: Reflections on Church and Mission. Essays to Honour Larry Nemer, SVD*, edited by Ross Fishburn, Michael Kelly, Christopher Monaghan, and Peter Price. Northcote, Victoria: Morningstar Publications, 29–48.

2014   "The Holy Spirit and Christian Mission Today." In *Excelling in Mission: A Festschrift in Honour of Dr. Joseph Puthenpurakal*, edited by Paul Vadakumpadan and José Varickasseril. Shillong, India: Sacred Heart Theological College, 78–93.

2014   "Missiology as Practical Theology: Understanding and Embodying Mission as Trinitarian Practice." In *Invitation to Practical Theology: Catholic Voices and Visions*, edited by Claire E. Wolfteich. Mahwah, NJ: Paulist Press, 253–74.

2014   "Mission des Heiligen Geistes." In *Mission, neu erklärt*, edited by Michael Biehl and Ulrich Dehn. Hamburg, Germany: Missionshilfe Verlag, 112–15.

2015   With Cathy Ross. "Introduction: Mission as Prophetic Dialogue." In Cathy Ross and Stephen Bevans, *Mission on the Road to Emmaus: Constants, Context, and Prophetic Dialogue.* Maryknoll, NY: Orbis Books.

2015   "Contextual Theology and Prophetic Dialogue." In Ross and Bevans, *Mission on the Road to Emmaus, 227–37.*

2015   "Mission as the Nature of the Church in Roman Catholic Contexts." In *Called to Unity for the Sake of Mission*, edited by John Gibaut and Knud Jørgensen. Oxford: Regnum Books, 128–40.

2015   "The Pact of the Catacombs: Implications for the Church's Mission. In *The Pact of the Catacombs: The Mission of the Poor in the Church*, edited by Xabier Pikaza and José Antunes da Silva. Pamplona, Spain:

Editorial Verbo Divino, 123–41. Translations in Portuguese, Spanish, and Italian.

2015   "Theological Education as Missionary Formation." In *Reflecting on and Equipping for Christian Mission,* edited by Stephen Bevans, Teresa Chai, Nelson Jennings, Knud Jørgensen, and Dietrich Werner. Oxford: Regnum Books, 93–105.

2015   "Prophetic Dialogue and Intercultural Mission. In *Intercultural Mission*, edited by Lazar T. Stanislaus and Martin Üffing. St. Augustin, Germany: Steyler Missionswissenschaftliches Institut / New Delhi: ISPK, 201–14.

2015   "The Social Dimension of Evangelization: Theological Foundations of *Evangelii Gaudium,* Chapter IV." In *Evangelizzare il Sociale: Prospettive per una Scelta Missionaria,* edited by Sandra Mazzolini. Rome: Urbaniana University Press, 9–16.

2015   "Beyond the New Evangelization: Toward a Missionary Ecclesiology for the Twenty-first Century." In *A Church with Open Doors: Catholic Ecclesiology for the Third Millennium,* edited by Richard R. Gaillardetz and Edward P. Hahnenberg. Collegeville, MN: Liturgical Press, 3–22.

2016   "A Prophetic Dialogue Approach" and "Response by Stephen B. Bevans." In *The Mission of the Church: Five Views in Conversation,* edited by Craig Ott. Grand Rapids, MI: Baker Academic, 3–20; 119–29.

2016   "Models of Contextual Theologizing in World Christianity." In *World Christianity: Perspectives and Insights*, edited by Jonathan Y. Tan and Ahn Q. Tran. Maryknoll, NY: Orbis Books, 146–60.

2016   "*Missio Dei* and *Missio Ecclesiae*: Trinitarian Mission, *Theosis,* and the Missionary Nature of the Church." In *Mission beyond* Ad Gentes, edited by Jacob Kavunka, SVD, and Christian Tauchner, SVD. Siegburg, Germany: Franz Schmitt Verlag, 17–30.

2016   "*Ad gentes divinitus*: Decree on the Church's Missionary Activity, December 7, 1965." In *A Liturgical Companion to the Documents of the Second Vatican Council.* Collegeville, MN: Liturgical Press, 83–87.

2016   With Ricky Manalo. "Contextual Preaching." In *A Handbook for Catholic Preaching,* edited by Edward Foley, Catherine Vincie, and Richard Fragomeni. Collegeville, MN: Liturgical Press, 233–43.

2016   With Daesung Lee. "Culture." In *Ecumenical Missiology: Changing Landscapes and New Concepts of Mission,* edited by Kenneth R.

Ross, Jooseop Keum, Kyriaki Avtzi, and Roderick R. Hewitt. Oxford: Regnum Books, 201–17.

2016   "*Together Towards Life* and *Evangelii Gaudium*: Life and Joy in Dialogue." In *Ecumenical Missiology: Changing Landscapes and New Conceptions of Mission*, edited by Kenneth R. Ross, Jooseop Keum, Kyriaki Avtzi, and Roderick R. Hewitt. Oxford: Regnum Books, 461–72.

2017   "The Holy Spirit and Christian Mission Today." In *A Light to the Nations: Explorations in Ecumenism, Missions, and Pentecostalism*, edited by Stanley M. Burgess and Paul W. Lewis. Eugene, OR: Pickwick Books, 155–69.

ARTICLES

1973   "Becoming a Filipino Theologian." *The Ilocos Review* (January–December): 208–14.

1975   "The Subject as Indigenous Theologian." *Philippine Priests' Forum* 7.2 (June): 51–56.

1976   "Singing the Lord's Song in a Foreign Land: The Foreigner as Theology Teacher." *South East Asia Journal of Theology* 17/2: 49–62.

1985   "Models of Contextual Theology." *Missiology: An International Review* 13/2 (April): 185–202. German translation: *Theologie der Gegenwart* 28/3 (1985): 135–47.

1987   "The Ministry of Jesus: What Was It All About?" *The Universe* (January 19).

1988   "A Local Theology in a World Church: Some US Catholic Contributions to Systematic Theology." *New Theology Review* 1/1 (February): 72–92.

1988   "US Systematic Theology: Doing Theology in a Postmodern World." *Revista Teologica Limense* 22/1: 123–42.

1988   "Acting Mission Minded: The Spirituality of Mission Sunday." *Church* (Fall): 28–32.

1988   "Contextual Theology: A First World Perspective." *Diwa: Studies in Philosophy and Theology* 13/2 (October): 69–87.

1989   "A Biblical-Theological Understanding of Stewardship: An Ecclesiological View." *Verbum SVD* 10/2: 103–14.

1991   "Seeing Mission through Images." *Missiology: An International Review* 19/1 (January): 45–57.

1991   With Norman E. Thomas, "Selected Annotated Bibliography on Missiology: Contextualization/Inculturation/Indigenization." *Missiology: An International Review* 19/1 (January): 105–8.

1991   "Eight Images of Mission." *Mission Outlook* 23/4 (Winter): 89–94.

1991   With Antonio M. Pernia and James W. Heisig (SVD Working Group). "Secularization, Dialogue, and Inculturation: Mission towards the Millennium and Beyond." *Sedos Bulletin* 23/8 (September 15): 240–46.

1992   "Eight Images of Mission." *IMU Report* (May-June): 4–5.

1992   With James A. Scherer. "Mission Statements: How They Are Developed and What They Tell Us." *International Bulletin of Missionary Research* 16/3 (July): 98–104.

1992   "The 1992 ASM Meeting: Final Thoughts." *Missiology: An International Review* 20/4: 539–40.

1994   "Taking Culture Seriously in Religious Education." *The Catholic World* (September-October): 236–40.

1995   "What Catholics Can Learn from Evangelical Mission Theology." *Missiology: An International Review* 23/2 (April): 155–64. Reprinted in *Sedos Bulletin* 28/4 (April 15): 108–12.

1995   "The Service of Ordering: Reflections on the Identity of the Priest." *Emmanuel* 101/7 (September): 397–406.

1995   "Reflections on *Keeping Faith* by Cornel West." *The Ecumenist* 2/4 (October-December): 63–64.

1996   "Images of the Priesthood in Today's Church." *Emmanuel* 102/7 (September): 389–98.

1996   "Inculturation of Theology in Asia: The Federation of Asian Bishops' Conferences, 1970–95." *Studia Missionalia* 45: 1–23. Reprinted: *Journal of Catholic Bishops' Conference of Japan,* Office of Research for Evangelization (1998): 47–66.

1996   "Similarities in Difference and Difference in Similarity: Protestants, Catholics, and Inculturation." *Japan Christian Review*: 5–17.

1996   "'Center, Means, and Aim': Contemporary Church Documents on Inculturation." *Verbum SVD* 17/4: 413–29.

1998   "God Inside Out: Toward a Missionary Theology of the Holy Spirit." *International Bulletin of Missionary Research* 22/3 (July): 102–5.

1998   "Jesus, Face of the Spirit: Reply to Dale Bruner." *International Bulletin of Missionary Research* 22/3 (July): 108–9.

1998   "Keeping Current: Cross Cultural Studies." *New Theology Review* 11/3 (August): 75–78.

1999   With Richard H. Bliese. "Dictionary of Mission: Theology, History, Perspecties." *Missiology: An International Review* 27/1 (January): 17–20.

1999   "Signs of the Times: Vital Statistics." *New Theology Review.* 12/3 (August): 65–68.

2001   "Wisdom from the Margins: Systematic Theology and the Missiological Imagination." *CTSA Proceedings*, 21–42. Also in *Verbum SVD* 43/1 (2002): 91–115; *Omnis Terra* 343 (January, 2004): 13–30 (*Omnis Terra* is in Portuguese, French, and Spanish.)

2001   "Inculturation and SVD Mission: Theological Foundations." *Verbum SVD* 42/3: 259–81.

2002   "A Spirituality of American Priesthood." Parts I and II. *Emmanuel* 108/2, 108/3 (May, June): 194–208, 260–75.

2003   "The Biblical Roots of Holy Orders." *The Bible Today* (May): 173–79.

2003   "Unraveling a 'Complex Reality': Six Elements of Mission." *International Bulletin of Missionary Research* 27/2 (April): 50–53.

2003   "Kirche-Sein in de letzten 'Supermacht.'" *Stadt Gottes* 126/7: 10–11.

2004   "The Church's Mission in the Third Millennium: Parts I and II: Religious and Lay Partnership for the Future." *Emmanuel* 109/6 and 110/1 (November/December): 420–46; (January/February): 4–13.

2007   "Learning to 'Flee from Bishops': The Charism of Priesthood in Formation for Religious Life." *Australian e-Journal of Theology* 10 (May).

2008   "DB4100: The God of Jesus Christ: A Case Study for a Missional Systematic Theology." *Theological Education* 43/2 (Summer): 105–14.

2009   "The Mission Has a Church, The Mission Has Ministry: Missiological Reflections on the Priest Shortage." *Compass* 43/3 (Spring): 1–14.

2009   "The Mission Has a Church: An Invitation to the Dance." *Australian e-Journal of Theology* 14 (August).

2009   "Church Teaching on Mission," "Six Elements of Mission in Contemporary Missiology," "Towards a Mission Spirituality." *The Cup of the New Covenant* [newsletter of the Missionaries of the Precious Blood] 29 (October): 1–5, 6–8, 9–11.

2010   "Signs of the Times: The Edinburgh Missionary Conference: Looking Back, Looking Forward." *New Theology Review* 23/1 (February): 79–81.

2010   "Thémes majeurs in missiologie nord américaine." *Spiritus* 201 (December): 457–68.

2011   With Gemma T. Cruz. "Introduction." *New Theology Review* 24/2 (May): 3–4.

2011   "A Missionary Parish: Beyond the Spiritual Service Station." *New Theology Review* 24/2 (May): 6–16.

2011   "Temas importantes en missionología norteamericano." *Spiritus* [Spanish edition] 52/1/202 (March): 79–89.

2011   "Missiology through the Back Door: Reflections of an SVD Mission Theologian." *Verbum SVD* 52/4: 367–77.

2011   "A Theology for the Ephesian Moment." *Anvil* 27/2 (November).

2012   "Lo Spirito Santo e la Missione Oggi." *Missione Oggi* 10 (January): 35–38.

2012   "Entering the Door of Faith: Preparing for the Year of Faith." *One Spirit: Newsletter of the Association of Catholic Religious in Taiwan* 10: 2–6 (English); 6–10 (Chinese).

2012   "Genesi e novità del decreto 'Ad Gentes.'" *Missione Oggi* 10 (December): 18–20.

2013   "Entering the Door of Faith: Preparing for the Year of Faith." *Emmanuel* 119/2 (March/April): 100–110.

2013   With Roger P. Schroeder. "Evangelization and the Tenor of Vatican II: A Review Essay." Review of Ralph Martin, *Will Many Be Saved? What Vatican II Actually Teaches and Its Implications for the New Evangelization* (Grand Rapids, MI: Eerdmans, 2012), *International Bulletin of Missionary Research* 37/2 (April): 94–95.

2013   "Revisiting Mission at Vatican II: Theology and Practice for Today's Missionary Church." *Theological Studies* 74/2 (June): 261–83.

2013   "'Scholar among Scholars, Hispanic among Hispanics': Justo's Legacy to the Church at Large." *Journal of Hispanic/Latino Theology* 18/2 (Spring): 20–28.

2013   "*Together towards Life*: Reflections on the Proposed WCC Mission Statement." *CMSM Forum* (August).

2014   "Mission, Vatican II, and Today's Missionary Church." *Mission Update* 23/1 (Spring): 6–10.

2014   "Roman Catholic Perspectives on Mission." *The Ecumenical Review* 66/1 (March): 65–71.

2014   "Mission of the Spirit." *International Review of Mission* 103/1 (April): 30–33.

2014   "Spreading the Joy of the Gospel." *Health Progress: Journal of the Catholic Health Association of the United States* (September-October): 23–27.

2014   "New Evangelization or Missionary Church? *Evangelii Gaudium* and the Call for Missionary Discipleship." *Verbum SVD* 55/2–3: 158–76.

2014   "Interfaith Engagement as Prophetic Dialogue." *Evangelical Interfaith Dialogue* (Fall).

2014   "Mission as the Nature of the Church: Development in Catholic Ecclesiology." *Australian eJournal of Theology* 21/3 (December): 184–96.

2014   "*Together towards Life*: Catholic Perspectives." *International Bulletin of Missionary Research* 38/4 (October): 195–96.

2014   "The Apostolic Exhortation *Evangelii Gaudium* on the Proclamation of the Gospel in Today's World: Implications and Prospects." *International Review of Mission* 103/2 (November): 297–308.

2015   "La Danza del Dialogo Profetico in *Evangelii Gaudium*." *Missione Oggi* (March): 18–20, 22.

2015   "Life, Joy, and Love: *Together towards Life* in Dialogue with *Evangelii Gaudium* and *The Cape Town Commitment*." *International Review of Mission* 104/2 (November): 193–202.

2016   "Transforming Discipleship: Missiological Reflections." *International Review of Mission* 105/1 (July): 75–85.

2016   "*The Church: Toward a Common Vision*: A Missiological Reading." *One in Christ* 50/2: 250–56.

2017   "Tribute to Bill Burrows." *Missiology: An International Review* 45/1l (January): 116–18.

2017   Review Article on *Apostolicity: The Ecumenical Question in World Christian Perspective* by John G. Flett. *International Bulletin of Mission Research* 41/2 (April): 102–6.

2017   "Élet, öröm és szeretet: missziói documentumok párbszéde." *Lelkipásztor* 92/2: 60–64.

2017   "Influences protestantes sur la conception catholique de la mission." *Spiritus* 227 (June): 171–84.

2017   "Inflencias protestantes en el concepto católico de la mission." *Spiritus* [Spanish edition] 227 (June): 23–38.

2017   "Protestant Influences on Catholic Mission Thinking." *Verbum SVD* 58/2–3: 150–62.

2017   "A Theology of Leadership, Not Management: Trinitarian Mission and Baptismal Discipleship." *Annales Missiologici Posnanienses* 22: 9–19.

PAMPHLETS

1991   With Antonio M. Pernia and James W. Heisig (SVD Working Group). *Secularization, Dialogue, and Inculturation: Mission toward the Millennium and Beyond.* Rome: SVD Generalate.

1993   *Cultural Expressions of Our Faith: Church Teachings and Pastoral Responses.* Washington, DC: United States Catholic Conference.

1996   *Inculturation of Theology in Asia: The Federation of Asian Bishops' Conferences, 1970–95.* FABC Papers. Hong Kong: FABC.

2010   *Constancy or Fidelity? Contextual Theology and Christian Tradition.* The 2009 Crowther Lecture, Church Mission Society. Oxford: Church Mission Society.

DICTIONARY AND ENCYCLOPEDIA ARTICLES

1990   "Engaged Encounter" and "The Religious Life." *Dictionary of Pastoral Care and Counseling.*

1997   "Common Witness." In *Dictionary of Mission: Theology, History, Perspectives,* edited by Karl Müller, Theo Sundermeier, Stephen B. Bevans, and Richard H. Bliese. Maryknoll, NY: Orbis Books, 72–73.

1997   "Bax, Jacques"; "Bermyn (*or* Bermijn), Alphonse"; "Bigandet, Paul Ambroise"; "Bonnand, Clement"; "Chavara, Kuriakose Elias"; "Dufresse, Jean-Gabriel-Taurin"; "Gregory I (the Great)"; "Grentrup, Theodor"; "Hahn, Henrich"; "Hanxleden, Johann Ernst"; "Müller, Karl"; "Ratisbonne, Marie-Théodore *and* Marie-Alphonse"; "Scherer, Henrich"; "Thérèse of Lisieux"; "Verbist, Théophile." In *Biographical Dictionary of Christian Missions,* edited by Gerald H. Anderson. New York: Macmillan Reference.

2000   With John Nyquist. "Roman Catholic Missions." In *Evangelical Dictionary of Christian Missions,* edited by A. Scott Moreau. Grand Rapids, MI: Baker Books, 837–41.

2000   "Schmidlin, Josef." In Moreau, *Evangelical Dictionary of Christian Mission,* 856.

2000   "Letting God and Speaking Out: A Spirituality of Inculturation." In *The Healing Circle: Essays in Honor of Claude Marie Barbour*, edited by Stephen Bevans, Eleanor Doidge, and Robert J. Schreiter. Chicago: CCGM Publications, 133–46.

2004   "Missions: Theology." In *International Mission Biography 1960–2000,* edited by Norman Thomas. ATLA Bibliographies No. 48. Lanham, MD, 79–119.

INTERVIEWS

2010   "Conversations: Steve Bevans." *Missiology: An International Review* 38/1 (January): 74–75.

2015   "Il Ruolo dei Missionari nella Genesi di *Ad Gentes*." Intervista a Stephen B. Bevans, a cura dei Mario Menin. *Missione Oggi* (October): 42–45.

2015   "Contextualization Revisited: Interview with Stephen Bevans." In *Evangelism and Diakonia in Context,* edited by Rose Dowsett, Isabel Phiri, Doug Birdsall, Dawit Olika Terfassa, Hwa Yung, and Knud Jørgensen. Oxford: Regnum Books, 251–56.

Index

acceptance model, in theology of religions, 220
accompaniment, mission of, 243
acculturation, 20
adaptation, 102
ad fontes, 58
Ad gentes (Declaration of Missionary Activity; Vatican II*)*, 22, 30, 33, 104–5, 197–98, 203, 211, 251–52
Africa
    Christians in, 69, 151
    Francophone theologians in, 112
    theological innovations in, 158
    Western missions to, 71
Africae terrarium (Paul VI), 105
African Americans, Christianity and, 139–42. *See also* black theology
African Independent/Initiated Churches, 156, 171n35
African slavery, in North America, 132
African theologies, 123, 162
African Traditional Religion, 156
Against the Heresy of the Ishmaelites (John Damascene), 218n22
aggiornamento, 235
AICs. *See* African Independent/Initiated Churches
Aikman, David, 171
Albert the Great, 30
Albert of Mainz, 56
All Africa Conference of Churches, 71
Althaus-Reid, Marcella, 181
Amaladoss, Michael, 29, 31, 167n27, 211n5
AMECEA. *See* Association of Member Episcopal Conferences of Eastern Africa
American Indians, 131–34, 139–42, 147

American Society of Missiology, 253
Anabaptists, 57, 58, 63
analogous Christians, 217n15
ancestor worship, Roman proscription of, 157
Anglican Church, 57, 63–64
Anselm of Canterbury, 18, 151, 209, 231
anthropological focus, 122
anthropological model, contextual theology and, 114
anthropological poverty, 194
anthropology of religion, 217
anticultural theologies, 159
anti-globalization movements, 112
Aparecida (homily; Benedict XVI), 239
Aparecida Document (CELAM), 34
apartheid, 108, 110–11, 112
Apess, William, 141
apocalyptic literature, 4–5
apophatic theology, 102
Apostolic Faith Mission (Los Angeles), 81
apostolicity, 45–46, 230, 234, 240–43
Aquinas, Thomas, 18, 30, 125n20, 209–10, 235n10
Arévalo, Catalino G., 251
Arndt, Jonathan, 63
Asia
    Christianity in, 69, 151
    theological innovations in, 158, 159
Asian religions, 123, 168, 212, 225
    Christian attention to, increasing, 217–18
    dialogue with, 213
ASM. *See* American Society of Missiology
Assemblies of God, 92
Association of Member Episcopal Conferences of Eastern Africa, 27

273

transcendental capabilities, 125
transcendental method, 250
transcendental model, contextual theology and, 115
transcendental realization, 122
transcultural theologies, 159
Transforming Mission (Bosch), 64
translation, 122, 220–21
translation model, contextual theology and, 113–14
Triadology, 42
tribal theology, 162
trinitarian theology, 27, 30–31, 41–42, 221
Trinity, centrality of, to mission, 23
triple dialogue, 184–87
True Christianity (Arndt), 63
True Jesus Church, 170
trust, mutual, principle of, 223–24
Tuddok (Pillars) movement (Philippines), 200–201
two-thirds world. *See* third world

Ueffing, Martin, 35
ujamaa, 108
Ultimate Mystery, encountering, 218
Union Theological Seminary (NYC), 72
United States
  Catholics in, and slavery, 143–44
  civil rights movement in, 145–46
  Civil War in, 144
  lynchings in, 144–45
  millennial role perceived for, 140–41
unity-in-diversity, 221
universality, 237. *See also* catholicity
urbanization, world mission conferences on, 253

Vatican II, 22–24, 75, 120–21, 127, 159, 232, 234
  audience for, 235
  on culture in church life, 195–97
  endorsing concept of culture, 104–5
  inculturation of, in Latin American context, 107
  meaning of, for Latin America, 106–7
  as missionary council, 252

recognizing theology as contextual, 235
vernacular, 38–39, 60, 74
vernacular hermeneutics, 194n10
Villa-Vicencio, Charles, 111–12
Vincent of Lérins, 154
Volf, Miroslav, 89
Voulgarakis, Elias, 40–41
Vuola, Elina, 179

Wallis, Jim, 147
Walls, Andrew, 122n9, 150
Ward, Graham, 241–42
Ward, Keith, 222
Ware, Kallistos, 44
Warneck, Gustav, 20, 64
waterbuffalo theology, 180
WCC. *See* World Council of Churches
Weber, Max, 109
Wei Zhuomin (Wei Cho Min; Francis Wei), 68
Wesley, John, 64
Whitefield, George, 139
Whitehead, Alfred North, 161
Whiteman, Darrell, 253
white privilege, 147
wider ecumenism, 227
Wijsen, Frans, 183
Williams, Roger, 137–38
witness
  as encounter, 72
  personal, 126
Wolanin, Adam, 32
Wood, Peter, 135–36
working class, movements for, 120
"world," meaning of, in modern thought, 119–20
world Christianity, 116, 149–50, 238n20, 254
  approach of, to God, 160–62
  biblical hermeneutics in, 153–54
  challenges to, 152
  Christology and, 163–67
  culture and, 155–57
  encountering other religions, 153
  and the Holy Spirit, 167–68
  impact of, on systematic theology, 150–52
  locations for, 169–72
  small traditions in, 156

The American Society of Missiology Series

1. *Protestant Pioneers in Korea*, Everett Nichols Hunt Jr.
2. *Catholic Politics in China and Korea*, Eric O. Hanson
3. *From the Rising of the Sun: Christians and Society in Contemporary Japan*, James M. Phillips
4. *Meaning across Cultures*, Eugene A. Nida and William D. Reyburn
5. *The Island Churches of the Pacific*, Charles W. Forman
6. *Henry Venn: Missionary Statesman*, Wilbert R. Shenk
7. *No Other Name? Christianity and Other World Religions*, Paul F. Knitter
8. *Toward a New Age in Christian Theology*, Richard Henry Drummond
9. *The Expectation of the Poor: Latin American Base Ecclesial Communities in Protest*, Guillermo Cook
10. *Eastern Orthodox Mission Theology Today*, James J. Stamoolis
11. *Confucius, the Buddha, and Christ: A History of the Gospel in China*, Ralph R. Covell
12. *The Church and Cultures: New Perspectives in Missiological Anthropology*, Louis J. Luzbetak, SVD
13. *Translating the Message: The Missionary Impact on Culture*, Lamin Sanneh
14. *An African Tree of Life*, Thomas G. Christensen
15. *Missions and Money: Affluence as a Western Missionary Problem . . . Revisited* (second edition), Jonathan J. Bonk
16. *Transforming Mission: Paradigm Shifts in Theology of Mission*, David J. Bosch
17. *Bread for the Journey: The Mission and Transformation of Mission*, Anthony J. Gittins, C.S.Sp.
18. *New Face of the Church in Latin America: Between Tradition and Change*, edited by Guillermo Cook
19. *Mission Legacies: Biographical Studies of Leaders of the Modern Missionary Movement*, edited by Gerald H. Anderson, Robert T. Coote, Norman A. Horner, and James M. Phillips
20. *Classic Texts in Mission and World Christianity*, edited by Norman E. Thomas
21. *Christian Mission: A Case Study Approach*, Alan Neely
22. *Understanding Spiritual Power: A Forgotten Dimension of Cross-Cultural Mission and Ministry*, Marguerite G. Kraft
23. *Missiological Education for the 21st Century: The Book, the Circle, and the Sandals*, edited by J. Dudley Woodberry, Charles Van Engen, and Edgar J. Elliston
24. *Dictionary of Mission: Theology, History, Perspectives*, edited by Karl Müller, SVD, Theo Sundermeier, Stephen B. Bevans, SVD, and Richard H. Bliese
25. *Earthen Vessels and Transcendent Power: American Presbyterians in China, 1837–1952*, G. Thompson Brown
26. *The Missionary Movement in American Catholic History*, Angelyn Dries, OSF
27. *Mission in the New Testament: An Evangelical Approach*, edited by William J. Larkin Jr. and Joel W. Williams